£50.50

D1628663

BSAVA

MANUAL OF EXOTIC PETS

New Edition 1991

636

Edited by

Peter H Beynon
BVSc MRCVS

and

John E Cooper
BVSc CertLAS DTVM FRCVS MRCPath FIBiol

Published by the
British Small Animal
Veterinary Association
Kingsley House, Church Lane,
Shurdington, Cheltenham,
Gloucestershire GL51 5TQ

Printed by KCO, Worthing
West Sussex.

First Published 1991
Reprinted 1992

ISBN 0 905214 15 3

CONTENTS

CONTENTS

FOREWORD

The Manual of Exotic Pets has proved to be one of the most successful of the BSAVA publications. It aims to provide the veterinary surgeon with information on some of the less familiar animals that he or she may encounter in veterinary practice or, if the species is not included by name, to outline basic principles and sources of relevant data. This is a third, fully revised edition of the manual and the contents reflect the advances that have been made in the field. No longer can some of the species covered really be considered 'exotic' or 'non-domesticated' since they include animals that are regularly kept or bred in captivity. However, others are, to the veterinary profession at any rate, 'unusual' or 'bizarre' and as such they fit the dictionary definition of 'exotic'. All of the animal groups covered are ones that receive relatively little attention on the undergraduate course.

No book is easy to edit but a multi-author text covering such diverse species is inevitably difficult. The close collaboration between the two editors has combined the meticulous organisational skills of Peter Beynon with the enthusiasm and expertise of John Cooper in the smooth and efficient production of this manual. We in the BSAVA are grateful to them both.

The authors of the various chapters are thanked for agreeing to contribute and (in most cases!) for submitting their manuscripts before the appointed deadline. All responded in a good-humoured and constructive fashion to requests for changes or additions to their chapters.

Many others have helped, directly or indirectly, in the production of this manual. Clare Knowler very kindly prepared the drawings for the cover and Alison Gray took a number of the photographs. Owen Davies, Carol Johnson, Nacho Marco, Elaine Penfold, Susan Spencer and Kathleen Tennant assisted in many ways including collating data. Ian Lyle and Anna Feistner commented on two of the chapters. Sally Dowsett undertook much of the supporting secretarial work.

The libraries of the Royal College of Surgeons and the Royal College of Veterinary Surgeons have provided copies of papers and helped locate relevant publications.

The Editors are indebted to their wives, Margaret Cooper and Paddy Beynon, for their support.

The BSAVA endorses the appreciation expressed by the Editors of the guidance and constant encouragement of Simon Orr, Chairman of Publications Committee, and the continued courtesy and co-operation of Michael Gorton Design.

It gives me great pleasure to be President of the BSAVA when this third edition of the Manual of Exotic Pets is to be published. Its success is indicative of the way in which small animal practice is developing, both in depth and breadth. The manual will, I know, prove as popular and as valuable as its predecessors.

COLIN J PRICE MA VetMB MRCVS
President 1990-91

CHAPTER ONE

INTRODUCTION

John E Cooper BVSc CertLAS DTVM FRCVS MRCPath FIBiol _____

"He prayeth well, who loveth well both man and bird and beast"
S.T. Coleridge

This is a third, fully revised, edition of the 'Manual of Exotic Pets'. While some parts have remained relatively unaltered — for example, the basic guidance offered in this introductory chapter — there are new subjects, new authors and new ideas. All the chapters have been either rewritten or revised.

This book deals with 'exotic pets' but the term is difficult to define. According to the Concise Oxford Dictionary 'exotic' means 'introduced from abroad; strange, bizarre, attractively strange or unusual' and none of these adequately describes all those species which are the subject of this manual. An alternative approach is to use the expression 'non-domesticated' but this also presents problems since several of the species covered — for example, ferrets, mice and canaries — have been bred in captivity for many generations (Mason, 1984) and as such do not warrant the description of non-domesticated. In the absence of a totally suitable term, therefore, the word 'exotic' has been used but it has been taken to imply animals which are less familiar to veterinary surgeons than those which form the basis of the undergraduate course, ie. dog, cat, horse, ox, sheep, pig, goat and fowl.

Further difficulties concern the term 'pet'. Many exotic species are kept for purposes other than companionship — for example, for agriculture, research or in zoos — but the manual is not concerned with these. Emphasis is put on those that are commonly kept for pleasure or exhibition and an effort has been made to ensure that these encompass the whole Animal Kingdom, from primates to praying mantids. Inevitably, however, some species or groups have had to be omitted. For this reason, the list of Further Reading includes some general references which may help in the care of species which are not covered *per se* in the manual.

DEALING WITH EXOTIC SPECIES

There are four important sets of questions which the veterinary surgeon must ask him/herself if presented with an exotic animal:-

1. What species is this? Do I know sufficient about its biology and natural history? If not, do I know where to obtain such information or to seek suitable advice?

2. Do I have adequate facilities, equipment and expertise/confidence to examine and treat the animal?

3. Do I have access to information about the diseases of this species?

4. Are there any special legal or ethical considerations of which I should be aware?

Each of these main headings is discussed more fully below. However, for detailed information individual chapters should be consulted.

CLASSIFICATION AND IDENTIFICATION

The veterinary surgeon who deals with exotic species must have some understanding of the classification of animals and their taxonomy. A simplified breakdown is given in Table 1. A number of points should be noted:-

1. Living things are best thought of as being in either the Animal or Plant Kingdom. Thus, all the species discussed in the manual are animals, whether mammals, birds, reptiles, amphibians, fish or invertebrates. Such expressions as 'animals and birds', still regularly used in reputable veterinary journals, are incorrect.

2. There are important differences between the five main groups of vertebrates. Of particular relevance is whether they are endothermic ('warm-blooded') — the mammals and birds — or ectothermic ('cold-blooded') — reptiles, amphibians and fish (plus invertebrates).

3. There are relatively few species of mammal compared with other Classes of vertebrate. Wood (1982) gave the following figures:

Mammals	4,008 species	Amphibians	2,400 species
Birds	8,900 species	Fish	30,000 species
Reptiles	5,175 species		

There are probably between 10 and 30 million species of invertebrate, which thus outnumber all other living things many times over.

Table 1
A simplified classification of living animals

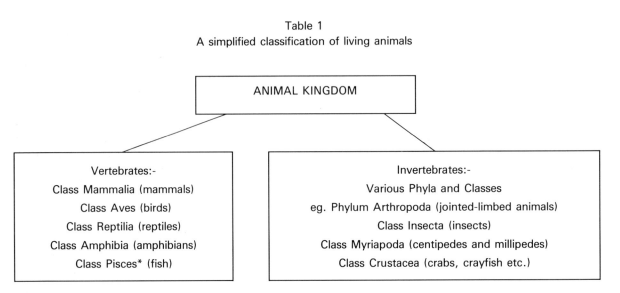

* Strictly there are three Classes of fish but for convenience they are grouped together in this Table.

Nomenclature sometimes presents problems. All living animals have a scientific name, usually of Latin or Greek origin. An International Code of Zoological Nomenclature exists to ensure that there is no duplication of names and to arbitrate over difficulties — for example, if the same species has been given two (or more) different names.

The first (generic) name has a capital, the second (trivial) name does not. The scientific name should be underlined: in books it is often put in italics. Other groupings, such as Family, Order and Class have a capital letter but should not be underlined. Three examples of classification, all species referred to directly or indirectly in this manual, are given below:-

	House mouse	Hermann's tortoise	Privet hawk moth
Kingdom	Animalia	Animalia	Animalia
Phylum	Chordata	Chordata	Arthropoda
Class	Mammalia	Reptilia	Insecta
Order	Rodentia	Chelonia	Lepidoptera
Family	Muridae	Testudinidae	Sphingidae
Genus	*Mus*	*Testudo*	*Sphinx*
Species	*musculus*	*hermanni*	*ligustri*

Some species have a third scientific name — for example, the ferret is usually called *Mustela putorius furo.* This means that it is a subspecies of the European polecat, *Mustela putorius.*

BIOLOGY AND NATURAL HISTORY

An understanding of the biology and natural history of a species can be of great value to the diagnosis and treatment of disease. To a certain extent an appreciation of the classification of the animal will assist in this respect. Thus, for example, if one knows that a patient is a salamander, in the Class Amphibia, this will immediately provide certain basic information — for example, that the animal favours a damp environment, has a soft sensitive skin and is likely to become torpid in cold weather.

Much of value can be learnt from appropriate books and journals including publications on the normal biology of various animals, as opposed to their diseases. Journals and magazines produced by specialist societies also warrant reference and consultation. It is worth remembering that the Library of the Royal College of Veterinary Surgeons can advise on publications, will lend books and journals and supply photocopies.

The best way of learning about the habits and requirements of a species is to keep it oneself. Veterinary surgeons and their staff should give serious thought to having a collection of exotic animals, either in the surgery or at home, so that expertise can be gained in such routine procedures as restraint, sexing, feeding and cleaning. Appropriate species include small rodents, cage birds, tortoises and fish. If this is not feasible, visits to premises where such animals are kept will prove of value, especially if an opportunity is taken not only to look at the creatures, but also to handle them. Insofar as small mammals are concerned, laboratory animal units are particularly recommended: the staff of such establishments are usually very experienced in handling and management and generally most willing to advise and demonstrate. Good petshops are also worth visiting and often a useful relationship between them and the practice can be developed. In this context the introduction of a Certificate Course in Pet Store Management is to be welcomed and it is encouraging to note the involvement of members of the veterinary profession in the compilation of the syllabus.

Information can often be obtained from specialist societies and the addresses of some of these are listed in the Appendix at the end of this manual. Membership of appropriate veterinary bodies, eg. the British Veterinary Zoological Society (BVZS), should be considered by anyone with a serious interest in exotic species. A subscription to a bird club or aquarist association may provide the practice with useful literature, valuable contacts and an opportunity to attend meetings and shows.

FACILITIES, EQUIPMENT AND EXPERTISE

Relatively few specialised items are needed for work with exotic pets assuming that the veterinary surgeon has basic facilities and equipment for work with dogs and cats. Most exotic species can be examined in the surgery but there is often merit in visiting the owner's premises in order to see caging and environment. A useful general tip, particularly when capturing or examining birds and small mammals, is to remember that most species are quieter in subdued light. Clinical examination is facilitated if it is carried out in a darkened room or if the patient's eyes are covered with a cloth. The ease with which many exotic species can escape has also to be borne in mind. Special attention must be paid to ensuring that windows and doors are closed and that boxes and nets are secure.

As many authors in the manual have emphasised, laboratory facilities are often needed for a definitive diagnosis. It may be best to send swabs, blood samples and biopsies elsewhere for processing but a number of simple procedures, such as examination of faeces for parasites, can and should be carried out in the practice.

Essential items of equipment for clinical work are as follows:-

Gloves. Ideally the veterinary surgeon should have a selection ranging from thin (gardening) gloves to the stouter leather version favoured by motorcyclists. Industrial elbow-length gloves are useful (see 'Appendix — Useful Addresses').

Scales or balance. One must be able to weigh the patient. Again, a range of balances or scales is desirable. Excellent spring balances are available from the British Trust for Ornithology (see 'Appendix — Useful Addresses').

Cloth bags. These are used to weigh and transport small animals: in addition, if placed over the head of a bird they tend to quieten it.

Nets. Various sizes should be available. Small nets of the type used by aquarists are ideal for invertebrates, fish, amphibians, cagebirds and rodents: larger (fishermen's) nets are needed for monkeys (see 'Appendix — Useful Addresses').

Suitable cages and containers. The veterinary surgeon should have a collection of rodent and bird cages, aquaria, glass and plastic containers etc. A supply of suitable food should also be readily obtainable.

Appropriate sized syringes and needles. Small syringes (1ml or less) and 25, 26 and 27G needles may be needed.

Certain drugs. Methoxyflurane, isoflurane, alphaxalone/alphadolone, propofol, fentanyl/fluanisone and diazepam or midazolam are amongst those preparations which are not necessarily part of the veterinary surgeon's usual range but which should be available.

In addition to the items above, the following will prove useful:-

Anaesthetic chamber. Can be made of perspex (Cooper, 1989), or fashioned from a bucket or icecream tub. Ether usually cannot be used with such materials.

Hospital cage or paediatric incubator. The former can be purchased from avicultural suppliers (see 'Appendix — Useful Addresses'); the latter can sometimes be obtained from a hospital. A range of heated containers for veterinary use is now available. Simpler methods of keeping patients warm, which should be available in any practice, include heating pads, infra-red bulbs, hot water bottles and aluminium foil.

Long forceps. These are ideal for emergency handling of tailed rodents, certain reptiles and invertebrates. The tips should be padded with rubber.

Wooden spatulae. Ice-lolly sticks are ideal.

Matchsticks and feather quills. Excellent for external splinting of fractures in small animals.

Butterfly attachments. These often prove preferable to needles, especially if the patient is fractious or liable to move.

Crush cage. Indispensable when dealing with the larger primates and certain other species. Can be purchased. Sometimes available secondhand from laboratory animal units.

Aquarists' testing kits. Invaluable when dealing with certain species of fish; very useful for aquatic amphibians and invertebrates (see 'Appendix — Useful Addresses').

Grabsticks. Useful for restraining and capturing reptiles.

Blowpipe/pole syringe. Primarily needed in zoo animal work, but may prove useful to immobilise primates or deer (see 'Appendix — Useful Addresses').

Rigid endoscope. Of increasing value as a diagnostic tool in mammals, birds and reptiles. Also used for surgical sexing. Flexible endoscopes are also useful (see 'Appendix — Useful Addresses').

Additional drugs. A number of special agents may be needed, eg. benzocaine anaesthetic for fish and amphibians.

Often equipment can be made or improvised. The value of an icecream tub as an anaesthetic chamber was mentioned earlier. Other examples include the use of a plastic syringe case as a gag (see 'Guinea Pigs') or facemask (see 'Gerbils').

Chemotherapeutic agents should be discussed since their use in exotic species can pose problems. Very few drugs are licensed for use in non-domesticated animals but this does not mean that they may not be prescribed or dispensed: the veterinary surgeon is reminded of the relevant part of the 'Guide to Professional Conduct' (RCVS, 1990) which states that 'A veterinary surgeon, in the exercise of his professional judgement, has the right to prescribe or supply any licensed product for any species of animal, regardless of whether the product was marketed initially for that species, for other species or for human use'.

Nevertheless, it would be a mistake to assume that one can automatically extrapolate from small (or large) domesticated animals. Often such an approach proves successful and safe but this is not always the case. There are four considerations:-

1. **Contra-indications.** Some drugs can prove toxic or dangerous to certain species. Details of these are given in the text, but examples include certain antibiotics which can prove lethal to rodents and the procaine group which may be hazardous in birds.

2. **Dosage.** Many of the exotic pets are considerably smaller than dogs or cats. This does not mean, however, that the dose of a drug for these species should be based on that for larger animals and then scaled down in a linear fashion. Many biological parameters, including metabolic rate, show a curved relationship when plotted against bodyweight and therefore a different approach to drug dosage is needed. In simple terms, small endothermic animals have a higher metabolic rate than larger ones and may require a relatively greater quantity of a drug per unit bodyweight, or the same dose repeated more frequently (see later). Kirkwood (1983a,b) and Kirkwood and Wathes (1984) discussed this in some detail and suggested that the formula $P = aW^{0.75}$ is applicable, where P is the dose, a is a constant and W the bodyweight. Put in another way, the duration of action of a compound in an animal increases with the ¼ power of weight ($W^{\frac{1}{4}}$). Thus, if one is dealing with two animals weighing 1kg and 100kg respectively, it can be assumed that a drug will be absorbed, metabolised and excreted $100:1^{\frac{1}{4}} = 3.16$ times faster in the former than in the latter. If the daily dose of the drug for the larger animal is 10mg/kg bodyweight then for the smaller specimen it will be 31.6mg/kg. The drug dosage in this case should be expressed as $31.6mg/kg^{\frac{3}{4}}$, a formula which will apply to the majority of endothermic vertebrates, rather than 10mg/kg which is strictly only correct for those individuals weighing 100kg. There is, of course, some variation between species in terms of the way in which chemotherapeutic agents are dealt with in the body and this may influence the equation. Nevertheless, the method of expressing dosages outlined above is clearly preferable to, and more exact than, the more conventional mg(mcg,g)/kg which has been in use for so long in veterinary medicine. If a clinician is unable to use this equation, a convenient, but rather inexact, rule of thumb for small, ie. less than 500g, mammals and birds is to work out the dose on a mg/kg bodyweight basis, using the recommendations for dogs and cats, and then to double this. It must be stressed, however, that this should not be used if there is any possibility of a species susceptibility to the agent in question.

3. **Frequency of administration.** As has been emphasised earlier, the metabolic rate of exotic species varies. In small birds and rodents the rate is usually considerably higher than in larger mammals, reptiles, amphibians and fish. The resultant differences in speed of drug absorption, metabolism and excretion mean that the frequency of administration must be carefully determined (Kirkwood, 1983a,b). This, clearly, is related to the total amount of drug given. In the example cited earlier the dose of 31.6mg/kg could either be given once a day or in divided doses — for example, 10mg/kg three times a day. In practice the latter is probably preferable since it reduces the volume of an agent which has to be administered at one time and is likely to produce effective tissue levels for a longer period. It must be stressed, however, that these calculations refer principally to endotherms (mammals and birds) since the smaller ectotherms tend to have a considerably lower metabolic rate, especially if they are temperate species at their preferred optimum temperature. Work on reptiles (Bush *et al*, 1978; Holt, 1981; Lawrence, 1983) has shown that when calculating the frequency of administration of a number of compounds the animal's ambient temperature must be taken into consideration and this is reflected in the chapters on reptiles, amphibians and fish in this manual.

4. **Route.** Although the oral route has much to commend it, especially when the owner is administering a drug, it is often far from ideal. In the case of small mammals and birds the gut transit time is rapid: agents given orally are often incompletely absorbed and blood and tissue levels may be inadequate. This can be overcome if the agent is given by injection but, as was mentioned earlier, the frequency of administration also has to be considered. Injections should always be given with as small a needle as possible and the volume of inoculum kept to a minimum. The choice of site is important: intramuscular injections in particular cause a surprising amount of tissue damage. Thus, it is generally wise to inject birds in the leg muscle rather than the pectorals since the latter are important in flight. Terrestrial species such as quail (*Coturnix* spp.), on the other hand, may be more adversely affected by an impaired gait than a drooping wing.

The whole question of drug dosage, route and frequency of administration is clearly of great relevance to work with exotic species and there is little doubt that the subject will attract far greater attention over the next few years.

Notwithstanding these points, a surprisingly wide range of chemotherapeutic agents can be used safely and successfully in exotic species. Recommendations are given in individual chapters but some general points might prove useful. A number of agents appear to be relatively safe across the spectrum: examples include liquid paraffin, halothane and several of the antimicrobial agents. Human paediatric preparations have much to commend them in that they are usually conveniently packed and often surprisingly palatable — disguising the taste is often essential when treating unco-operative patients. There is merit in preparing small quantities of some of the more familiar compounds — for example, vitamin and mineral supplements, bonemeal, dextrose saline — which can then be easily dispensed to the client.

Some general rules for the veterinary surgeon who is presented with an exotic species and wishes to administer a given drug are as follows:-

1. Check the data sheet: are there any specific contra-indications?

2. Contact the manufacturers: do they have any information on the use of their product in the species in question?

3. Consult the literature (including this and other manuals).

4. Seek advice from colleagues who may have experience of the compound and/or species.

5. When appropriate, proceed to administer/dispense the drug but —

    a. warn the client that there might be an unexpected effect;

    b. if several animals are involved, carry out test dosing of a small number initially;

    c. observe the animal(s) carefully for any adverse sequelae;

    d. err on the side of safety.

CLINICAL PROCEDURES

The clinical examination of exotic animals cannot be discussed in detail: so much depends upon the species involved. As a general rule, however, much is gained by visiting the animals or hospitalising them, rather than having them brought to the surgery. The reason for this is clear. As several authors in the manual have emphasised, many diseases of exotic species are associated with husbandry factors and the latter can only be properly investigated on the owner's premises. It is particularly important to check the animals' environment when they are being kept in a school, hospital, prison or similar institution, where there may be close contact with the animals by many different people. For the same reason such animals should be properly screened for disease (see later).

A proper clinical history is of the greatest importance when dealing with exotic species. All too often the veterinary surgeon is presented with an animal which is reported to be 'off-colour' and there is little or no information on its origin, age, diet or accommodation. The owners of exotic species must be encouraged to keep careful records and to produce these when required. Regular weighing of animals is wise and these figures will often serve as a guide to the animal's health and development.

The handling and restraint of exotic animals are of great importance. It is not sufficient for a veterinary surgeon to restrict himself to peering at a bird in a cage or a tropical fish in a tank and then pronouncing on the animal's state of health. Observation of the patient is, of course, essential but this must be a prelude to a full clinical examination. The latter implies handling and/or restraint and that is why considerable emphasis is laid upon this throughout the manual.

The ability to hold a species properly is something that can only be learned by experience. Sometimes protective clothing may be needed — for instance, gloves for monkeys — or specialised equipment has to be employed — for example, grabsticks for snakes, nets for fish, transparent examination containers for invertebrates. Special precautions apply to certain species — some species of lizard may shed their tails, chinchillas tend to lose fur, while hedgehogs need encouraging if they are to uncurl and be handled comfortably.

There are various aids to clinical examination which are of value in exotic species. The familiar stethoscope can be usefully employed when examining mammals, birds, reptiles and amphibians. Radiography is often of particular value and frequently has to be used to **make,** rather than **confirm**, a diagnosis.

Treatment of exotic species can be carried out in a variety of ways but, as in domesticated animals, the four main approaches are a) administration of chemotherapeutic agents, b) surgery, c) attention to management and d) supportive care. In many instances the third of these is the most important: particular examples are fish and amphibians in which disease is very frequently attributable to, or precipitated by, an adverse environment. Chemotherapy was mentioned earlier and is discussed in considerable detail in each chapter. Surgery can be carried out, to a greater or lesser extent, in all types of animal. A vital consideration in this context, however, is the prevention of unnecessary pain. Relatively little information is available on the use of analgesics in exotic species other than certain mammals (Flecknell, 1987). For this reason is it usually advisable to use general anaesthesia when surgery is carried out.

Some form of anaesthesia is probably a legal requirement for surgery insofar as the vertebrates are concerned (see 'Legislation') but should also be considered for invertebrates. Hypothermia must never be used in an attempt to anaesthetise ectothermic species: their response to stimuli may be delayed when they are chilled but there is no evidence that their pain threshold is in any way altered.

Supportive care is very often as important as chemotherapy, surgery and attention to management. Many exotic species are small and thus particularly susceptible to changes in temperature, fluid loss and tissue damage. Nursing of the patient is usually of prime importance and it is fortunate that many veterinary nurses find exotic animals interesting and challenging.

Health monitoring of exotic species for pathogens is not specifically covered in this manual but is alluded to in a number of chapters. The veterinary surgeon should be prepared to advise upon quarantining (isolation) of incoming animals and screening for pathogens. Such precautions, coupled with regular health checks, are especially important when animals are kept in institutions.

A special mention should be made here about wild animal casualties. Although many exotic species are kept and bred in captivity a number of those presented for veterinary attention are casualties — for example, orphaned birds, sick hedgehogs or injured toads. The important point to remember, regardless of the species, is that wild animals are particularly prone to 'shock' and therefore supportive care is of the utmost importance. In the case of the endothermic species this means keeping the patient warm, administering fluids, providing food (by force-feeding if necessary) and avoiding unnecessary disturbance. Warmth is of less importance when nursing ectothermic animals — the aim should be to maintain them at their preferred body temperature (PBT) — but the fluids and food remain essential. The prognosis for wildlife animal casualties must always be guarded.

Another topic which has not been covered in detail in this manual is captive breeding. Part of the changing pattern of exotic pet keeping is a tendency for fewer animals to be imported — often as a result of concern over welfare and/or conservation (see 'Legislation') — and for a greater emphasis to be put on breeding in captivity. The past few years have seen an encouraging increase in this trend and a number of species, particularly reptiles and birds, are now being regularly and successfully bred. Nevertheless, many problems remain unsolved — for example, infertility, early embryonic death and hand-rearing — and this is a field in which the veterinary surgeon with an interest in exotic species and their protection can play a valuable role.

Euthanasia is mentioned in some, but not all, of the chapters. It is an important topic since the ability to kill an animal humanely is one of the most important skills that a veterinary surgeon has. It is a regrettable fact that many owners of exotic animals, especially children, still tend to assume that a 'visit to the vet' means that their animal is to be 'put to sleep'. For too long veterinary surgeons with little interest in non-domesticated animals — and even less sensitivity towards their owners — have taken the easy way out and advocated euthanasia rather than a proper examination and attempt at treatment. The climate of opinion has now changed for the better and many members of the profession, particularly recent graduates, take a serious and sympathetic interest in exotic species. Nevertheless, some animals still have to be killed and it is important that this is done humanely. As with other species, either chemical or physical methods can be used. The choice depends on the circumstances but the cardinal rule is that the animal must come first: a method which is aesthetically pleasant may not be humane. Chemical methods are probably the easiest to carry out: in most cases they consist of an overdose of an appropriate anaesthetic agent. Physical methods often require a certain amount of expertise: for example, no-one should try to dislocate the neck of a rabbit or a mouse unless he or she has received adequate training and practised on dead animals. Decapitation is probably satisfactory in mammals and birds but there is doubt about its humanity in reptiles (UFAW/WSPA, 1989) and, probably, other ectotherms.

LEGAL AND ETHICAL CONSIDERATIONS

Legislation which is of relevance to the care and treatment of exotic pets is discussed later in the manual (see 'Legislation'). Suffice it to say that these species are subject to many of the statutes relating to domesticated animals but, in addition, specific legislation may be applicable, eg. Dangerous Wild Animals Act, 1976 (Cooper, 1987).

Quite apart from legal considerations, ethical questions may arise when dealing with these species. These mainly concern welfare and conservation. Although many of the animals discussed in this manual are now 'domesticated', in the sense that they have been bred in captivity for several generations, others may still need to be imported from overseas. The veterinary surgeon may well disapprove of this trade but can probably best contribute towards reducing it by a) ensuring that imported animals are properly looked after and receive optimum veterinary attention and b) by encouraging and contributing to captive breeding programmes.

Quite apart from the question of importation, however, there are those who condemn the keeping of any non-domesticated animals, on the grounds that they (the animals) often do not fare well in captivity and, in some cases, are potentially hazardous to humans. Certain of the arguments in this respect were put forward by Keymer (1972). The contrary view is that some less familiar species frequently prove to be excellent pets, especially for children or those who have limited facilities, because of their size or ease of maintenance (Cooper, 1976; 1986; Cooper and Gibson, 1976). At a time when there is great interest in the 'human-animal bond' this aspect cannot be ignored. Perhaps it is too simplistic to think in terms of 'exotic' versus 'domesticated': after all, certain species such as the golden hamster (*Mesocricetus auratus*) and budgerigar (*Melopsittacus undulatus*) have only been domesticated for a few decades and yet are now well established and popular pets.

There can be no doubt that the veterinary profession must be prepared to deal with exotic species, however uninteresting or distasteful such work may appear to some. As is emphasised in a later chapter (see 'Legislation') the Veterinary Surgeons Act imposes limitations on those who may diagnose and treat diseases or injuries in mammals, birds and reptiles: there are no legal restrictions on amphibians, fish and invertebrates but members of the profession are regularly consulted over the first two of these — and increasingly so over the third — and this is a responsibility which should be taken seriously. The 'Guide to Professional Conduct' (RCVS, 1990) makes this very clear in Paragraph 1.5.1. (Treatment of species not normally dealt with) where it states, *inter alia*:-

> "Every veterinarian . . . will, from time to time, find himself in the position of being presented with an animal for treatment which is an animal of a species with which he does not normally deal. It is accepted that he could be unwise to administer any treatment or give any advice which he does not feel professionally competent to offer. At the same time he has an obligation as a veterinarian to provide first-aid whenever necessary and is better qualified to do so than any lay person."

The Guide goes on to emphasise the importance, when necessary, of referring an animal to another member of the profession more conversant with the species, or, if a case is not actually presented, of giving clear and specific advice to the owner as to where and how he can contact someone with suitable experience. It stresses, however, that 'Animal owners should not be directed to members of the profession who are not in practice without the prior consent of the member having been obtained'. This is an important point: although recent years have seen an increase in the number of veterinary surgeons with experience of exotic species, such persons are usually already heavily committed. Most will readily give advice to their professional colleagues by letter or telephone and many will see referrals. What the vast majority dislike, however, is having their name, address and telephone number given to members of the public by veterinary surgeons who quite clearly are not interested in the case and are anxious to pass the client and the exotic animal on to someone else as quickly as possible. Quite apart from the discourtesy of such an approach it may, in the long run, be counterproductive. There are strong indications that trends in pet-keeping are changing and the profession is likely to see more, rather than fewer, non-domestic animals in future. In these circumstances it would seem prudent for veterinary surgeons to foster a greater interest in, and awareness of, such species and, rather than depending entirely on the experience of colleagues, to develop expertise and confidence with them themselves.

Readers will find that the best way to use this manual is to refer to the Index as well as the main chapter headings. Information about a particular disease or diagnostic technique is not necessarily repeated and therefore the answer to a query about hamsters may be found under 'Gerbils' or 'Rats and Mice'. The manual clearly cannot cover all aspects of exotic pets but will, it is hoped, prove a useful source of information and guidance to those who work with these species.

A number of abbreviations are used in this manual in order to save space and facilitate ease of reading. The most important ones are:-

s/c	subcutaneous	sid	once daily
i/m	intramuscular	bid	twice daily
i/v	intravenous	tid	three times daily
i/p	intraperitoneal		

REFERENCES

BUSH, M., SMELLER, J. M., CHARACHE, P. and ARTHUR, R. (1978). Biological half-life of gentamicin in gopher snakes. *American Journal of Veterinary Research* **39**, 171.

COOPER, J. E. (1976). Pets in hospitals. *British Medical Journal* **i**, 698.

COOPER, J. E. (1989). Anaesthesia of exotic species. In: *Manual of Anaesthesia for Small Animal Practice* (Ed. A. D. R. Hilbery) BSAVA, Cheltenham.

COOPER. J. E. (1986). Animals in schools. *Journal of Small Animal Practice* **27**, 839.

COOPER, J. E. and GIBSON, L. W. (1976). 'Exotic' not always 'unsuitable'. *Veterinary Record* **98**, 37.

COOPER, M. E. (1987). *An Introduction to Animal Law.* Academic Press, London.

FLECKNELL, P. (1987). *Laboratory Animal Anaesthesia.* Academic Press, London.

HOLT, P. E. (1981). Drugs and dosages. In: *Diseases of the Reptilia.* Vol. 2. (Eds. J. E. Cooper, and O. F. Jackson) Academic Press, London.

KEYMER, I. F. (1972). The unsuitability of non-domesticated animals as pets. *Veterinary Record* **91**, 373.

KIRKWOOD, J. K. (1983a). Dosing exotic species. *Veterinary Record* **112**, 486.

KIRKWOOD, J. K. (1983b). Influence of body size on health and disease. *Veterinary Record* **113**, 287.

KIRKWOOD, J. K. and WATHES, C. M. (1984). Size, time, ketamine and birds. *Veterinary Record* **115**, 390.

LAWRENCE, K. (1983). The use of antibiotics in reptiles: a review. *Journal of Small Animal Practice* **24**, 741.

MASON, I. L. (1984). Ed. *Evolution of Domesticated Animals.* Longman, London.

ROYAL COLLEGE OF VETERINARY SURGEONS (1990). *Guide to Professional Conduct.* RCVS, London.

UNIVERSITIES FEDERATION FOR ANIMAL WELFARE/WORLD SOCIETY FOR THE PROTECTION OF ANIMALS (1989). *Euthanasia of Amphibians and Reptiles.* UFAW, Potters Bar.

WOOD, G. L. (1982). Ed. *Guinness Book of Animal Facts and Feats.* Guinness Superlatives, Enfield.

FURTHER READING

BREARLEY, M. J., COOPER, J. E. and SULLIVAN, M. (1991). *A Colour Atlas of Small Animal Endoscopy.* Wolfe, London.

COOPER, J. E. (1984). Anaesthesia of exotic animals. *Animal Technology* **35**, 13.

COOPER, J. E. (1986). Veterinary work with non-domesticated pets. I, II, III and IV. *British Veterinary Journal* **142**, 411, 420; **143**, 21, 193.

FOWLER, M. E. (1986). Ed. *Zoo and Wild Animal Medicine.* 2nd Edn. W. B. Saunders, Philadelphia.

GABRISCH, K. and ZWART, P. (1985). Eds. *Krankheiten der Heimtiere.* Schlütersche, Hannover.

GABRISCH, K. and ZWART, P. (1987). Eds. *Krankheiten der Wildtiere.* Schlütersche, Hannover.

GREEN. C. J. (1979). *Animal Anaesthesia.* Laboratory Animals Limited, London.

HARKNESS, J. E. (1987). Ed. *Exotic Pet Medicine.* The Veterinary Clinics of North America, W. B. Saunders, Philadelphia.

JACOBSON, E. R. and KOLLIAS, G. V. (1988). Eds. *Exotic Animals.* Churchill Livingstone, New York.

JOHNSTON, D. E. (1986). Ed. *Exotic Animal Medicine Practice.* The Compendium Collection Veterinary Learning Systems, New Jersey.

KLÖS, H. G. and LANG, E. M. (1982). Eds. *Handbook of Zoo Medicine.* Van Nostrand Reinhold Company, New York.

KNIGHT, M. and GREEN, W. (1983). *Keeping Pets.* Treasure Press, London.

POOLE, T. B. (1987). Ed. *The UFAW Handbook on the Care and Management of Laboratory Animals.* 6th Edn. Longman, Harlow.

WALLACH, J. D. and BOEVER, W. J. (1983). *Diseases of Exotic Animals.* W. B. Saunders, Philadelphia.

CHAPTER TWO

CHINCHILLAS

Richard A Webb BVSc MRCVS

Two species of chinchilla are recognised, *Chinchilla laniger* and *Chinchilla brevicaudata.* They are hystrichomorph rodents closely related to the porcupine, coypu, guinea pig and viscacha. They all originate from South America. Chinchillas inhabit the Andes of Peru, Bolivia, Chile and Argentina, living at altitudes of 4,500 metres. They have been bred in captivity since 1923 when numbers were caught alive by Mathias Chapman.

Chinchilla laniger is the main species bred today. It is a small squirrel-like rodent with endearing characteristics. Although shy and easily frightened, it makes a clean, odourless and friendly pet for the older child or adult who has had experience in handling other less lively animals. Its fur, for which it was trapped almost to extinction, is a beautiful bluish grey. Colour mutations now exist including white, silver, beige and black. The photograph shows an adult grey and an adult white chinchilla (see Figure 1).

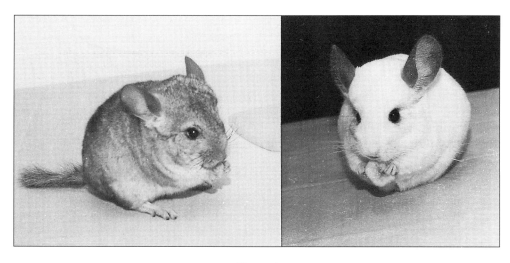

Figure 1

BIOLOGICAL DATA

Adult weight	400-500g, female larger than male
Birth weight	30—60g
Number born	1—5, usually 2
Gestation	111 days
Weaning age	6—8 weeks
Life-span	10 years — up to 18 years has been recorded
Sexual maturity	8 months
Body temperature	38° — 39°C
Pulse	100—150 per minute
Respiratory rate	40—80 per minute

Chinchillas are basically nocturnal but can be quite active during the day.

HOUSING

A well lit and ventilated room or building kept between 10°C and 20°C is necessary. Chinchillas gnaw a great deal and make light work of wooden cages. Welded wire mesh cages of 15mm by 15mm mesh are usually provided, with or without solid floors. Chinchillas are very active, acrobatic animals and require a lot of space. Ideally an enclosure of at least 2m x 2m x 1m should be provided with a wooden nestbox 30cm x 25cm x 20cm. Many breeders use smaller cages but the author believes these active animals need as much room as possible for exercise.

Dust baths should be given daily. These must be deep enough to allow the animal to roll over. A finely powdered volcanic rock is used to keep the fur clean and well groomed. Chinchillas can be kept in pairs, colonies or polygamous units with one male having access to about five females maintained in separate cages. The male has a tunnel along the back of the cages which enables him to enter any cage. The females cannot pass through the tunnel because they are each fitted with a light plastic or metal collar which is just a little wider than the opening to the cage. The male feeds in any one of the cages.

Chinchillas can survive very low temperatures (0°C) if they are kept in a dry atmosphere free from draughts. High temperatures must be avoided. Low relative humidity (under 50%) and temperatures under 18°C favour fur growth (Kraft, 1966).

FEEDING

Little is known about the diet of the wild chinchilla except that it will eat a wide range of vegetable food. In captivity a standard rabbit or guinea pig pellet is useful. If the pellets are made longer than normal this will enable chinchillas to pick up the food with their forefeet and eat while sitting on their haunches. An average analysis of such pellets would be:- crude protein 16—20%, fat 2—5%, moisture 10%.

The pellets should provide about 11.34 KJ (2,700 calories)/kg of diet (Davis and Hoff, 1982). Good hay should be fed. Clover hays are better sources of calcium and other minerals. All hay must be free from mould and vermin contamination. Water must be provided by bottle or automatic drinkers. Dried fruit and nuts are especially liked. Fresh carrot, cut grass and well washed green vegetables can also be given. Pellets may be fed *ad libitum* or given at intervals during the day. Any change of diet, even the introduction of a new supply of hay or pellets, should be done slowly.

HANDLING

Chinchillas are not difficult to handle and rarely bite. They may be picked up by holding them round the shoulders, but it must be remembered that grasping the fur or rough handling will result in the animals shedding patches of fur. This is called 'fur slip'. In order to avoid this the chinchilla can be picked up by its tail close to the body. The body is then supported by the other hand. If this cannot be achieved because the animal is too lively, an ear may be held to discourage jumping whilst the tail is grasped. Chinchillas should not be lifted by an ear alone.

REPRODUCTION

Although chinchillas will breed throughout the year, they are essentially seasonally polyoestrous, the main breeding season being between November and May in the Northern hemisphere.

Oestrous cycles vary from 30 — 50 days. When in oestrus, the normally tightly-sealed vulva is open and mucus is generally visible. After mating, a copulatory plug or 'stopper' is passed by the female. This is thought to consist of coagulated vesicular and prostatic gland secretions in a casing of vaginal cells.

The gestation period is 111 days and births generally occur in the early morning. The young, usually two, are precocious, being fully furred and able to see and move about easily. The female suckles her young from her pectoral mammary glands in the first instance, only using the more caudal ones when a larger litter has to be fed. If the dam has no milk, a foster mother can be tried; even a guinea pig may be suitable. Failing this, hand-rearing must be undertaken. Evaporated milk, diluted equally with boiled water, can be fed to appetite with an eye dropper or syringe. A piece of bicycle valve-rubber attached to the end of the dropper makes an ideal teat. Vitamin drops and cereals can be added after one week. Newly born kits can be quite aggressive to each other, particularly when there are more than two. Clipping the incisor teeth may be necessary to prevent serious injury to siblings. Weaning can take place at 6—8 weeks.

A *post-partum* oestrus occurs within the first 24 hours after birth.

Dystocias due to schistomsome fetuses have been recorded on a number of occasions. Caesarean section using atropine premedication followed by halothane induction and maintenance has been very successful (Jones, 1990; Stephenson, 1990).

SEXING

Females

The urethral orifice is at the end of a genital papilla at the base of which is the slit-like vulva. The vulva is normally sealed unless in season when it is open for 3—5 days. Immediately caudal to the urogenital openings is the anus (see Figure 2).

Males

The penis is separated from the anus by a considerable distance (see Figure 2).

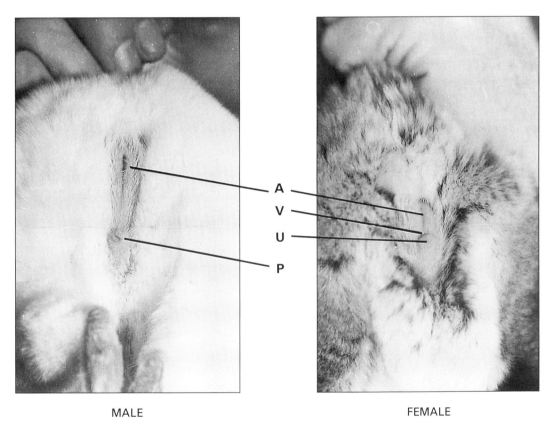

MALE   FEMALE

Figure 2
External genitalia of adult chinchillas.
A = anus, P = tip of prepuce, U = urethral opening, V = vulva.

CASTRATION

When castrating a chinchilla it is necessary to suture the cremasteric sac with its outer layer of internal abdominal oblique muscle, as there is no internal inguinal ring to prevent loss of abdominal contents (Ashdown *et al*, 1967) (see also 'Guinea Pigs').

DISEASES/CLINICAL CONDITIONS

Non-Infectious Diseases

Malocclusions or 'slobbers'

Probably, this is the most commonly presented condition of chinchillas. The molar teeth become overgrown, as do the incisors which lose their orange pigment and become ridged. A constant clinical sign in the later stages is excessive drooling with wet fur around the chin, chest and forepaws. The roots of the molars begin to extend into the orbit which causes lachrymation. The upper molars curve downwards and outwards, the inner edges of the lower molars grow and project inwards, towards the tongue (see Figure 3).

Inspection of the mouth and teeth can be carried out using a standard metal aural speculum. The use of a woollen sock with a part of the toe cut out is an easy means of restraint. The chinchilla is put into the sock head first and the head only allowed to emerge at the cut-off end.

Treatment of malocclusions gives disappointing results as the molar arcade remains abnormal. However, under sedation with acepromazine and atropine (see Anaesthesia), the molar spurs can be trimmed with a pair of narrow electrician's pliers and smoothed with small files. Overgrown incisors can be shortened easily where necessary.

Improvement in the mineral balance, possibly using Vionate Powder (Ciba-Geigy), and the provision of sufficient wood or pumice stone on which to gnaw, may help. Breeding from affected stock should be avoided as there may be an inherited predisposition to this condition.

ABNORMAL   NORMAL

Figure 3
Malocclusions in a chinchilla.

'Fur ring'

Adult males may suffer from paraphimosis. This is often caused by the presence of a ring of fur around the penis inside the prepuce. The penis should be carefully withdrawn and lubricated. The ring of fur can be slipped off or carefully cut away.

'Fur slip'

Chinchillas slip areas of fur when roughly handled or when in fights. The skin is left clean and smooth. Regrowth may take from 4—6 months (Mainwaring, 1962).

'Fur chewing'

Here the animal chews its own or its mate's fur leaving the coat with a motheaten appearance. The cause or causes of this are not fully determined but a low roughage diet, boredom, dirty fur, dietary imbalances and hereditary factors may be involved.

Colic

Various factors, including gastric tympany, intussusception and impaction of the caecum and large intestine, have been implicated. In the last condition hard contents can be palpated in the large intestine. The animal will be seen stretching and rolling about in obvious distress. Treatment necessitates softening the bowel contents with liquid paraffin given by mouth and warm soapy liquids by enema. Intussusception requires surgery. To treat gastric tympany, a stomach tube may be passed or the gas released by paracentesis.

'Shock'

Progressive weakness and inco-ordination may be early signs of shock. Treatment will necessitate removal of the stress factors if known, keeping the animal in a very warm, quiet, dimly lit room and giving corticosteroids and circulatory stimulants such as etamiphylline camsylate (Millophylline-V, Arnolds). The dose should be based on that recommended for cats and dogs.

Infectious diseases

Definitive diagnosis of many infectious diseases requires laboratory investigation. There are likely to be differences between the diseases seen in children's pets and those in large establishments. However, a similar clinical approach should be followed to that adopted for a cat or dog. The following notes may give the reader some indication of the likely diseases to be seen in chinchillas (see Further Reading; Bowden, 1959; Dall, 1962).

Pseudotuberculosis caused by *Yersinia pseudotuberculosis*

This disease may be acute or chronic in nature. Clinical signs are very variable and include listlessness, loss of weight and diarrhoea. Loss of appetite is not consistently seen. Infection is probably introduced by food contamination by wild rodents. The use of tetracyclines in the drinking water can prevent the transmission in chinchilla herds.

Clostridial enterotoxaemia caused by *Clostridium perfringens*

The production of type A enterotoxin causes gastro-intestinal disturbances, prolapsed rectum, flatulence and severe diarrhoea leading to death within 24—48 hours (Bartoszcze *et al,* 1990).

Listeriosis caused by *Listeriosis monocytogenes*

The chinchilla is highly susceptible to this disease. Encephalitic and enteric forms are encountered. Treatment is unlikely to be effective. Prevention is most important. Rodent contaminated food or fomites must be avoided. Signs include depression, inappetence, diarrhoea and loss of weight. Death may occur within a few days from septicaemia or there may be illness for one to two weeks. *Post-mortem* examination frequently reveals whitish miliary nodules, approximately 1mm in diameter, throughout the liver and mesentery.

Following diagnosis and antibiotic sensitivity, treatment with appropriate antibiotics could be given to other animals at risk.

Enteritis

Causes of enteritis are numerous, including coccidia, *Clostridium* spp., *E. coli, Proteus, Pseudomonas, Staphylococcus* and *Salmonella* spp. Identification of the causal organism from faecal samples and antimicrobial sensitivity testing is required. Oral antibiotics can be safely given for short periods, but care must be taken with a number of injectable agents (see also 'Gerbils', 'Guinea Pigs', 'Hamsters', 'Rabbits' and 'Rats and Mice').

Pneumonia

Again, various bacteria have been implicated including *Pseudomonas* and *Pasteurella* spp. Damp, draughty housing may predispose to this condition.

Ringworm

The chinchilla is susceptible to infection with *Trichophyton mentagrophytes* and *Microsporum* spp. This can be treated with griseofulvin (Grisovin, Coopers Pitman-Moore) (25mg/kg bodyweight orally once a day for 3 weeks).

Other parasites

Nematodes, cestodes (*Hymenolepis* sp.), *Giardia* spp. and coccidia are occasionally seen. They are rarely pathogenic. Where *Giardia* spp. are thought to be influencing the course of an enteritis, treatment can be given using metronidazole (Torgyl, RMB) in the drinking water at the rate of 4ml/kg for 5—7 days.

DRUG ADMINISTRATION

Injection technique

Intramuscular injections can be given into the quadriceps femoris or the semitendinosus semi-membranosus muscles, using a 23—25 gauge needle. No more than 0.3ml of a solution should be given at a single site to an adult animal. Insulin syringes have 25 gauge needles and are ideal for accurate administration.

Subcutaneous injections using a 23 gauge needle can be given under the skin of the neck or flank. One should remember that 'fur-slip' occurs if the fur is pulled (see earlier).

Intraperitoneal injections of up to 10ml of fluid can be given by the usual methods (see also 'Guinea Pigs' and 'Rats and Mice').

Intravenous injections. No information is available on suitable sites.

Oral drops of sweetened or human paediatric medicines can be given by syringe. Powders can be concealed inside sultanas.

DRUG DOSAGES

Owners must be advised that the drugs to be discussed are not licensed for use in chinchillas.

Anthelmintics

The following drugs have been used to control nematodes and cestodes in chinchillas, though these are not commonly found in pet animals.

Ivermectin (Ivomec, MSD)	0.1% solution at a dose rate of 0.1ml per 500g either s/c or orally.
Metroniphate (Neguvon, Bayer)	100mg/kg given in a syrup. Is better tolerated than thiabendazole.
Niclosamide (Yomesan, Bayer)	200mg/kg is effective against tapeworms.
Thiabendazole (MSD)	100mg/kg is effective against trichostrongyles but can be toxic (Stampa and Hobbs, 1966).

Antibiotics

Among the many that can be used are:-

Cephalosporin (Ceporex, Coopers Pitman-Moore)	25—100mg/kg orally qid. The injectable suspension is too thick to be delivered through a 23—25 gauge needle.
Chloramphenicol	50mg/kg i/m bid.
Chloramphenicol palmitate	50mg/kg orally bid.
Chlortetracycline	50mg/kg orally bid.
Cotrimoxazole syrup or injection	25mg/kg of combined active material bid.
Griseofulvin	25mg/kg orally sid.
Oxytetracycline	50—100mg/kg orally bid.
Tetracycline	50mg/kg orally bid. It has been suggested that this may be used to treat pseudotuberculosis and listeriosis.

ANAESTHESIA AND SURGERY

As chinchillas are extremely susceptible to stress, surgery should be undertaken with caution. Premedication with atropine (0.5mg/kg) and acepromazine (0.5mg/kg) should be given for operations other than caesarean section when acepromazine must not be given.

Inhalation anaesthetics

Halothane by a mask or through a small box with a glass side (see 'Introduction'). This agent is suitable for long procedures. **Ether** can be used but is not so well tolerated. **Methoxyflurane** (Metofane, C-Vet) is safe but induction can be prolonged.

Non-volatile agents

Alphaxalone/alphadolone (Saffan, Coopers Pitman-Moore). The large volumes needed make it unsuitable for intramuscular use.

Ketamine hydrochloride (Vetalar, Parke-Davis) (40mg/kg) plus acepromazine (0.5mg/kg) intramuscularly (Morgan *et al*, 1981). Induction takes approximately 5 minutes, duration of surgical anaesthesia is 40—60 minutes and complete recovery occurs in 2—5 hours.

During recovery the animal should be kept in a warm place and handled occasionally to stimulate return of consciousness. Fluids may be helpful. Up to 10ml of warm saline or Hartmann's solution can be given subcutaneously depending on the size of the animal.

A request for further information

Little has been published on the veterinary care of chinchillas. The experience of practitioners and others can be most valuable, and the author would appreciate communications from others who have worked with these species.

REFERENCES

ASHDOWN, R. R., WEBB, R. A. and COOPER, J. E. (1967). The anatomy of the abdominal muscles of the chinchilla. *Research in Veterinary Science* **8**, 227.

BARTOSZCZE, M., NOWAKOWSKI, M., ROSZKOWSKI, J., MATRAS, J., PALEC, S. and WYSTUPE, E. (1990). Chinchilla deaths due to *Clostridium perfringens* A enterotoxin. *Veterinary Record* **126**, 341.

DAVIS, J. W. and HOFF, G. L. (1982). *Non-infectious Diseases of Wildlife.* Iowa State University Press, Ames.

JONES, A. K. (1990). Caesarian section in a chinchilla. *Veterinary Record* **126**, 441.

KRAFT, H. (1966). Chinchilla diseases. *Blue Book for the Veterinary Profession* **11**, 7.

MAINWARING, U. (1962). The handling and management of the chinchilla. *Journal of Small Animal Practice* **4**, 197.

MORGAN, R. J., EDDY, L. B., SOLIE, T. N. and TURBES, C. C. (1981). Ketamine-acepromazine as an anaesthetic agent of chinchillas. *Laboratory Animals* **15**, 218.

STAMPA, S. and HOBSON, N. K. (1966). Control of some internal parasites of chinchillas. *Journal of the American Veterinary Medical Association* **149**, 929.

STEPHENSON, R. S. (1990). Caesarian section in a chinchilla. *Veterinary Record* **126**, 370.

FURTHER READING

BOWDEN, R. S. T. (1959). Diseases of chinchillas. *Veterinary Record* **71**, 1033.

BRITISH VETERINARY ASSOCIATION (1970). *Handbook of the Treatment of Exotic Pets: Part 2, Chinchillas.* BVA, London.

DALL, J. (1962). Diseases of the chinchilla. *Journal of Small Animal Practice* **4**, 207.

DUPHAR VETERINARY LIMITED. *The Management of Exotic Animals — a Duphar Guide: Chinchillas.* Duphar Veterinary Limited, Southampton.

SNOW, C. F. (1959). *Chinchilla Breeding.* Foyles Handbooks, London.

UNIVERSITIES FEDERATION FOR ANIMAL WELFARE (1987). *The UFAW Handbook on the Care and Management of Laboratory Animals.* 6th Edn. (Ed. T. B. Poole) Longman, Harlow.

CHAPTER THREE   # CHIPMUNKS

K Elizabeth Gillett

J David Temple MA VetMB MRCVS

Figure 1
Siberian chipmunk identified by dorsal stripes continuing to tail root
and white-tipped hairs on tail.

There are 24 species of chipmunks within the Genus *Tamias* (Honacki *et al*, 1982). However, only colonies of the relatively large Siberian (or Asian) species, *Tamias (Eutamias) sibiricus* (see Figure 1), also known as the Korean or Japanese squirrel or Burunduk, were found in the UK during a survey (Blake and Gillett, 1984). Presumably earlier colonies of North American species had died out and although more Siberian chipmunks are now being imported from Korea via the Continent, there are no reports of further introductions from North America. The chipmunk is a diurnal, alert and very active burrowing rodent which is also an agile climber. In both morphology and behaviour it is intermediate between the tree squirrel and the ground squirrel (marmots, prairie dogs etc). In the wild these chipmunks are associated with forests (Ognev, 1940). They live in loose colonies with individual burrows (Kawamichi, 1989). Prior to 1971, most of the original stock was probably imported from Korea and Japan but these two races are now interbred. Albinos are appearing in some colonies; in others with close selective pairing, pale cream-coloured chipmunks with stripes just visible are being bred.

BIOLOGICAL DATA

Adult weight	72-120g
Adult length	head and body, 12—19cm; tail, 11cm approx.
Respiratory rate	75 per minute approx. (resting)
Body temperature	38°C when awake; a few degrees above environmental temperature when in hibernation
Longevity in captivity	average according to survey: male 2.7 years though some live to 8 years female 4.1 years but can live up to 12 years
Longevity in the wild	8 years or longer (Snyder, 1982)

HOUSING

Chipmunks may be kept in a house, shed or outside aviary and can be caged singly, in pairs or in trios of one male with two females. It has now been found that if several animals are caged together, after a while only the dominant female breeds and eventually the colony dies out.

Cages

Cages should be as large as possible with base + length + height totalling 3.5m for an indoor cage and 4.5m for an outside cage. Upright supports of metal or untreated wood are covered with wire, fixed internally to prevent gnawing. Inside cages should have one or more solid sides with the solid base covered with paper, wood shavings or dry peat (sawdust causes sneezing). As chipmunks are enthusiastic burrowers, the bases of outside cages should be made of well-drained concrete, unpointed bricks or wire mesh. The base should then be covered with soil or peat. One end of the cage should be solid and covered for protection against the weather. It is advisable to have a double entrance to prevent escapes and upstand boards should be placed around the base to keep the cage litter inside. The wiring mesh should be no larger than 2.5 x 1.3cm and 16 gauge is recommended. 2.5 x 2.5cm mesh permits escape and 22 gauge chicken netting can be bitten through. All cage doors should be bolted top and bottom. Hook and eye fastenings shake undone as the animal runs up and down the wiring. To provide both an interesting environment and hiding places, branches, rocks, shelves, pipes, an empty cardboard box, dry grass and leaves and extra nestboxes must be added to the cage. If inside cages are positioned by a window, the chipmunks will spend much time watching what goes on outside, though they should be shaded against hot sunshine.

NB. Particular care is needed to ensure that the mesh is sound and that there are no tiny gaps at the joins or between the mesh and the base of the cage. Chipmunks can push through very small holes to escape as many have already done.

Chipmunks are clean animals; they will use one particular spot in a cage as a latrine. Apart from removing old fruit, cleaning of outside cages is not necessary, although the soil base can be changed once a year. Inside cages should be cleaned every 1—4 weeks as needed and depending upon the base covering used. It is easier to do this when the animals are asleep at night. Too much disturbance should be avoided.

Nestboxes

One nestbox per adult is required in each cage. This should measure approximately 15 x 20 x 15cm for indoor cages and larger for outside cages to allow space for extra insulation in winter. It can be sited on the ground or slightly above with the 5cm entrance hole turned away from the light source. The nestboxes should be filled with hay, shredded paper or leaves. Nestboxes must be cleaned after weaning; in addition they should be cleaned at least once up to a maximum of three times per year. It is better to leave them untouched in winter. Some seeds should be added to replace the hoards removed when cleaning. Extra nesting material must be provided in early autumn in preparation for winter and should also be available for a mother with young. Artificial heating is not necessary, but good ventilation is important.

FEEDING

In the wild, Siberian chipmunks are primarily vegetarians and seed eaters, 72.6% of their food being seeds, with buds, leaves and flowers making up 23.6%. Some insects are eaten but this is thought to be incidental (Kawamichi, 1980). In captivity a balanced diet is important but acceptance of individual foods other than seeds varies over the year.

Seeds

Chipmunks will eat sunflower seeds, wheat, maize, rolled oats, plain canary seed and buckwheat. Commercial bird seed or hamster mix can also be offered. Peanuts are better avoided and the sharp points of whole oats may damage the pouches of chipmunks.

Fruit

Chipmunks eat a wide variety of fruit, eg. oranges, apples, grapes, gooseberries, blackberries, raspberries, cherries, plums, hips, haws etc. Raisins, sultanas and dried banana slices are also taken. Plum stones should not be given as these are potentially toxic.

Vegetables

Lettuce, dandelion leaves and flowers, peapods, corn cobs, tomatoes, chickenweed, groundsel and clover may be given.

Nuts

Acorns, beech mast, walnuts (cracked), cob, hazel, pine and sweet chestnut are all enjoyed by chipmunks.

Other foods

Branches and twigs to gnaw are necessary to keep the constantly growing teeth in trim; cooked bones can also be given. Foods supplying supplementary protein should be provided if needed, particularly for pregnant and/or lactating females. These may be in the form of a gruel made with milk, honey and baby cereal such as Mylupa (Mylupa Infant Foods), puppy biscuit, day-old chick legs or cooked chicken drumsticks. Some chipmunks will eat insects and their larvae; the poisonous tiger- striped caterpillars of the cinnabar moth must be avoided, as should those with urticating hairs. Water, to which a vitamin preparation can be added, should always be available, preferably in water-bottles with a metal spout. A calcium block may be provided in the cage.

HANDLING AND BEHAVIOUR

In captivity the avoidance of both aggression and stress is important, for unless controlled either could be fatal. Hyperactivity indicates stress and some individuals of either sex are naturally aggressive; the signs are frequent chasing of the subdominant animal and preventing it from eating. It is advisable not to put a new animal into a cage already occupied by another, but to put both into a fresh cage. The exception to this is that a male may be introduced into the cage of a female on heat. It is best to cage pairs or trios together at the age of six weeks if possible.

Generally, chipmunks do not like being handled and may bite hard, though some which have been hand-reared may be picked up in cupped hands or quickly by the large scruff of the neck (making sure that the cheek pouches are empty) and held supported by the other hand against the handler's body. A lightweight butterfly net can be used for wilder animals, which must be promptly but gently gathered into the base of the net when caught. A long continuous chase without a break is very stressful and must be avoided. A repeated cycle of activity can become a habit and to avoid this further diversifications should be added to the cage (Zoological Society of London, 1974). For example, an inside cage could be moved nearer a window.

Hibernation

In winter, some animals kept indoors may become torpid and remain in their nestboxes for several days with the entrance hole plugged with bedding, before resuming normal activity. Outside, some chipmunks may hibernate while others will remain active. If provided with 50cm depth of soil and leaves etc. for bedding, chipmunks will hibernate from October to April, awakening every few days to eat from their hoards and to excrete without emerging. The survival rate is higher where there is no hibernation.

Escapes

If a chipmunk escapes, it will return to its cage of its own accord if the way is clear, but cats — and dogs — are a danger.

Transport

Healthy animals travel well in suitable boxes. If these are used as temporary nestboxes before and after a journey this lessens the stress. There should be minimum disturbance for the first few days after a move. Following a purchase, it is recommended that diet details are obtained from the seller so that no abrupt changes are made in the food offered.

Television (TV)

Animals caged near a television set can suffer from severe stress. Prolonged exposure can result in death or the loss of litters. It is suspected that the radiation from the 15.6kHz time-based oscillator is responsible. There would be electromagnetic radiation and probably sonic radiation at this frequency, which is in the sensitive area of chipmunks' hearing range.

SEXING

The penis is visible in males, and in the breeding season the scrotum is much enlarged. The distance between the anus and the urogenital papilla is greater in males than in females. Litters can be sexed at one week of age when the female is out of the nestbox.

REPRODUCTION

Young born	March—September
Oestrous cycle	usually 13—14 days (range 11—21 days)
Gestation	usually 31—32 days (range 28—35 days)
Emergence of young	about 35 days (range 28—35 days)
Weaning	about 1 week after emergence
Litter size	usually 3—5 but may vary from 1—10
Mammary glands	4 pairs

There are one or sometimes two litters per year; the second litter is smaller, born about three months after the first. It is rare for a female to have three litters in one season. Males and females breed from 1-7 years of age. The overall sex ratio is even at birth. The male's testes descend into the scrotum about the beginning of January and are retracted into the abdomen by the end of September. Females have a three-day cycle when the males are attracted. On the second day the female calls, chirping repeatedly throughout the day from a perch in the cage. She will allow the male to approach her on this day and successful copulation usually occurs. Some chipmunks of both sexes may be in breeding condition for only the first few months of the breeding season. There is no *post-partum* oestrus (Blake and Gillett, 1988). Females are normally active during pregnancy. They are not often seen on the day of parturition but might emerge briefly in the late day, when the teats are prominent. The young are born naked and blind and are 3cm long. They are fully furred at 16 days and the eyes open at about 26—29 days (Saddington, 1966). The young squeak from birth for about 14 days after which they are generally silent until emergence. Most litters survive but should the mother become stressed, eg. TV emission, human disturbance, strange loud noises or because of some unknown factor, the neonates may die and be abandoned or eaten, possibly because lactation has not been established. Another sign of stress is the mother running around the cage carrying one or more neonates in her mouth before returning them to the nestbox. The young usually survive this treatment.

Hand-rearing

Young have been successfully reared by hand from one week on a mixture of 3 teaspoonfuls baby cereal such as Mylupa, 1 teaspoonful evaporated milk and 1/2 teaspoonful honey mixed together with water to the consistency of a thin gruel. A vitamin supplement can be added. A dropper or teat used for kittens may be used for feeding, which must be carried out very slowly.

Feeding routine: every 4 hours at age 1-2 weeks
every 6 hours at age 2-3 weeks
every 8 hours from 3 weeks to weaning

Should bubbles appear at the nostrils or choking occur, the young chipmunk should be held up by its hindlegs, while its body is supported with a finger, until respiration has returned to normal. To aid elimination of fluid, the abdomen may be gently stroked with a piece of cotton-wool squeezed out in tepid water.

DISEASES/CLINICAL CONDITIONS

As long as chipmunks are provided with good housing and diet, they are tough little animals and usually stay healthy. There appears to be no specific illness to which they are prone. Lacerations following fighting are probably the most common cause of death. Should the end of the tail become caught, the skin sloughs off leaving the bone exposed, which the chipmunk removes itself. The tail does not grow again and no treatment is needed. A sick animal is inactive, sits with its fur fluffed up and is inappetent. Chipmunks appear to recognise potential weakness in others. Recently weaned young may receive a fatal bite. Older, chronically ill animals die from stress after relentless chasing. Although such animals may show little outward signs of illness, *post-mortem* examination will reveal serious pathological conditions. Some chipmunks are allergic to cow's milk.

Skin and associated structures

Abscesses

These occur and may be treated using trimethoprin/sulphadiazine (Tribressin, Coopers Pitman-Moore). One quarter of a Tribressin 80 tablet can be dissolved in water and the resulting solution divided into 12 equal parts. Each part thus contains 10mg of active ingredient of trimethoprin/sulphadiazine which is the daily dose for a 100g chipmunk.

Alopecia

This condition may respond to corticosteroid injections but, first, other possible causes, eg. parasites, should be excluded.

Lacerations

These may result from fighting or faulty cage wiring. Potentiated sulphonamides (see Abscesses) will reduce the risk of infection. Severe lacerations may need suturing. Deep wounds may result in marked swelling and oedema. There is little bleeding from these wounds. However, if a claw is torn off or if a digit is bitten, bleeding may continue for many minutes.

Parasites

Mange. Bromocyclen powder (Alugan, Hoechst) sprinkled in the nestbox and on the animal itself appears to cure this problem. The identity of the parasite involved is not clear.

Fleas and harvest mites. Fleas may be introduced by rodents and, in the summer, harvest mite larvae may be introduced on clothing. Bromocyclen is an effective treatment.

Endoparasites. These are rare in chipmunks.

Respiratory conditions

Emphysema

The clinical signs of emphysema and peribronchial cuffing are gasping sounds lasting up to 20 minutes with a very rapid respiration rate (around 150 per minute). Traces of blood may be seen around the nostrils. The animal gradually grows weaker until death supervenes. The cause and pathogenesis of this condition are not clear.

Pneumonia

This may occur as a result of stress following a change of environment (see Transport, Handling and Behaviour). Predisposing factors are bad housing and damp conditions. Good ventilation is important. Oxytetracycline powder (Terramycin Soluble Powder 5.5%, Pfizer) at a dose rate of 40mg of powder (ie. 2.2mg oxytetracycline active ingredient) per chipmunk per day given orally for 5 days is often effective.

Deaths in chipmunks have occurred folowing exposure to human influenza virus (C. Moiser, personal communication).

Other clinical conditions

Cataracts

These may occur in older animals, particularly males, and are of unknown aetiology. Partial or complete blindness is shown by the animals' running into objects and by hesitancy when climbing.

Enteritis

Bacterial enteritis is not uncommon and may be treated with antibiotics (see Pneumonia for example and dose) or potentiated sulphonamides (see Abscesses). The water in which whole grain rice has been boiled, or arrowroot cakes, may be an effective ancillary treatment. *Salmonella* spp. may be implicated. Transmission by mice is suspected.

Epilepsy

This condition is rare and the pathogenesis is not clear. The animal is seen to race round and round before dropping quivering and losing consciousness. There may be several such fits before death occurs.

Fractures

Falls may occur without harm resulting, but fractures may result if the landing is on a hard object. If the vertebral column is fractured death usually follows, but long bones will heal naturally. Radiography can be carried out with the chipmunk placed in a large transparent plastic bag with suitable small air holes. General anaesthesia is not normally necessary: it can cause considerable stress in chipmunks. However, if radiography is necessary this should be done as quickly as possible to minimise stress. The chipmunk should be confined in a very small cage for 3 — 4 weeks, then moved to a larger one for a further 7 — 10 days before being returned to its normal enclosure. Some time may elapse before full confidence returns and the chipmunk climbs freely again.

Hepatic lesions

Cirrhosis, bile duct proliferation and degenerative changes in the liver have been noted in *post-mortem* specimens as have fatty change and variation in size and appearance of hepatocytes (J.E. Cooper, personal communication). The significance of these changes is unknown.

Hypocalcaemia

This occurs most commonly after parturition at the beginning of lactation. It has been recorded in a young male chipmunk. The clinical signs are partial posterior paralysis, straining, apparent constipation, general lack of coordination and tiredness progressing to semi-consciousness. Treatment must be given as soon as possible using 0.5ml of 10% calcium borogluconate injected subcutaneously. Alternatively, Sandocal (Sandoz) has been shown to be quickly effective given orally (½ tablet in 100ml water). One should avoid using a bottle with a metal spout as deposits are left on the metal. Sandocal is available from chemists without prescription.

Lymphoedema

The lymph nodes or lymphatics above the forelegs may become very swollen and can interfere with climbing. In hibernating animals the swelling decreases over winter; in others it persists throughout the year, gradually increasing in size. 1/80th part of a 40mg frusemide tablet (Lasix, Hoechst) per day given orally helps to reduce this condition. It is probably genetic in origin.

Meningitis

This is probably caused by bacteria or viruses. It has occurred recently in young chipmunks, which showed fits followed by paralysis and death.

Metritis

This may result if a fetus is retained after parturition. There follows a general loss of condition. The urine becomes very dark and the abdomen greatly enlarged and painful. Peritonitis and toxaemia may follow. Sometimes after parturition no young chipmunks may be seen or heard, presumably because the mother has eaten them.

Pyometra

The animal will appear off colour with swelling and pain in the caudal abdomen. The uterus must be removed surgically under general anaesthetic and recovery prospects are good.

Tumours

These may be either benign and circumscribed or more irregular and malignant. The mammary gland is the most common site and the tumours are usually fibro-adenomas (J.E. Cooper, personal communication).

Urethritis and cystitis

Clinical signs are small cries emitted when urinating. The penis of the male is swollen and protruded from the prepuce. The faeces may be larger than normal. There is loss of appetite and vomiting may occur as the general condition deteriorates. Suggested treatment is as for other bacterial infections (see Abscesses and Pneumonia).

Dental disorders

Overgrown teeth

The incisor teeth may become overgrown. If these are left untreated, death will occur due to starvation or the tongue becoming caught against the roof of the mouth. Rhinitis can develop. The condition may be caused by too much soft food. Alternatively, the teeth may become loose in the gums. The teeth can be clipped under a light transient general anaesthetic. If no nuts, twigs or bones are available in the diet, wholemeal macaroni will help to prevent this condition. Either the upper or lower incisors may drop out. The remaining pair must then be clipped regularly. The chipmunk will live normally if fed on a soft diet of fruit and finely ground dehusked sunflower seed. The latter may be obtained from health food shops.

Periodontal disease

This condition can be caused by fragments of wood, plastic or even food being forced up between the incisors. This may lead to chronic suppurative periodontal disease with rhinitis, followed by necrotic rhinitis and generalised toxaemia. Clinical signs are a constantly running nose with noisy respiration when asleep. The animal may wash its face frequently. These signs progress to profuse watering of the eyes and gasping.

GENERAL POINTS

Oral medicines, if not added to the drinking water, can be mixed with cold pureed apple or placed on a dampened or oiled walnut or other favoured food item. If a chipmunk is off colour generally, Wysoy (Wyeth) is useful given at a dilution of 1 part Wysoy to 6 parts water. Visits to a veterinary surgery are very stressful, after which some chipmunks may become quiescent before resuming normal activity 24 hours later.

ANAESTHESIA

Inhalation mixtures such as **oxygen/halothane** or **oxygen/methoxyflurane** may be administered via a tube from a small animal anaesthetic machine vaporiser into a sealed transparent box containing the chipmunk. Once the animal becomes recumbent it is removed from the box and short procedures can be carried out before it recovers.

Alphaxalone/alphadolone (Saffan, Coopers Pitman-Moore) used at a rate of 40mg/kg i/m (ie. 0.33mg for a 100g chipmunk) is suitable for longer procedures.

REFERENCES

BLAKE, B. H. and GILLETT, K. E. (1984). Reproduction of Asian chipmunks (*Tamias sibiricus*) in captivity. *Zoo Biology* **3**, 47.

BLAKE, B. H. and GILLETT, K. E. (1988). Estrous cycle and related aspects of reproduction in captive Asian chipmunks, *Tamias sibiricus. Journal of Mammalogy 69* **3**, 598.

HONACKI, J. H., KINMAN, K. E. and KOEPPL, J. W. (1982). *Mammal Species of the World*. Allen Press Inc. and the Association of Systematics Collections, Kansas.

KAWAMICHI, M. (1980). Food, food hoarding and seasonal changes of Siberian chipmunks. *Japanese Journal of Ecology* **30**, 211.

KAWAMICHI, M. (1989). Nest structure dynamics and seasonal use of nests by Siberian chipmunks (*Eutamias sibiricus*). *Journal of Mammalogy 70* **1**, 44.

OGNEV, S. I. (1940).*Mammals of the USSR and Adjacent Countries. Volume IV, Rodents*. Translated by Israel Program for Scientific Translations, Jerusalem, 1966.

SADDINGTON, G. M. (1966). Notes on the breeding of the Siberian chipmunk, *Tamias sibiricus*, in captivity. *International Zoo Yearbook* **6**, 165.

SNYDER, D. P. (1982). *Tamias striatus, Mammalian species 168*. Leaflet published by the American Society of Mammalogists.

ZOOLOGICAL SOCIETY OF LONDON (1974). *Chipmunks No. 11* (leaflet). Zoological Society of London, London.

FURTHER READING

GILLETT, K. E. (1988). *Chipmunks, the Siberian Chipmunk in Captivity*. Bassett Publications, Plymouth.

HANNEY, P. W. (1975). *Rodents, their Lives and Habits*. David and Charles, Newton Abbot.

WISHNER, L. A. (1982). *Eastern Chipmunks, Secrets of their Solitary Lives*. Smithsonian Institution Press, Washington DC.

CHAPTER FOUR

GERBILS

Christopher D West BVetMed CertLAS MRCVS MIBiol

The most commonly kept species of the Family Gerbillidae, Order Rodentia, is the Mongolian gerbil (*Meriones unguiculatus*). The name 'gerbil' in common usage may be replaced by the term 'jird'.

In the wild this species lives in desert areas of Mongolia and China and evolution for this type of habitat must always be borne in mind when considering environmental conditions in captivity. As pets gerbils are clean, relatively odourless, inquisitive and easy to handle. Most are of a natural, sandy brown colour (agouti) with a black tip to the furred tail, but an albino variety is available and, more recently, colour mutations termed piebald, dove and cinnamon have been bred. Black gerbils are not uncommon. Gerbils are nocturnal, naturally monogamous, have very well developed water-conserving abilities and can tolerate wide temperature fluctuations.

HOUSING

Gerbils are usually kept in solid-floored plastic or metal cages designed for other small rodents. The presence of metal bars should be avoided because attempts at burrowing can lead to abrasion of the nose. Glass aquaria are also suitable containers. The height of the cage should be more than adequate for animals to stand on their hind limbs. Provision of the correct type of bedding, in sufficient depth for burrowing, is vital. Wood-shavings, sawdust, shredded paper and peat can all be used. The best combination is probably to use peat as a substrate (to 3—5cm depth) and shredded paper in the nesting area. Sand, whilst 'natural', can cause facial abrasions and artificial fibres may cause problems by wrapping about limbs and restricting blood supply leading to gangrene, or by causing intestinal impaction after ingestion. Since gerbils produce very small amounts of urine, cage cleaning usually need not be carried out more than every 1—2 weeks depending on the numbers of animals kept together.

Although in the wild gerbils would be subjected to daily temperature fluctuations of approximately 0°—32°C, a range of 15°—20°C is recommended for pets. Relative humidity should not exceed 50% so as to prevent a matted and greasy appearance. Pairs or groups of animals kept together since before sexual maturity tend to co-exist satisfactorily.

If animals are removed and then reunited they are liable to fight. Risks of injury can be minimised by anaesthetising animals and allowing them to recover together in a new cage (Harkness and Wagner, 1977) or placing hiding places in a cage for subordinate animals. Females are often more aggressive than males.

FEEDING

Proprietary rodent diets for rats and mice are suitable for gerbils; adults will consume approximately 10—15g daily. Gerbils will show a preference for sunflower seeds so these must only be given as occasional treats. If too many sunflower seeds are given the low levels of calcium and high fat content can lead to metabolic problems, notably osteodystrophies/osteoporosis, in turn leading to skeletal abnormalities and fractures. Similarly, the proportion of green food in the diet should be rationed to achieve a balanced intake of nutrients.

Fresh water should always be available *ad libitum,* although gerbils, with their water conservation capabilities, require only small amounts, particularly if fed some green food. The average adult daily consumption is about 4—5ml.

Young gerbils start to eat solid food from about two weeks of age so need to be given softened/moistened pellets and some green food. They also start to drink water so the sipper tube needs to be within reach and a water bottle used which requires very little suction.

HANDLING

Gerbils rarely bite but they may struggle and can jump prodigiously in efforts to escape. They should never be picked up near the tip of the tail as this may lead to stripping of the skin of the tail. They may be picked up by placing cupped hands over the animal, or the base of the tail may be held gently by one hand, with support provided by placing the palm of the other hand under the animal's body and limbs. Firmer restraint can be achieved by grasping the loose skin at the scruff of the neck and applying downward pressure. Gerbils resent being held on their backs so procedures such as injections are best carried out with the animal restrained in a different position.

PROCEDURES

The most humane method of collecting blood from gerbils is to carry out cardiac puncture on an anaesthetised animal. Other methods have been described such as orbital sinus bleeding, toe nail clipping and tail vein cutting. All of these have possible adverse side-effects or welfare drawbacks.

Reference should be made to Table 1 in the chapter on hamsters for information about injection techniques. In gerbils, intravenous injection is easier than in hamsters as the lateral tail vein is available.

Medication can be supplied in the drinking water and oral dosing (1 — 10ml) can also be carried out using a plastic pipette or dropper-bottle.

SEXING

In adult gerbils the easiest way of sexing animals is to assess the anogenital distance (see Figure 1). This is best achieved by gently lifting the front limbs so that the animal is vertical, rather than trying to roll it on to its back. The distance in males will be approximately 10mm and in females 5mm. Other

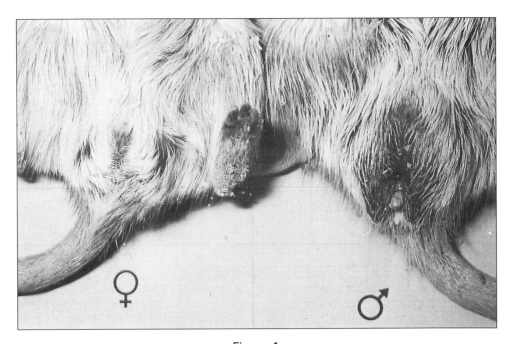

Figure 1
External genitalia of adult male and female gerbils.

indicators are that males are generally larger and have a more pronounced tan-coloured, ventral mid-line, sebaceous scent gland and dark scrotal sacs. The scent gland produces a dark yellow, musky smelling secretion which is rubbed on to objects for the purpose of defining territories. Urination and defaecation are also territory-markers. The male is more active in marking than females and demonstrates 'foot drumming' behaviour more frequently.

REPRODUCTION

TABLE 1

Reproductive parameters.

Parameter	Age/weight/time	Comments
Sexual maturity	10 weeks	
Duration of oestrus	4—6 days	Polyoestrous.
Mating		Evenings.
Ovulation		Spontaneous.
Implantation		May be delayed if mates whilst suckling.
Gestation	24—26 days	Up to 42 days if delayed implantation.
Litter size	4—6	
Birth weight	2.5—3.5g	
Weaning	3.3—6.0g/21—24 days	
Average reproductive life span	18 months	

In captivity with controlled 12—14 hour daylight, gerbils will breed all year round (Marston, 1976) and females can produce a litter every 30—40 days. Females in oestrus are restless and may have a congested vulva. It is better to keep animals as a monogamous pair because, although polygamous 'harem' groups can be formed from animals under eight weeks of age, fighting is much more likely. Males can be kept with the female and pups and, as a consequence of this, fertile matings often occur during a *post-partum* oestrus. However, if more than two pups are being suckled delayed implantation is likely.

Very small litters may be eaten by the female, which arrests lactation and allows more rapid recycling, mating and production of a larger number of young (Harkness and Wagner, 1977). Normal sized litters may be eaten if the mother is excessively disturbed or suffering from nutritional or lactational problems, eg. agalactia, mastitis, but generally gerbils are less 'sensitive' mothers than hamsters. Infertile matings may lead to a pseudopregnancy of 14—16 days duration. A copulation plug is formed during mating but being small and positioned deep in the vagina it is not readily observed. In the event of death of the mother, cross-fostering and hand-rearing are usually both impracticable and rarely successful.

Successful caesarian sections have been recorded (Mighell and Baker, 1990).

TABLE 2

Physiological data.

Data		Comments
Adult life span	3—5 years	Females greater than males.
Adult bodyweight	50—60g	Males greater than females.
Respiration rate/min	90—140	
Heart rate/min	250—500	
Rectal temperature	37.4°—39°C	
Blood volume ml	3—4	
Packed cell volume	48 (41—52)%	
Red blood cell count $\times 10^{12}$/l	8.5 (7.0—10.0)	Half-life (approx 10 days).
Haemoglobin g/dl	15 (12.1—16.9)	
White blood cell count $\times 10^9$/l	11 (4.3—21.6)	
Neutrophils %	29.9	
Lymphocytes %	73.5	
Daily water intake ml	4—5	Dependent on moisture in food.
Daily food consumption g	10—15	

DISEASES/CLINICAL CONDITIONS

Gerbils are relatively robust and appear to suffer from fewer disease problems than other rodents kept as pets. Reference will be made in this section to similar conditions in the hamster.

Digestive system

Tyzzer's disease, due to *Bacillus piliformis,* is the infection which most frequently causes fatal disease in gerbils — notably weanling young and *post-partum* females. It is seldom characterised by diarrhoea, in contrast to the situation in other rodents and rabbits, but is most likely to produce lethargy, anorexia, loss of weight and piloerection. The course of the disease is usually 1 — 3 days, after a 10 day incubation period, but peracute deaths do occur.

Diagnosis is by *post-mortem* examination and demonstration of a characteristicly enlarged liver with numerous pale yellow foci about 2mm in diameter (Carter *et al,* 1969) and oedematous and haemorrhagic intestines, particularly in the region of the ileocaecal junction. Confirmation of diagnosis is by silver/Warthin-Starry staining of liver and gut lesions to reveal pleomorphic, filamentous, Gram-negative organisms.

Treatment can be attempted (see 'Hamsters') but it is unlikely to be successful as the organism is intra-cellular and the course of infection is acute. If more than one animal is kept it must be borne in mind that there is a danger of Tyzzer's disease spreading swiftly, particularly via contaminated bedding, as demonstrated by Port (1970). If an outbreak is suspected affected animals should be isolated, confirmation of diagnosis achieved by histopathology and culling should be seriously considered. Bedding must be carefully removed and cages and feeding and drinking equipment sterilised to reduce the risk of persistence of spores.

'Wet tail' (see 'Hamsters'). This condition is much less common in gerbils than hamsters; it is usually encountered in individuals prior to weaning but occasionally later (Marston, 1976). It is considered to have a multifactorial cause, with stress as a triggering agent. In older animals Marston (1976) suggested a possible dietary cause.

Salmonellosis. Both *S.enteritidis* and *S.typhimurium* have been recognised as pathogens in the gerbil, usually as a result of contact with food or bedding contaminated by rodents. As with other species, the clinical signs of salmonellosis are moderate to severe diarrhoea, a staring coat, dehydration and weight loss. Mortality levels may be high and the course of the disease may be peracute so that animals are found dead without any premonitory signs. At *post-mortem* examination the main lesions are gastro-intestinal distension, congestion of the liver and peritoneal exudates and abscesses. The liver is characteristically covered with multiple foci of inflammation and necrosis. These are usually small but may become large and granulomatous with caseous centres.

Treatment of animals with salmonellosis is not recommended because of the zoonotic risks. Recovered animals often become carriers.

Dental problems (see 'Hamsters')

Infestation with endoparasites

Cestodes. *Hymenolepis nana* (see 'Hamsters').

Nematodes. Although several species have been identified in gerbils, none has been regarded as pathogenic. *Syphacia muris* and *S.obvelata* are readily transmitted from rats and mice respectively, particularly to young gerbils. Another oxyurid, *Demtostomella translucida,* may be found in the proximal small intestine.

Respiratory system

Pneumonias. Lower respiratory tract infections are relatively uncommon in gerbils.

Upper respiratory tract infections. Various signs can be exhibited, from an oculonasal discharge and sneezing to torticollis and circling. Likely aetiological agents are ubiquitous staphylococci or streptococci. Other bacteria, mycoplasmas and viruses should not be discounted and any possible routes of contamination or infection from other species should be investigated. One predisposing factor is that inappropriate substrates, eg. sand or cage materials, may cause facial abrasions.

This problem can be remedied by altering the substrate, observing scrupulous hygiene standards and using a topical antibiotic ointment, eg. Panalog, Ciba-Geigy.

Animals showing torticollis, circling and loss of balance are suffering from **otitis media** as a sequel to respiratory infection. Treatment is by parenteral or oral administration of an antibiotic such as oxytetracycline (oxytetracycline in water — 390mg/100ml for 14 days) (Peckham, 1974).

Skin

Staphylococcal infections. It is more likely that infected abrasions or bald noses will lead to a more general staphylococcal or streptococcal dermatitis than respiratory problems. Lesions usually spread from around the external nares to the feet, legs and ventrum. Any bite wounds will exacerbate the condition. An acute moist dermatitis in the absence of any preceding nose abrasions has been reported (Peckham, 1974), and the causative agent was *Staphylococcus aureus.* In weanlings a 25% mortality is possible. Recommended treatments include oxytetracycline (see earlier) or chloramphenicol parenterally and antibiotic ointments.

Acariasis *(Demodex merioni)* can cause alopecia, scaliness and ulcerations on the tail and hind limbs (Schwartzbrott *et al,* 1974). Mite infestation usually only becomes clinically significant in undernourished young, geriatric or pregnant individuals or those that are otherwise immunocompromised. Diagnosis is by skin scrapings and treatment is as for hamsters.

Ringworm. In gerbils ringworm results from contamination from bedding or other pets or humans. It can be recognised by loss of hair, brittle hair, dry skin and hyperkeratosis. The most common cause is *Trichophyton mentagrophytes* but infection with *Microsporum* sp., eg. *M.gypseum*, also occurs. Diagnosis is by appearance of the lesions, skin scraping and microscopic examination, or culture and possible fluorescence *(Microsporum)* under a Wood's lamp.

An outbreak of ringworm may indicate poor husbandry standards. Animals should be treated with griseofulvin (see 'Hamsters'), affected areas clipped, bedding disposed of and caging cleaned thoroughly.

Swollen sebaceous glands. The large ventral abdominal sebaceous gland may become inflamed, swollen and infected, particularly in the male. The condition usually responds rapidly to topical administration of corticosteroids and antibiotics, eg. Betsolan Cream, Coopers Pitman-Moore. Badly infected glands may need to be debrided. In older animals, tumours (adenomas or carcinomas) of this gland can occur. Surgical removal is possible.

Neoplasia

There is quite a high incidence of spontaneous neoplasia in gerbils over two years old — approaching 25% (Vincent *et al,* 1975). This constitutes a significant cause of clinical problems and death in ageing animals. The most commonly affected organs are the ovaries, skin (squamous cell carcinomas), sebaceous glands, kidney and adrenal gland.

Miscellaneous conditions

Cystic ovaries. Ageing female gerbils have a high incidence of cystic ovaries — approaching 50% over 400 days (Norris and Adams, 1972) with a third of the individuals being affected bilaterally. The cysts may reach 50mm in diameter and can severely depress reproductive performance. Females with particularly large cysts are sometimes thought to be pregnant.

Antibiotic toxicity

Unlike hamsters and guinea pigs, gerbils are not thought to develop a fatal enterotoxaemia if treated with antibiotics such as penicillin which are active against Gram-positive organisms. However, gerbils will suffer toxic effects if treated with streptomycin and dihydrostreptomycin and these drugs should be avoided.

Epilepsy

Gerbils subjected to acute stress such as a change of environment, loud noises or unaccustomed handling may go into convulsions or a cataleptic state which lasts for one or two minutes. No treatment is required but there is a familial trait, so badly affected animals may not be suitable for breeding.

TABLE 3
Therapeutic regimes.

Drug	Purpose	Dosage/Route/Frequency
Acepromazine	Sedative	0.5—1.0mg/kg i/m
Cephaloridine	Antibiotic	30mg/kg i/m bid for 5—7 days
Chloramphenicol	Antibiotic	30mg/kg i/m or s/c bid for 5—7 days
Dimetronidazole	Antibiotic	0.25—1.0% in water for 5—7 days
Diazepam	Sedative	5—10mg/kg i/m
Griseofulvin	Antifungal	25—30mg/kg per os sid for 3 weeks
Neomycin	Antibiotic	100mg/kg per os sid for 5—7 days
Niclosamide	Anthelmintic (cestodes)	100mg/kg per os
Oxytocin	Uterine stimulation	0.2—3.0iu/kg i/m or s/c
Piperazine	Anthelmintic (nematodes)	2—3mg/ml in water for one week, rest for one week then re-treat (lower dose for juveniles)
Streptomycin	TOXIC	
Tylosin	Antibiotic	10mg/kg i/m or s/c for 5—7 days

ANAESTHESIA

As with other species, a variety of options is available.

Gaseous (gases and volatile liquids)

As in the hamster the recommended agent is **methoxyflurane** (Metofane, C-Vet) administered via an Ayre's T-piece circuit and face mask. **Halothane** or **isoflurane** can be used with care.

Injectable

Use of a variety of agents, in combination and alone, has been described in the gerbil. Significant individual variation may be encountered. Recommended agents are listed in Table 4. They may be given for induction, followed by maintenance with an inhalation agent, eg. methoxyflurane, or incrementally to maintain appropriate anaesthetic depth for the whole procedure.

The use of pentobarbitone is not recommended because of its poor analgesic and severe respiratory depressant effects, leading to high mortality rates.

TABLE 4
Injectable anaesthetic agents.

Agent	Dosage	Route	Duration	Comments
Ketamine (Vetalar, Parke-Davis) and xylazine (Rompun, Bayer)	50mg/kg + 2mg/kg	i/m	approx 30 mins	May not provide completely adequate analgesia. Will cause diuresis.
Ketamine and diazepam (Valium, Roche)	50mg/kg + 2.5mg/kg	i/p	approx 30 mins	Need to monitor analgesia carefully.
Fentanyl/fluanisone (Hypnorm, Janssen) + midazolam (Hypnovel, Roche)	2 – 4 ml/kg (of the mixture)	i/p	approx 30 mins	Generally good analgesia. Monitor respiratory depression.
Metomidate (Hypnodil, Janssen) + fentanyl (Sublimaze, Janssen)	50mg/kg + 0.05mg/kg	s/c or i/p	30 – 60 mins	Agents of choice if available (Flecknell, 1983, 1987).

If chemical immobilisation is required for sedation or pre-medication the recommended regime is fentanyl/fluanisone (Hypnorm, Janssen) at a dosage of 1.0ml/kg i/m (Flecknell, 1978).

Analgesia and supportive therapy

As for hamsters except that the dosage level of buprenorphine (Temgesic, Reckitt and Colman) is 0.1 – 0.3mg/kg injected s/c tid.

REFERENCES AND FURTHER READING

CARTER, G. R., WHITENACH, D. L. and JULIUS, L. A. (1969). Natural Tyzzer's disease in Mongolian gerbils *(Meriones unguiculatus)*. *Laboratory Animal Care* **19**, 648.

FLECKNELL, P. A., JOHN, M., MITCHELL, M. and SHIREY. C. (1983). Injectable anaesthetic techniques in two species of gerbil, *Meriones libycus* and *Meriones unguiculatus. Laboratory Animals* **17**, 118.

FLECKNELL, P. A. (1983). Restraint, anaesthesia and treatment of children's pets. *In Practice* **5**, 85.

FLECKNELL, P. A. (1987). *Laboratory Animal Anaesthesia.* Academic Press, London.

HARKNESS, J. E. and WAGNER, J. E. (1977). *The Biology and Medicine of Rabbits and Rodents.* Lea and Febiger, Philadelphia.

JANESEN, V. (1968). The Mongolian gerbil. *Journal of the Institute of Animal Technicians* **19**, 56.

LOEW, F. M. (1971). The management and diseases of gerbils. In: *Current Veterinary Therapy IV. Small Animal Practice.* (Ed. R. W. Kirk) W. B. Saunders, Philadelphia.

MARSTON, J. H. (1976). The Mongolian gerbil. In: *The UFAW Handbook on the Care and Management of Laboratory Animals.* 5th Edn. (Ed. UFAW) Churchill Livingstone, Edinburgh.

MIGHELL, J. S. and BAKER, A. E. (1990). Caesarian section in a gerbil. *Veterinary Record* **126**, 441.

NORRIS, M. L. and ADAMS, C. E. (1972). Mortality from birth to weaning in the Mongolian gerbil, *Meriones unguiculatus. Laboratory Animals* **6**, 295.

PECKHAM, J. L. (1974). Staphylococcal dermatitis in Mongolian gerbils *(Meriones unguiculatus). Laboratory Animal Science* **24**, 43.

PORT, C. D. (1970). Tyzzer's disease in the gerbil. *Laboratory Animal Care* **24**, 109.

SCHWARTZBROTT, S. S., WAGNER, J. E. and FRISK, C. S. (1974). Demodicosis in the Mongolian gerbil: a case report. *Laboratory Animal Science* **24**, 666.

VINCENT, A. L., PORTER, D.D. and ASH, C. R. (1975). Spontaneous lesions and parasites of the Mongolian gerbil, *Meriones unguiculatus. Laboratory Animal Science* **25**, 711.

CHAPTER FIVE

HAMSTERS

Christopher D West BVetMed CertLAS MRCVS MIBiol

Hamsters are small rodents belonging to the Family Cricetidae. Members of the Family may be found in the wild in Eastern Europe, the Middle East, North Africa, China and Siberia. In captivity hamsters have simple needs and are relatively odourless. As pets they are appealing, nocturnal animals which generally need to be kept alone to prevent fighting, can inflict a painful bite and have well developed gnawing capabilities which may lead to escapes.

The species most likely to be encountered are:-
Golden (Syrian) hamster *(Mesocricetus auratus)*
Chinese (striped) hamster *(Cricetulus griseus)*
European hamster *(Cricetus cricetus)*
Djungarian (hairy-footed or Russian) hamster *(Phodopus sungorus)*

Of these the first is the species most frequently kept in captivity and about which most is known. Information presented in this chapter will be based on the golden hamster with indications of any differences from the next most frequently kept species - the Chinese.

In the wild, the golden hamster has a short, thick, reddish brown coat. Domesticated animals are descended from one male and two female siblings imported into the UK from Syria in 1931 (Alder, 1948). A variety of hair colours and coat patterns has resulted from mutations and the most popular strains now are agouti (commonest), cinammon, cream, white and piebald. A long-haired variety is becoming increasingly popular.

HOUSING

The basic caging requirements of sufficient space, privacy, warmth and opportunities for activity in an easily cleaned environment hold true for hamsters. The material used for cages needs to be without sharp projections and not liable to splinter, robust (escape-proof) and should enhance warmth by being a poor thermal conductor. Commercially available plastic or polypropylene cages are probably best, whether they are of a simple rectangular 'shoe box' design or are built up from modules with inter-connecting tubes.

Metal cages, whilst gnaw-proof and easy to clean, are rather cold. Wooden cages are not so easy to clean and can produce splinter-trauma when gnawed.

Hamsters require suitable bedding material as a substrate to absorb moisture. Sawdust is most frequently used but some owners find peat is satisfactory. The material should be free of contamination by toxins or pathogens. The frequency of cleaning depends on the size of the cage and the number and/or size of the animals contained. Once weekly to fortnightly should provide the correct balance between hygiene and disturbance. Hamsters also require nesting material in a secluded area of the cage for sleeping during the day; this is of particular importance if breeding is intended. Suitable materials include hay, shredded paper, wood shavings or cellulose wadding. Cotton-wool should not be used because of the risk of constipation and care should be taken with any material comprising strands, whether natural such as hay, or artificial, to avoid tangling around legs and resultant circulatory problems (Henderson *et al,* 1977; Wells, 1977).

Apart from the fabric of caging and bedding other physical parameters need to be considered. Hamsters should be kept in a temperature range of 19°—23°C. At ambient temperatures below 5°C hamsters become torpid and enter hibernation. The body temperature drops to one or two degrees above the ambient temperature and heart and respiratory rates decrease so as to become almost imperceptible. If ambient temperatures increase a hibernating hamster will wake up rapidly. For this reason, fresh food should always be available.

The range of relative humidity should be 55% +/- 10%. It is important that there are no pronounced fluctuations or variations in the microclimate of the cage.

Hamsters are crepuscular or nocturnal in activity so bright lighting is unnecessary; a maximum of 350—400 lux is cited. They are also sensitive to noise disturbance.

With regard to the social environment of domesticated hamsters, it is difficult to keep more than one hamster in the same cage because of fighting. It is possible to maintain animals of one sex from the same litter together but generally they are best kept alone. This reflects the social organisation of wild hamsters. When breeding hamsters one must observe the male and female closely and separate them if a fight breaks out (see Reproduction).

Male hamsters carry out territorial scent-marking using glands on the costovertebral area which can be seen as areas of dark pigmentation and coarse hair (Magalhaes, 1968). Excessive cleaning of cages may not only cause direct disturbance stress but may also disrupt territorial marking.

FEEDING

Hamsters are generally assumed to have similar dietary requirements to other small rodents such as rats or mice, or to be suited to a combination of rat and rabbit diet. Often, hamsters are offered unbalanced recipes consisting of copious amounts of vegetables and/or sunflower seeds. Hamsters differ from other rodents in having a well defined forestomach in which preliminary fermentation occurs. This enhances the breakdown of proteins and carbohydrates but generally increases the requirements for minerals and vitamins (Newberne and McConnell, 1979).

Of the 5—10g of food consumed per day by adult hamsters (male and female) the proportions of dietary constituents should be: protein 16—24%, carbohydrate 60—65% and fat 5—7%.

In practice, most proprietary pelleted hamster diets are satisfactory providing they are fresh. Supplementation with seeds, grains, fruit and green vegetables is recommended to provide variety but should not imbalance the intake of nutrients. Any fresh food that could be contaminated with pathogens should be washed in dilute antiseptic solution, eg. Savlon, ICI, and rinsed afterwards. Apples and lettuce have been reported to be effective in reducing the incidence of cannibalism of babies (Poiley, 1950).

Food can be presented in metal, plastic or ceramic bowls or in hoppers from the side or roof of the cage. Hamsters prefer to eat from the cage floor (Harkness *et al*, 1977) and this is perfectly satisfactory. Faecal contamination of food is of little importance in a species which is naturally coprophagic. Coprophagy enhances absorption of vitamins B and K.

Water should be provided fresh and *ad libitum*. The adult requirement is approximately 30ml per day. The easiest way of supplying water is in a glass or plastic bottle mounted on the cage side or top. A metal sipper tube should be used because a glass one will be bitten and the tip of the tube must be low enough so that babies approaching weaning age can reach it.

HANDLING

Physical restraint of hamsters is generally regarded as being fraught with the risk of being bitten. Hamsters do bite if startled or subjected to pain or discomfort when not held firmly. For non-painful and non-stressful procedures such as moving cages or clinical examination, hamsters can be lifted and held in two cupped hands. A hamster may even remain asleep in the warmth of the hands although it is often prudent to wake it first (Van Hoosier and Ladiges, 1984). For firmer restraint hamsters should be held by the scruff taking in as much loose skin as possible between forefinger and thumb. Wearing gloves is not recommended as it prevents a good grip.

If a hamster, despite being approached calmly, quietly and deliberately, is still sitting on its haunches and 'chittering' aggressively, it can be transported using a container, even a clean tin can. Alternatively, one could consider chemical restraint (see Anaesthesia).

PROCEDURES

Collection of blood and injection with therapeutic agents are the commonest procedures carried out on hamsters. Blood can be collected by using a scalpel blade to cut into a lateral tail artery. This produces a very small volume for clinical chemistry and haematological analysis, is subject to contamination, but more importantly is now considered to be a crude and stressful technique (RSPCA Working Party - Bleeding Techniques - in press).

A more humane technique is to carry out intracardiac puncture under general anaesthesia (Van Hoosier and Ladiges, 1984). This entails some risk of intrathoracic trauma and serious haemorrhage. The maximum volume that should be removed at one time from an average adult hamster is 1.5—2ml (see Table 3 for haematological parameters).

In the past, nail clipping has been widely used to provide small volumes for blood smears or packed cell volume measurements. Before using this technique, consideration should be given to the likely benefits versus the undoubted crudity and painful nature of the technique.

Table 1 summarises information about injection techniques which may be used for administration of antibiotics, analgesics and anaesthetics.

Table 1
Injection techniques in hamsters.

Route	Site	Limit volume*	Comments	
Intravenous	saphenous	0.2ml	Difficult access.	(General
Intravenous	penile	0.2ml	Very difficult access.	anaesthesia required).
Intramuscular	quadriceps	0.1ml	Difficult restraint. Painful.	
Subcutaneous	scruff	1.0ml	Eased by amount of loose skin.	
Intraperitoneal		4.0—5.0ml		

*for an adult (120g) hamster

Therapeutic regimes can also be based on drug-delivery via drinking water. Consideration must be given to stability of the agent in water and its effect on potability. A check must be made on whether water intake has been adversely affected.

Other procedures include measurement of body temperature, pulse or heart rate and respiration rate. With careful restraint and good lubrication a standard clinical thermometer can be used to measure rectal temperature. Alternatively, and preferably, commercially available rectal probes/thermocouples can be used. Respiration rate can be measured by visual observation. Heart rate can be measured by placing forefinger and thumb across an animal's thorax. This will prove easier when an animal is torpid/hibernating, moribund or anaesthetised when heart rate and strength will give a useful indication of prognosis.

SEXING

The sexing of adult hamsters is straightforward and can usually be done without any need for handling by observing the animals from above. Males have a visibly extended, rounded scrotal sac and females have a much 'blunter' rear end. In younger animals the best guide is the anogenital distance — as with rats and mice this is considerably larger in males (see Figure 1).

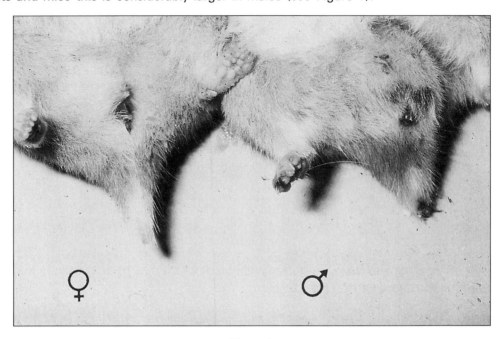

Figure 1
External genitalia of adult male and female hampsters.

REPRODUCTION

Table 2
Reproductive parameters for the golden hamster.

Parameter	Age/Weight/Time
Age/weight sexual maturity ♂	6—8 weeks/80—120g
♀	4 weeks/80—120g — tend not to be receptive until 8—12 weeks (14 weeks for Chinese hamster)
Duration of oestrous cycle	4 days
Ovulation	1—2 hours after dark on day 1 of oestrus
Implantation	Day 6 after onset of oestrus
Gestation period	15—18 days (21 days for Chinese hamster)
Litter size	4—12
Weight at birth	2—5g
Weaning age	21 days
Average reproductive lifespan	15 months

The female hamster will cycle all year except when hibernating. Fertility appears to decrease in the winter related to light intensity. Males' testes may retract during the winter. Sexual maturity can be observed behaviourally as individuals show more aggression. Females will start to attack males apart from when in oestrus and for this reason, if breeding is intended and a male and female are placed together, it should always be under supervision. The encounter should either be in neutral territory or the female should be taken to the male. The early hours of darkness are most likely to coincide with ovulation.

Onset of oestrus can be recognised by the presence of a vaginal discharge. By day 2 there is a copious, grey-white, odoriferous, post-ovulatory discharge. Pregnancy is confirmed by the absence of subsequent post-ovulatory discharges on days 5 and 9. There is no obvious vaginal plug as seen, for example, in the guinea pig (see 'Guinea Pigs').

If a female is kept with other females and/or in a cage with a mesh floor, it is advisable, on confirmation of pregnancy, to move her to a separate cage with a discrete nesting area. Cannibalism is more likely to occur if there is undue disturbance during the first week after parturition. There is no *post-partum* oestrus but there is often a post-weaning oestrus. If the mother is unable to feed her babies, fostering or hand-rearing can be attempted but is rarely successful.

Table 3
Physiological data for the golden hamster.

Life span	2—3 years
Adult weight/g ♂	85—140g
♀	95—120g
Respiration rate/min	74 (33—127)
Heart rate/min	280—412
Rectal temperature	36.2°—37.5°C
Blood volume ml/kg	70—75
Packed cell volume (PCV)	45%
Red blood cell count x10^{12}/l	7.5
Haemoglobin g/dl	16.8
White blood cell count x10^9/l	7.62
Neutrophils %	29.9
Lymphocytes %	73.5
Daily water intake	30ml
Daily food consumption	10—15g

DISEASES AND CLINICAL CONDITIONS

Digestive system

'Wet tail' (proliferative ileitis, transmissible ileal hyperplasia)

Hamsters of all species are susceptible to enteric disorders of uncertain aetiology characterised by severe diarrhoea and very high mortality rates. Enteric disorders constitute the most frequently recorded disease category in the golden hamster. Watery diarrhoea causing soiling of the tail, perineum and ventral abdomen is a characteristic clinical sign requiring prompt veterinary attention.

Presenting signs also include lethargy, irritability and anorexia leading to emaciation and death. The disease is generally acute (3—5 days) but may be more prolonged.

Aetiology. Wet tail has been described as a colibacillosis (Frisk and Wagner, 1977) and *E.coli* is certainly cultured in a majority of cases. However, it is felt that it is a multifactorial disease. *Campylobacter fetus* var *jejunum* has been isolated from normal and affected hamsters (Fox *et al*, 1981). It is possible that the two organisms act synergistically and cause disease after a 'trigger event' such as stress, viral infection or parasitic infestation.

Transmission. The disease is rapidly transmitted by direct contact and, experimentally, oral inoculation has resulted in disease (Amend *et al*, 1976). Animals in the post-weaning period up to 8 weeks of age are most often affected.

Post-mortem findings. Grossly the ileum is likely to be thickened, the mesenteric lymph nodes enlarged and the peritoneum inflamed with adhesions. In animals that have shown milder clinical signs but have succumbed during a prolonged 'recovery' phase, there may be evidence of intussusception, intestinal obstruction or rectal prolapse.

Treatment and prevention. If animals are being kept together any individuals showing signs of diarrhoea should be immediately isolated. Treatment is rarely successful in severe cases. A variety of antibiotics has been tried, including neomycin (Neobiotic P Aquadrops, Upjohn), diluted 1:3 with water given as one drop orally/110mg bodyweight twice daily (Sheffield and Beveridge, 1962), tetracyclines in the drinking water (La Regina et al, 1980) and metronidazole (Jacoby and Johnson, 1981). None has proved consistently successful.

Supportive therapy should be given to reduce the effects of dehydration and shock. Isotonic saline or lactated Ringer's solution (10% bodyweight) can be given either subcutaneously or intraperitoneally and oral rehydration solutions, eg. Lectade, SmithKline Beecham, may be administered. Fasting for 24 hours is recommended to reduce gut activity. Multivitamin and corticosteroid injections will aid recovery in those animals that survive. Affected animals should be kept in a warm environment (Sebesteny, 1979). Prevention is largely a matter of good hygiene, especially in cages housing recently weaned animals; it is also important to reduce stress.

Differential diagnoses. Tyzzer's disease and salmonellosis are the two most likely alternative causes of infectious diarrhoea and antibiotic-related enteritis may result from treatment for another problem.

Tyzzer's disease

This is a condition more frequently encountered in mice (see 'Rats and Mice') but which can infect all species of hamsters and other animals (Ganaway et al, 1971). It should be considered as a possible cause of acute diarrhoea and death — especially in weanling animals and if mice are present in the same environment. The causative agent is *Bacillus piliformis*, an obligate intracellular bacterium which cannot be cultured. Diagnosis can only be confirmed by *post-mortem* examination and subsequent histopathology. Typical features are gross lesions of enterocolitis, enlarged mesenteric lymph nodes and necrotising hepatitis - shown by multiple pale foci and myocardial necrosis. *Bacillus piliformis* is best viewed with the aid of silver stains. Treatment is not likely to be successful but a similar regime to that described for wet tail may be attempted.

Salmonellosis

Very few outbreaks have been recorded of salmonellosis in the hamster and all appear to have been ascribed to *S.enteritidis.* The disease has an acute onset and high mortality. In groups of animals it spreads very rapidly. Diarrhoea is not a typical sign and *post-mortem* multifocal necrosis of the liver is the main feature. Because of the zoonotic risks associated with salmonellosis euthanasia rather than treatment is recommended. If more than one animal is kept steps must be taken to identify the source of contamination — probably food or bedding — and eliminate it.

Dental problems

Being rodents, hamsters have teeth with open roots that grow continuously. Problems can arise with both the incisors and cheek teeth if insufficient wear is provided by the diet or if malocclusion occurs, for example as a result of gnawing on a metal-barred cage. Increased wear on teeth can be encouraged by placing pieces of wood in the cage. Malocclusions have to be corrected by regular clipping using nail clippers (see 'Guinea Pigs').

Impacted cheek pouches

Hamsters may be presented with unilateral or bilateral swellings on the face. Whilst these may be the result of dental problems they are more likely to be impacted cheek pouches. The lining of the pouches is dry so some types of food may adhere to them. The pouches should be gently emptied and flushed with water.

Constipation

This condition can occur in hamsters of all species and is generally related to an inappropriate diet, either in terms of constituents such as cotton-wool or because there is inadequate moisture. Exceptionally, it may be the result of parasitic infestation. Young hamsters of about two weeks of age are particularly susceptible as they start to eat solid food. If only dry food is offered constipation can occur. Affected animals present with a swollen abdomen, discomfort and inappetance. Severe cases need an enema; less severe cases respond to a change of diet to include green vegetables and fruit.

Infestation with endoparasites

Cestodes. *Hymenolepis nana,* the dwarf tapeworm, is the most significant endoparasite in hamsters. The host range extends to other rodents and primates including man. Normally, infestation is of the small intestine and is asymptomatic but enteritis and loss of condition can occur and very large numbers of parasites can lead to intestinal obstruction. *H.nana* can have either a direct or indirect lifecycle and auto-infection can occur. Indirect transmission is via flour beetles (various species) or fleas and direct transmission is by ingestion of ova in faeces, resulting in tissue migration in the new host.

Diagnosis is confirmed by the presence of ova with hooked scolices in the faeces. The presence of hooks distinguishes *H.nana* from *H.diminuta,* a closely related, but rarer, species.

Treatment with niclosamide (Yomesan, Bayer) (100mg/100g bodyweight orally repeated after 7 days) is consistently effective (Ronald and Wagner, 1975). Prevention and containment are achieved by good standards of hygiene and control of fleas and other insects.

Nematodes. The mouse pinworm, *Syphacia obvelata,* is found in hamsters although at very low levels (Wontland,1955). The pinworms occupy the caecum and their presence can be confirmed by the presence of characteristically 'banana-shaped' ova in the faeces. They are not thought to be pathogenic. The recommended treatment is 2 repeated 7 day courses of piperazine citrate in drinking water (10mg/ml) with a 5 day interval between.

Antibiotic-related enteritis

Hamsters treated with certain antibiotics may become anorexic, show signs of diarrhoea and die. The problem antibiotics are those that are selective for Gram-positive organisms and include penicillin, cephalosporins, lincomycin and erythromycin (recommended antibiotics are referred to in Table 4). It is thought that enterocolitis is due to overgrowth of toxin-producing clostridia, particularly *Clostridium difficile* (Bartlett *et al,* 1978).

Streptomycin and dihydrostreptomycin do not cause enteritis but are known to be directly toxic in Syrian hamsters and should be avoided in all other species of hamster.

Respiratory system

After diarrhoea, pneumonias are numerically the most significant diseases in hamsters. There are several possible aetiologies; viral, bacterial and mycoplasma and combinations of all three.

Viral pneumonias. Sendai virus (Parainfluenza Type 1) is predominantly a pathogen of mice but can naturally infect hamsters (Matsumoto *et al,* 1954). Sendai infection alone is generally regarded as being asymptomatic in adult hamsters but may cause death in young animals under approximately three weeks of age. Clinically unaffected animals may show lesions *post mortem* — characteristically plum-coloured patches of consolidation of the lungs. Sendai infection can lead to secondary bacterial infection.

Bacterial pneumonias. *Pasteurella pneumotropica* and *Streptococcus* spp., particularly *S. pneumoniae,* are causative agents of bacterial pneumonia in hamsters. These organisms are found in healthy hamsters and, indeed, also in humans, so underlying environmental stressors, eg. temperature fluctuations, or concurrent viral infections need to be considered. Disease is usually acute in onset with characteristic signs of oculonasal discharge, inappetence and dyspnoea. Culture and sensitivity testing can indicate an effective antibiotic but the possibility of antibiotic-related enteritis must always be borne in mind. Supportive treatment, especially provision of warmth, is recommended. Prevention is by avoidance of stressful situations and immediate separation of affected individuals - if kept in a group.

Mycoplasma pneumonias. Pneumonia due to mycoplasmas is rarely diagnosed because of the more obvious presence of the bacteria listed earlier.

Skin

Hamsters may be presented for examination suffering from alopecia, dry dermatitis, erythema, hyperpigmentation and self-trauma, either alone or in combination. The most likely aetiology for such skin diseases is ectoparasitic infestation, although some aged individuals may develop bilateral alopecia on the back which often spreads. It has been suggested that this may have an endocrine basis but no convincing evidence has been reported.

Acariaris. Cases of alopecia, often on the rump and associated with dry, scaly skin, are usually due to infestation with one of two species of *Demodex* mite. Both *D. criceti* and *D. aurati* are present on hamsters but only become clinically significant when immunity is compromised by concurrent infections, treatment with immunosuppressant drugs, age or pregnancy. Males seem to be more susceptible than females (Chesney *et al,* 1971). Diagnosis can be confirmed by taking skin scrapings although it should be borne in mind that *Demodex* mites may be present in 'normal' animals.

Treatment can be carried out successfully using an appropriate mange-wash, eg. Derasect, SmithKline Beecham, applied to one third of the skin surface daily until skin scrapings are negative (Chesney *et al,* 1971; Owen and Young, 1975). Rarely, sarcoptic mange can be seen in hamsters usually as a result of poor hygiene. It is responsible for more severe lesions as it leads to vigorous self-trauma. Badly affected animals should be euthanased. Those suffering less discomfort can be treated using 0.5% bromocyclen washes (Alugan, Hoechst) (Scott 1958).

Ringworm. Ringworm in hamsters results from contamination from bedding (hay), other pets or humans. *Trichophyton mentagrophytes* is the most commonly identified cause but infection with *Microsporum* sp. also occurs and can be diagnosed with the aid of a Wood's lamp. Ringworm lesions are characterised by loss of hair, brittle hair, dry skin and hyperkeratosis, especially of the ears. Affected animals should be isolated and the cage thoroughly cleaned. The recommended treatment is griseofulvin, (Grisovin, Coopers Pitman-Moore) (25—30mg/kg for three weeks or longer) (Young, 1974). Reference should be made to the precautions listed on this product's data sheet.

Neoplasia

Spontaneously occurring tumours are relatively common, especially in older animals and, for some tumour types, with a marked preponderance in males. The most frequently reported benign tumours are intestinal polyps and adrenal cortex adenomas (Van Hoosier and Trentin, 1979). The most frequently reported malignant tumour-type is lymphosarcoma. Cooper *et al,* (1991) have reported a high incidence of multiple tumours in Russian hamsters, mainly in the Cambridge area.

Miscellaneous conditions

Amyloidosis. Hamsters have a high incidence of a generalised, primary amyloidosis. Deposition of amyloid starts at under one year and the condition progresses with age.

Cage paralysis. A hamster may appear paralysed or paretic because of spinal trauma (normally subsequent to being dropped), lack of exercise or nutritional myopathy. Lack of exercise can be corrected by providing suitable activities such as a wheel and myopathies can usually be reversed by supplementing vitamins D and E. Deficiencies are unlikely to occur if appropriate proprietary food is offered. A sex-linked cage paralysis has been reported in 8—10 month old males. It is much rarer and milder in females (Nixon and Connelly, 1968).

Polycystic disease. This is a condition seen in animals over one year of age. Cysts develop in the liver, pancreas, epididymis and seminal vesicles. The aetiology is unknown and the condition is usually discovered at *post mortem.*

Trauma.   Injuries may result from fighting or falling/dropping on to hard surfaces. Fractured long bones, unless compound, are often best left to heal conservatively as neither external nor internal fixation is usually very successful. Stainless steel hypodermic needles can be improvised as intramedullary pins. Self-trauma can be minimised by use of analgesic agents (see Analgesia and Supportive Therapy).

Lymphocytic choriomeningitis (LCM).   LCM virus is a natural infection of wild rodents. In the hamster it is asymptomatic, producing a persistent low-level infection with excretion of virus in urine and saliva. The virus can be transmitted to humans in which it may cause signs ranging from mild influenza to a fatal meningitis (Maetz *et al,* 1976). Despite a widely publicised outbreak of several human cases of LCM contracted from pet hamsters in 1974, mice are regarded as being a more likely source of infection than hamsters. It is possible to exclude LCM from rodent colonies, and schools, petshops and similar bodies should be encouraged to obtain animals from such sources (see'Introduction').

Table 4
Therapeutic regimes.

Drug	Purpose	Dosage/Route/Frequency
Acepromazine	Sedative	0.5—1.0mg/kg i/m
Ampicillin	TOXIC	
Amoxycillin	TOXIC	
Atropine	Anaesthetic pre-medication	0.1—3.0mg/kg s/c
Cephaloridine	Antibiotic	30mg/kg i/m bid
Chloramphenicol	Antibiotic	20mg/kg i/m bid
Clindamycin	TOXIC	
Diazepam	Sedative	5—10mg/kg i/m
Dimetronidazole	Antibiotic	0.25—0.1% in water for 5—7 days
Griseofulvin	Antifungal	25—30mg/kg per os sid for 3 wks
Lincomycin	TOXIC	
Naloxone	Opiate antagonist	0.01—0.1mg/kg i/p or i/v
Niclosamide	Anthelmintic (cestodes)	100mg/kg per os
Oxytocin	Uterine stimulation	0.2—3.0 iu/kg i/m or s/c
Pethidine	Analgesic	20mg/kg i/m every 2 hours
Piperazine	Anthelmintic (nematodes)	2—3mg/ml in water for 1 week, rest for 1 week then re-treat
Temgesic	Analgesic	0.5mg/kg s/c tid
Tetracycline	TOXIC	
Trimethoprim/sulphadiazine	Antibiotic	0.2ml/kg s/c sid for 5—7 days
Tylosin	Antibiotic	10mg/kg i/m or s/c sid for 5—7 days

ANAESTHESIA

The choice of anaesthetic regime will depend on the intended purpose so that very short-term immobilisation for a minor procedure will entail far less anaesthetic 'sophistication' than a prolonged, invasive surgical operation.

Gaseous

The safest 'gaseous' anaesthetic for hamsters is **methoxyflurane** (Metofane, C-Vet) which can be administered via an inhalation chamber for induction and a face mask for maintenance. Methoxyflurane provides good analgesia and produces rapid, stress-free recovery. It is the agent of choice for short, mild procedures. **Halothane** is an effective agent but must be used under close observation because its potency heightens the risk of overdosage. **Ether** should not be used because of its excessive irritancy. **Isoflurane** is proving safe and effective.

Injectable

Use of a variety of agents, in combination and alone, has been described (see Table 5).

Table 5
Injection anaesthetic agents.

Agent	Dosage	Route	Duration	Comments
Ketamine (Vetalar, Parke-Davis)	200mg/kg	i/p	variable	Poor analgesia and muscle relaxation. Can be used for chemical restraint but not for painful procedures.
Ketamine, plus xylazine (Rompun, Bayer)	200mg/kg 10mg/kg	i/p i/p		Addition of xylazine promotes a smoother recovery.
Alphaxalone/ alphadolone (Saffan, Coopers Pitman-Moore)	150mg/kg	i/p	20—60min	Deep sedation — variable analgesia. Limited usefulness.
*Fentanyl/fluanisone and midazolam (Hypnorm, Janssen and Hypnovel, Roche)	4ml/kg (of the mixture)	i/p	60min	Good surgical anaesthetic. Some respiratory depression. Make up as two parts sterile water: one part Hypnorm: one part Hypovel (5mg/ml).
Pentobarbitone				Not recommended. Poor analgesia. Pronounced respiratory depression.

*(Flecknell, 1987)

The regime of choice for surgical anaesthesia is fentanyl/fluanisone and to reduce the effects of respiratory depression oxygen can be delivered via a face mask. At the end of the procedure the fentanyl can be reversed by naloxone (Narcan, Winthrop) (0.01mg/kg by injection by any parenteral route). Buprenorphine (Temgesic, Reckitt and Colman), an opioid, is a partial agonist and if given for post-operative pain relief will effect some reversal of fentanyl and speed recovery. If the degree of respiratory depression causes concern during anaesthesia, stimulation of the medullary respiratory centre can be achieved using doxapram (Dopram-V, Willows Francis) either by injection (10-15mg/kg s/c or i/m) or by application of drops under the tongue. Doxapram has a relatively short duration of action (5-15 minutes) so repeated administration may be necessary.

ANALGESIA AND SUPPORTIVE THERAPY

Whenever carrying out surgical procedures which are likely to produce pain on recovery from anaesthesia an analgesic should be administered. The agent of choice is buprenorphine (Temgesic, Reckitt and Colman) (0.5mg/kg s/c) because of its long duration of action of 6—8 hours. Administration of an analgesic enhances food and water intake during the post-operative period and, therefore, accelerates recovery.

Recovery should take place in an area which has subdued lighting and is warm and quiet. Warmth can be provided by use of lamps or heating pads but care must be taken not to allow overheating, so rectal and environmental temperatures should be monitored. Animals should not be placed back in cages directly onto a substrate of wood-shavings or sawdust which could stick in the nose, mouth and eyes. A small piece of towel or synthetic sheepskin (Vetbeds, Alfred Cox) is ideal.

If respiratory depression persists supplementary oxygen via a face mask is beneficial, particularly in conjunction with administration of doxapram. It may be necessary to compensate for blood loss during an operation or to provide fluid therapy in cases of dehydration due to other causes. The required volume will be in the order of 8—10ml/day. In a conscious animal fluid may be given by the oral route but if this is too stressful, subcutaneous or intraperitoneal injections of dextrose saline (4% dextrose, 0.18% saline) or saline (0.9%) may be given (Flecknell, 1987).

REFERENCES

ALDER, S. (1948). Origin of the Golden hamster *(Cricetus auratus)* as a laboratory animal. *Nature* **162**, 256.

AMEND, N., LOEFFLER, D., WARD, B. and VAN HOOSIER, G. L. JNR. (1976). Transmission of enteritis in the Syrian hamster. *Laboratory Animal Science* **26** (4), 566.

BARTLETT, J. G., CHANG, T., MOON, N. and ONDERDONK, A. B. (1978). Antibiotic-induced lethal enterocolitis in hamsters : studies with eleven agents and evidence to support the pathogenic role of toxin-producing clostridia. *American Journal of Veterinary Research* **39** (9), 1525.

COOPER, J. E., KNOWLER, C. and PEARSON, J. A. (1991). Tumours in Russian hamsters *(Phodopus sungorus)*. *Veterinary Record*.

CHESNEY, C. J., ESTES, P. C., RICHTER, C. B. and FRANKLIN, J. A. (1971). Demodectic mange in the Golden hamster. *Laboratory Animal Science* **13**, 305.

FLECKNELL, P. A. (1987). *Laboratory Animal Anaesthesia.* Academic Press, London.

FOX, J.G., ZANOTTI, S. and JORDAN, H. V. (1981). The hamster as a reservoir of *Campylobacter fetus* subspecies *jejuni. Journal of Infectious Disease* **143** (6), 856.

FRISK, C. S. and WAGNER, J. E. (1987). Hamster enteritis: a review. *Laboratory Animals* **11**, 79.

GANAWAY, J. R., ALLEN, A. M. and MOORE, T. D. (1971). Tyzzer's disease. *American Journal of Pathology* **64** (3), 717.

HARKNESS, J. E., WAGNER, J. E., KUSEWITT, D. F. and FRISK, C. S. (1977). Weight loss and impaired reproduction in the hamster attributable to an unsuitable feeding apparatus. *Laboratory Animal Science* **27** (1), 117.

HENDERSON, G. L. B., KEYWOOD, E. K., WRIGHT, J. M. and ARUNDEL, B. L. (1977). Unsuitable bedding material. *Veterinary Record* **100**, 458.

JACOBY, R. O. and JOHNSON, E. A. (1981). Transmissable ileal hyperplasia. In: *Hamster Immune Responses in Infections and Oncologic Diseases.* (Eds. J. Streilein, D. Hart, J. Stein-Streilein, W. Suncan and R. Billingham) Plenum Press, New York.

LA REGINA, M., FALES, W. H. and WAGNER, J. E. (1980). Effects of antibiotic treatment on the occurence of experimentally induced ileitics of hamsters. *Laboratory Animal Science* **30** (1), 38.

MAETZ, H. M., SELLERS, C. A., BAILEY, W. C. and HARDY, G. E. (1976). Lymphocytic choriomeningitis from pet hamster exposure : a local public health experience. *American Journal of Public Health* **66**, 1082.

MAGALHAES, H. (1968). Gross anatomy. In: *The Golden Hamster, its Biology and Use in Medical Research.* (Eds. R. A. Hoffmann, P. F. Robinson and H. Magalhaes) Iowa State University Press, Ames.

MATSUMOTO, T., NAGATA. I., KARIYA, Y. and OHASKI, K. (1954). Studies on a strain of pneumotropic virus of hamster. *Nagoya Journal of Medical Science* **17** (2), 93.

NEWBERNE, P.M. and McCONNELL, R. G. (1979). Nutrition of the Syrian hamster. *Progress in Experimental Tumour Research* **24**, 127.

NIXON, C. W. and CONNELLY, M. E. (1968). Hind leg paralysis : a new sex-linked mutation in the Syrian hamster. *Journal of Heredity* **59**, 276.

OWEN, D. and YOUNG, C. (1973). The occurrence of *Demodex aurati* and *Demodex criceti* in the Syrian hamster in the United Kingdom. *Veterinary Record* **92**, 282.

POILEY, S. M. (1950). Breeding and care of the Syrian hamster. In: *The Care and Breeding of Laboratory Animals.* (Ed. E. J. Farris) John Wiley and Sons, New York.

RONALD, N. C. and WAGNER, J. E. (1975). Treatment of *Hymenolepis nana* in hamsters with Yomesan. *Laboratory Animal Science* **25**, 219.

SCOTT, H. G. (1958). Control of mites on hamsters. *Journal of Ecology and Entomology* **51**, 412.

SEBESTENY, A. (1979). Syrian hamsters. In: *Handbook of Diseases of Laboratory Animals.* (Eds. J. M. Hime and P.N. O'Donoghue) Heinemann Veterinary Books, London.

SHEFFIELD, F. W. and BEVERIDGE, E. (1962). Prophylaxis of wet tail in hamsters. *Nature* **196**, 294.

VAN HOOSIER, G. L. and LADIGES, W, C. (1984). *Biology and Diseases of Hamsters in Laboratory Animal Medicine.* (Eds. J. G. Fox, B. J. Cohen and F. M. Loew) Academic Press, New York.

VAN HOOSIER, G. L. JNR. and TRENTIN, J. J. (1979). Naturally occurring tumours of the Syrian hamster. *Progress in Experimental Tumour Research* **23**, 1.

WARNER, R. G. and EHLE, F. R. (1976). Nutritional idiosyncracies of the Golden hamster *(Mesocricetus auratus). Laboratory Animal Science* **26** (4), 670.

WELLS, G. A. H. (1977). Unsuitable bedding material. *Veterinary Record* **100**, 537.

WONTLAND, W. W. (1955). Parasitic fauna of the Golden hamster. *Journal of Dental Research* **34**, 631.

YOUNG, C. (1974). *Trichophyton metagrophytes* infection in the Djungarian hamster. *Veterinary Record* **94**, 287.

FURTHER READING

HARKNESS, J. E. and WAGNER, J. E. (1989). *The Biology and Medicine of Rabbits and Rodents.* 3rd Edn. Lea and Febiger, Philadelphia.

CHAPTER SIX

GUINEA PIGS

Paul A Flecknell MA VetMB PhD DLAS MRCVS

Guinea pigs (cavies) *(Cavia porcellus)* make good pets for children since they are quiet and clean when well kept, relatively docile and easy to handle. Three main breeds are seen in the UK:- English, which are the most common, having short, fine hair; Abyssinian, which have a rough, wiry coat thrown into rosettes; and Peruvian, which are very long-haired and should be regarded as show animals rather than as pets. A wide range of colour varieties is produced. Self-coloured guinea pigs have a single solid hair colour of black, white, cream, golden, beige, lilac, red or chocolate. Agoutis have a ticked coat pattern similar to Abyssinian cats; golden and silver are the most common colours, but chocolate, cinnamon, lemon and salmon are occasionally seen. Dutch guinea pigs are smooth-coated with white cheeks and a white blaze and white forequarters, thorax and abdomen. The hindquarters and the rest of the head are either red, black, chocolate, cream, golden, silver or agouti. Tortoiseshell guinea pigs have distinct blocks of red and black hair. Tortoiseshell and white animals are similarly patterned but with the addition of blocks of white hair. When these patterns are bred in other colour combinations, the animals are described as bi-colours or tri-colours. Himalayans are an attractive variety which have a white body and black or chocolate nose, ears and feet. Brindles have an even mixture of black and white hairs, roans of black and red. Most of the above colour patterns can be seen in all three main breeds. For further information on less common varieties and illustrations of different coat colours, reference should be made to Elward (1980).

HOUSING

A wide range of different hutch and pen designs has been used successfully for housing guinea pigs. Whilst it is possible to maintain animals outdoors in the UK, it is preferable to move them into a garage or outbuilding during the winter months and to provide plenty of bedding and a well insulated hutch. During the warmer months animals may be housed outdoors and it is often convenient to use a mobile run which can be moved around the lawn.

Pens should be at least 25cm high to avoid escapes and, if outdoors, they should be covered with wire mesh to keep out cats. Cages can be of the "rabbit-hutch" type; at least 30cm high with about 0.2m² of floor area for each guinea pig. Shoebox type cages are often used and are quite satisfactory; a nestbox is not essential, but plenty of bedding should be provided for animals to hide in when startled. Guinea pigs are social animals and are best kept in small groups. Fighting is rarely a problem, but it is usually preferable to keep single-sex groups to avoid the production of large numbers of offspring.

If large numbers of guinea pigs are kept they may be housed in cages with mesh floors. The mesh must be of a suitable size to prevent the animal from trapping its feet in the grid; a rectangular mesh about 1.25 x 3.5cm will usually minimise such problems.

Bedding can either be woodshavings, straw or shredded paper. Hay is ideal as this will also act as a dietary supplement, but it must be fresh, dry and of good quality. Guinea pigs will tolerate a wide range of temperatures, especially if acclimatised gradually. The preferred range is 12°—20°C; temperatures about 27°—30°C may cause heatstroke, particularly in overweight or pregnant animals (Harkness and Wagner, 1989).

FEEDING

Commercial pelleted feed should form the basis of the diet and this may be supplemented with hay and green food. Guinea pigs must receive adequate vitamin C — at least 10mg/kg/day, increasing to 30mg/kg/day during pregnancy. This should be provided by most commercial diets, but prolonged storage, particularly under poor conditions, can lead to a reduction of the vitamin C content. Diets for laboratory guinea pigs have additional vitamin C included and have a shelf-life of three months. It is likely that unfortified diets will contain adequate vitamin C for a much shorter period. Guinea pigs are fairly fastidious in their choice of food and changing the diet too suddenly may cause them to stop eating. Sudden alterations in the type of diet, eg. increasing or decreasing the percentage of fresh food, can result in digestive disturbances.

Water must be provided *ad libitum* and bowls cleaned regularly. Guinea pigs may defaecate into floor mounted bowls, so suspending the water container slightly above floor level may be helpful. Changing the watering arrangements must be a gradual process as the animals may not drink from unfamiliar containers.

HANDLING

Guinea pigs are fairly non-aggressive, but a frightened animal will run around its cage at high speed, making safe handling difficult. Subdued lighting will help quieten the animal, as will covering its eyes. Owners should be encouraged to bring animals to the surgery in small boxes (a shoe box is ideal) with a minimum of bedding. A guinea pig should be picked up by placing one hand round the shoulders (see Figure 1) and lifting it clear of the cage, while the hindquarters are supported with the other hand (see Figure 2). Following restraint as described above, a second person can carry out any examination or manipulations that may be required.

Injection technique

Intramuscular injections are best made into the quadriceps, using a 26—23 gauge needle. No more than 0.3ml of material should be administered at a single site to an adult guinea pig.

Subcutaneous injection using a 23 gauge needle can be made under the skin overlying the neck and thorax. Up to 10ml of material can be administered by this route.

Intraperitoneal injections are best made with the animal restrained by an assistant as shown (see Figure 3) and the needle directed along the line of the hind limb to enter the abdomen in the centre of one caudal quadrant. This avoids puncturing either the bladder or the liver. A 25—23 gauge needle should be used and up to 15ml of fluid can be administered by this route.

Intravenous injection is difficult in guinea pigs, since there are few superficial veins. Adult animals may have ear veins that are large enough to be entered with a 26 or 25 gauge needle, but movement of the animal in response to venepuncture often results in damage to the fragile vessels. Application of local anaesthetic cream (EMLA, Astra) 30 minutes prior to venepuncture will overcome the problem (Flecknell *et al*, 1990). Alternatively, a forelimb may be shaved and use made of the brachiocephalic vein. Small blood samples can be obtained by nicking the ear vein, or clipping a nail.

Oral dosing of guinea pigs should be carried out by passing a catheter (1.5—2mm, 3—4 French gauge) into the back of the pharynx and on into the oesophagus or stomach if this is thought necessary. If material is to be regularly administered, a small gag can be made by drilling a hole through the side of a plastic case from a 1ml disposable syringe. The catheter can then be passed through the hole in the gag, so preventing the animal from biting through it.

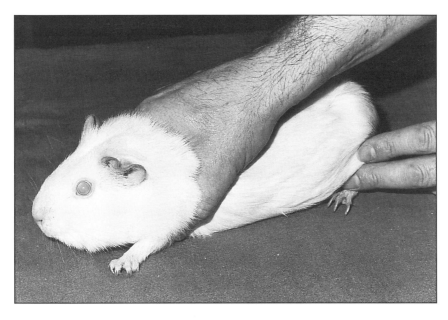

Figure 1
The guinea pig should be restrained and picked up
with one hand around the shoulders.

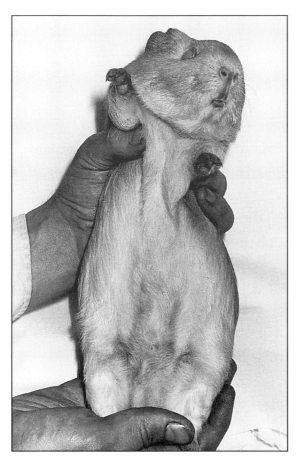

Figure 2
As the animal is lifted clear of its cage,
the hindquarters should be supported.

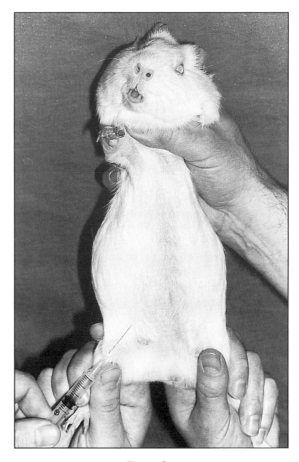

Figure 3
Guinea pig restrained for
intraperitoneal injection.

SEXING

Both male and female guinea pigs have a single pair of nipples in the inguinal region, and the external genitalia are superficially very similar. In males, the penis can be protruded by gently pressing on either side of the genital opening (see Figure 4). In very young animals, the penis can be palpated just cranial to the genital opening in the midline. Females have a shallow vaginal groove between the urethral orifice and anus (see Figure 5), the vagina being closed by a membrane except during oestrus and parturition. Gentle pressure will part the genital opening and expose the vaginal membrane.

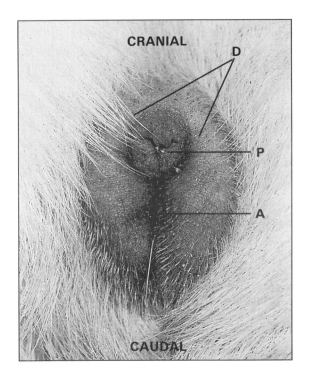

Figure 4
External genitalia of an adult male guinea pig.
A = anus. Digital pressure at D will extrude penis at P.

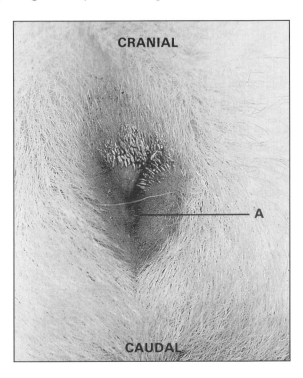

Figure 5
External genitalia of an adult female guinea pig.
A = anus.

REPRODUCTION

Female guinea pigs are usually sexually mature at about six weeks of age, but mating should be delayed until they are about twelve weeks old. Guinea pigs are polyoestrous and spontaneous ovulators (Hafez, 1970); normal reproductive parameters are summarised in Table 1. The oestrous cycle lasts 15—17 days, and is characterised by adoption of the lordosis posture when the back and rump are stroked and by mounting of other females. Oestrus lasts about eight hours; the vaginal membrane frequently ruptures on the day before oestrus and remains open for 3—4 days. Following mating, a plug of ejaculate usually forms in the vagina (a 'vaginal plug'); this is shed during the next day or so, and may be found by the owner.

Table 1
Reproductive parameters in the guinea pig.

Sexual maturity — male	9—10 weeks
— female	4—6 weeks
Oestrous cycle	16 days
Duration of oestrus	1—16 hours
Gestation period	59—72 days (depending on litter size — see text)
Litter size	1—6 (average 3—4)
Weaning age	3 weeks

Pregnancy can be diagnosed by gentle abdominal palpation at about 4—5 weeks and also by the considerable increase in bodyweight during gestation. Females will often double their bodyweight by full term. The length of gestation varies from 59—72 days and is usually influenced by litter size — the larger the litter the shorter the gestation period. A *post-partum* oestrus occurs 24—48 hours after parturition.

Litter size ranges from 1—6, with an average of 3—4 offspring. The young are delivered at an advanced state of development, with normal body hair, eyes open and able to take solid food within the first day of life. The onset of parturition is difficult to predict and is not preceded by any nest-building activity. Palpation of the pubic symphysis should enable the detection of a gradual relaxation of the pubic ligaments and separation of the symphyses. Once the gap is about 15mm (finger width), parturition is imminent and, if necessary, can usually be induced by injection of oxytocin (1—2iu intramuscularly). If breeding has been delayed and the female is over one year old, separation of the symphysis will be impaired and Caesarean section may be required. Dystocia is relatively common in obese females and may also occur because of oversized fetuses. Since the length of gestation varies, it is difficult to predict accurately the time of parturition and pregnant females should be observed carefully for any signs of ill health. Depression, inappetence and the presence of a bloody or olive-green vaginal discharge are indications of dystocia. Caesarean section should be undertaken as rapidly as possible, using a midline approach. The surgical technique is similar to that employed in the dog and the cat, but anaesthesia and post-operative care are of critical importance (see later). If the mother dies following Caesarean section or normal parturition, baby guinea pigs should be fed on a mash of commercial pellets and on diluted cow's milk using a dropper or syringe.

It is preferable to separate pregnant females from other animals and to house the sow and her litter separately until weaning. If several animals and their litters are kept together, the adults may inadvertently trample on the young and injure them. One advantage of group housing of breeding females is that the young will be cross-suckled by sows and this can help overcome problems caused by individual sows which have a reduced milk supply. Care must be taken, however, to ensure that newborn animals are not deprived of milk by older individuals sucking from their dam.

DISEASES/CLINICAL CONDITIONS

Normal physiological variables are summarised in Table 2 (see also Mitruka and Rawnsley, 1977 and Sanderson and Phillips, 1982).

Table 2
Physiological data in the guinea pig.

Average life-span	4—8 years
Adult bodyweight	750—1000g
Respiratory rate	90—150 per minute
Tidal volume	1.0—4.0ml
Heart rate	130—190 per minute
Rectal temperature	38.6°C (37.2°—39.5°C)
Blood volume	75ml/kg bodyweight
Haematocrit	0.40 (0.35—0.45) l/l
Red blood cell count	5.0×10^{12} /l
Haemoglobin	14.3 g/dl
White blood count	11.2×10^9 /l
Neutrophils	37%
Lymphocytes	56%
Average daily water intake	10ml/100g bodyweight

Skin and associated structures

Hair loss and skin lesions may be caused by several agents as well as by non-infectious factors.

Mites

Mite infestations (commonly *Trixacarus caviae*, a sarcoptid mite) can cause extensive pruritus. Diagnosis can be confirmed by examination of skin scrapings, and the condition usually responds to treatment with bromocyclen dusting powder (Alugan, Hoechst). In severe cases pruritus may be accompanied by nervous signs and bromocyclen may not be effective. Diazepam (Valium, Roche) (1—2mg/kg bodyweight) will help to control the clinical signs. Ivermectin (Ivomec, MSD) (200μg/kg s/c) can also be used successfully to treat this condition, but as this product is not licensed for use in rodents, care must be taken.

Lice

Louse infestation may occur but this does not usually cause pruritus unless infestation is severe. Lice can normally be seen in the fur, or are detectable on microscopic examination of hair and skin scrapings. Bromocyclen powder is usually very effective in eliminating the parasites.

Ringworm

Ringworm is fairly common in guinea pigs, producing patches of hair loss. The affected skin is usually scaly, but may be markedly inflamed and pruritic. *Trichophyton mentagrophytes* is the most frequently isolated dermatophyte so ultraviolet fluorescence is not usually diagnostic. Direct microscopic examination of the skin and hair from lesions together with culture on Sabouraud's agar will confirm the diagnosis. Treatment with griseofulvin (Grisovin, Coopers Pitman-Moore) (25mg/kg — about 0.8mg/kg of feed for adult animals) for 4—6 weeks is usually effective. Since guinea pigs are usually owned by children who often practise less than perfect personal hygiene, the desirability of treatment should be considered carefully.

'Barbering' and alopecia

Hair loss without obvious pruritus can result from hair chewing by other guinea pigs, or it may be self-inflicted. If self-inflicted, the head and neck will not be affected. Changing of the animals' caging and bedding materials may discourage the habit, but there is often little response to such manipulations. In young guinea pigs, excessive grooming and hair chewing by the mother may produce almost complete hair loss and in these instances weaning should be carried out as soon as is practicable. Female guinea pigs frequently develop severe alopecia in late pregnancy; the cause is not known but hair growth usually resumes following parturition.

Pododermatitis

Bacterial infection of the feet, usually with *Staphylococcus aureus*, can cause pronounced swelling and ulceration of the foot pads. The condition is generally associated with rough, infrequently cleaned cage flooring. Changing to softer bedding and a smooth floored cage will help to prevent further outbreaks. Treatment of existing infections is rarely successful once severe swelling has occurred. Systemic antibiotics (see Table 3) and local application of corticosteroid/antibiotic ointment may produce some improvement in the condition.

Abscesses/skin wounds

Localised abscesses are frequently seen in guinea pigs, and both these and scratches and bite wounds may result when several adult animals are housed together. Damaged food containers and water bowls and rough sides of cages may also abrade the skin and cause localised infection. It is important to open the abscess and to clean it thoroughly — simple lancing will usually be ineffective and hence the animal should be sedated (see later). If the animal is otherwise healthy, systemic antibiotics are best avoided and topical application of antibiotic-containing ointments or powders or the use of multicleansing agents, eg. Dermisol, SmithKline Beecham, is preferable. More extensive abscessation may result from infection with *Streptococcus zooepidemicus* (see later).

Table 3
Dose rates of antibacterial agents in the guinea pig.

Agent	Dose/Comments
Cephaloridine	15mg/kg i/m bid
Cephalexin	15mg/kg i/m bid
Chloramphenicol injectable suspension oral preparations	20mg/kg i/m bid 50mg/kg tid
Neomycin injectable solution oral preparations	30mg/kg s/c sid 5mg/kg
Sulphadimidine (33⅓% solution)	2% solution in drinking water for 7—10 days
Trimethoprim 40mg, sulphadiazine 200mg per ml (Tribrissen 24%)	0.5ml/kg s/c
Not recommended Ampicillin Erythromycin Lincomycin Oxytetracycline Penicillin Tetracycline	Toxicity, resulting in enterotoxaemia and death in a high proportion of animals, has been reported.

Cervical lymphadenitis ('lumps')

Cervical lymphadenitis is usually caused by infection with *Streptococcus zooepidemicus,* although the condition must be differentiated from pseudotuberculosis (see later) and localised abscesses following skin trauma. The lymph nodes of the neck are most frequently affected and they can then readily be palpated. The infected lymph nodes often burst and discharge yellow-white pus. Individual animals may be treated by systemic administration of cephaloridine for 14 days (see Table 3); however, if a breeding group of animals is kept the disease will become enzootic. In addition to the chronic abscessation, occasional animals may die suddenly with septicaemia or with severe, acute pneumonia.

Respiratory system

Respiratory disease is relatively common in guinea pigs and may be caused by a variety of agents, the most common of these being the bacterium *Bordetella bronchiseptica.* Clinical signs include dyspnoea, abnormal respiratory sounds, sneezing, nasal discharge, weight loss, inappetence, depression and death. Most animals are presented for treatment only when severely affected and therapy is often unsuccessful. Early or milder cases often respond well to broad spectrum antibiotics such as chloramphenicol (see Table 3) but animals that survive an acute infection frequently carry organisms in the upper respiratory tract and may act as a reservoir of infection (Trahan *et al,* 1987). If large numbers of animals are infected with *B. bronchiseptica*, use of an autogenous vaccine has been claimed to be effective (Ganaway *et al,* 1965). An alternative vaccination regimen using porcine *B. bronchiseptica* vaccine has also been shown to prevent acute disease (Matherne *et al,* 1987), but vaccinated animals become carriers of the organism.

Adenovirus pneumonia

Pneumonia caused by an adenovirus has been described in guinea pigs (Naumann *et al,* 1981; Kunstyr *et al,* 1984). In laboratory colonies clinical disease seems only to occur in stressed animals.

Streptococcal pneumonia

Streptococcus pneumoniae may cause a fatal pneumonia in guinea pigs. Pregnant animals may abort or give birth to still-born offspring. The organism is frequently carried in clinically normal animals. Affected guinea pigs are usually presented too late in the course of the disease for treatment to be effective, but antibiotic therapy of less severely affected individuals is occasionally effective. Other bacteria such as *Klebsiella* sp. have also been associated with pneumonia. Outbreaks of clinical disease with these bacterial pathogens are often associated with overcrowding, poor husbandry and adverse environmental conditions. Inadequate diet, especially marginal vitamin C deficiency, may also predispose to infection.

Gastro-intestinal system

Malocclusions

A guinea pig's teeth are all open-rooted and they grow continuously throughout the animal's life. Malocclusion of either the incisors or the cheek teeth can occur. Once one group of teeth has become affected, the abnormal jaw position will tend to cause the other group of teeth to overgrow. Affected animals stop eating and usually drool saliva profusely. The mouth can be held open with artery forceps to inspect the teeth, although this is more easily achieved if the animal is sedated. An aural speculum (preferably made of metal) is useful for carrying out an initial examination of the cheek teeth. It is important to perform a thorough inspection of the teeth, and this is best achieved by anaesthetising the animal and using a purpose-made mouth gag or laryngoscope to examine the oral cavity. Particular attention should be paid to the lower molars and premolars, as small spurs often develop which abrade the tongue. The consequent pain reduces food intake and may cause drooling of saliva. The teeth should be clipped back to their normal length, although the condition tends to recur and repeated clipping will be required. Cuticle nippers are suitable for this purpose, or a dental burr may be used.

Diarrhoea

Digestive disturbances are a relatively common problem in guinea pigs, but often such conditions are of uncertain aetiology.

Coccidiosis (usually due to *Eimeria caviae*) can occur, but this parasite may be a secondary problem, developing as a sequel to some initial intestinal disorder. If large numbers of oocysts are seen on examination of faecal samples, treatment with sulphadimidine (Sulphamethazine Solution 33 ⅓ %, ICI) (2% in drinking water for 7—10 days) is usually effective in treating the condition. In addition, the standard of cage cleaning should be improved and increased in frequency to help minimise reinfection.

Salmonella. Diarrhoea may result from *Salmonella* infection, but this organism is more likely to cause septicaemia and sudden death and abortions. More chronic infections result in a generalised loss of weight and of condition. If *Salmonella* spp. are isolated from faecal samples it is probably best to kill the animals in view of the public health hazard.

Pseudotuberculosis (yersiniosis) can cause diarrhoea and weight loss and death after a 3—4 week period of illness. Other animals may die of acute septicaemia in 24—48 hours or develop non-fatal infections restricted to the cervical lymph nodes. Animals that die after developing the more chronic form of the disease frequently have enlarged mesenteric and abdominal lymph nodes and focal necrosis of the liver and spleen. Diagnosis can be confirmed by culture of *Yersinia pseudotuberculosis* from blood or lymph nodes. The disease is believed to be transmitted to guinea pigs by contamination of their green feed by wild rodents or birds. Since the bacteria may infect man, affected pet animals should be killed and the cages disinfected before new animals are introduced.

'Non-specific' diarrhoea often develops following stress or dietary changes. Treatment of such conditions is by standardising the diet, avoiding environmental stress, eg. extremes of temperature, and giving symptomatic treatment with neomycin/kaolin preparations. The condition may resolve more or less spontaneously, but a guarded prognosis should be given. *Bacillus piliformis* (Tyzzer's disease) and *Campylobacter* sp. are rare causes of gastro-intestinal disease in guinea pigs.

Antibiotic-induced diarrhoea. The administration of certain antibiotics has been reported to produce a fatal enteritis and diarrhoea in guinea pigs. It is probable that this results from colonisation of the gut with enterotoxin-producing *Clostridium* spp. following the imbalance in normal gut flora caused by administration of the antibiotic. There is considerable variation in the agents associated with this syndrome, and it may be that other environmental factors are involved in its development. In general, all antibiotics should be regarded as potentially hazardous to guinea pigs. Ampicillin, for example, caused enterocolitis in 20—30% of animals and, in addition, had such a short half-life that it was considered to be ineffective clinically (Young *et al*, 1987). Single doses of cefazolin (50mg/kg i/m) appeared safe, but repeated doses caused a 25% mortality (Fritz *et al*, 1987). This antibiotic also had an extremely short half-life and was thought unlikely to be effective clinically. Given the uncertainties of the safety and efficacy of antibiotics in guinea pigs, it is difficult to provide clear guidelines. In general, broad-spectrum agents seem less toxic than narrower-spectrum drugs, and oral administration more hazardous than intramuscular or subcutaneous injection, although administration by any of these routes may result in enterotoxaemia. Available data concerning antibiotic administration are summarised in Table 3.

Musculoskeletal system

'Scurvy' (hypovitaminosis C)

Clinical signs of deficiency can develop within 2—3 weeks of restriction of vitamin C intake. In severely affected animals, the limb joints become swollen and painful, the animals refuse to move, lose condition and die. At *post-mortem* examination, multiple haemorrhages can be seen in the muscles and around the joints. Scurvy should also be suspected in individuals which show non-specific signs such as dullness, inappetence and reluctance to move or which develop abnormalities of gait. Treatment is with vitamin C (100 mg/day), preferably as drops directly into the mouth to ensure adequate intake, until the animal is clinically normal. As a precautionary measure, soluble vitamin C tablets can be added to the drinking water once or twice a week.

Miscellaneous conditions

Pregnancy toxaemia

Pregnancy toxaemia occurs during the last 1—2 weeks of pregnancy, or during the first four days *post partum*. Animals develop a ketoacidosis and are depressed, anorexic and often dyspnoeic. Death is usually rapid once clinical signs have been seen. Obese animals appear more susceptible and hence overfeeding of pregnant animals should be avoided. Minimising stress (such as a visit to a veterinary surgeon) late in pregnancy is also important. Treatment is rarely successful, although intraperitoneal or subcutaneous dextrose/saline and intramuscular corticosteroids may be of value.

Mastitis

The factors which predispose to the development of mastitis in guinea pigs are probably similar to those in other species, and hence improved hygiene and more frequent cage cleaning often help to prevent the condition. A number of different bacteria have been isolated, including *Streptococcus zooepidemicus, E. coli* and *Klebsiella pneumoniae.* Treatment with broad-spectrum antibiotics for 7—10 days is often successful. If severe ulceration and necrosis of the gland have occurred this should be treated topically with a suitable multicleansing agent, eg. Dermisol, SmithKline Beecham.

Conjunctivitis

This may be associated with respiratory infection, but usually appears to be secondary to local trauma or irritation. Infection with *Chlamydia* sp. may also cause severe conjunctivitis in guinea pigs. Treatment should be with topical ophthalmic ointments.

Otitis media

Middle ear disease is relatively common in guinea pigs, but animals with purulent otitis media may fail to show clinical signs of disease (Boot and Walvoort, 1986). A range of bacteria including *Bordetella bronchiseptica, Streptococcus zooepidemicus, Streptococcus pneumoniae, Pasteurella* sp. and *Actinobacillus* sp. may all cause infection. Treatment of clinically affected animals with antibiotics is occasionally successful.

ANAESTHESIA

Guinea pigs are among the most difficult rodents in which to achieve safe and effective anaesthesia. Their response to many injectable agents is very variable and post-anaesthetic complications such as respiratory infections, digestive disturbances and generalised depression and inappetence are frequently seen (Flecknell, 1987). Many of these problems can be avoided by careful selection of anaesthetic agents and a high level of intra and post-operative nursing care.

Sedation/light anaesthesia

Restraint and sedation sufficient for minor procedures such as examination and clipping of teeth and opening, draining and cleaning of abscesses can be achieved by the administration of fentanyl/fluanisone (Hypnorm, Janssen) (1.0ml/kg i/m). Ketamine (Vetalar, Parke-Davis) (25—100mg/kg i/m) immobilises guinea pigs but does not produce good analgesia. Alphaxalone/alphadolone (Saffan, Coopers Pitman-Moore) (40mg/kg i/m) produces deep sedation but the large volume of drug required (2—3ml/guinea pig) is a serious disadvantage.

Surgical anaesthesia

Whichever agents are used, it is very important to minimise loss of body heat and so prevent the development of hypothermia, which, if severe, can cause shock and subsequent death (see 'Introduction'). The animals should be placed on a heated pad, if available, or at least on a thick towel rather than directly on to the operating table. Extra insulation can be provided by wrapping in aluminium foil and then cutting an opening over the operative site. Effective insulation can also be provided by using 'bubble packing' or with purpose-made materials such as 'Flectabed' (Wyvern). Shaving of the hair and use of skin disinfectants should be kept to a minimum to avoid cooling and whenever possible supplemental heating, eg. with an anglepoise electric light, should be provided. Depth of anaesthesia may be assessed by pinching the web of the toes or the ears. A lack of response to these stimuli indicates the onset of surgical levels of anaesthesia.

Volatile anaesthetics

Methoxyflurane (Metofane, C-Vet) is the volatile anaesthetic agent of choice for anaesthesia of guinea pigs. Induction can be easily achieved using a small facemask (either a human paediatric mask or 'home-made' from a plastic syringe case) or by placing the animal in a purpose-made anaesthetic chamber (see 'Rats and Mice'). Anaesthesia should be maintained with 1:1 nitrous oxide and oxygen and the minimum concentrations of methoxyflurane compatible with adequate analgesia (about 0.5—1.0%). A suitable sized Ayre's T-piece and small cone-shaped facemask is the best circuit for use in the guinea pig.

Halothane (Fluothane, ICI; Halothane, RMB) can be used successfully in guinea pigs, but the margin of safety is considerably less than with methoxyflurane and particular care must be taken to avoid overdose during induction. Induction concentrations should not exceed 3% and anaesthesia can usually be maintained with 1.5% halothane.

Isoflurane (Forane, Abbott) can also be used to provide effective surgical anaesthesia in guinea pigs, although it is essential to use a calibrated vaporiser and to avoid excessively high concentrations during induction. Safe induction concentrations are 2.5—3.0% and anaesthesia can be maintained with 1.5—2% isoflurane.

Ether is unsuitable for use in guinea pigs since it is highly irritant to the respiratory tract, producing increased bronchial secretions that tend to occlude the narrow airways. In addition, bronchospasm may occur during induction.

Injectable agents

The absence of accessible superficial veins limits administration of injectable anaesthetics to the intra-peritoneal, subcutaneous or intramuscular routes. When using these routes it is not possible to administer drugs incrementally to achieve the desired depth of anaesthesia. For this reason, anaesthetics with a wide margin of safety are to be preferred. It is also preferable to select agents which can be reversed rapidly using specific antagonists. The animals should be carefully weighed and dose rates calculated accurately. If a guinea pig is in poor condition or has been inappetent for a prolonged period, the drug dosage should be reduced. If possible, warmed (38°C) lactated Ringer's solution (Hartmann's) (30 ml/kg i/p) should be administered a few hours prior to anaesthesia.

Fentanyl/fluanisone. The anaesthetic combination of choice is fentanyl/fluanisone, 1.0ml/kg i/m, plus diazepam (Valium, Roche), 2.5mg/kg i/p. Alternatively, a mixture of 1 part fentanyl/fluanisone, 1 part sterile water, 1 part midazolam (Hypnovel, Roche) and 1 part sterile water can be given as a single intraperitoneal injection (8.0ml/kg). It is important to dilute the fentanyl/fluanisone and midazolam before mixing these two components. These combinations both provide surgical anaesthesia with good muscle relaxation, lasting for about 45 minutes. If a longer period of anaesthesia is required, further doses of fentanyl/fluanisone can be given (about 0.5ml/kg every 20—30 minutes), although care must be taken to avoid serious respiratory depression and consequent acidosis. At the end of the operative procedure, anaesthesia should be reversed by administration of buprenorphine (Temgesic, Reckitt and Colman) (0.1—0.5mg/kg i/m) an opioid which reverses the respiratory depressant action of fentanyl, but maintains analgesia through its own activity (Flecknell *et al,* 1989).

Ketamine (40mg/kg i/m) combined with xylazine (Rompun, Bayer) (5mg/kg i/m) produces light to medium surgical anaesthesia, but the degree of analgesia may be insufficient for major surgery. Similar results can be obtained with ketamine (40mg/kg i/m) and medetomidine (Domitor, SmithKline Beecham) (0.5mg/kg i/m). A disadvantage of these combinations is the glycosuria and polyuria produced by the xylazine and medetomidine, but a major advantage is that the effects of these compounds can be reversed using atipamezole (Antisedan, SmithKline Beecham) (1mg/kg s/c). The effects of ketamine alone are relatively minor, so that rapid recovery usually occurs following reversal of the xylazine or medetomidine.

Pentobarbitone. If pentobarbitone is to be used, this is best administered at a dose rate of 25mg/kg i/p to sedate and immobilise the animal, and anaesthesia should be deepened using methoxyflurane. As soon as surgery has been completed, a respiratory stimulant should be administered, eg. doxapram (Dopram V, Willows Francis).

Post operative recovery is aided by administering warmed dextrose/saline (0.18% saline, 4% dextrose) (20—30 ml/kg s/c or i/p) to correct any fluid deficit. A warm (25°—30°C) recovery area should be provided and the animal given additional subcutaneous fluid for the next few days if its appetite is depressed. It is advisable to weigh the animal prior to surgery both to allow accurate calculation of drug dosages and to provide a means of assessing post-operative weight loss. Following surgery, analgesics such as buprenorphine (0.05mg/kg i/m, 6—12 hourly) should be administered for 24 to 48 hours. As with many other species, company — in the form of another guinea pig — appears to aid recovery and encourages feeding. It is also helpful to give a good quantity of dry hay both to provide warmth and to enable the animal to hide.

SURGICAL PROCEDURES

Castration

Castration of the guinea pig is complicated by the presence of an open inguinal canal which allows the testis to move easily between the scrotum and the abdomen. Provided that the guinea pig is adequately anaesthetised, the testes should remain in the scrotum. In an adult animal, a 2cm skin incision should be made in the scrotum, about 1cm lateral to the penis, in a cranio-caudal direction. The underlying muscle should be incised and the testis removed. In older animals it is necessary to separate the caudal tip of the testis from the muscle by blunt dissection. The fat surrounding the blood vessels can be gently manipulated to allow a secure ligature to be placed around the spermatic vessels. The testis can then be removed and the muscle and skin closed with interrupted sutures. The procedure is then repeated with the remaining testis.

Although the inguinal canal remains patent, herniation of the bowel does not seem to be a problem, possibly due to the large seminal vesicles which partially occlude the entrance to the inguinal canal. Although some people advocate closing the canal, this is probably not necessary.

REFERENCES AND FURTHER READING

BERGHOGG, P. C. (1990). *Les Petits Animaux Familiers et leur Maladies.* Maloire, Paris.

BOOT, R. and WALVOORT, H. C. (1986). Otitis media in guinea pigs: pathology and bacteriology. *Laboratory Animals* **20**, 242.

CANADIAN COUNCIL ON ANIMAL CARE (1980). *Guide to the Care and Use of Experimental Animals 1.* Canadian Council on Animal Care, Ottawa.

COLES, E. H. (1986). *Veterinary Clinical Pathology.* W. B. Saunders, Eastbourne.

COOPER, J. E. (1989).Anaesthesia of exotic species. In: *Manual of Anaesthesia for Small Animal Practice.* 3rd Edn. (Ed. A. D. R. Hilbery), BSAVA, Cheltenham.

ELWARD, M. (1980). *Encyclopedia of Guinea Pigs.* TFH Publications, Reigate.

FLECKNELL, P. A. (1987). *Laboratory Animal Anaesthesia.* Academic Press, London.

FLECKNELL, P. A., LILES, J. H. and WILLIAMSON, H. A. (1990). The use of lignocaine-prilocaine local anaesthetic cream for pain-free venepuncture in laboratory animals. *Laboratory Animals* **24**, 142.

FLECKNELL, P. A., LILES, J. H. and WOOTTON, R. (1989). Reversal of fentanyl/fluanisone neuroleptanalgesia in the rabbit using mixed agonist/antagonist opioids. *Laboratory Animals* **23**, 147.

FRITZ, P. E., HURST, W. J., WHITE, W. J., and LANG, C. M. (1987). Pharmacokinetics of cefazolin in guinea pigs. *Laboratory Animal Science* **37**, 646.

GABRISCH, K. and ZWART, P. (1985). *Krankheiten der Heimtiere.* Schlütersche, Hanover.

GANAWAY, J. R., ALLEN, A. M. and McPHERSON, C. W. (1965). Prevention of acute *Bordetella bronchiseptica* pneumonia in a guinea pig colony. *Laboratory Animal Care* **15**, 156.

HAFEZ, E. S. E. (1970). *Reproduction and Breeding Techniques for Laboratory Animals.* Lea and Febiger, Philadelphia.

HARKNESS, J. E. and WAGNER, J. E. (1989). *The Biology and Medicine of Rabbits and Rodents.* 3rd Edn. Lea and Febiger, Philadelphia.

HIME, J. M. and O'DONOGHUE, P. N. (1979). Eds. *Handbook of Diseases of Laboratory Animals.* Heinemann Veterinary Books, London.

INGLIS, J. K. (1980). *Introduction to Laboratory Animal Science and Technology.* Pergamon Press, Oxford.

KUNSTYR, I., MAESS, J., NAUMANN, S., KAUP, F. J., KRAFT, V. and KNOCKE, K. W. (1984). Adenovirus pneumonia in guinea pigs: an experimental reproduction of the disease. *Laboratory Animals* **18**, 55.

MANNING, P. J., WAGNER, J. E. and HARKNESS, J. E. (1984). Biology and diseases of guinea pigs. In: *Laboratory Animal Medicine.* (Eds. J. G. Fox, B. J. Cohen and F. M. Loew) Academic Press, New York.

MATHERNE, C. M., STEFFEN, E. K. and WAGNER, J. E. (1987). Efficacy of commercial vaccines for protecting guinea pigs against *Bordetella bronchiseptica* pneumonia. *Laboratory Animal Science* **37**, 191.

MITRUKA, B. M. and RAWNSLEY, H. M. (1977). *Clinical Biochemical and Hematological Reference Values in Normal Experimental Animals.* Masson Publishing USA Inc., New York.

NAUMANN, S., JUNSTYR, I., LANGER, I., MAESS, J. and HORNING, R.(1981). Lethal pneumonia in guinea pigs associated with a virus. *Laboratory Animals* **15**, 235.

SANDERSON, J. H. and PHILLIPS, C. E. (1982). *An Atlas of Laboratory Animal Haematology.* Oxford University Press, Oxford.

TRAHAN, C. J., STEPHENSON, E. H., EZZELL, J. W. and MITCHELL, W. C. (1987). Airborne-induced experimental *Bordetella bronchiseptica* pneumonia in strain 13 guinea pigs. *Laboratory Animals* **21**, 226.

WAGNER, J. E. and MANNING, P. J. (1976). *Biology of the Guinea Pig.* Academic Press, New York.

YOUNG, J. D., HURST, W. J., WHITE, W. J. and LANG, C. M. (1987). An evaluation of ampicillin pharmacokinetics and toxicity in guinea pigs. *Laboratory Animal Science* **37**, 652.

CHAPTER SEVEN

HEDGEHOGS

Martin W Gregory BVSc PhD MRCVS DipIEMVT MIBiol
Les Stocker

Erinaceus europaeus is the only species of hedgehog that occurs naturally in the UK. Its natural diet includes insects, slugs, snails, earthworms, small vertebrates and fruit. Hedgehogs are of great value to the gardener and in several European countries they are protected by law. Their enemies include road vehicles, badgers and foxes. Many die in garden ponds, not because they cannot swim but because they cannot climb out.

Adults usually weigh between 800g and 1200g. Life expectancy in the wild is three to four years but captive animals can live for ten years. Hedgehogs are normally nocturnal; activity in broad daylight is usually a sign of ill-health. They are solitary for most of the year. Mating starts in March—April and involves long and noisy courtship. Usually three to five young are born after about five weeks' gestation.

At birth the spines are white and are hidden by oedematous skin. New brown spines soon start to appear and by the time the eyes open at twelve to eighteen days, the white spines are hardly visible. The young may start to take solid food at twenty one days or even earlier, but they continue suckling until about forty days, when the bodyweight is approximately 230g. Transmission of maternal immunoglobulins continues throughout the suckling period (Morris and Rudge, 1970). Late litters are often born in August/September.

Rectal temperature is normally in the range of 34°—37°C. Hibernation usually occurs if the environmental temperature falls below about 9°C. Body temperature is then maintained at about 6°C. It is not harmful to arouse hedgehogs in midwinter, but the process of waking up (which takes two to five hours) uses much energy, and therefore they need to eat and drink within a short time. Hedgehogs need not hibernate and they will not do so if kept warm and fed. Even in wild animals, hibernation may only be brief or spasmodic.

The hedgehog curls up into a spiny ball by means of a circular muscle that acts as a purse-string. It is simple-stomached, and has no caecum.

HANDLING

Some hedgehogs obstinately refuse to unroll. Different authors have each found their own ways of persuading hedgehogs to do so. It is most important to avoid sharp noises.

Wroot (personal communication) bounces the animal in his hands and says this always works immediately. Poduschka (personal communication) finds that by heavy backward stroking of the spines over the rump, the hedgehog is always persuaded to uncurl.

One method (see Figures 1—4) is to hold the rolled-up hedgehog head-downwards over a flat surface. It then usually unrolls cautiously and tries to reach the surface. The back legs can then be grasped gently and the animal can be held by them and examined at leisure while it strives to reach the ground. Intraperitoneal injections can also be given in this position. This is an ideal method for checking injuries to the hind legs. If all else fails, the hedgehog can be anaesthetised (see later).

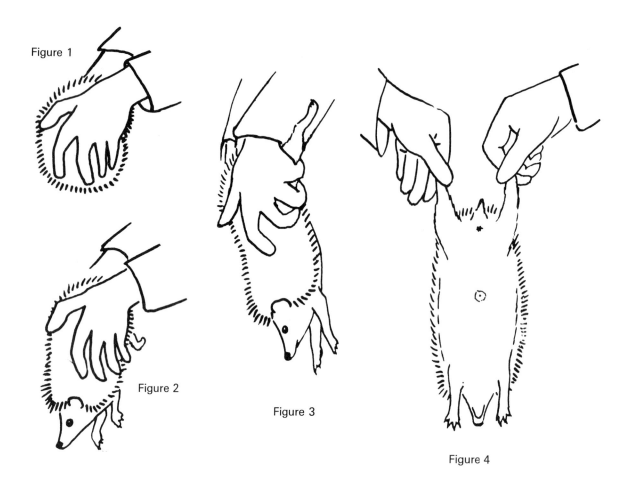

Figure 1

Figure 2

Figure 3

Figure 4

Unrolling a hedgehog.

SEXING

The preputial opening of the male is near the middle of the belly (see Figure 4). The vulva of the female is only a short distance from the anus. In newborn animals the prepuce is also near the anus; it migrates forwards as the animal matures. The testes remain intra-abdominal throughout life.

MANAGEMENT

Mature females should not be taken into captivity because of the risk of separation from their young. As a general rule a hedgehog should only be brought into captivity if it is sick or injured.

Accommodation

Disabled hedgehogs can be kept in a walled garden, which they will keep free of pests, but they will need a feed supplement. This is an ideal way to keep hedgehogs that would not survive in the wild. However, their natural home range is wide, and the need to mate is strong, so they are liable to climb over fences.

Injured hedgehogs can be kept in netting enclosures if there is a 20cm overhang along the top of the netting. A similar infolding of the netting around the bottom will stop them from digging their way out, but they may get sore feet in the attempt. Alternatively, the netting can be buried 20cm below ground level, but this means that the enclosure cannot be moved. A shelter is needed where the animals can sleep in dry leaves, hay, newspaper or other bedding.

Hedgehogs can be kept in small indoor cages, but unless they are already tame, they may refuse to eat for a long time. They will not breed in close confinement. Hedgehogs of either sex are liable to fight.

Food

The diet should be as varied as possible. Hedgehogs will readily take meaty household scraps and tinned petfoods. Chicken carcases, raw or cooked, are much appreciated, and the bones help to balance the diet and keep the teeth free of tartar. Soft fruit, nuts, soaked dog biscuits and bread scraps can be offered as well. Bread and cow's milk are liable to cause digestive upsets, particularly in young hedgehogs. Tartar can be a major problem: any adult hedgehog should have a dental inspection, especially of the molars.

Abandoned babies

The natural orifices and the eyes must be checked for blowfly eggs and maggots (see later). The baby must be kept warm. Goat's milk (2 parts) and goat's colostrum (1 part) make a good milk substitute. A vitamin and mineral supplement is also recommended. A very small animal should be fed every 3—4 hours, and after each meal its belly and genitals should be massaged and its anus cleaned. Tinned petfoods should be offered from the start. A hedgehog should weigh at least 450g before being released in the late autumn, otherwise it has little chance of surviving the winter months (Morris, 1983, 1984). More detailed information is to be found in Stocker (1987a).

DRUG ADMINISTRATION

Subcutaneous injections can be given in the back and flank and intramuscular injections in the thigh. Intraperitoneal injections can be administered while holding the animal by the hind legs (see earlier) or by the forelegs if it is seriously debilitated. Edwards (1957) used the external saphena vein over the hock for intravenous chloral hydrate anaesthesia.

DISEASES/CLINICAL CONDITIONS

Ectoparasites

Fleas

Most wild hedgehogs carry large numbers of the hedgehog flea *(Archaeopsylla erinacei)* (Jordan and Hughes, 1982). They usually cause little harm to the hedgehog and are unlikely to bite people. They can be killed with dusting powder such as pyrethrum (Rid-Mite, Johnsons) or bromocyclen (Alugan, Hoechst) applied to the animal and its bedding. Aerosol sprays tend to be toxic. Schicht (1982) recommends washing off the spray after application.

Mites

Caparina tripilis and *Notoedres* spp. can cause severe mange (see Figure 5) and, often predispose to ringworm infection. Treatment with acaricidal dips, eg. bromocyclen, are effective and early trials with ivermectin (Ivomec, MSD) (1 part ivermectin mixed with 9 parts propylene glycol; 0.2mg/kg s/c) are promising (Wildlife Hospital Trust, unpublished).

Figure 5
Mange mites in a hedgehog often predisposes to ringworm infection.

Ticks

Ticks are commonly found, particularly *Ixodes hexagonus*. They can usually be removed with forceps without untoward effects.

Blowfly maggots

Blowfly maggots or eggs may be found on young abandoned hedgehogs or old and ailing animals. The eyes, mouth, nostrils, ears, anus, prepuce and vulva must all be checked, as well as skin folds elsewhere. Both maggots and eggs can be removed with forceps or, in adults, coumaphos (Negasunt, Bayer) or acaricidal ear drops.

Endoparasites

Helminths

Many species occur but only *Crenosoma striatum* commonly causes serious disease. It affects the lungs, causing coughing, rattling breath, bronchopneumonia and death. Because of this parasite, Schicht (1982) recommended immediate treatment of all hedgehogs brought in to the surgery (see Table 1 for details). Early trials with ivermectin are producing promising results (The Wildlife Hospital Trust, unpublished).

Protozoa

Coccidia occasionally cause dysentery. Recommended treatment is sulphadimidine at a dose rate of 100 — 200mg/kg bodyweight subcutaneously on three successive days, or combined preparations such as Kaobiotic tablets (Upjohn) or Neo-sulphentrin (Willows Francis).

Table 1
Helminths of the hedgehog.

Classification	Name	Site	Transmission	Treatment
Trematoda	*Brachylaemus erinacei*	Intestine and bile ducts.	via slugs and snails	Praziquantel 10 — 15mg orally or niclosamide 200mg/kg (Schicht, 1982).
Cestoda	*Hymenolepis erinacei*	Intestine	via arthropods	None necessary.
	Mesocestoides spp.	Mesentery and liver (cysts).	via arthropods and dogs	
Nematoda	*Crenosoma striatum*	Lungs	via slugs and snails	Mebendazole 100mg/kg daily for 5 days in food or levamisole 1% 10mg/kg s/c, repeated after 48 hours (Schicht, 1982) or febantel 0.5ml/kg of 10% suspension daily for 5 days (Koch, 1981).
	Capillaria aerophila	Lungs	direct or via earthworms	
	Physaloptera clausa	Oesophagus	? direct	Levamisole, as above, is probably effective (Poduschka and Kieliger, 1972).
	Capillaria spp.	Intestine	?	As for *Crenosoma* (Schicht, 1982).
Acanthocephala	*Moniliformis* and other genera.	Intestine and mesentery.	? via insects	Levamisole, as above (Poduschka, personal communication).

Other clinical conditions

Fungi

Trichophyton erinacei (Arthroderma benhamii) is carried by about 25% of hedgehogs (Morris and English, 1969), but they usually show little evidence of infection. As *Trichophyton* does not fluoresce, confirmation of infection is obtained with Dermatophyte Test Medium (Fungassay, C-Vet). Occasionally this organism causes a troublesome dermatitis in people. The lesion in humans is not typical of ringworm and may not be recognised immediately by medical practitioners. It is intensely irritating but usually heals spontaneously in 2—3 weeks. In the authors' experience clotrimazole fungicidal cream (Canesten, Bayer) can be effective in man.

Bacteria

Bordetella bronchiseptica is sometimes involved in pneumonia — usually in association with *Crenosoma striatum.* Schicht (1982) recommended oxytetracycline, 50mg/kg bodyweight daily in food for five days. Amoxycillin (Clamoxyl, SmithKline Beecham), penicillin and lincomycin (Lincocin, Upjohn) can also be used for bacterial infections (Stocker and Kilshaw, 1987). Various bacteria may be carried including *Salmonella enteritidis, Leptospira* spp. and *Pasteurella* spp. Such infections are more prevalent in mature hedgehogs and are liable to become apparent under stress, such as in captivity.

Viruses

Hedgehogs are renowned for their susceptibility to foot and mouth disease (McLauchlan and Henderson, 1947) but this is of little practical importance. Other viruses may be carried (Smith, 1968) but their significance is not known.

Nutritional disorders

Schicht (1982) and Poduschka and Kieliger (1972) put great emphasis on vitamin deficiency, particularly in hedgehogs just emerging from hibernation. It appears that multivitamin therapy can be beneficial in cases of weakness and sometimes also of lameness. Rickets also occurs in captivity if the diet is unbalanced (Edwards, 1957).

Fractures

Multiple fractures to legs and head are not uncommon. Most will respond well to supportive treatment with the larger limb bones being readily receptive to intramedullary pinning. Spinal injuries should be evaluated radiographically before resorting to euthanasia.

Hernias

Some road casualties experience abdominal hernias which respond well to surgery.

Skin wounds

Skin wounds amongst the spines can be approached for suturing by cutting the spines short with dressing scissors. Normal electric clippers are not effective and may be damaged.

Euthanasia

Anaesthesia prior to injection will facilitate access to preferred points of entry.

Poisoning

Hedgehogs are relatively resistant to the effects of many natural and synthetic toxins. They are susceptible to poisoning by metaldehyde but are usually unharmed by eating slugs that have been killed by it (Schicht, 1982; Morris, 1983).

ANAESTHESIA

Poduschka and Saupe (1981) recommend **halothane** or **methoxyflurane** for short anaesthesia and **ketamine** (Vetalar, Parke-Davis) (20mg/kg i/m) or **fentanyl/fluanisone** (Hypnorm, Janssen) (1—2ml/kg i/m) for prolonged anaesthesia. Schicht (1982) reported variable success with ketamine. Intraperitoneal **pentobarbitone sodium** (25mg/kg) is usually effective and, in the authors' experience, safe. There is no mention of the use of **alphaxalone/alphadolone** (Saffan, Coopers Pitman-Moore) in the hedgehog literature; it would be well worth trying intramuscularly at 15mg/kg.

ANALGESIA

Buprenorphine (Temgesic, Reckitt and Colman) can be used intramuscularly at 0.04ml/kg every 6—8 hours.

RELEASE

Hedgehogs are unlikely to become tame and unless disabled should always be released, preferably in deciduous woodland or with access to at least ten gardens. They will revert to completely natural behaviour.

A request for further information

Little has been published on the veterinary care of hedgehogs. The experience of practitioners and others can be most valuable, and the authors would appreciate communications from those who have worked with this species. The Wildlife Hospitals Trust at Aylesbury treats many hundreds of hedgehogs. They are always willing to advise or take on casualties and would appreciate any correspondence on hedgehog conditions and treatments.

REFERENCES AND FURTHER READING

EDWARDS, J. T. G. (1957). The European hedgehog (*Erinaceus europaeus*). In: *The UFAW Handbook on the Care and Management of Laboratory Animals.* 2nd Edn. (Eds. A. N. Worden and W. Lane-Petter) Churchill Livingstone, Edinburgh.

JORDAN, W. J. and HUGHES, J. (1982). *Care of the Wild.* Macdonald, London.

KOCH, J. (1981). Worm control in hedgehogs *(Erinaceus europaeus). Veterinary Medical Review* **2**, 150.

McLAUCHLAN, J. D. and HENDERSON, W. M. (1947). The occurrence of foot and mouth disease in the hedgehog under natural conditions. *Journal of Hygiene* **45**, 474.

MAJEED, S. K. and COOPER, J. E. (1984). Lesions associated with a Capillaria infestation in the European Hedgehog *(Erinaceus europaeus). Journal of Comparative Pathology* **94**, 625.

MORRIS, P. (1983). *Hedgehogs.* Whittet Books, Weybridge.

MORRIS, P. (1984). An estimate of the minimum body weight necessary for hedgehogs *(Erinaceus europaeus)* to survive hibernation. *Journal of Zoology* London **203**, 291.

MORRIS, P. and ENGLISH, M. P. (1969). *Trichophyton mentagrophytes* var *erinacei* in British hedgehogs. *Sabouraudia* **7**, 122.

MORRIS, B. and RUDGE, G. (1970). Serum proteins in young hedgehogs. *Journal of Zoology London* **162**, 461.

PODUSCHKA, W. and KIELIGER, F. (1972). Zur medizinische Betreuung des Igels *(Erinaceus europaeus* und *Erinaceus europaeus roumanicus). Kleintier-Praxis* **17**(7), 192.

PODUSCHKA, W. and SAUPE, E. (1981). *Das Igel Brevier.* 5th Edn. Deutscher Tierschutzbund, Bonn.

RANSON, R. M. (1941). New laboratory animals from wild species. Breeding a laboratory stock of hedgehogs *(Erinaceus europaeus). Journal of Hygiene* **41**, 131.

SAUPE, E. and PODUSCHKA, W. (1984). Igel. In: *Krankheiten der Heimtiere.* (Eds. K. Gabrisch and P. Zwart) Schlütersche, Hannover.

SCHICHT, M. (1982). Der Igel als gelegentlicher Patient in der Kleintierpraxis. *Monatshefte für Veterinärmedizin* **37**, 829.

SMITH, J. M. B. (1968). Diseases of hedgehogs. *Veterinary Bulletin* **38**, 425.

STOCKER, L. (1987a). Artificial Rearing of Orphaned Hedgehogs. *Proceedings of Veterinary Zoological Society Meeting, London.*

STOCKER, L. (1987b). *The Complete Hedgehog.* Chatto and Windus, London.

STOCKER, L. and KILSHAW, R. (1987). *Medication for Use in the Treatment of Hedgehogs.* Wildlife Hospitals Trust, Aylesbury.

CHAPTER EIGHT

RABBITS

Paul A Flecknell MA VetMB PhD DLAS MRCVS

Domestic rabbits *(Oryctolagus cuniculus)* are kept as pets, as show animals and are bred commercially for meat production. Although pet animals are usually of mixed origin, a large number of distinct breeds are available and extensive show standards have been produced by the British Rabbit Council (see 'Appendix — Useful Addresses').

The various breeds of rabbits fall into two broad groups — fancy breeds and fur breeds. The latter are divided into three sections — normal fur breeds in which the coat consists of an undercoat of down hairs and an outer coat of longer guard hairs; rex breeds, in which the guard hairs are shortened, producing a flat, velvety coat; and satin breeds, in which the structure of all the hair fibres is altered. Body conformation and size vary considerably amongst the fancy breeds, ranging from the Netherland dwarf, which weighs about 1kg when adult, to the Flemish giant which can weigh over 8kg. A full list of rabbit breed classification is given in Sandford (1986). Descriptions of the more frequently seen breeds, together with much useful general information for the rabbit owner, are given in Nightingale (1979).

HOUSING

A great many different designs of rabbit hutch are seen – both commercially-produced and home-made. Whilst some of these designs are good, others are far from adequate. A floor area of at least 0.3m² should be provided for a single small rabbit and 0.2m² per animal if several are kept in the same hutch. For animals over 2kg in weight, the floor space should be increased by about 0.1–0.2m² per extra kilogram of bodyweight. The floor dimensions should be sufficient to allow the animal to lie at full stretch. The hutch height should be sufficient to allow the animal to raise itself vertically on its hindquarters, ie. it should be 45cm to 90cm high, depending upon the size of the rabbit. Most pet rabbits are housed in solid floored cages, which help to provide a more weather-proof environment for animals housed outdoors. If rabbits are housed indoors, then mesh or perforated-grid floors are preferable since these have the advantage of needing less frequent cleaning and also help to minimise the build-up of endoparasites. Frequent cleaning (preferably daily) should be encouraged to prevent a build-up of faecal matter and solid floored cages should have a covering of newspaper, sawdust, wood shavings, straw or hay. A separate nestbox should be provided and this should contain plenty of clean, dry hay as bedding. In the UK most pet rabbits are housed outdoors throughout the year. This is satisfactory provided that the hutch is well insulated to prevent extremes of cold in the winter and suitably shaded to prevent overheating in summer. It should also be dry and draught-free. Temperatures above 27°C are likely to produce heatstroke or precipitate an acute episode of respiratory disease (see Diseases). Male rabbits should not generally be housed together as they are likely to fight. Does and bucks should also be housed separately. Does reared together from weaning can be housed in the same hutch, provided that overcrowding is avoided. Housing of rabbits in small groups should be encouraged so that the animals can engage in social activities.

FEEDING

Rabbits are best fed on a commercial pelleted ration, which will provide a balanced diet. This may be supplemented with hay (as bedding) and small quantities of green food, carrots, cabbage and salad crops to provide some variety. Allowing the animal out of its hutch (under supervision) to browse on grass and other plants is to be encouraged, but feeding of grass clippings or anything other than freshly collected plant material must be avoided as this may result in digestive disturbances. Rabbits should never be fed waste salad crops and vegetables which are considered unfit for human consumption. Sudden changes in diet can also cause digestive problems and so must be avoided. Water must be freely available and both water and food bowls cleaned daily. Water bottles can be suspended on the wall of the cage to help ensure a continuous supply of clean water.

HANDLING

Rabbits are generally fairly docile but the occasional aggressive animal will be encountered and such rabbits can inflict painful bites and scratches. Aggression is usually caused by fear — most rabbits are easily frightened and, if improperly handled, they may struggle violently and suffer serious injury to their vertebral column, resulting in permanent posterior paralysis. Severe stress and fear can also cause cardiac arrest. For these reasons rabbits must be handled carefully and quietly. They should be grasped by the scruff if fractious, or held with one hand under the thorax, gripping each fore leg separately with thumb and two fingers and the hindquarters supported with the other hand as they are lifted clear of the ground (see Figure 1). The animal should be held close to the handler's chest when being carried (see Figure 2) and must be put down immediately on a firm, non-slip surface if it struggles violently or starts to squeal. The rabbit should be placed on a firm surface and restrained by the scruff to enable clinical examination or minor manipulation to be undertaken. However, tame pet rabbits may resent being scruffed and can be held gently but firmly with a hand under the thorax, as described above. Very excitable or aggressive animals can be restrained by administration of diazepam (Valium, Roche) (1mg/kg i/m), fentanyl/fluanisone (Hypnorm, Janssen) (0.3ml/kg i/m) or ketamine (Vetalar, Parke-Davis) (25mg/kg i/m).

INJECTION TECHNIQUES

Intramuscular injections are best made into the quadriceps using a 23 gauge needle; 0.25 − 1.0ml of material can be administered by this route (depending upon the size of the rabbit).

Subcutaneous injections can easily be given under the skin overlying the neck and thorax using a 21 or 23 gauge needle. Large volumes of fluid may be administered by this route — for example 50−70ml of dextrose saline for the treatment of dehydration.

Intraperitoneal injections are best carried out with the animal restrained by an assistant as shown in Figure 3. The needle should be introduced at right angles to the body wall just lateral to the midline, at a point equidistant between the xiphisternum and pubis. This positioning should avoid accidental puncture of the bladder or stomach. A short (2.5cm) needle should be used. If no assistance is available the rabbit should be restrained by the scruff and the injection made at a point just cranial to the hindlimb in the lower third of the abdomen. This is a less satisfactory technique as sudden movement by the rabbit could lead to damage of the abdominal viscera.

Intravenous injection is a relatively simple technique in rabbits. The marginal ear vein is used and the overlying hair should first be shaved so that the vessel is clearly visible. If assistance is available the vein should be compressed at the base of the ear, so that it dilates along the rest of its length. The ear is held firmly in one hand and the needle inserted gently into the vein. Most rabbits will react with slight head movement at this point and the needle can easily be dislodged from the vein. For this reason, it is often easier to use a butterfly infusion set — the flexible coupling between the needle and syringe will enable the needle to be maintained in the vein. If the rabbit reacts strongly to attempted venepuncture then either a sedative/analgesic drug such as fentanyl/fluanisone can be administered or the skin overlying the ear can be anaesthetised using local anaesthetic cream (EMLA, Astra) (Flecknell et al, 1990). The ear veins are fairly fragile and if repeated injections are to be made (for example when using an intravenous anaesthetic) an indwelling flexible catheter (such as Abbocath, Abbot Ireland, or Quickcath, Travenol Laboratories) should be used.

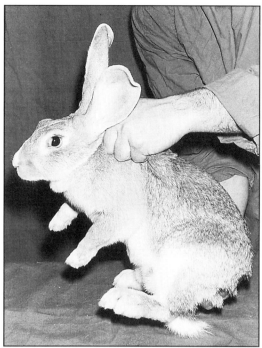

Figure 1
Restraint of the rabbit.
The rabbit is grasped by the scruff and
its weight supported under the hindquarters.

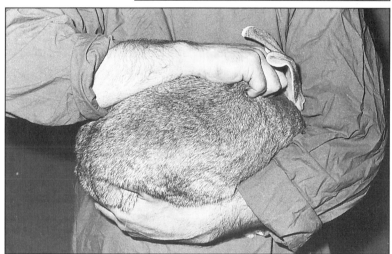

Figure 2
To carry a rabbit the animal's
head should be tucked into
the handler's arm, and the
handler's forearms used to
provide support both along the
back and beneath the rabbit.

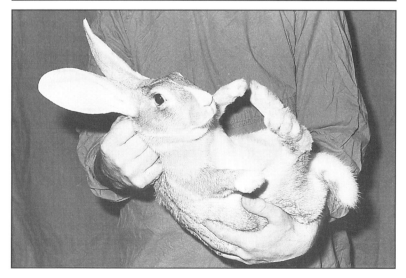

Figure 3
Method of restraint for
intraperitoneal injection.

Oral dosing of rabbits is usually straightforward provided that the material is not too unpalatable. The animal should be wrapped in a towel to ensure good restraint, with its head exposed. The nozzle of a syringe can then be introduced into the corner of the mouth and small (0.25—0.5ml) boluses of fluid administered, allowing time for swallowing between each mouthful. If the animal refuses to swallow then a stomach tube can be passed; a 3.0mm outside diameter (8.0 French Gauge) soft polythene catheter is a suitable size for most rabbits. A gag is usually necessary as rabbits will rapidly chew through most tubes — a suitable one can be made by drilling a hole through the sides of the plastic case provided with some types of disposable syringes. Alternatively, a commercial gag can be used.

SEXING

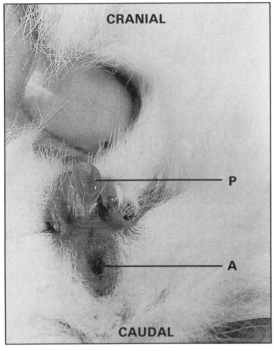

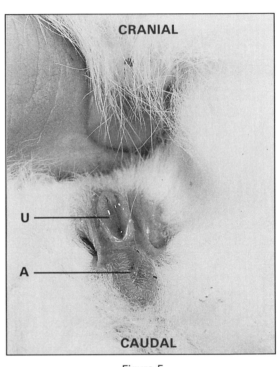

Figure 4
External genitalia of a young male rabbit. In adult animals the penis (P) can be protruded by gentle pressure on either side of the genital opening. A = anus.

Figure 5
External genitalia of a young female rabbit.
A = anus, U = urethra.

Sexing of young rabbits is very difficult and requires considerable practice. Young males have a pointed, protruding genital opening (see Figure 4) and the female a short, slit-shaped opening (see Figure 5). In adult males the penis can be protruded by gentle pressure on either side of the genital opening, and the scrotal sacs may be seen lateral and cranial to the penis. To examine the external genitalia of an adult rabbit, the animal should be restrained as shown in Figure 6.

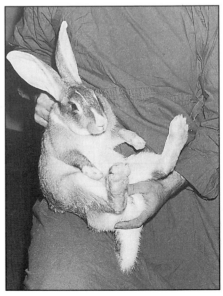

Figure 6
Method of restraint of an adult rabbit to allow examination of the external genitalia. The rabbit's back and hindquarters are supported on the handler's thigh.

REPRODUCTION

Rabbits are sexually mature at between 16—24 weeks of age, smaller breeds tending to mature earlier than larger breeds. Normal reproductive parameters are summarised in Table 1. Rabbits do not have regular oestrous cycles, but may show long periods of oestrus (Hafez, 1970). If mating does not take place the ovarian follicles regress and new follicles mature. During this stage a short period of lack of receptivity (lasting 1—2 days) may occur (roughly every 12—16 days). If the doe is in poor condition, lactating, moulting, or stressed in other ways, then oestrus is often suppressed.

Table 1
Reproductive parameters in the rabbit.

Sexual maturity	16—24 weeks
Oestrous cycle	See text (induced ovulation)
Gestation period	30—33 days
Litter size	4—12 (average 7)
Weaning age	7—8 weeks

The buck may be attacked by the doe if he is introduced into her hutch. For this reason they should be housed separately and the doe taken to the buck's hutch for mating. Following successful mating she should be returned to her own hutch. Ovulation is triggered by mating but it may also occur following mounting by other does. If the mating is unsuccessful, pseudopregnancy can result. This condition lasts for about 18 days and is usually associated with mammary gland enlargement and nest-building behaviour.

Normal pregnancy lasts 30—33 days, and can be diagnosed by abdominal palpation at around 12—14 days of gestation. During the final week of pregnancy nest-building activity commences, when the doe usually pulls hair from her abdomen and flanks to line the nest. Mammary development is rapid during the last week of pregnancy, but milk secretion is usually delayed until after parturition. Litter size varies considerably, commonly ranging from 4—12, with an average of 7. Smaller breeds tend to have fewer young. Following parturition, the doe and her young should not be disturbed, except to provide food and water and to clean the hutch — the nestbox should not be cleaned. Weaning can generally be completed when the young are 7—8 weeks old. It is possible to hand-rear orphaned rabbits using commercial puppy milk substitutes, eg. Welpi, Vetbed, but aspiration pneumonia and diarrhoea frequently occur and often prove fatal.

Table 2
Physiological data in the rabbit.

Average life span	8—12 years
Adult bodyweight	1—8kg (varies with breed and sex)
Respiratory rate	35—60 per minute
Tidal volume	20ml (3.0kg rabbit)
Heart rate	220 per minute
Rectal temperature	38.3°C, range 37°—39.4°C
Blood volume	70ml/kg bodyweight
Haematocrit	0.41 l/l
Red blood cell count	6.5×10^{12}/l
Haemoglobin	13.5g/dl
White blood cell count	8.6×10^9/l
Neutrophils*	45%
Lymphocyte	40%
Average daily water intake	100ml/kg bodyweight

*Rabbit neutrophils have prominent cytoplasmic granules which resemble those seen in eosinophils (Sanderson and Phillips, 1982).

DISEASES/CLINICAL CONDITIONS

Many of the conditions seen in pet rabbits result from poor husbandry and it is particularly important to obtain an accurate history of the housing and feeding of the animal. Normal physiological variables which may assist in clinical and laboratory examinations are summarised in Table 2. It should be remembered that rabbits are easily frightened and that this will produce a marked tachycardia and tachypnoea. Drug dose rates are listed in Table 3.

Table 3
Dose rates of antibacterial drugs in the rabbit.

Antibacterial agent	Dose/Comments
Ampicillin: injection, 15% w/v : oral preparations	25mg/kg i/m or s/c sid or bid 15mg/kg bid
Cephaloridine	15mg/kg i/m bid
Cephalexin	15mg/kg s/c bid
Chloramphenicol: injectable suspension : tablets	15mg/kg i/m bid 50mg/kg sid
Chlortetracycline: soluble powder	1mg/ml drinking water
Gentamicin	4mg/kg i/m sid
Oxytetracycline: injection, 50mg/ml : Terramycin LA, Pfizer : soluble powder	115mg/kg i/m or s/c bid 30mg/kg i/m or s/c every 3 days 1mg/ml in drinking water or 60mg/kg (per day) in divided doses
Potentiated sulphonamides eg. trimethoprim/sulphadiazine, Tribrissen 24% (Coopers Pitman-Moore)	0.2ml/kg s/c sid or bid
NOT RECOMMENDED Lincomycin	Toxic, produces enterotoxaemia.

Skin and associated structures

Hair loss and skin irritation may be caused by a range of different agents. It should be noted that pregnant and pseudopregnant rabbits may pull large quantities of fur from their flanks and abdomens in order to make a nest.

Ringworm

Ringworm, usually caused by *Trichophyton* spp., produces areas of hair loss with scaling of the skin. In some instances severe pruritus occurs and the lesions may be encrusted with exudate. Direct microscopic examination of the hairs or culture on Sabouraud's agar should confirm the diagnosis. Treatment with griseofulvin (25mg/kg by mouth for 28 days) is usually effective.

Mites

Mite infestation can cause severe pruritus. *Psoroptes cuniculi* is the parasite most frequently involved. Usually only the ear canal is affected. However, in severe cases the lesions may extend to involve most of the pinnae. The ear canal becomes reddened and ulcerated and plugged with brownish exudate. Treatment with ear drops containing an acaricide, eg. GAC, Arnolds, is usually effective, but cleaning of the debris is best delayed for a few days to avoid further damage to the ulcerated ear canal. After several days treatment the waxy exudate will have softened and it can more easily be removed. To prevent any pain during this procedure, the rabbit should be sedated with fentanyl/fluanisone. Treatment should continue for seven days and be repeated at fortnightly intervals for six weeks. Since the hutch may be contaminated with mites, it must be thoroughly cleaned. An alternative to the use of topical treatment is to administer ivermectin (Ivomec, MSD), (400µg/kg) (Harkness, 1987). More generalised dermatitis can be caused by *Cheyletiella parasitivorax* infestations, which often cause the hairs to be lost in tufts with a very noticeable accumulation of skin flakes and debris at their base. The underlying skin is often reddened and sore. Dermatitis can also be caused by sarcoptic and notoedric mange mites. Examination of skin scrapings or of hair samples (for *Cheyletiella*) should confirm the diagnosis, and the condition can then be treated with bromocyclen dusting powder (Alugan, Hoechst).

Skin wounds/abscesses

Skin wounds and abscesses can result both from fights with cage mates and from injuries caused by other animals — suspected dog, cat and fox bites are all seen fairly frequently. After administration of a sedative/analgesic such as fentanyl/fluanisone, wounds should be cleaned and, unless very severe, should not be sutured but left open to allow good drainage. Twice daily cleaning with sterile saline, wound cleaning solution (Dermisol, SmithKline Beecham) or antiseptic is usually sufficient to prevent serious infection developing. Abscesses should be opened and cleaned under light anaesthesia — it is particularly important in rabbits to establish good drainage otherwise the cavity may reseal and the abscess recur. Careful flushing with saline or a wound cleaning preparation is recommended to help promote rapid healing. In warm weather an insecticidal powder should be applied to the coat around the wound to prevent myiasis. Abscesses in the mandibular region may involve deeper tissues including bone. These lesions respond very poorly to treatment. Careful exposure of all of the infected tissue under general anaesthesia to establish drainage, followed by a 2—3 week course of treatment with systemic antibiotics may be successful in less severely affected animals.

Necrobacillosis

Necrotic skin lesions can be produced by *Fusobacterium necrophorum* infection. The disease progresses gradually, the rabbit loses condition and eventually becomes severely emaciated and dies. Diagnosis follows examination of smears taken from the area beneath the skin lesions for the presence of the causal organism. Successful treatment has not been reported and affected animals are probably best humanely killed. The underlying cause of infection is usually poor husbandry, with soiling of the rabbit's skin with urine and faeces.

Sore hocks

Hair loss and ulceration of the skin on the plantar aspects of both hind limbs can result from trauma due to badly designed wire mesh floors, or to constant exposure to damp and dirty solid floors. Occasionally the forelimbs may also be affected. The wounds should be cleaned and the rabbit housed in a solid-floored pen with plenty of clean, dry bedding. Bandaging of the area with a padded dressing for 7—10 days may help to prevent further damage and encourage healing. Under no circumstances should attempts be made to débride and excise the lesions.

Bacterial dermatitis

Areas of reddened and ulcerated skin often occur on the ventral abdomen and inguinal region of rabbits which are housed in poor conditions. A range of different bacteria may be cultured from such wounds, including *Staphylococcus* and *Pseudomonas* spp. Correction of the husbandry and treatment of the wounds with cleansing solutions or antibiotic/antiseptic ointments usually result in a cure. Rabbits may also develop localised dermatitis in the medial canthus of the eye, or around the chin, caused by habitual rubbing on the spout of a water bottle. Symptomatic treatment should be given and the type of water bottle changed.

Gastro-intestinal disorders

Overgrown teeth (malocclusions)

Abnormal wear of the incisors or molars can result in excessive growth of the teeth and prevention of normal jaw movements. Affected animals drool saliva and have an impaired appetite. The incisor teeth can be inspected in conscious rabbits, but it is very difficult to carry out a thorough examination of the cheek teeth without anaesthetising the animal. Use of an aural speculum in lightly sedated or very tractable conscious animals may be possible and is worth attempting if anaesthesia is considered hazardous. The teeth can be clipped back to their normal length using either nail clippers or a dental burr. In smaller rabbits, cuticle clippers can be used to clip the cheek teeth. It is important always to examine the molars and premolars if the incisor teeth are overgrown. The condition tends to recur and since it may be an inherited abnormality, affected animals should not be used for breeding. Repeated clipping is worth undertaking, as even some apparent congenital malocclusions may eventually resolve.

Gastric hairball

Excessive grooming and ingestion of hair may occasionally lead to the production of a large hair or furball in the stomach. Affected animals are inappetent and often develop diarrhoea due to secondary digestive tract disturbances. The hairball may be palpable, but radiographic examination following the administration of barium will confirm the diagnosis. Treatment with liquid paraffin is usually ineffective, although it is occasionally successful if combined with gentle massage of the stomach through the body wall to try to break up the hairball. It is usually necessary to remove the hairball surgically. Provided secondary digestive tract disturbances are not too severe, the prognosis for such animals is quite good. Small furballs are a common incidental finding at *post-mortem* examination and appear to be of little significance.

Diarrhoea/enteritis

A range of different factors can produce diarrhoea or enteritis in rabbits. Careful consideration of the husbandry of the animal, its diet and any recent environmental stress may assist in determining the cause or causes of the condition. Faecal examination for endoparasites and culture to identify potentially pathogenic bacteria may be helpful. A number of specific causes of enteritis have been reported, including *E. coli, Bacillus piliformis,* salmonellae and coccidia (Kraus *et al,* 1984). However, most cases are of uncertain aetiology and are collectively referred to as the 'enteritis complex'.

Enteritis complex. This syndrome may be caused by a wide range of factors, including poor husbandry, diet and bacterial, protozoal and fungal agents. In young rabbits severe losses can occur, particularly at 5—7 weeks and 10 weeks of age (Whitney, 1976). Affected animals are depressed, have faecal staining of the perineum and the abdomen often feels 'watery' when palpated. Treatment should concentrate on maintaining food intake — this may require hand-feeding of homogenised food of high fibre content. Hay should be fed and fresh green food in the diet reduced to a minimum. Although coccidial oocysts are frequently seen in the faeces of affected animals, these are probably not the prime cause of the disorder, but treatment with sulphadimidine (Sulphamethazine Solution 33 ⅓ % ICI) (0.2% in drinking water for 7—14 days) may be helpful. Treatment with oral antibiotics should be undertaken only if dietary changes are proving ineffective or if the animal develops other clinical signs of disease such as lethargy and depression. Neomycin and methscopolamine (Neobiotic P Aquadrops, Upjohn) (2ml/4.5kg daily in divided doses) appears successful in some animals. Loperamide (Immodium, Janssen) (0.1mg/kg tid for 3 days) has been recommended for treating rabbits with *E. coli* diarrhoea (Banerjee *et al,* 1987). Kaolin preparations, eg. Kaopectate, Upjohn (2ml/kg bodyweight daily in frequent small doses), may also prove effective. Fluid therapy is especially important, and in addition to intravenous or subcutaneous administration, oral rehydration using glucose and electrolyte solutions (Lectade, SmithKline Beecham; Life Aid, Norbrook) can be extremely effective. Provided that therapy can be started early in the course of the condition, a reasonably good prognosis can be given. Unfortunately, many rabbits are presented for treatment late in the course of the disease when they have become severely dehydrated and emaciated. Under these circumstances, therapy is less likely to be successful.

Some authors have differentiated a second clinical syndrome, termed 'mucoid enteropathy' (Kraus *et al,* 1984). This condition usually occurs in young animals, particularly following weaning. Although diarrhoea is a common clinical sign, some animals may develop a distended abdomen and be found dead. Other rabbits become inappetent and pass both normal faeces and a clear gelatinous material. On *post-mortem* examination clear mucus is often found in the colon. The cause of this syndrome is uncertain and treatment can only be symptomatic and is generally ineffective.

Coccidiosis. Although, as mentioned earlier, coccidial oocysts are frequently found in faeces in 'non-specific' enteritis in rabbits, primary coccidial infections may also occur. The species of greatest clinical significance are *Eimeria magna, E. perforans, E. media* and *E. irresidua.* If large numbers of oocysts are found on faecal examination, treatment with sulphonamides should commence (sulphadimidine 0.2% in drinking water). It must be remembered that apparently healthy rabbits frequently shed large numbers of oocysts, and so the involvement of other factors should always be considered.

Clostridial enterotoxaemia. Clostridial infections may be clinically indistinguishable from other causes of enteritis, but usually have a more acute onset and course. Affected animals may be found dead, or die with acute diarrhoea within 24 hours of first developing clinical signs of disease. At *post-mortem* examination, the caecum is often haemorrhagic and oedematous.

Salmonellosis. *Salmonella* spp. (frequently *S. typhimurium*) may cause enteritis with high mortality in young rabbits. Diagnosis is by isolation of *Salmonella* spp. from faecal samples. In view of the risk of infection to man, affected animals should be killed. In-contact adult animals should be screened as they may harbour the organisms and carrier animals should also be culled.

Tyzzer's disease. This condition is caused by *Bacillus piliformis* and results in either anorexia and acute diarrhoea which may be haemorrhagic and associated with a high mortality, or a more chronic illness with progressive loss of condition. *Post-mortem* examination may show focal necrosis of the liver and the diagnosis can be confirmed by histological examination to demonstrate *B. piliformis* in the tissues (see also 'Rats and Mice'). Treatment with oxytetracycline may reduce mortality but will not eliminate the condition.

Endoparasite infestation. Rarely, the presence of large numbers of *Passalurus ambiguus,* the most commonly seen rabbit nematode, may be associated with diarrhoea. Treatment with piperazine (200mg/kg bodyweight) will control the condition.

Pseudotuberculosis (Yersiniosis) (see also 'Guinea Pigs'). This disease is rare in domestic pets and is believed to be transmitted by food contaminated with faeces of birds or wild rodents containing the causative organism, *Yersinia pseudotuberculosis.* Clinical signs include loss of condition and the development of caseous nodules in the abdomen. Diagnosis is confirmed by the demonstration of the organism in smears from these nodules. The condition is transmissible to man, and animals suspected of having the disease should be killed.

Hepatic coccidiosis. This condition is caused by *Eimeria stiedae,* which parasitises the bile-ducts and can produce severe liver damage. Clinical signs are either absent or non-specific, poor growth and loss of condition occurring in severe cases. Examination of bile from the gall-bladder *post mortem* should show the presence of large numbers of oocysts. Treatment is with sulphonamides.

Respiratory diseases

Pasteurellosis

This syndrome is probably the most frequent single cause of illness in pet rabbits. The causative agent, *Pasteurella multocida,* is found in the respiratory tract of most conventionally reared rabbits. Clinical disease may be triggered by environmental stress, pregnancy and lactation, or other concurrent illness. Rhinitis and conjunctivitis leading to the development of a purulent discharge are the most frequently seen clinical signs. The animals' forelimbs should be inspected, as affected animals may completely clean the discharge from their noses and eyes when grooming. The disease may be chronic or result in sudden death due to rapid onset of severe bronchopneumonia. *Pasteurella* infection may also cause middle ear disease or genital infection with testicular abscessation or pyometra. In some instances pulmonary or pericardial abscesses may occur, or acute septicaemic episodes. Animals which appear to have only mild upper respiratory tract infection may rapidly develop severe pneumonia if stressed.

Treatment with broad-spectrum antimicrobial agents such as cephaloridine or trimethoprim/sulphonamide may help to control the clinical disease but are rarely effective in eliminating the infection. Conjunctival infection should be treated with chloramphenicol or tetracycline eye ointment; steroid preparations should be avoided. The most effective means of treatment is to sedate the rabbit with fentanyl/fluanisone and to flush the tear ducts and nasal chambers either with saline or antibiotic solutions (Petersen-Jones and Carrington, 1988). Severe nasal congestion can also be eased by the use of mucolytics (such as Bisolvon, Boehringer Ingelheim) at a dose rate of 0.3g of 1% powder by mouth once daily.

Although treatment may produce complete remission of clinical signs, subsequent stress may cause recurrence of the condition. Many rabbits appear to have undergone a pulmonary infection with *Pasteurella* when young, resulting in the production of a chronic bronchopneumonia and this increases the risks associated with anaesthesia. Improving general husbandry and avoiding stress, particularly that caused by high environmental temperatures, poor ventilation and overcrowding, will help to minimise the incidence of clinical disease.

Bordetella infections

Bordetella bronchiseptica may cause an acute bronchopneumonia in rabbits; treatment is with broad-spectrum antimicrobial agents as for pasteurellosis.

Neurological disorders

Middle and inner ear disease

This is most frequently caused by *Pasteurella multocida* and is best considered as part of the 'Pasteurellosis syndrome'. Treatment is generally ineffective, although prolonged administration of broad-spectrum antibiotics may aid remission in some cases.

Encephalitozoon (Nosema) cuniculi

This parasite, which affects the central nervous system and kidney, is of little clinical significance and very rarely causes clinical illness. Occasional generalised CNS disturbance or renal dysfunction has been reported and renal lesions — a pronounced interstitial nephritis — may be seen at *post-mortem* examination.

Toxoplasmosis

Toxoplasma gondii rarely causes clinical disease in domestic rabbits. Paralysis or convulsions following a period of depression and inappetence may be seen, followed by death a few days later. Diagnosis is made by histological examination *post mortem.*

Posterior paralysis

Damage to the lumbar spine may result from struggling during handling, or may occur following violent exertion. Radiographic examination of the spinal column may assist in determining the degree of injury. Fractures or displacement of vertebrae usually produce severe damage to the spinal cord, and recovery of function is unlikely. Less severe lesions occasionally improve following cage rest and corticosteroid administration.

Miscellaneous conditions

Myxomatosis

Myxomatosis is a viral disease enzootic in much of the wild rabbit population in the UK. Transmission from wild rabbits to domestic pets via the rabbit flea *(Spilopsyllus cuniculi)* may occur if wild rabbits enter gardens in which pet animals are housed. The incubation period of the disease is 2—8 days and this is followed by the development of a purulent conjunctivitis with swelling of the eyelids and peri-orbital tissue, often causing partial closure of the eye. Subcutaneous swelling then usually develops on the head, neck and anogenital region. Death occurs 11—18 days after the onset of clinical signs, although occasionally an animal may survive. Vaccination can protect against the disease — vaccine is available from Mansi Laboratories Ltd., Weybridge, Surrey.

Rabbit syphilis

This condition, caused by *Treponema cuniculi,* produces inflammation and ulceration of the genital region. In some rabbits secondary lesions may occur on the face and paws. The organism is transmitted at mating, and is thus primarily a problem of large breeding groups, and not of single pet animals. The disease is usually self-limiting and can be treated with ampicillin (see Table 3). It is not transmissible to humans.

Mastitis

Mastitis is most often seen when a female's litter is abruptly weaned, particularly if this is done at 3—4 weeks rather than at 7—8 weeks *post partum.* Poor husbandry increases the incidence of the condition. Treatment with broad-spectrum antibiotics for 7—10 days is usually successful.

Pregnancy toxaemia

This is a rare condition which results in collapse, dyspnoea and sudden death during the last few days of pregnancy. The cause of the disorder is uncertain, but subcutaneous dextrose/saline and corticosteroids may be of value if the doe is presented in the early stages of the condition.

Haematuria

Rabbit urine varies considerably in colour and may be clear, straw coloured, brown, reddish brown or bright red. The colouration is believed to be caused by porphyrins and bile pigments derived from plant material. The urine may also be extremely turbid. It is important to differentiate this common, normal colouration from haematuria or haemoglobinuria. Urine can be collected for analysis by placing the rabbit in a grid-bottomed cage or the rabbit can be heavily sedated and catheterised. Catheterisation is a relatively straightforward procedure in male rabbits, but extremely difficult in females. Blood in the urine may be caused by cystitis, uterine adenocarcinoma, uterine polyps or renal infarcts (Garibaldi *et al,* 1987). Radiography may show the presence of calculi, but large quantities of fine, sandy material are a frequent incidental finding in normal rabbits. Single or multiple large calculi are much more likely to be associated with cystitis and these should be removed surgically.

ANAESTHESIA

Rabbits are difficult animals in which to achieve safe and effective anaesthesia. They are easily stressed during induction, and this may contribute to cardiac or respiratory arrest (Flecknell, 1987). The frequent presence of pre-existing lung damage may cause respiratory failure during the period of anaesthesia. In addition, the stress of surgery and anaesthesia, particularly if irritant agents such as ether are used, can result in the exacerbation of respiratory infections with *Pasteurella* and the production of severe clinical illness post-operatively. Recovery from anaesthesia is often slow, particularly following the use of pentobarbitone and the prolonged inappetence that is a frequent post-operative complication can result in serious gastro-intestinal disturbances.

The incidence of these potentially serious problems can be minimised by careful selection of the anaesthetic regime, avoidance of stress pre-operatively and post-operatively and by maintaining high standards of intra- and post-operative care.

Sedation/light anaesthesia

Rabbits can be immobilised and sedated for minor procedures such as clipping of teeth and draining and cleaning of abscesses with fentanyl/fluanisone (Hypnorm, Janssen)(0.2—0.5ml), ketamine (Vetalar, Parke-Davis)(25mg/kg) or alphaxalone/alphadolone (Saffan, Coopers Pitman-Moore)(12mg/kg) all administered by the intramuscular route.

Surgical anaesthesia

Whichever agent is used, handling of the animal during induction of anaesthesia must always be gentle and exposure to sudden noises or bright lights should be avoided. Heat loss will be minimised by insulating the animal with aluminium foil or towels, or by the use of heating pads. Depth of anaesthesia may be assessed by pinching the ear — lack of a head shake in response to this stimulus indicates the onset of surgical anaesthesia.

Volatile anaesthetics

Methoxyflurane (Metofane, C-Vet) is the volatile anaesthetic agent of choice; it is non-irritant and can be used to maintain anaesthesia safely for long periods. Induction using a facemask can be hazardous, however, because of the stress involved and it is preferable to induce anaesthesia with an injectable agent. Alternatively, the rabbit can be sedated with a low dose of fentanyl/fluanisone or ketamine (see earlier), followed by induction of anaesthesia with methoxyflurane. A suitably sized Ayre's T-piece or unmodified Bain's circuit are the best anaesthetic circuits to use with rabbits, connection to the animal being by means of a close fitting mask or endotracheal tube.

Endotracheal intubation in rabbits requires practice — the narrow mouth obstructs the view of the larynx and laryngospasm and laryngeal haemorrhage are common complications of inexpert intubation. If intubation is to be attempted, the larynx should be sprayed with lignocaine (Xylocaine, Astra) and a 2.5—3.5mm tube passed under direct vision using a laryngoscope fitted with a straight paediatric blade. A size 1 Wisconsin blade (Penlon Ltd., Abingdon, Oxon.) is ideal, since its design prevents the cheeks from obscuring the view of the larynx. Alternatively, visualisation of the larynx can be improved if an assistant applies gentle traction to the cheeks with tissue forceps. Recently, commercial rabbit gags have become available and these are highly recommended for any procedures requiring visualisation of the oropharynx.

Halothane or isoflurane can be used successfully to maintain anaesthesia in rabbits, although the margin of safety is considerably less than that of methoxyflurane. Induction using a facemask is not recommended unless a sedative is administered to prevent excitement and distress.

Ether is an unsuitable anaesthetic agent for use in rabbits — its irritant nature can result in laryngospasm during induction and it frequently exacerbates pre-existing respiratory disease.

Injectable agents

Fentanyl/fluanisone. The anaesthetic combination of choice for rabbits is fentanyl/fluanisone (Hypnorm, Janssen) at a dose rate of 0.3ml/kg i/m, together with either diazepam (Valium, Roche) or midazolam (Hypnovel, Roche) at a dose rate of 1mg/kg i/m or i/v. This combination provides good surgical anaesthesia with excellent muscle relaxation lasting about 20—40 minutes. Longer periods of anaesthesia can be achieved by the administration of additional doses of fentanyl/fluanisone (about 0.1ml/kg i/m every 30—40 minutes). Following the completion of surgery, anaesthesia can be reversed using naloxone (Narcan, Du Pont) at a dose rate of 0.1mg/kg i/v — although this will also reverse any analgesic effects of the fentanyl. It is preferable to use a mixed agonist-antagonist opioid such as buprenorphine (Temgesic, Reckitt and Colman) (0.05mg/kg i/v or i/m) or nalbuphine (Nubain, Du Pont) (1—2mg/kg i/v or i/m), as these compounds will reverse the respiratory depression caused by fentanyl/fluanisone and also provide post-operative analgesia (Flecknell *et al*, 1989).

Alternative agents include **xylazine** (Rompun, Bayer) (5mg/kg i/m) or **medetomidine** (Domitor, SmithKline Beecham) (0.5mg/kg i/m), in combination with ketamine (35mg/kg i/m) (Nevalainen *et al*, 1989). The two compounds can be premixed and given as a single injection. This combination provides about 30 minutes of surgical anaesthesia. Recovery time can be reduced by reversal of the medetomidine or xylazine with atipamezole (1mg/kg i/m) (Antisedan, SmithKline Beecham) A 1.25% solution of **thiopentone** (Intraval, RMB) at a dose rate of 30mg/kg i/v or a 1% solution of **methohexitone** (Brietal, Elanco) at a dose rate of 10—15mg/kg i/v will produce 5—10 minutes anaesthesia and are useful for induction followed by maintenance using methoxyflurane or halothane.

Alphaxalone/alphadolone (Saffan, Coopers Pitman-Moore) at a dose rate of 6—9mg/kg i/v produces light surgical anaesthesia, but must be administered with great care as sudden apnoea and cardiac arrest can occur even with normal induction doses. This agent is perhaps best used at low doses to sedate the animal to enable smooth induction via a facemask with volatile anaesthetics.

Propofol (Rapinovet, Coopers Pitman-Moore) (10mg/kg i/v) produces light anaesthesia, but increasing the dose rate usually results in respiratory arrest before the onset of surgical anaesthesia.

Pentobarbitone should be diluted to provide a 30mg/ml solution and up to 30—45mg/kg administered slowly, to effect, by the intravenous route. Respiratory arrest and death frequently occur with this regime and the drug is best avoided in rabbits.

Whichever agent is used, post-operative recovery is aided by the administration of warmed dextrose/saline s/c and by provision of a warm recovery area of 20°—25°C. Respiration can be stimulated by the use of doxapram (Dopram V, Willows Francis) at a dose rate of 5—10mg/kg i/v.

SURGICAL PROCEDURES

Castration of male rabbits is carried out both to prevent breeding and to reduce aggression. The surgical procedure is complicated by the presence of an open inguinal ring. It is preferable to carry out a closed castration via a scrotal incision, placing transfixation ligatures in the tunica vaginalis to close the inguinal canal and ligate the spermatic vessels. Increasing the depth of anaesthesia will usually allow the testes to be manipulated into the scrotum.

Occasionally, problems are encountered due to retraction of the testes into the inguinal canal. Raising the forequarters or manipulating the inguinal canal will usually position the testes in the scrotum. If this does not prove possible, it is often indicative of poor anaesthesia, with insufficient muscle relaxation.

Ovariohysterectomy is a relatively simple procedure in rabbits. A 5—6 cm midline incision is made just cranial to the pelvic brim. If the viscera are displaced cranially, the uterine horns can be located on either side of the bladder. It is advisable to ligate both the ovarian and uterine vessels prior to removal of the uterus. Placing the rabbit on a sloping table with the head in the lower position may help to expose the uterus; however, care must be taken that the forward displacement of abdominal viscera does not interfere with respiratory movements.

REFERENCES AND FURTHER READING

BANERJEE, A. K., ANGULO, A. F., DHASMANA, K. M. and KONG-A-SAN, J. (1987). Acute diarrhoeal disease in rabbits: bacteriological diagnosis and efficacy of oral rehydration in combination with loperamide hydrochloride. *Laboratory Animals* **21**, 314.

BERGHOFF, P. C. (1990). *Les Petits Animaux Familiers et leurs Maladies.* Maloine, Paris.

CANADIAN COUNCIL ON ANIMAL CARE (1980). *Guide to the Care and Use of Experimental Animals.* Canadian Council on Animal Care, Ottawa.

COLES, E. H. (1980). *Veterinary Clinical Pathology.* Saunders, Eastbourne.

FLECKNELL, P. A. (1987). *Laboratory Animal Anaesthesia.* Academic Press, London.

FLECKNELL, P. A., LILES, J. H. and WILLIAMSON, H. A. (1990). The use of lignocaine-prilocaine local anaesthetic cream for pain-free venepuncture in laboratory animals. *Laboratory Animals* **24**, 142.

FLECKNELL, P. A., LILES, J. H. and WOOTTON, R. (1989). Reversal of fentanyl/fluanisone neuroleptanalgesia in the rabbit using mixed agonist/antagonist opioids. *Laboratory Animals* **23**, 147.

GABRISCH, K. and ZWART, P. (1985). Eds. *Krankheiten der Heimtiere.* Schlütersche, Hanover.

GARIBALDI, B. A., FOX, J. G., OTTO, G., MURPHY, J. C. and PECQUET-GOAD, M. E. (1987). Hematuria in rabbits. *Laboratory Animal Science* **37**, 769.

HAFEZ, E. S. E. (1970). *Reproduction and Breeding Techniques for Laboratory Animals.* Lea and Febiger, Philadelphia.

HARKNESS, J. E. (1987). Rabbit husbandry and medicine. *Veterinary Clinics of North America: Small Animal Practice* **17**, 1019.

HARKNESS, J. E. and WAGNER, J. E. (1989). *The Biology and Medicine of Rabbits and Rodents.* 3rd Edn. Lea and Febiger, Philadelphia.

HIME, J. M. and O'DONOGHUE, P. N. (1979). Eds. *Handbook of Diseases of Laboratory Animals.* Heinemann Veterinary Books, London.

INGLIS, J. K. (1980). *Introduction to Laboratory Animal Science and Technology.* Pergamon Press, Oxford.

KRAUS, A. L., WEISBROTH, S. H., FLATT, R. E. and BREWER, N. (1984). Biology and diseases of rabbits. In: *Laboratory Animal Medicine.* (Eds. J. G. Fox, B. J. Cohen and F.M. Loew) Academic Press, New York.

LOEB, W. F. and QUINBY, F. W. (1989). *The Clinical Chemistry of Laboratory Animals.* Pergamon Press, New York.

NEVALAINEN, T., PYHALA, L., HANNA-MAIJA, V. and VIRTANEN, R. (1989). Evaluation of anaesthetic potency of medetomidine-ketamine combinations in rats, guinea pigs and rabbits. *(Acta Veterinaria scandinavica Supplement* **85**, 139.

NIGHTINGALE, G. (1979). *Rabbit Keeping.* Bartholomew and Son, Edinburgh.

PETERSEN-JONES, S. M. and CARRINGTON, S. D. (1988). *Pasteurella* dacryocystitis in rabbits. *Veterinary Record* **21**, 514.

SANDERSON, J. H. and PHILLIPS, C. E. (1982). *An Atlas of Laboratory Animal Haematology.* Oxford University Press, Oxford.

SANDFORD, J. C. (1986). *The Domestic Rabbit.* 4th Edn. Collins, London.

WHITNEY, J. C. (1976). A review of non-specific enteritis in the rabbit. *Laboratory Animals* **10** 209.

WHITNEY, J. C. (1979). Rabbits. In: *Handbook of Diseases of Laboratory Animals.* (Eds. J. M. Hime and P. N. O'Donoghue) Heinemann Veterinary Books, London.

CHAPTER NINE

RATS AND MICE

Paul A Flecknell MA VetMB PhD DLAS MRCVS

Rats and mice are kept both as children's pets and for show purposes. Rats in particular make excellent pets, soon becoming accustomed to handling and being easy to train.

Most mice kept in the UK are *Mus musculus,* although other species are occasionally seen. Deer mice *(Peromyscus leucopus)* have been introduced as pets; they are similar in size to *M. musculus* but have a dark brown or sandy coat, a white abdomen and white feet.

Dormice belong to a separate Family, the Gliridae, rats and mice being members of the Muridae. Two species are occasionally seen as pets; the common or hazel dormouse *(Muscardinus ovellanarius),* which is a small rounded animal with a long, fur-covered tail, and the fat or edible dormouse *(Glis glis),* a much larger animal (30-35cm long including the tail) which is rather squirrel-like. Dormice will hibernate in winter in the UK unless maintained at an even, warm temperature.

Other wild species are occasionally seen as pets, including the harvest mouse *(Micromys minutus),* the wood or long-tailed field mouse *(Apodemus sylvaticus)* and the yellow-necked mouse *(Apodemus flavicollis).*

Species of rat other than *Rattus norvegicus* do not usually make suitable pets, although the kangaroo rat *(Dipodomys desertii)* is occasionally seen.

Although mice which are sold as children's pets are usually white, a large number of other colour varieties are available. These fall into four main groups. 'Selfs' have a single solid body colour and include blacks, whites, blues, chocolates, fawns, doves, creams, champagnes and silvers. 'Tans' have one colour on the upper body and a tan underside, the two colours showing a distinct demarcation. All of the self colours can be seen with tan, eg. black and tan, cream and tan, etc. Various colour patterns make up the 'marked' animals; these are basically white mice with different colour patches. Recognised varieties of marked animals include 'broken', 'even', 'variegated', 'Dutch', 'Himalayan' and 'tri-coloured'. A final group is classed as 'Any Other Variety' (AOV) and includes all the other possible colour and coat types, such as agoutis, chinchillas, long haired, and a wide range of others.

Rats are also available in many colour varieties; those more commonly seen include a range of 'self' (solid) colours and a group of 'hooded' animals. These latter varieties include the Irish black, distinguished by an equilateral triangle of white fur on its chest and by its white feet, and the Japanese hooded rats which have a solid coloured head and shoulders and a stripe along the back to the tail, the rest of the body being white. Capped rats lack the stripe of the Japanese hooded.

Showing of rats and mice is organised by the National Mouse Club and the National Rat Club (see 'Appendix — Useful Addresses').

HOUSING

Rats and mice can be successfully housed in either commercially produced or home-made cages. It should be remembered, however, that they are likely to chew through wooden or plastic containers, so that metal or glass cages are to be preferred. A separate sleeping compartment is usually provided in commercially made cages, although this is not necessary if plenty of suitable bedding is available.

Caging often tends to be too small. Rats and mice make entertaining pets if given room for 'additions' to their environment such as exercise wheels, ladders, hollow tubes and climbing frames etc., which encourage exercise and help prevent boredom. A cage size of 45 x 30 x 25cm high could house two or three mice or one rat, but since rats, like mice, are sociable animals, it is best to obtain a larger cage and keep two or three animals together. Increasing the floor area by about 50% would enable twice the number of animals to be housed. This should not be continued *pro rata*, however; several smaller cages are to be preferred to one very large one.

Bedding should be soft wood shavings, tissue paper or sawdust and cages should be cleaned frequently (two to three times a week) to minimise odours (particularly with mice) and to help to minimise the risk of disease. Rats and mice should be housed indoors, ideally at temperatures of 15°–27°C. Temperatures above 30°C may cause heatstroke, particularly in overcrowded conditions. If cage lids are made of metal mesh, this must be fine enough to prevent escape of young animals, but strong enough to resist being chewed through by adults (one wire per cm for mice, one per 1.5cm for rats, should be satisfactory).

FEEDING

Rats and mice should be fed a commercially produced complete ration as their basic diet and this may be occasionally supplemented with small amounts of varied food such as biscuit, apples, tomatoes and dog biscuits. Rats are particularly fond of chocolate and cakes and small quantities of these items are useful in encouraging the animal to respond to its owner. Rats and mice are very tolerant of changes in their diet, but this may lead to feeding of an imbalanced diet, or to overfeeding which can result in obesity. Water must be made available *ad libitum* either in small bowls or in commercially produced dispensers.

HANDLING

Mice

Whilst most pet mice are amenable to handling by their owner, mice in unfamiliar surroundings will bite if given the opportunity and so should be handled with care. The owner should be encouraged to bring the animal to the surgery in a small container, or, if it is in its normal cage, asked to transfer it to a small box. Once the animal is clearly visible, it can be picked up by its tail and transferred on to a rough surface. It will instinctively pull away, allowing the skin of the 'scruff' to be grasped with the other hand (see Figure 1). It can then be lifted clear and the grip on the tail transferred to the third and fourth fingers (see Figure 2).

Rats

Rats rarely bite, unless frightened or in pain, and should be picked up by placing a hand around the shoulders (see Figure 3). The thumb should be positioned under the mandible so that pressure can be used to prevent biting if a painful clinical procedure is to be carried out (see Figure 4). It is important to hold the animal firmly but to avoid grasping it so tightly that it is prevented from breathing. If this occurs the rat will panic and may bite the handler. If the animal appears aggressive it can be handled in the same manner as a mouse, although care should be taken when lifting a rat by the base of its tail as it may grasp its cage tightly. If this occurs its claws should be gently dislodged to avoid damaging them. The animal having been placed on a rough surface, it should be grasped around the shoulders and lifted to be examined. Picking up a rat by the scruff will often cause it considerable distress and so should be avoided.

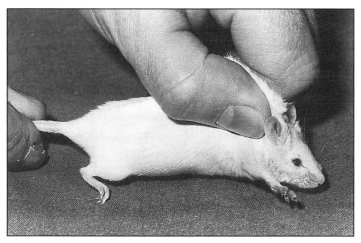

Figure 1
Restraint of the mouse. The mouse is lifted from its cage by the base of the tail and allowed to grip a rough surface. The scruff can then be grasped and the mouse lifted clear.

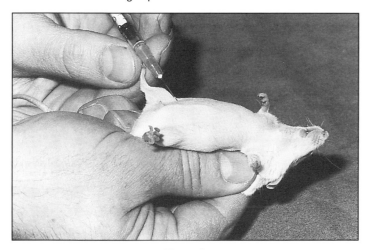

Figure 2
Restraint of the mouse. The grip on the scruff is maintained and an assistant can extend one hind leg and carry out an intraperitoneal injection.

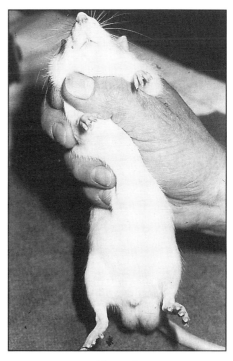

Figure 4
The thumb is positioned below the mandible to prevent the animal from biting.

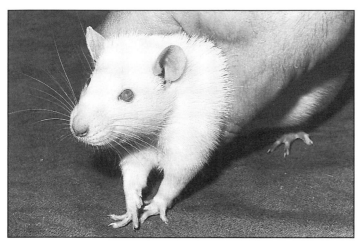

Figure 3. Restraint of the rat.
The rat can be picked up around its shoulders.

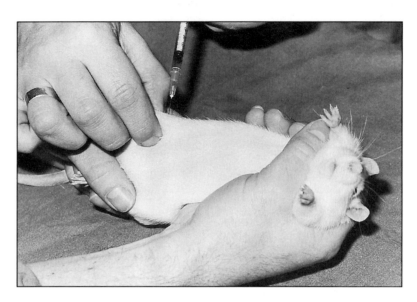

Figure 5
The rat is restrained so that an assistant can inject
into the quadriceps muscles.

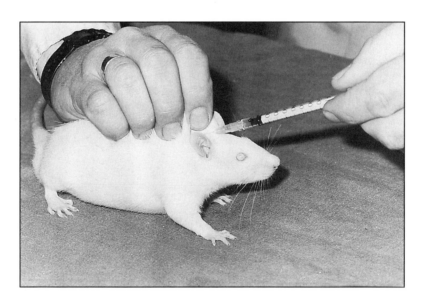

Figure 6
Subcutaneous injections can easily be made into the scruff.

Injection techniques

Intramuscular injections are best made into the quadriceps using a 25—23 gauge needle (see Figure 5). Because of the small muscle mass no greater volume than 0.05ml (mouse) or 0.2ml (rat) should be injected at any one site.

Subcutaneous injections can easily be made under the skin overlying the neck or thorax using a 25—23 gauge needle (see Figure 6). About 2—3ml of material can be administered to mice, 5ml to rats.

Intraperitoneal injections are best carried out with the animal restrained by an assistant as shown (see Figure 2, mouse; Figure 5, rat). One hind limb should be extended and the needle (23G or narrower) introduced along the line of the leg into the centre of that posterior quadrant of the abdomen, so avoiding the bladder and liver. Approximately 1—2ml of fluid may be administered to mice, 5ml to rats. If no assistance is available, use can be made of simple, disposable polythene rat restrainers (see Figure 7).

Intravenous injection is a difficult technique to carry out in rats and mice, but with practice the lateral tail vein can be entered using a 25 gauge needle. Venepuncture is much easier if the tail has been warmed. This can be done by placing the animal in a box under a 60 watt lightbulb for 10—15 minutes, in an incubator maintained at 35°C, or in a bowl or beaker which is then immersed in warm water (30°—35°C), for about 15 minutes. The dilated vessels will now be clearly visible in mice and young rats. In old rats the thickened skin of the tail makes venepuncture even more difficult, but careful cleaning of the skin will make the underlying vessels more clearly visible. Disposable insulin syringes are a convenient size and have a suitable needle (25G) both for venepuncture and injection of drugs by other routes in rats and mice.

Oral administration of drugs can be via a small (20 gauge) catheter, eg. Medicut, Argyle, or, if the material is palatable, it may be lapped from the end of a syringe. Alternatively, it can be injected into food (small pieces of doughnut seem particularly useful for this purpose).

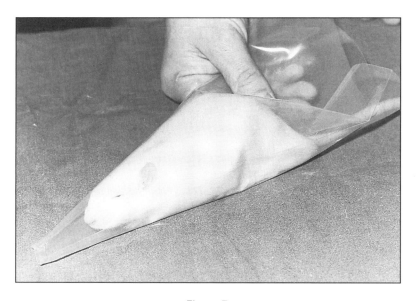

Figure 7
If assistance is not available, rats can be held in disposable
polythene restrainers to carry out i/p, s/c or i/v injections.

SEXING

Mice

The appearance of the external genitalia of adult mice usually enables the sexes to be distinguished (see Figure 8). Sexing newborn or juvenile animals requires some experience — the anogenital distance in males is approximately twice that in females and, if animals of both sexes are available, comparison may enable the distinction to be made.

Rats

Rats are considerably easier to sex than mice since the testes are visible even in juvenile animals. If problems are experienced the animal should be held vertically, which will cause the testes to pass from the inguinal canal into the scrotum. Neonatal rats are difficult to sex. As with mice, the anogenital distance is greater (about double) in males than in females, although careful comparison is needed to distinguish the sexes.

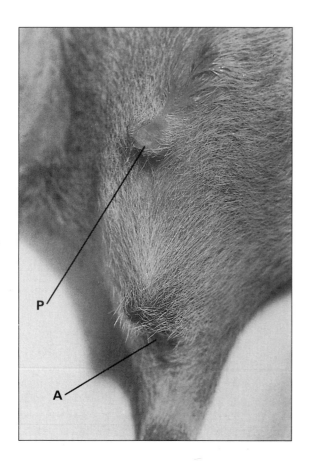
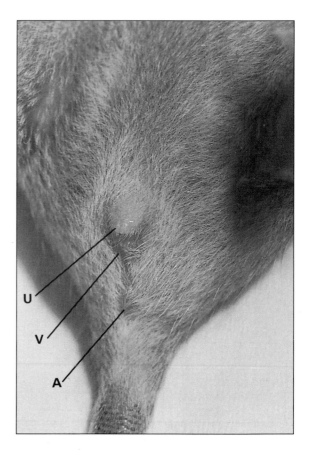

MALE   **FEMALE**

Figure 8
External genitalia of adult mice. The anogenital difference in males is approximately twice that in females.
A = anus, P = tip of penis, U = urethral opening, V = vulva.

REPRODUCTION

Normal reproductive parameters are summarised in Table 1. Both rats and mice are polyoestrous, with no specific breeding season. The oestrous cycle lasts 4—5 days in both species and the different stages of the cycle can be determined by microscopic examination of vaginal smears (Inglis, 1980). Following mating, a plug of ejaculate forms in the vagina (the 'vaginal plug'). In the rat the plug soon shrinks and falls out of the vagina after 12—24 hours, but it may persist for up to two days in mice.

Table 1
Reproductive parameters in the rat and mouse.

	Rat	Mouse
Sexual maturity	8—10 weeks	6—7 weeks
Oestrous cycle	4—5 days	4—5 days
Duration of oestrus	14 hours	14 hours
Gestation period	20—22 days	19—21 days
Litter size	6—16 (average 10)	8—12 (average 10)
Weaning age	3—4 weeks	3—4 weeks

Pregnancy can be diagnosed (with practice) by gentle abdominal palpation in the last third of gestation. Mammary development is usually pronounced by day 15—16 in rats and mice. Nest-building activity suddenly increases a few days *pre partum*, and large nests of bedding material are prepared. Following birth, the mother should be left undisturbed for 2—3 days, since excessive handling may cause the female to eat her young. This is a particular danger with rats. Rat and mouse pups are relatively immature at birth and are blind and hairless. They grow rapidly, however, and can be weaned at around three weeks *post partum.*

With most pet rats and mice, a 'population explosion' can be a major problem. To avoid excessive production of young, ideally only single sex groups should be kept, preferably females. Since both rats and mice are social animals, they should be maintained at least in groups of two or more. If a breeding pair is kept, it is important to separate the male and female before the young are born, otherwise the parents are likely to mate within 12 hours of parturition (the *'post-partum* oestrous'), leading to overproduction of young.

DISEASES/CLINICAL CONDITIONS

Pet rats and mice may develop a range of clinical conditions similar to those seen in more familiar species such as the dog and cat. For example, pyometra, cardiac failure, renal disease, hepatic disorders and arthritis may all occur in pet rodents. Extrapolation of techniques from the more familiar species will often enable diagnosis and treatment of such conditions. Diagnostic tests are less likely to be undertaken in small rodents than in dogs and cats and hence, although such investigations are often extremely useful, treatment will usually be symptomatic and based only on the result of clinical examination. Signs of ill health are frequently reflected in the external appearance of rats and mice — the coat becomes ruffled and the animal often remains immobile, even when handled. A reddish-brown encrustation is often seen around the nose and eyes in rats. This material is secreted from the Harderian glands and should not be confused with dried blood. It is a non-specific response to stress and disease and is not necessarily indicative of respiratory disease. Soiling of the perineum is usually obvious when diarrhoea is present and ocular and nasal discharges may be seen in cases of respiratory infection. Other clinical signs may indicate involvement of particular organs or systems.

In all instances, it is of considerable importance to ensure that the animals are housed and cared for adequately, since poor husbandry is the most frequent cause of ill health. Normal physiological variables which may assist in clinical and laboratory examinations are listed in Table 2 (see also Mitruka and Rawnsley, 1977; Sanderson and Phillips, 1982; Loeb and Quinby, 1989). Descriptions of the more commonly seen diseases are given below, together with details of any specific treatments.

Table 2
Physiological data in the rat and mouse.

	Rat	Mouse
Average life span	3—4 years	2—3 years
Adult bodyweight	400—800g	20—40g
Respiratory rate	70—150 per minute	100—250 per minute
Tidal volume	1.5—1.8ml	0.15ml
Heart rate	260—450 per minute	500—600 per minute
Rectal temperature	38.0°C	37.5°C
Blood volume	50ml/kg	80ml/kg
Haematocrit (PCV)	0.46l/l	0.40l/l
Red blood cell count	8.5×10^{12}/l	9.3×10^{12}/l
Haemoglobin	14.2g/dl	11.1g/dl
White blood cell count	9.8×10^9/l	13.6×10^9/l
Neutrophils	25%	17%
Lymphocytes	74%	72%
Average daily water intake	10ml/100g	15ml/100g

Skin and associated structures

Skin wounds/abscesses

Male mice should not normally be housed together or they may fight. Animals from the same litter, or animals reared together since weaning, may be more compatible, but fighting is still likely to occur. The lesions produced may either be small puncture wounds that may develop into an abscess, or, more frequently, areas of hair loss and ulceration of the skin which may become very extensive. These ulcerated areas may also result from self-inflicted injury, possibly arising due to stress. Less severe lesions can be produced by mice gnawing each other's fur, and particularly their whiskers ('barbering'), producing small circumscribed bald spots, usually bilaterally symmetrical, that should not be confused with ringworm. Rats fight less frequently than mice and also rarely produce extensive skin lesions due to self trauma. Ectoparasite infestation can produce crusty, pruritic lesions, particularly on the head and neck. Mites can usually be seen if animals are examined under a low power (x20) microscope or hand lens. If no parasites are visible, skin scrapings from affected areas should be examined for evidence of burrowing mites (Hsu, 1979).

Ringworm

Ringworm is occasionally seen in both mice and rats. *Microsporum* spp. are usually involved and hence fluoresce when examined using a Wood's lamp. In addition, skin and hair may be sampled for culture or microscopic examination. Skin lesions caused by dermatophytes are usually scaly areas of hair loss, but occasionally the patches may be reddened and pruritic.

If a specific cause of skin disease can be established, appropriate treatment may be instigated. Ectoparasite infestations should be controlled by use of bromocyclen dusting powder (Alugan, Hoechst) or by injection with ivermectin (Ivomec, MSD) (200μg/kg s/c). Ringworm should be treated with oral griseofulvin (Grisovin, Coopers Pitman-Moore) (25mg/kg for 28—42 days).

Abscesses should be opened and cleaned under light anaesthesia; the use of a multicleansing agent (Dermisol, SmithKline Beecham), or topical antibiotic-containing powder or ointment may be sufficient to produce healing. Alternatively, an antibacterial agent may be administered for 5—7 days (see Table 3). Advice should be given on general husbandry and on housing of animals that are fighting.

There will remain a group of dermatoses in which no clear aetiology can be determined. Treatment with topical corticosteroids and antibiotics, or with systemic antibiotics if infection appears severe, may be helpful. As a last resort, systemic corticosteroids can be administered to reduce pruritus, eg. betamethasone 0.1mg/kg bodyweight subcutaneously. Unfortunately, these may precipitate disease by activating latent organisms and so must be used with caution. It is particularly important that animals with non-specific dermatoses are kept under ideal conditions, since environmental stress and dietary imbalance may predispose to the development of such lesions.

Table 3
Dose rates of antibacterial agents in the rat and mouse.

Antibacterial agent	Dose/comments
Sulfamerazine	0.02% in drinking water
Sulphadimidine	0.2% in drinking water (Sulphamethazine Solution 33 ⅓ %, ICI)
Tetracycline: oral preparations injection 50 mg/ml	5mg/ml orally in drinking water (Panmycin, Upjohn, is a convenient aqueous preparation) 100 mg/kg s/c
Oxytetracycline long acting injection (Terramycin LA, Pfizer)	60mg/kg s/c or i/m every 3 days.
Cephalexin	60mg/kg orally 30mg/kg s/c (mouse) 15mg/kg s/c (rat)
Cephaloridine	30mg/kg i/m daily
Chloramphenicol suspension oral preparations	50mg/kg i/m bid (mouse) 10mg/kg i/m bid (rat) 200mg/kg tid (mouse) 20—50mg/kg bid (rat)
Ampicillin: injection, 15% w/v oral preparations	50—150mg/kg s/c 200mg/kg orally (Penbritin Soluble Powder, SmithKline Beecham)
Amoxycillin	150mg/kg i/m (rat) 100 mg/kg s/c (mouse)
Neomycin oral preparations	50mg/kg s/c (rat) 2.5g/l in drinking water (mouse) 2.0g/l in drinking water (rat)
Clavulanate-potentiated amoxycillin (Synulox, SmithKline Beecham)	2ml/kg orally
Potentiated sulphonamides (eg. trimethoprim/sulphadiazine, Tribrissen 24%, Coopers Pitman-Moore)	0.5ml/kg s/c
Tylosin	10mg/kg s/c
NOT RECOMMENDED Streptomycin Procaine penicillin	Toxic reaction reported. Procaine toxic to rats and mice.

Mammary glands

Mastitis

Mastitis is infrequent in both rats and mice and must be differentiated from mammary tumours which are not uncommon in these species. Treatment with systemic antibiotics is usually successful in resolving mastitis. Any ulcerative areas should be treated with appropriate topical preparations.

Mammary tumours

Mammary tumours must be removed surgically. In mice they are usually malignant and the prognosis is poor. In the rat they are frequently benign, but can become very large, and removal may be difficult. If the lesions are successfully removed, however, a good prognosis may be given.

Gastro-intestinal diseases

Malocclusions

Overgrowth of the incisor teeth results in inappetence and weight loss, although the characteristic drooling of saliva seen in other species (rabbit and guinea pig) is rarely noted in rats and mice. The teeth can be clipped to their normal length with nail cutters, although recurrence of the condition is likely.

Diarrhoea

Diarrhoea is a common clinical sign of ill health in rats and mice, and can be caused by a wide range of organisms.

Protozoa. Faeces should be examined for the presence of endoparasites. *Entamoeba muris, Trichomonas muris* and *Giardia muris* are frequently seen in mice and rats, but are generally considered non-pathogenic. Very large numbers of these parasites may cause mild enteritis, however, and this may be treated with metronidazole or dimetridazole (2.5mg/ml of drinking water). The palatability of this preparation is improved by adding 1% sucrose (Roach *et al,* 1988).

Coccidial infection with *Eimeria* spp. is also a common coincidental finding in rats and mice. Occasionally, coccidia can cause disease in animals kept in poor conditions, or be a secondary cause of diarrhoea. Treatment with sulphonamides in the drinking water for 7—10 days (see Table 3) will control infection.

Cestodes and nematodes. Heavy infestations of cestodes *(Hymenolepis* sp.) and nematodes *(Syphacia obvelata* and *Aspiculuris* sp.) can result in loss of condition and occasionally in diarrhoea. *Syphacia* infestation may also cause rectal prolapse in mice. Examination for roundworms is best carried out by pressing a small piece of adhesive tape, eg. 'Sellotape', on to the perianal region, then removing it and sticking it on a slide for microscopic examination. Any eggs will be easily visible. Roundworms can be treated with piperazine (3mg/ml of drinking water or 200mg/kg daily) for seven days, repeated seven days later for a further week. Cestodes may be controlled by niclosamide (100mg/kg orally).

Bacteria. Faeces should be cultured to ensure that diarrhoea is not due to *Salmonella* spp: if several mice are owned, then in addition to diarrhoea, generalised loss of condition and occasionally sudden death of an animal may be seen. Other bacteria are associated with diarrhoea but, as with other species, these are often normal gut organisms. If bacterial involvement is thought likely then treatment with neomycin (see Table 3) for 5—7 days may be effective.

Tyzzer's disease (caused by *Bacillus piliformis)* may produce diarrhoea together with generalised illness and death (see also 'Gerbils' and 'Hamsters'). Poor husbandry or other stress may trigger latent disease. If several mice or rats are involved, treatment with tetracycline (see Table 3) may help to control the disease. Affected individuals almost invariably die.

If the cause of the diarrhoea cannot be determined, or the expense of laboratory tests is not thought to be warranted, general symptomatic treatment may be given with a kaolin-based preparation, eg. Keosul Suspension, Syntex, (0.5—1.0ml daily/rat, 0.1ml daily/mouse, in two divided doses).

Respiratory system

Respiratory disease is one of the commonest problems of rats and mice. Many animals are found to have extensive pneumonic lesions at autopsy, but often the affected animal will have been completely asymptomatic. Clinical respiratory disease is typified by dyspnoea, weight loss, rhinitis, abnormal respiratory sounds and, as the disease progresses, the adoption of a 'hunched-up' posture. Many different agents may be involved in the aetiology of the condition including *Mycoplasma pulmonis,* Sendai virus, Pneumonia virus of mice, and several species of bacteria — for example, *Pasteurella pneumotropica* and *Bordetella bronchiseptica.* Environmental stress, caused by poor husbandry, overcrowding and dirty caging, may exacerbate subclinical infections. Treatment of affected individuals is rarely successful. High doses of tetracyclines (see Table 3) have been reported to be successful in treating *Mycoplasma* infections and may be helpful in control. Long-acting oxytetracycline has been reported to produce effective plasma concentrations for 72 hours in rats (Curl *et al,* 1988). Tylosin, cephalosporins and potentiated sulphonamides may all occasionally be effective in treating clinical cases (see Table 3).

Neurological disorders

Several viral diseases can cause paralysis in mice, although most of these occur very rarely. Lymphocytic choriomeningitis (LCM) is a zoonotic infection which is usually asymptomatic in mice, although death, with or without paralysis, can occur (Lehmann-Grube, 1982). Mouse (Theiler's) encephalomyelitis virus can produce progressive paralysis of the hindquarters and general signs of ill health, but clinical disease is rare (Downs, 1982). Any animals showing signs of central nervous disease should be killed and, if possible, examined for LCM in view of the public health hazard.

Middle (Inner) ear disease

Typical clinical signs of head tilt, circling and loss of balance are observed in rats with middle ear disease. The condition is less frequently seen in mice and in both species is usually caused by bacterial or mycoplasmal infection. Treatment with antibiotics (tetracycline 100mg/kg s/c for 7 days) is successful in some cases, although more prolonged treatment may be needed to produce permanent remission of clinical signs.

ANAESTHESIA

Because of the small size of these animals, administration of injectable anaesthetics by the intravenous route is difficult, and use must be made of the i/p, i/m or s/c routes. When using these routes it is not possible to administer drugs 'to effect' because of the slow onset of action in comparison with intravenous injection. There is a very wide range of variation in response to anaesthetics between different strains of laboratory rodents and it seems likely that this variation will also occur amongst the pet rodent population. For this reason drugs that have a wide margin of safety are to be preferred and, if possible, an anaesthetic which can be reversed using a specific antagonist should be selected. It is often preferable to use a volatile anaesthetic since this allows better control of the depth of anaesthesia, provided that a calibrated vaporiser is used. If injectable anaesthetics are administered, oxygen should be provided via a face-mask throughout the anaesthetic period.

The small size of rats and mice makes them extremely susceptible to hypothermia when anaesthetised, and every effort must be made to minimise heat loss (see 'Guinea Pigs' for suggested methods).

Volatile anaesthetics

Whichever volatile anaesthetic agent is to be used, induction should be carried out in a suitable anaesthetic chamber (Cooper, 1984; Flecknell, 1987). Anaesthetic gases should be piped from an anaesthetic machine, using a calibrated vaporiser to ensure that a safe concentration for induction of anaesthesia is delivered. The surplus gas or vapour should be ducted out of the chamber using a suitable gas scavenging system. Placing cotton-wool impregnated with liquid anaesthetic into a jam-jar or similar container should be used only as a last resort. Using this anachronistic technique will not allow an accurate vapour concentration to be delivered and will not usually enable the waste anaesthetic gases to be removed safely.

Methoxyflurane (Metofane, C-Vet) is the volatile anaesthetic agent of choice in rats and mice, as it is in other small rodents. After induction in an anaesthetic chamber with 3.5% methoxyflurane, the animal can be removed and short procedures (less than a few minutes) undertaken immediately. Otherwise, the animal should be maintained on a facemask and T-piece with 0.5—1% methoxyflurane and 1:1 nitrous oxide and oxygen.

Halothane is also suitable for induction and maintenance of anaesthesia, but must only be administered using a calibrated vaporiser. Care must be taken to avoid overdosage but, provided excessively high vapour concentrations (>4%) are avoided, it is a safe and effective anaesthetic. Concentrations of 1.5—2% are usually adequate for maintaining anaesthesia in small rodents.

Isoflurane can be used to anaesthetise rats and mice provided that a calibrated vaporiser is used. For induction of anaesthesia, a concentration of 3.5—4.0% should be used and this can be reduced to 2.0—2.5% for maintenance.

Ether is much less suitable for anaesthesia of rats and mice. It is irritant to the respiratory tract and the consequent increase in bronchial secretions can impair respiration. Such irritation exacerbates any pre-existing (subclinical) respiratory diseases which may lead to serious illness post-operatively.

Injectable anaesthetics

Fentanyl/fluanisone with diazepam or midazolam The anaesthetic combination of choice is fentanyl/fluanisone (Hypnorm, Janssen) together with diazepam (Valium, Roche) (for a mouse, 0.1ml/30g of a 1:10 dilution of fentanyl/fluanisone i/p plus diazepam 5mg/kg by the same route; for a rat 0.3ml/kg i/m of fentanyl/fluanisone and 2.5mg/kg diazepam i/p). Fentanyl/fluanisone and midazolam (Hypnovel, Roche) can be combined if prediluted with water. A mixture of one part fentanyl/fluanisone plus one part water and one part midazolam plus one part water is stable for at least two months and can be given as a single intraperitoneal injection to produce good surgical anaesthesia in rats and mice (0.2—0.3ml/30g mouse; 1.0ml/300g rat).

Etorphine/methotrimeprazine (Immobilon Small Animal, C-Vet) may also be used to produce surgical anaesthesia in rats (0.1 of a 1:1 dilution of etorphine/methotrimeprazine/100g bodyweight intramuscularly) although a considerably greater degree of respiratory depression is produced than with the combinations using fentanyl/fluanisone. In both cases respiratory depression can be reversed at the end of surgery using either naloxone (Narcan Neonatal, Du Pont) at a dose rate of 0.1mg/kg, buprenorphine (Temgesic, Reckitt and Colman) (0.05mg/kg i/m or i/p) or diprenorphine (Revivon, C-Vet) (equal volume to that of the etorphine/methotrimeprazine).

Ketamine (Vetalar, Parke-Davis), **with xylazine** (Rompun, Bayer) **or medetomidine** (Domitor, SmithKline Beecham) can be used to provide surgical anaesthesia in rats and mice. The degree of analgesia may be insufficient for major surgery in some animals, but these combinations have the advantage that the xylazine or medetomidine can be reversed using atipamezole (Antesedan, SmithKline Beecham) (1mg/kg s/c or i/p). Since ketamine alone has very little anaesthetic effect in rats and mice, animals rapidly recover consciousness and regain their righting reflex after administration of the antagonist drug (Nevalainen et al, 1989). Ketamine should be administered to mice at a dose of 150mg/kg i/p and to rats at a dose rate of 90mg/kg i/p. This should be accompanied by either xylazine (10mg/kg i/p) or medetomidine (0.5mg/kg). The solutions can be pre-mixed and given as a single intraperitoneal injection.

Pentobarbitone may be employed to produce anaesthesia, but the amount used will be close to the lethal dose in many animals. If attempts are made to induce surgical anaesthesia with pentobarbitone as the sole anaesthetic, an unacceptably high mortality rate will occur. Pentobarbitone should only be administered at low doses (40mg/kg) to provide light anaesthesia, which can then be deepened using inhalational agents.

At the completion of surgery, anaesthesia should either be reversed using specific antagonists (see earlier) or a general respiratory stimulant such as doxapram (Dopram V, Willows Francis) (10−15mg/kg s/c or i/m). Post-operative mortality can often be reduced by the administration of warmed dextrose/saline (0.18% NaCl, 4% dextrose) (1.0ml/mouse, 5.0ml/rat s/c) since many animals fail to maintain an adequate fluid intake after surgery and some are dehydrated as a result of it. The animal should have been weighed prior to induction of anaesthesia, both to enable accurate calculation of drug dosages and also to enable an assessment to be made of the severity of any post-operative weight loss. Following surgical procedures, analgesics such as buprenorphine should be administered for 24−48 hours to control post-operative pain (0.05mg/kg s/c tid) (Flecknell, 1987).

Surgical procedures

Castration

Both rats and mice have open inguinal canals and the testes move easily between the abdomen and scrotum. The testes can be removed via a scrotal incision and the vas deferens and spermatic blood vessels ligated. The wall of the scrotum and the skin should be closed in separate layers in the rat; in the mouse it is only possible to close the incision in a single layer. The use of an open technique of castration does not seem to be associated with herniation of viscera into the inguinal canal and scrotum in these species, presumably because of effective closure of the canal by the remaining adipose tissue.

Ovariohysterectomy

Ovariohysterectomy is a relatively straightforward technique in both the rat and the mouse. A midline approach should be used and both the ovarian and uterine vessels ligated together with the associated connective tissue and the cervix. The abdominal incision should be closed in two layers. If possible, 4/0 suture material should be used for the skin, as this seems to minimise the incidence of interference with the sutures post-operatively.

REFERENCES AND FURTHER READING

BAKER, H. J., LINDSEY, J. R. and WEISBROTH, S. H. (1979). *The Laboratory Rat. Vol. 1. Biology and Diseases.* Academic Press, New York.

BERGHOFF, P. C. (1990). *Les Petits Animaux Familiers et leurs Maladies.* Maloine, Paris.

CANADIAN COUNCIL ON ANIMAL CARE (1980). *Guide to the Care and Use of Experimental Animals.* Canadian Council on Animal Care, Ottawa.

COLES, E. H. (1980). *Veterinary Clinical Pathology.* W. B. Saunders, Eastbourne.

COOPER, J. E. (1984). Anaesthesia of exotic animals. *Animal Technology* **35**, 13.

CURL, J. L., CURL, J. S., and HARRISON, J. K. (1988). Pharmacokinetics of long acting oxytetracycline in the laboratory rat. *Laboratory Animal Science* **38**, 430.

DOWNS, W. G. (1982). Mouse encephalomyelitis virus. In: *The Mouse in Biomedical Research.* (Eds. H. L. Foster, D. J. Small and J. G. Fox) Academic Press, New York.

FLECKNELL, P. A. (1987). *Laboratory Animal Anaesthesia.* Academic Press, London.

FOSTER, H. L., SMALL, D. J. and FOX, J. G. (1982). *The Mouse in Biomedical Research. Vol. II. Diseases.* Academic Press, New York.

GABRISCH, K. and ZWART, P. (1985). Eds. *Krankheiten der Heimtiere.* Schlütersche, Hanover.

GREEN, C. J. (1979). *Animal Anaesthesia.* Laboratory Animals Limited, London.

HAFEZ, E. S. E. (1970). *Reproduction and Breeding Techniques for Laboratory Animals.* Lea and Febiger, Philadelphia.

HARKNESS, J. E. and WAGNER, J. E. (1983). *The Biology and Medicine of Rabbits and Rodents.* Lea and Febiger, Philadelphia.

HIME, J. M. and O'DONOGHUE, P. N. (1979). Eds. *Handbook of Diseases of Laboratory Animals.* Heinemann Veterinary Books, London.

HSU, C-K, (1979). Parasitic diseases. In: *The Laboratory Rat. Vol. 1.* (Eds. H. J. Baker, J. R. Lindsey and S. H. Weinsbroth) Academic Press, New York.

INGLIS, J. K. (1980). *Introduction to Laboratory Animal Science and Technology.* Pergamon Press, Oxford.

JACOBY, R. O. and FOX, J. G. (1984). Biology and diseases of mice. In: *Laboratory Animal Medicine.* (Eds. J. G. Fox, B. J. Cohen and F. M. Loew) Academic Press, New York.

KOHN, D. F. and BARTHOLD, S. W. (1984). Biology and diseases of rats. In: *Laboratory Animal Medicine.* (Eds. J. G. Fox, B. J. Cohen and F. M. Loew) Academic Press, New York.

LEHMANN-GRUBE, F. (1982). Lymphocytic choriomeningitis virus. In: *The Mouse in Biomedical Research.* (Eds. H. L. Foster, D. J. Small and J. G. Fox) Academic Press, New York.

LOEB, W. F. and QUINBY, F. W. (1989). *The Clinical Chemistry of Laboratory Animals.* Pergamon Press, New York.

MITRUKA, B. M. and RAWNSLEY, H. M. (1977). *Clinical Biochemical and Hematological Reference Values in Normal Experimental Animals.* Masson Publishing USA Inc., New York.

NEVALAINEN, T., PYHALA, L., HANNA-MAIJA, V. and VIRTANEN, R. (1989). Evaluation of anaesthetic potency of medetomidine-ketamine combinations in rats, guinea pigs and rabbits. *Acta Veterinaria scandinavica Supplement* **85**, 139.

ROACH, P. D., WALLIS, P. M. and OLSON, M. E. (1988). The use of metronidazole, tinidazole and dimetridazole in eliminating trichomonads from laboratory mice. *Laboratory Animals* **22**, 361.

SANDERSON, J. H. and PHILLIPS, C. E. (1982). *An Atlas of Laboratory Animal Haematology.* Oxford University Press, Oxford.

SMITH, K. E. (1976). *Mice and Rats.* Bartholomew and Son, Edinburgh.

CHAPTER TEN

FERRETS

Michael Oxenham BVetMed MRCVS

The ferret *(Mustela putorius furo)* is almost certainly the domesticated descendant of the European polecat *(Mustela putorius)*. Behavioural changes from the wild polecat have occurred through selective breeding over a very long time, but the ferret is still completely interfertile with its wild ancestor. There are records in the literature of its domestication for hunting from 2,000 years ago, notably in the writings of Aristotle (c. 350 BC), Strobo (c. 63 B.C.—24 AD) and Pliny (23—79 AD).

The ferret has been used for rabbiting in Britain from the time of the Norman conquest and possibly by the Romans 1,000 years earlier (Marchington, 1978; Owen, 1984; Wellstead, 1981; Whittaker, 1978).

Nomenclature is sometimes confused mainly due to the colour variations that occur, eg. the albino or white form being called the ferret, and the natural buff and dark points colour, the fitch or polecat ferret. Other local names include fitchet, fitchew, futrit, foulmarten or foumart. The albino phenotype and other colour mutants (ginger, silver-mitt, panda, cinnamon etc.) are recessive to the normal polecat colour.

Males are referred to as hobs, females as jills, the very young as kits and castrated males as hobbles.

USES AND ACTIVITIES

Ferreting

Rabbit hunting continues to be a popular pastime and is well described by Porter and Brown (1985) and McKay (1989). Ferrets are also used for ratting, although this is probably now less common.

Domestic pets

Ferrets are becoming popular as household pets, particularly with older children. Many ferret owners are members of local clubs affiliated to the National Ferret Welfare Society (NFWS) (see 'Appendix — Useful Addresses'). In association with the NFWS it is estimated that the working and pet ferret population of the UK is approximately 250,000 — of these about 65% are working ferrets and 35% pets. The colour distribution is estimated to be 40% natural polecat, 20% albino and 40% other colour variations. In the USA ferrets are kept mainly as pets, hunting with them being illegal in many states.

Ferret racing

Clubs arrange races at country fairs and shows, creating much interest and entertainment. The ferrets race along 12—16 metre lengths of plastic pipe, which have 2 or 3 mesh windows at intervals so that spectators can observe their progress. Each race is generally between 4 or 6 ferrets. The small bets placed by the punters increase the interest and the proceeds assist the club's funds.

Shows

Clubs arrange shows and the ferrets are judged on conformation, condition, behaviour, quality of coat and cleanliness.

Fur ranching

The ferret has been ranched in the UK but this practice is now declining with the general trends in the fur trade. However, it still continues in other parts of Europe, the USA, Canada and New Zealand. It is the practice of some ranches to breed male mink with female ferrets in order to obtain two litters per year compared with the female mink's one litter. The offspring are infertile hybrids with a better quality fur than the pure ferret.

Biomedical research

For many decades the ferret has been widely used in research including studies into virology, reproductive physiology, endocrinology, pharmacology, toxicology and teratology.

Ferret legging

This is often referred to as a sport in other texts (Fox, 1988; McKay, 1989). It involves people putting a ferret or ferrets down their trousers, with the trousers tied at the ankle, to see who can tolerate their presence for the longest length of time. The NFWS does not approve of this activity as it can cause needless fear and stress in ferrets, which may induce them to bite or scratch the participant.

BEHAVIOUR

Ferrets have a reputation for being unpredictable in temperament, but the majority presented to veterinary surgeons are very tame and accustomed to handling. Most owners will not keep one that is aggressive or dangerous to humans. It is important to handle kits regularly from four weeks of age to encourage socialisation. They can be trained to litter boxes. Ferrets are very sociable, although males may fight when in season. When used for rabbiting or ratting, ferrets are instinctively aggressive and determined in seeking out their quarry. There is no natural animosity between dogs or cats and ferrets but each can inflict wounds on the other if aroused.

HOUSING

Suitable housing is described by Wilson and O'Donoghue (1982), Porter and Brown (1985) and McKay (1989). Constructed of good quality hardwood and weldmesh (2.5cm square mesh size), a cage for two ferrets should measure 1.5m long, 0.5m high and 0.5m deep with a nestbox of 25% of that area. Hay or straw is suitable for bedding and wood shavings for the litter area. The cage can be kept in an unheated garage or shed through the winter as the ferret can withstand a temperature near freezing point. In the summer the cage should not be in the direct sun as ferrets are very susceptible to heat stress. Optimum environmental temperature is 15°−21°C. Larger exercise areas should be available with an emphasis on secure construction.

NUTRITION

The ferret is a true carnivore and can be maintained successfully on good quality tinned or pelleted cat food (Fox,1988). The basic need is a high protein (30%), high fat (30%), low carbohydrate/fibre diet with vitamin/mineral supplement, such as SA 37 (Intervet). Whole day-old chicks are now widely used but should be supplemented with cat food, which has a higher protein content than dog food. Some fresh raw meat is beneficial, particularly for the teeth, but can be a source of *Salmonella, Campylobacter* and *Listeria* spp. which are all zoonotic. Botulism has been reported (Harrison and Borland, 1973) from using decomposing raw meats. Small amounts of milk are beneficial, but a mainly bread and milk diet is unacceptable. Commercial pellet diets are available for laboratory ferrets. The normal consumption of an adult ferret is about 90−120g of semi-moist food daily. Obesity can occur, although it is normal for ferrets to gain weight in the winter. It is usual to feed once daily, preferably in the evening. Water *ad libitum* is essential.

HANDLING, RESTRAINT AND DRUG ADMINISTRATION

To pick up a ferret its attention should be attracted with one hand and then the neck quickly grasped with the thumb under the chin. The hind quarters should be supported (see Figure 1). For subcutaneous injection of small volumes, the animal should be held by the scruff of the neck and injected over the shoulder area (see Figure 2). The owner or an assistant should restrain the ferret for intramuscular injection with one hand behind the head, the other over the lumbar area and pinning the animal to the table. For intravenous routes, reference should be made to the section on blood sampling. Liquids can be given orally by syringe while the animal is held by the neck (see Figure 3).

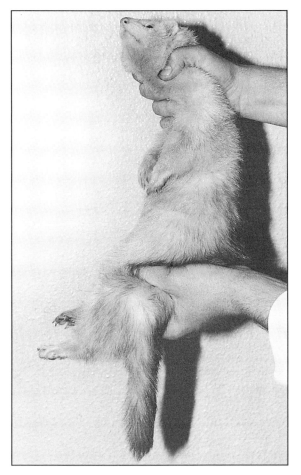

Figure 1
Manual restraint of the ferret.

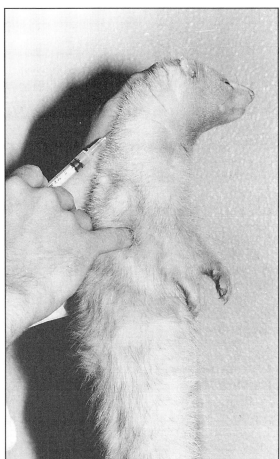

Figure 2
Giving a subcutaneous injection.

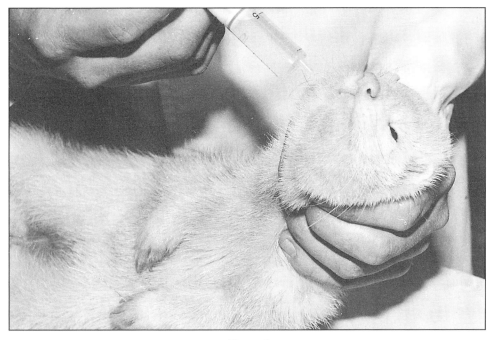

Figure 3
Oral dosing of a ferret.

BIOLOGICAL DATA

Average life span	5—11 years
Adult weight	Male: 700—2000g: Female: 600—900g
Birth weight	5—15g
Weaning weight	300—500g
Rectal temperature	38.6°C. Range 37.8°—40.0°C
Heart rate	300—400 per minute
Respiratory rate	30—40 per minute

Haematology	Male		Female	
	Mean	Range	Mean	Range
PCV (l/l)	0.43	0.36—0.5	0.48	0.47—0.51
Haemoglobin (g/l)	143	120—163	159	152—174
§Erythrocyte Count (10^{12}/l)	10.23	7.3—12.2	8.11	6.8—9.8
Leucocyte Count (10^9/l)	11.3	7.7—15.4	5.9	2.5—8.6
Neutrophils (%)	40.1	24—78	31.1	12—41
Lymphocytes (%)	49.7	28—69	58.0	25—95
Monocytes (%)	6.6	3.4—8.2	4.5	1.7—6.3
Eosinophils (%)	2.3	0—7	3.6	1—9
Basophils (%)	0.7	0—2.7	0.8	0—2.9
§Platelets (10^9/l)	453	297—730	545	310—910

Biochemistry	Mean	Range
Total protein (g/l)	59.0	53.0—72.0
*Globulin (g/l)	22.0	20—29
Glucose (mmol/l)	5.656	3.5—7.504
Urea (mmol/l)	10.08	4.32—15.48
Creatinine (μmol/l)	35.36	17.68—53.04
*ALP Alkaline phosphatase (iu/l)	42	31—64
*AST (GOT) (iu/l)	117	74—248
*ALT (GPT) (iu/l)	109	78—149

The results of the ALP, AST and ALT tests will depend on which method the laboratory uses for its reference values. Data from: —

    Lee *et al* (1982). Natural polecat colour ferrets.
    §Thornton *et al* (1979). Albino ferrets.
    *Fox *et al* (1986a). Natural polecat colour male ferrets.
The values quoted in these texts have been converted, where appropriate, to SI units.

BLEEDING TECHNIQUES

Blood samples may be needed for routine haematology or serological tests and the quantity needed will determine the method to be used. Toe-nail clipping will yield a few drops of blood sufficient for a capillary tube (see Figure 4). An experienced assistant is required to restrain the ferret if a larger amount of blood is needed. Alternatively, light anaesthesia can be used. The jugular vein is the most convenient and safe site for venepuncture using a 23 gauge needle. Other sites used are the caudal tail vein, cranial vena cava and cardiac puncture, the last of which can be hazardous.

REPRODUCTION

Males (hobs)

Puberty occurs at 5 to 9 months of age during the spring after birth. The hob is in season from January to August when the testicles enlarge and descend into the scrotum. From September to December the testicles atrophy and retract into the inguinal area or abdomen. There is a J-shaped os penis which makes catheterisation difficult.

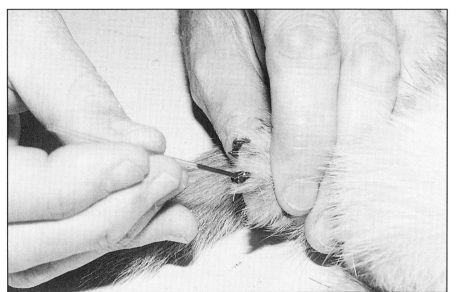

Figure 4
Taking a blood sample
from a toe-nail.

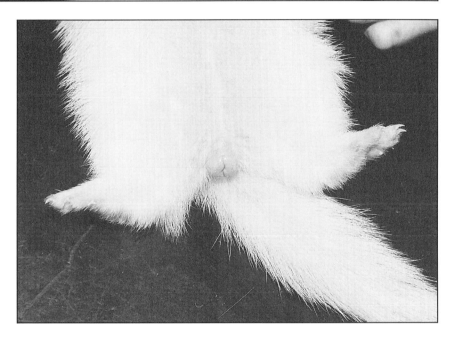

Figure 5
The swollen vulva
of a jill in oestrus.

Females (jills)

Puberty occurs during the spring after birth. The jill is seasonally polyoestrous, commencing the last week of March and lasting until September. Onset of oestrus may be much earlier if the jill is subjected to artificial light. Oestrus is recognised by a swollen vulva (see Figure 5) and will persist for 6 months or until ovulation is induced by mating. Coitus is notable for the aggressive neck gripping by the hob, which, together with mounting and intromission, is essential to induce ovulation. Coitus can last for 1 — 3 hours. Fetuses can be palpated at 14 — 21 days. Gestation is 38 — 44 days (average 42). An infertile mating or one with a vasectomised hob may result in a pseudopregnancy which also lasts about 42 days. Litter size is 5 — 13 kits (average 8). Young are born very underdeveloped and are almost impossible to hand-rear before 1 week of age. Dystocia is rarely a problem but oxytocin (3 iu i/m) can be given if necessary. Kits are born up to 30 minutes apart. Disturbance during the first week after birth may cause cannibalism. New born kits are subject to harm by wide fluctuations in temperature. They commence eating solid food at 3 weeks and the eyes open between 4 and 5 weeks. Weaning age is 6 — 8 weeks. Jills return to oestrus shortly after weaning and can have two litters per year.

DISEASES AND CLINICAL CONDITIONS

Reproductive disorders

Oestrogen-induced anaemia

The high levels of endogenous oestrogens, which are present during the prolonged oestrus of the unmated jill, may cause progressive depression of the bone marrow. This results in a debilitating and potentially fatal pancytopoenia (Kociba and Caputo, 1981; Cooper *et al*, 1985). Clinical signs include weight loss, anorexia, alopecia, pale mucous membranes, laboured respiration and, later, melaena and subcutaneous petechial haemorrhages on the abdomen and flanks. Secondary infections often occur. The PCV can be less than 0.10. Treatment is unlikely to be successful in the advanced stages, but either spaying or hormonal treatment to stop oestrus, together with supportive therapy, can be attempted if the PCV is above 0.15. Repeated transfusions of 10ml fresh whole blood containing 1ml sodium citrate have been used (Ryland, 1982). Crossmatching does not appear to be necessary as evidence of blood groups could not be detected by Manning and Bell (1990).

Control of oestrus is, therefore, important in non-breeding jills. This can be achieved by spaying, the use of vasectomised hobs or by hormonal means. Mating with a vasectomised hob will usually induce a pseudopregnancy lasting about 42 days and is repeated when the jill returns to oestrus. Proligestone (Delvosteron, Mycofarm; Covinan, Intervet) can be given from the end of March or when oestrus commences, if earlier. The dose is 0.5ml subcutaneously. In 91.6% of jills this will suppress oestrus for the rest of the summer (Oxenham, 1990a). If the jill returns to oestrus, a second dose can be given. Jills breed satisfactorily the year following use of this hormone. No cases of pyometra have been seen by the author following its use.

Chorionic gonadotrophins will induce ovulation followed by a pseudopregnancy of 40—50 days duration. This may be useful if an owner wants to breed the jill in the middle of the summer. The following can be used for this purpose:—

> Human chorionic gonadotrophin (Chorulon,Intervet) (20iu i/m) or
> buserelin (Receptal, Hoechst) (0.25ml i/m) which has a follicle stimulating/luteinising function
> (Wilson, personal communication).

Pyometra

This is an uncommon condition but can occur soon after the start of the pseudopregnancy phase. A variety of organisms has been isolated from infected uteri including *Streptococcus* spp., *Staphylococcus* spp., *E.coli* and *Corynebacterium* spp. The ferret will be anorexic, depressed and often febrile. The enlarged uterus is palpable. Rupture of the uterus and peritonitis can follow, so ovariohysterectomy is required urgently.

Hypocalcaemia

This can occur 3—4 weeks *post partum*. Signs include hyperaesthesia, posterior paresis and convulsions. Intraperitoneal injection of calcium borogluconate gives a quick response, with subsequent additions of calcium supplements to the diet.

Pregnancy toxaemia

This causes sudden death of the jill a few days before parturition. The main autopsy finding is a fatty liver. The cause is unknown but there may be a nutritional factor.

Mastitis

This occurs in the early lactation phase. The glands quickly become swollen and hard. The jill is lethargic, anorexic and pyrexic and will cease to feed the kits. The condition requires urgent treatment with antibiotics. The usual causal agent is *E.coli* and ampicillin (10mg/kg i/m bid) or gentamicin (5mg/kg i/m sid) are indicated.

Viral diseases

Canine distemper (CD)

Ferrets are highly susceptible to the distemper virus. The usual source is the dog and the incubation period is 7—9 days. Clinical signs are similar to those in the dog with mucopurulent ocular and nasal discharge, high temperature (40.6°—41.1°C) and anorexia. This is followed by a rash under the chin and inguinal area. The terminal phase is marked by central nervous signs, convulsions and death. Distemper must be regarded as 100% fatal in the ferret and euthanasia should be recommended once diagnosis is certain. There is no ferret distemper vaccine currently licensed for use in the UK. Most of the dog vaccines available are either insufficiently attenuated for ferret use or have other live virus components such as adenovirus, parvovirus and parainfluenza virus which are unnecessary for this species.

The use of an unsuitable vaccine can cause clinical distemper with a fatal result. A vaccine which has been used widely and without ill-effect is Vaxitas D (Coopers Pitman-Moore). This is a live vaccine using the Rockborn strain distemper virus, grown in the Vero continuous line of African green monkey cells (Willoughby, personal communication). Half the dog dose is sufficient for the ferret and annual boosters should be given (Oxenham, 1990b).

For ferrets which have been exposed to CD infection, Maxaglobin (Hoechst) is licensed for use in this species. This is a solution of immunoglobulin containing neutralising antibodies against distemper virus and gives a passive immunity for 2—3 weeks. The dose rate for prophylaxis is 0.2ml/kg bodyweight given by subcutaneous or intramuscular injection.

Influenza virus (human)

Several strains of this virus cause mild upper respiratory disease in adult ferrets, but in young kits it may be 100% fatal. The ferret may be anorexic, listless and febrile, with a nasal discharge (Bell and Dudgeon, 1948). Recovery is often spontaneous, but antibiotics may be needed to control secondary infection.

There is evidence that the disease can be transmitted to humans from ferrets (Smith and Stuart-Harris, 1936).

Aleutian disease (AD)

The causal agent is a parvovirus. Aleutian disease is a serious problem on mink farms and the virus can cause persistent infection in ferrets, occasionally causing serious disease (Ohshima *et al*, 1978; Porter *et al*, 1982; Oxenham, 1990c). Infection may be more common than previously suspected. The disease is immune-mediated and also causes a degree of immunodepression. The signs are, therefore, variable. Recorded signs include black tarry faeces, recurrent fevers, weight loss, behaviour changes such as being more aggressive or hyperaesthetic, thyroiditis, posterior paralysis and eventually death. It might also cause sudden death in stressed animals. Transmission is both vertical and horizontal. Asymptomatic carriers, particularly breeding jills, can spread the disease. There is no specific treatment but antibiotics and steroids may give temporary relief.

Diagnosis is confirmed by serology and *post-mortem* histopathology. Infection should be suspected if the gammaglobulins are more than 20% of the total serum protein. Liver enzyme levels are not raised by AD. The specific test is done by counter-current immuno-electrophoresis (CIEP or CEP). Blood for this is collected into a heparinised capillary tube by the toe-nail clipping method (see earlier). At least a quarter of a tube of blood is needed. The test is carried out by Harlan Olac Ltd. (see 'Appendix — Useful Addresses') who can give further information. Some importing countries request that this test is done before admitting a ferret. Samples should be taken either before CD vaccination or more than two months after, in order to reduce levels of non-specific binding in the CIEP test.

There is no cross antigenicity between AD and feline or canine parvovirus vaccines and there is no specific vaccine due to the immune-mediated nature of the disease.

Control presents some difficult choices and will depend upon how many ferrets the owner has, whether any breeding is carried out and whether any exchange of stock takes place. If an owner has a number of ferrets with which some breeding is done and a small percentage of them are CIEP test positive, then there is a strong case for culling those few animals. In order to ensure effective eradication, the ferrets remaining in a colony following the culling of positive animals should be retested twice at intervals of not less than three weeks. The reason for this is that sero-conversion takes up to 21 days. But if the whole stock is positive and they are good working ferrets, the owner may wish to keep them for their natural life, in which case he or she should cease breeding the ferrets and not exchange any stock. All serious ferret owners should regularly (once yearly) test their stock and, in the case of positive results, take suitable action. Only a small percentage of CIEP positive ferrets will develop serious illness but they must be regarded as potentially infective to other ferrets and should therefore, at the very least, be strictly isolated.

Rabies

Cases of rabies in ferrets are recorded in countries where the disease is enzootic. Clinical signs include anxiety, lethargy and, occasionally, posterior paralysis. Mortality, however, is not always 100% and it is interesting to note that Blancou *et al* (1982) were unable to demonstrate that the virus is not present in the saliva of experimentally infected animals. There is no vaccine licensed for ferret use and if a live canine vaccine is used, rabies may be induced (Burke, 1989). Ferrets are subject to 6 months rabies quarantine restrictions on entering the UK (see 'Legislation').

Note. Ferrets are not susceptible to feline panleucopoenia virus, canine parvovirus or canine viral hepatitis and, therefore, vaccination for these conditions cannot be justified.

Bacterial diseases

Many types of bacterial infections have been recorded, some of which only occur in laboratory and ranch colonies. Those most likely to be encountered in the working or pet ferret will be discussed here.

Abscesses

These are common in the submandibular area and are often caused by *Staphylococcus* spp. or *Streptococcus* spp. They probably arise through damage to the buccal mucosa by sharp bones in the diet. Treatment is by drainage under anaesthetic followed by a broad-spectrum antibiotic such as ampicillin.

Enteritis

This is a common condition particularly in young ferrets and is often the cause of sudden death. In the author's experience haemolytic *E. coli* is the most common causative organism.

Campylobacter spp. have been associated with proliferative colitis and gastric ulceration (Fox, 1988). The faeces of ferrets vary in consistency and the animal is not necessarily ill or in danger if the faeces are less solid than usual. It is probable that dietary factors play a part in starting cases of enteritis, such as decomposition, contamination or sudden changes of food, so attention must be given to this aspect of the condition. The treatment chosen will depend upon culture and sensitivity tests. There is usually a wide choice of broad-spectrum antibiotics for *E. coli*, but for *Campylobacter* spp. chloramphenicol or gentamicin are likely to be more effective. Fluid and electrolyte replacement are necessary in very sick animals and this is achieved by oral administration of Lectade (SmithKline Beecham) (25ml/kg tid).

Actinomycosis

In the author's experience, actinomycosis takes the form of a fairly acute diffuse hard swelling of the whole of the ventral neck. The ferret is listless, anorexic and febrile — up to 40.8°C — and may have been fed a diet, such as day-old chicks, which caused abrasions of the oesophagus. Injections of cephalosporin (Ceporex, Coopers Pitman-Moore) (0.5ml i/m sid) achieve a good response, together with liquid feeding.

Botulism

Ferrets are very susceptible to *Clostridium botulinum* type C. Central nervous signs and paralysis are rapidly followed by death. The organism is a natural contaminant of some wild bird carcases. Most cases occur in commercial ranches where food hygiene is poor. Annual toxoid vaccination can be given when there is considered to be a risk (Fox, 1988).

Tuberculosis and salmonellosis have been recorded (Symmers *et al*, 1953; Coburn and Morris, 1949), mainly in association with ranched or laboratory colonies. There have been no recently recorded cases in pet or working ferrets in the UK.

Leptospirosis

The question of vaccination for leptospirosis often arises. Studies carried out in New Zealand (Hathaway and Blackmore, 1981) and Denmark (Fennestad and Borg-Petersen, 1972) indicate that the ferret has a natural resistance to infection, even when used for rodent control. To date, therefore, there is no substantiated reason for advising vaccination, although some veterinary surgeons use (killed) canine vaccine and report no ill effects.

Skin conditions

A comprehensive review has been published by Cooper(1990). The conditions most likely to be seen fall under the following headings:-

Parasitic

Fleas (*Ctenocephalides* spp.), contracted from dogs, cats and wild animals, are very common from July to October. Insecticidal preparations used for the dog and cat are safe for the ferret. Heavy infestations of ticks, usually *Ixodes ricinus*, occur during the summer months, particularly in escaped and feral ferrets. Care must be taken to ensure that the mouthparts of the tick are fully removed from the skin.

Ear mites (*Otodectes cynotis*) are common and can be treated with ear drops containing gamma BHC or by injection of ivermectin (Ivomec, MSD Agvet) (1.0mg/kg s/c) repeated after two weeks.

Mites (*Sarcoptes scabiei*) can cause two forms of mange, a generalised condition with alopecia and intense pruritus, or just foot and toe lesions (Ryland *et al*, 1983). Mange should be treated with a parasiticidal wash such as bromocyclen (Alugan, Hoechst) or ivermectin injections. Ivermectin can cause congenital deformities if used in the first month of pregnancy (Burke, 1989).

The harvest mite *(Trombicula autumnalis)* causes small multiple lesions mainly on the underside of the neck and trunk during August and September. It can be treated with Alugan wash.

Dermatophytosis (ringworm)

This is uncommon. *Microsporum canis* infection is only contracted by the ferret if it is in contact with an infected cat, or, more rarely, a dog. The lesions are similar to those in the cat. Treatment is with griseofulvin (Grisovin, Coopers Pitman-Moore), 25mg/kg daily for three weeks.

Alopecia

There are many possible causes of alopecia including seasonal environmental conditions, dietary imbalances, hyperoestrogenism and endocrine imbalances secondary to various neoplastic conditions. The clinical history and examination should give a guide as to the probable cause and treatment (see Nutrition, Reproductive Disorders and Neoplasia). Iatrogenic alopecia can occur following the use of proligestone for oestrus control. A small (1.5cm diameter) area of alopecia occurs in about 5% of cases at the injection site and persists for a variable length of time (Oxenham, 1990a). The incidence of this will be reduced if the injection site is carefully massaged.

Skin neoplasia

This occurs frequently. The most common neoplasms of the skin are mast cell tumours, squamous cell carcinomas and sebaceous gland adenomas. Surgery is indicated as early as possible, but they can prove recurrent. Others recorded are adenocarcinomas, histiocytomas and multiple benign warts. Histopathology is important for differential diagnosis and prognosis.

In the author's experience immune-mediated skin disease, which is seen so frequently in the dog and cat, is not a clinical problem in the ferret.

Miscellaneous conditions

Dental disease

A number of conditions in this category have been recognised (Andrews *et al*, 1979; Berkovitz and Poole, 1977). The most common condition is periodontal disease caused by accumulation of dental calculus. Nutritional factors are probably important in its aetiology, particularly when ferrets are fed bread and milk or soft processed food to the exclusion of a more natural diet (see Nutrition). Regular teeth scaling under anaesthetic is necessary in some animals. Teeth damaged by various causes, such as chewing metal parts of a cage, may need extraction.

Osteodystrophy

This is due to hyperphosphorosis associated with an all meat diet and a consequent calcium deficiency. In the author's experience it usually occurs in the 6—12 week age group and affects the whole litter. The ferrets are unable to stand and characteristically the front legs are abducted. They move about with a seal-like gait. The bones are soft and deformed. Ferrets that recover are often left with deformed legs and spine. Mortality can be high. Urgent dietary correction is needed — supplemented with a vitamin/mineral product such as SA 37 (Intervet). Radiography will assist diagnosis and differentiate from congenital abnormalities.

Thiamine deficiency

In the author's experience, this condition is associated with feeding a diet consisting of an excessive proportion of day-old chicks and/or eggs or fish and is usually seen in the 8—12 week age group. The signs are lethargy, anorexia, hindquarter weakness and, later, convulsions. Response to injections of vitamin B complex (5mg sid s/c for 3 days) is usually rapid.

Posterior paralysis

This is a common presenting sign which experienced ferreters call the 'staggers'. There are several possible causes which are not always easy to distinguish clinically. It may be due to intervertebral disc disease, hypocalcaemia in a nursing jill, viral myelitis, Aleutian disease, vertebral trauma, spinal neoplasia, bone marrow depression or dietary imbalance such as thiamine deficiency. Clinical history, serology, blood chemistry and radiography will assist diagnosis. Response to steroids and vitamin therapy will be observed in appropriate cases, but reference should be made to other relevant sections of this chapter. Secondary cystitis associated with urinary incontinence must also be treated in these cases.

Urolithiasis

Struvite calculi varying in size from sand to single large stones occur in association with urinary tract infection. Treatment includes antibiotics, surgery and special diet using stone dissolving cat food, such as Feline Prescription Diet s/d (Hill's Pet Products).

Zinc toxicity

Ferrets are very susceptible to zinc toxicity. This can arise from the use of galvanised feeding dishes or by licking cage bars (Straube *et al*, 1980). The signs are lethargy, anaemia and weakness of the hind legs followed by renal and hepatic failure. The prognosis is poor and there is no specific treatment.

Endoparasites

Toxocara and *Toxascaris* spp. occasionally occur but are not generally a problem. The following anthelmintics can be given orally:

> fenbenzadole (Panacur Wormer 22% granules,Hoechst), 0.5g/kg in a single dose or mebendazole (Telmin KH 100mg tablet, Janssen), 50mg/kg bid for 2 days.

Other parasites recorded which can cause clinical disease are heartworms (in the USA), coccidia, *Toxoplasma* and *Pneumocystis*. The clinical signs and treatment are reviewed by Fox (1988).

Internal neoplasia

A wide variety of neoplasms have been recorded (Chesterton and Pomerance, 1965) and the literature is fully reviewed by Fox (1988). Many of the recorded cases of spontaneous tumours have occurred in ferrets kept in research institutions. The prevalence of neoplasias in pet and working ferrets is difficult to assess, as many owners do not seek attention for ailing and aged animals. Lymphosarcoma is probably the most common type (Fox *et al*, 1986b), followed by tumours of the reproductive tract (Cotchin, 1980), pancreatic islet cell (Lumeij *et al*, 1987) and the adrenal gland. Various treatment regimes using surgery, steroids and cytotoxic agents have been used in the USA (Brown, 1989). Remissions have been recorded but the long-term prognosis in many cases is poor.

ANAESTHESIA

Ferrets should be carefully examined and weighed before sedation or anaesthesia. If the body condition is poor or there is any possibility of a septicaemic condition, the dose of injectable agents should be reduced by 25%. Animals should be fasted for 6—12 hours before anaesthesia. Water should not be withdrawn. Atropine sulphate (0.5mg/kg s/c) should be given routinely as a premedicant.

Sedation/Light an aesthesia

Ketamine hydrochloride (Vetalar, Parke-Davis; Ketaset, Willows Francis).

An intramuscular dose of 25mg/kg bodyweight gives moderate sedation in 4 minutes; 40mg/kg gives deep sedation sufficient for minor procedures such as radiography or lancing of abscesses. Muscle relaxation will be improved by giving diazepam (Valium,Roche) or midazolam (Hypnovel, Roche) (1—2mg/kg i/m).

Xylazine (Rompun, Bayer).

A subcutaneous dose of 4mg/kg gives sedation as above in 10—15 minutes.

Fentanyl/fluanisone (Hypnorm, Janssen) (0.3mg/kg i/m) or **alphaxalone/alphadolone** (Saffan, Coopers Pitman-Moore) (10mg/kg i/m) can also be used for sedation and as a premedicant for inhalation agents.

Surgical anaesthesia

This can be achieved using any of the sedative agents mentioned earlier in combination with an inhalation anaesthetic, such as **methoxyflurane, isoflurane, halothane** or **ether,** given with oxygen and face mask to effect. Isoflurane can be used on its own; it is particularly safe as it has a short induction and recovery phase. Ferrets are easy to intubate.

Ketamine/xylazine (25mg/kg ketamine/2mg/kg xylazine i/m) gives satisfactory surgical anaesthesia which lasts for 30—40 minutes (Fox 1988; Engh and Smith, 1989). This combination can be hazardous if the ferret is not in good health.

Pentobarbitone (30—35mg/kg i/p) is not recommended because of the risk of damage to the abdominal viscera and the long recovery phase. It is a poor analgesic.

The depth of anaesthesia is monitored by observation of the palpebral and pedal reflexes together with the heart and respiratory rates. The ferret should be kept warm during the recovery phase.

EUTHANASIA

Intraperitoneal pentobarbitone is the chemical method of choice.

SURGICAL PROCEDURES

Castration

Castration reduces aggression between males and the characteristic musky body odour; this is done preferably from January to September, when the hob is in season and the testicles are descended. A closed technique,as for the dog, should be used, and the skin is best sutured with fine monofilament nylon.

Vasectomy

Vasectomy is requested when an owner has a number of jills in which he or she wishes to induce ovulation followed by a pseudopregnancy. Again, this is best performed when the hob is in season. An optical aid is useful as the vas deferens is small. Two incisions are made either side of the mid-line, 3cm cranial to the testicles. The spermatic cords are located by blunt dissection and the vasa are isolated with fine instruments. Each end of the vas is ligated with 4/0 gut. The hob cannot be assumed to be sterile until 7 weeks after surgery. If there is any doubt about the tissue removed, it can be submitted for histology.

Ovariohysterectomy

This operation can be carried out from 6 months of age during either anoestrus or oestrus without ill-effect. A 4cm mid-line incision is made. The uterus is about 4cm long and the ovaries are usually concealed by a fat capsule. After ligation, the capsule should be opened to ensure that all of the ovary has been removed, otherwise the jill will have problems associated with prolonged oestrus (see earlier). The abdomen is closed as for the cat.

Trauma

Most injuries are the result of fighting, hunting or dog attacks and are dealt with as for a small cat. Ferrets manage satisfactorily after amputation of a leg.

Neoplasia

Tumours for which surgery is indicated mainly involve the skin (see earlier). The most common sites are the feet, legs and trunk. Most types of tumour are likely to recur unless removed in the early stages.

Foreign bodies

Gastro-intestinal foreign bodies cause vomiting, anorexia and malaise. Diagnosis is made or suspected by palpation and radiography. Rubber or plastic material is the most frequent offending object. Fabrics and hairballs have also been recorded. Routine gastrotomy or enterotomy is performed. As there is a slight risk of breakdown in these cases, the peritoneum and abdominal muscle are best sutured with monofilament nylon, which is also used for the skin. It should be noted that the ferret does not possess a caecum and the ileocolic junction cannot be identified from the outside of the bowel. Care should be taken not to extend the laparotomy incision too far cranially, as it is possible to create an accidental pneumothorax (Lumeij *et al*, 1987).

Congenital hernia

Inguinal hernias can be very large and need surgery at an early age (6—8 weeks). The hernial ring is closed with monofilament nylon.

Anal gland removal

This may be requested in the belief that the operation will reduce the ferret's natural odour. This is a false premise, since the animal's musky odour is produced by skin secretions and by the stronger smelling urine of the hob. 'Descenting' is indisputedly a mutilation and is not to be recommended. An undesirable sequel to the operation can be impairment of the function of the anal sphincter muscle. If surgery is indicated on medical grounds the operation is best performed as described by Fox (1988).

Acknowledgement

The author is indebted to Hazel Oxenham for her assistance in the preparation of this chapter.

REFERENCES AND FURTHER READING

ANDREWS, P. L. R., BOWER, A. J. and ILLMAN, O. (1979). Some aspects of the physiology and anatomy of the cardiovascular system of the ferret *Mustela putorius furo. Laboratory Animals* **13**, 215.

BERKOVITZ, B. K. B. and POOLE, D. F. G. (1977). Attrition of the teeth in ferrets. *Journal of Zoology London* **183**, 411.

BELL, F. R. and DUDGEON, J. A. (1948). An epizootic of influenza A in a ferret colony. *Journal of Comparative Pathology* **58**, 167.

BLANCOU, J., AUBERT, M. F. A. and ARTOIS, M. (1982). Rage expérimentale du furet *(Mustela putorius furo). Revue de Médecine Vétèrinaire* **133**, 553.

BROWN, S. A. (1989).(Unpublished). Paper to Seminar, Royal College of Surgeons, London.

BURKE, T. J. (1989). (Unpublished). Paper to Western Veterinary Convention, USA

CHESTERMAN, F. C. and POMERANCE, A. (1965). Spontaneous neoplasms in ferrets and polecats. *Journal of Pathology and Bacteriology* **89**, 529.

COBURN, D. R. and MORRIS, J. A. (1949). The treatment of *Salmonella typhimurium* infection in ferrets. *Cornell Veterinarian* **39**, 198.

COOPER, J. E., BREARLEY, M. J. and CUNNINGHAM, A. (1985). Oestrus associated anaemia in the ferret. *Veterinary Record* **117**, 395.

COOPER, J. E. (1990). Skin diseases of ferrets. In: *The Veterinary Annual.* (Eds. C. S. G. Grunsell, F. W. G. Hill and M-E. Raw) Scientechnica, London.

COTCHIN, E. (1990). Smooth muscle hyperplasia and neoplasia in the ovaries of domestic ferrets. *Journal of Pathology* **130**, 163.

ENGH, E. and SMITH, A. (1989). Anaesthesia and sedation of the ferret. (In Norwegian) *Norsk Veterinaertidsskrift* **101**, (8/9), 693.

FENNESTAD, K. L. and BORG-PETERSEN, C. (1972). Leptospires in Danish wild animals. *Journal of Wildlife Diseases* **8**, 343.

FOX, J. G. (1988). *Biology and Diseases of the Ferret.* Lea and Febiger, Philadelphia.

FOX, J. G., HOTALING, L., ACKERMAN, B. P. and HEWES, K. (1986). Serum chemistry and haematology reference values in the ferret (*Mustela putorius furo*). *Laboratory Animal Science* **36**, 583.

FOX, J. G., LIPMAN, N. S. and MURPHY, J. C. (1986b). Lymphoma in the ferret. *Laboratory Animal Science* **36**, 562.

HARRISON, S. G. and BORLAND, E. D. (1973). Deaths in ferrets (*Mustela putorius*) due to *Clostridium botulinum* type C. *Veterinary Record* **93**, 576.

HATHAWAY, S. C. and BLACKMORE, D. K. (1981). Failure to demonstrate the maintenance of leptospires by free living carnivores. *New Zealand Veterinary Journal* **29**, 115.

KOCIBA, G. J. and CAPUTO, C. A. (1981). Aplastic anemia associated with estrus in pet ferrets. *Journal of the American Veterinary Medical Association* **178**, 1293.

LEE, E. J., MOORE, W. E., FRYER, H. C. and MINORCHA, H. C. (1982). Haematological and serum chemistry profiles of ferrets *(Mustela putorius furo). Laboratory Animals* **16**, 133.

LUMEIJ, J. T., van der HAGE, M. H., DORRESTEIN, G. M. and van SLUIJS, F. J. (1987). Hypoglycaemia due to a functional pancreatic islet cell tumour (insulinoma) in a ferret (*Mustela putorius furo*). *Veterinary Record* **120**, 129.

MANNING, D. D. and BELL, J. A. (1990). Lack of detectable blood groups in domestic ferrets: implications for transfusion. *Journal of the American Veterinary Medical Association* **197**, 84.

MARCHINGTON, J. (1978). *Pugs and Drummers*. Faber and Faber, London.

McKAY, J. (1989). *The Ferret and Ferreting Handbook*. The Crowood Press, Marlborough.

OHSHIMA, K., SHEN, D. T., HENSON, J. B. and GORHAM, J. R. (1978). Comparison of the lesions of Aleutian disease in mink and hypergammaglobulinemia in ferrets. *American Journal of Veterinary Research* **39**, 653.

OWEN, C. (1984). Ferret. In: *Evolution of Domesticated Animals.* (Ed. I. L. Mason) Longman, London.

OXENHAM, M. (1990a). Oestrus control in the ferret. *Veterinary Record* **126**, 148.

OXENHAM, M. (1990b). Distemper vaccination in ferrets. *Veterinary Record* **126**, 67.

OXENHAM, M. (1990c). Aleutian disease in the ferret. *Veterinary Record* **126**, 585.

PORTER, V. and BROWN, N. (1985). *The Complete Book of Ferrets*. Pelham Books, London.

PORTER, H. G., PORTER, D. D. and LARSEN, A. E. (1982). Aleutian disease in ferrets. *Infection and Immunity* **36**, 379.

RYLAND, L. M. (1982). Remission of estrus-associated anemia following ovariohysterectomy and multiple blood transfusions in a ferret. *Journal of the American Veterinary Medical Association* **181**, 820.

RYLAND, L. M., BERNARD, S. L. and GORHAM, J. R. (1983). A clinical guide to the pet ferret. *The Compendium of Continuing Education* **5**, 25.

SMITH, W. and STUART-HARRIS, C. H. (1936). Influenza infection of man from the ferret. *Lancet* **21**, 121.

STRAUBE, E. F., SCHUSTER, N. H. and SINCLAIR, A. J. (1980). Zinc toxicity in the ferret. *Journal of Comparative Pathology* **90**, 355.

SYMMERS, W. S. T. C., THOMSON, A. P. D. and ILAND, C. N. (1953). Observations on tuberculosis in the ferret (*Mustela furo L.*). *Journal of Comparative Pathology* **63**, 20.

THORNTON, P. C., WRIGHT, P. A., SACRA, P. J. and GOODIER, T. E. W. (1979). The ferret, *Mustela putorius furo*, as a new species in toxicology. *Laboratory Animals* **16**, 119.

WELLSTEAD, G. (1981). *The Ferret and Ferreting Guide*. David and Charles, Newton Abbot.

WHITTAKER, P. (1978). *Ferrets and Ferreting.* Pugs and Drummers Publication, Friary Press, Dorchester.

WILSON, M. S. and O'DONOGHUE, P. N. (1982). A mobile rack of cages for ferrets (*Mustela putorius furo*). *Laboratory Animals* **16**, 278.

CHAPTER ELEVEN

PRIMATES

Anthony W Sainsbury BVetMed CertLAS MRCVS

This chapter has been based on that written by Miss W. Mary Brancker, published in the second edition of the *Manual of Exotic Pets.*

CLASSIFICATION

Primates are classified as follows:

Suborder Prosimii (Prosimians) (African and Asian)

Lemur	Genus *Lemur*	Arboreal.
Loris	Genus *Loris*	Nocturnal/insectivorous.
Bushbaby	Genus *Galago*	Nocturnal/insectivorous.

Suborder Anthropoidea (Simians)

New World monkeys (Platyrrhini) (South American)

Marmoset	Genus *Callithrix*	
Tamarin	Genus *Saguinus*	
Squirrel	Genus *Saimiri*	
Woolly	Genus *Lagothrix*	
Spider	Genus *Ateles*	} Prehensile tails.
Capuchin	Genus *Cebus*	

Old World monkeys (Cercopithecidae) (African and Asian)

Patas	Genus *Erythrocebus*	} Cheek pouches.
Baboon	Genus *Papio*	Ischial pads.
Macaque	Genus *Macaca*	
Colobus	Genus *Colobus*	Leaf-eating, sacculated stomach.

Lesser Apes (Hylobatinae) (Asian)

Gibbons	Genus *Hylobates*	No tail, long arms and legs, frequently walk upright.

Great Apes (Pongidae) (African and Asian)

Orangutan	Genus *Pongo*	No tails, long
Gorilla	Genus *Gorilla*	} arms and short
Chimpanzee	Genus *Pan*	legs, large and powerful.

Martin (1990) should be consulted for a more complete classification. Marmosets are increasingly kept as pets and (only the marmosets of the all primates) have the advantage, from the owner's point of view, that they are not covered by the Dangerous Wild Animals Act 1976 (as amended by The Dangerous Wild Animals Act 1976 (Modification) Order 1984) (see 'Legislation'). Macaques and marmosets are commonly kept in laboratories.

BIOLOGICAL DATA

Heart rate, respiratory rate and body temperature have limited clinical use because of the excitability of most species. However, the following approximate figures may be of value (see Lapin *et al* (1972) for further details).

Rectal temperature	large species 38°C
	small species 38.5° – 40.0°C
Heart rate	small species 200 – 300 per minute
Respiratory rate	large species 30 – 50 per minute
	small species 50 – 70 per minute
Approximate adult weight ranges	Common marmoset 350 – 400g
	Squirrel monkey male 700 – 1100g
	Squirrel monkey female 500 – 750g
	Rhesus macaque male 6 – 11kg
	Rhesus macaque female 4 – 9kg

HOUSING

Most primates originate in warm climates and an indoor enclosure maintained at between 15° – 24°C for Old World monkeys and 20° – 28°C for New World monkeys must always be available.

When considering the design of housing, the behaviour and social organisation of the species to be housed must be taken into account. Primates require a complex and stimulating environment and should not be housed alone for long periods. Attention must be paid to cage furnishings to avoid boredom and reduce aggression. There are many methods of achieving this: devices to increase foraging time, swings, ropes etc (Poole, 1988; Segal, 1989). Bedding, such as woodchips and woodwool, in which food is placed for foraging is useful for many species. Most furnishings should be easily replaced since primates are destructive, but drinking and feeding devices will need to be durable. Locks on cages must be escape-proof and checked regularly. Many primates have a vertical flight reaction and the height of the house should cater for this. It is important for animals which are housed in groups to be able to avoid visual contact with others. Most small species, eg. marmosets and tamarins, should be provided with a nest-box.

The welfare of primates should be monitored closely. 'Abnormal' behaviour such as stereotypic locomotion and self-inflicted injury should be used as an indicator that changes in their environment are required (Poole, 1988; Segal, 1989).

FEEDING

Incorrect nutrition is a common cause of disease in pet primates. It is frequently not appreciated that the majority of non-human primates are omnivorous and require animal protein as well as fruit and vegetables. However, there are some specialised feeders, for example the colobus monkey, which is a leaf-eater. The National Research Council (1978) has published some detailed information on the nutritional requirements of primates and Ullrey (1986) has provided some notes on diets in the wild. It is not possible to recommend a standard diet for all primates but it usually includes some of the following constituents: primate pellets (Special Diet Services, Witham), cereal mixes, pink mice, insects, hard-boiled eggs, fruit and vegetables. Pelleted diets are usually well balanced but have low palatability. It is important to ensure that sufficient of the pellets are eaten but not at the expense of a varied diet. Pellets can be soaked in condensed milk, or other sweet liquids, to increase palatability although this may lead to increased dental disease.

All primates require a source of vitamin C in their diet. New World primates require vitamin D_3 since they are unable to convert D_2. Vitamin D_3 is available in pelleted diets and vitamin/mineral supplements (100iu/kg bodyweight daily is sufficient in young animals).

Food should be presented in such a way as to stimulate 'natural' foraging activity and on at least two occasions each day.

HANDLING

Caution is necessary because primates may harbour zoonoses; they can, and are usually prepared to, inflict serious bites and they have great strength for their size. Leather gloves or gauntlets are often required for handling, which should not be attempted single-handed with animals weighing more than 5kg. Figures 1 and 2 show examples of handling methods. Other types of physical restraint which can be employed include nets, crush-back (or squeeze-back) cages or training systems (Sainsbury *et al*, 1989).

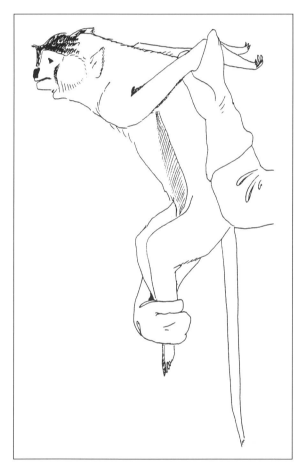

Figure 1
Method of restraint for a macaque-sized monkey.

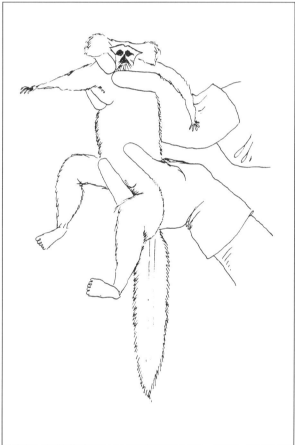

Figure 2
Handling a marmoset in the correct manner.

SEXING

Certain female monkeys resemble males superficially because the lips of the vulva are elongated and appear to be like a prepuce. However, on closer examination they are distinguishable. All primates carry their testes in the scrotum from an early age.

REPRODUCTION

There are wide variations in primate breeding systems and the following authors should be consulted for detailed information: Bearder and Pitts (1987), Hearn (1987), Whitney and Wickings (1987). The Table below gives basic information.

Species	Oestrous/Menstrual cycle (days)	Gestation (days)	Age at puberty (external signs)
Bushbaby	28—49	111—138	—
Marmoset/Tamarin	14—30	128—170	8—18 months
Capuchin	15—22	162—180	3—4 years
Squirrel	7—13	145—182	2.5—3.5 years
Woolly	23—26	139—225	4 years
Macaque	25—32	146—210	3—6 years
Baboon	30—36	154—270	2.5—4 years (sex skin)
Chimpanzee	31—40	210—270	7—10 years (perineal swelling)

DISEASES/CLINICAL CONDITIONS

Many of the conditions described below are zoonoses or potential zoonoses (Brack, 1987). When working with primates one must be aware of the risks involved and maintain stringent hygiene practices, eg. by wearing rubber gloves when handling primates or their tissues. Care must be taken with the disposal of the latter. People with signs of infectious disease should not be allowed to work with primates. A personnel health programme should be considered (Medical Research Council, 1985).

Nutritional bone disease

This is a very common condition in pet monkeys and those young animals that are affected show a predisposition to secondary infection. Nutritional bone disease can be attributed to prolonged deficiencies of calcium or vitamin D or a high ratio of phosphorus compared with calcium in the diet (Fowler, 1986). Either rickets or osteomalacia may occur with or without fibrous osteodystrophy.

Clinical signs

Clinical signs include lethargy, anorexia, pain, inability to jump (often described as 'cage paralysis'), vertebral damage/spinal cord dysfunction, facial deformity and a pliable jaw ('rubber jaw').

Diagnosis

Radiological examination, carried out after careful sedation, may reveal any of the following conditions: pathological fractures, thinning of the cortices, old healed fractures, bowing or folding of bones.

Treatment

The diet will need to be corrected (see Feeding). Where appropriate, intramuscular injections of vitamin D_3 (cholecalciferol)(1,000—3,000iu/kg) should be given every two weeks and sterilized bone flour added to the diet. Ultraviolet emitting fluorescent lamps are useful if animals do not have access to sunlight (Richter et al, 1984). Concurrent disease should be treated and suitable exercise encouraged to develop the limb muscles. Progress should be monitored by a further radiograph after four to six weeks. Surgical treatment of pathological fractures is usually contraindicated. Recovery will be good if the bone loss is not too great (40% of the mineral has been resorbed in bones that appear radiolucent).

Enteric conditions

Diarrhoea

Loose faeces may be passed by primates subjected to stressors or those fed an incorrect diet.

Bacteria. *Shigella* and *Salmonella* spp. are the most important causes of bacterial diarrhoea or dysentery, though recently *Campylobacter fetus* var *jejuni* has been increasingly isolated (Renquist, 1987). All these bacteria are zoonotic and the first two may be present in the carrier state, which must be considered when initiating treatment. Antibiotic treatment should only be attempted following sensitivity tests.

Protozoa. Enteric flagellates often occur in large numbers when primates have diarrhoea. However, they are generally believed to be non-pathogenic and may not be the initiating factor (Frenkel, 1980). Treatment with metronidazole (Flagyl, May and Baker) (20mg/kg for 5 days) may temporarily resolve the condition.

New World primates are particularly susceptible to toxoplasmosis and should not be fed raw meat. Clinical signs are non-specific and may comprise death without prior signs. *Entamoeba histolytica* infection should be considered as a differential diagnosis for diarrhoea in New World monkeys. *Balantidium coli* can cause severe colitis in Old World simians, including humans, but can be found in apparently healthy animals. It can survive in the environment for long periods and is therefore difficult to eradicate.

Helminths. *Strongyloides, Oesophagostomum* and *Trichostrongylus* spp. can cause enteritis. The acanthocephalan worm, *Prosthenorchis,* is common in South American primates and can cause damage to the intestines and occasionally peritonitis. Cockroaches are the intermediate hosts and these should be controlled.

Enterobius vermicularis, the human pinworm, is common and causes peri-anal irritation, digestive problems and diarrhoea. Piperazine (100mg/kg) is an effective treatment but infection may be difficult to eliminate completely.

Of the cestodes, the dwarf tapeworm, *Hymenolepis nana,* is of note because it can have a direct lifecycle and therefore poses greater zoonotic risks.

Treatment of helminths

Nematodes	Fenbendazole 20—50mg/kg orally for 5 days
	Mebendazole 15mg/kg orally for 2 consecutive days or 3mg/kg for 10 consecutive days
	Ivermectin 200µg/kg - single injection
Cestodes	Dichlorophen 0.5g/3kg orally
	Niclosamide (Yomesan, Bayer) 0.5g/4kg orally following 12 hours starvation

In cases where no pathogen is found, diarrhoea may respond to an increase in dietary fibre. Reseeding the gut with *Lactobacillus* spp. by feeding yogurt may also be useful. Toft (1986) should be consulted for a review of primate parasitology.

Chronic colitis. Persistent diarrhoea associated with inflammation of the colon, the cause of which is uncertain, is often reported in marmosets and tamarins (Richter *et al,* 1984). Supportive treatment is indicated but animals frequently fail to recover. In the cotton-top tamarin (*Saguinus oedipus),* chronic colitis has been associated with adenocarcinoma of the colon.

Acute gastric dilatation

The aetiology of this condition is unknown but it has been associated with an overgrowth of *Clostridium perfringens* in the stomach and it occurs principally in macaques. Its prevalence has been reduced by altering feeding practices (Richter *et al,* 1984). The condition is rapidly fatal but may be relieved in early cases by passing a stomach tube.

Intussusception and rectal prolapse

These conditions are not uncommon in primates and are associated with tenesmus and severe diarrhoea. Recurrence of a prolapse can usually be prevented by placing a purse-string suture around the anus.

Tuberculosis

Mycobacterium tuberculosis and *M. bovis* can cause disease in primates. New World primates are much less susceptible than Old World (Martin *et al*, 1986). Atypical mycobacteria can also infect primates (Renquist, 1987; Calle *et al*, 1989).

M. tuberculosis infection runs a course of six months or more, is transmissible to and from humans and can remain occult until it becomes terminal. Diagnosis may be difficult and it is wise in any case of intractable pneumonia, chronic cough or loss of weight to suspect tuberculosis. When a primate has been in contact with a known human case the animal should be kept under close observation for at least six months.

The six months rabies quarantine for mammals (see 'Legislation') will probably eliminate many cases of tuberculosis contracted outside the UK.

Diagnosis can sometimes be confirmed by the use of the tuberculin test in the abdominal skin or the eyelid (Martin *et al*, 1986; Richter *et al*, 1984). Chest radiography is particularly useful in advanced cases which may give false negative results to the tuberculin test. False positive results may result from sensitisation to mycobacteria other than *M. tuberculosis* and *M. bovis* and this is common in orangutans (Calle *et al*, 1989). Laparoscopy may reveal abdominal lesions and should be considered in suspect cases.

Tuberculosis lesions are most commonly found in the lungs, liver and spleen. Treatment is inadvisable.

Pseudotuberculosis (Yersiniosis)

Wild birds and rodents are the reservoir hosts for *Yersinia pseudotuberculosis.* Contaminated food can act as the source of the infection but, where animals are kept outdoors, the whole environment may be contaminated. Vegetables and fruit should be washed before feeding. Stressors may predispose animals to the disease. Clinical signs include loss of condition, anorexia and, sometimes, acute death. Palpation of the abdomen may reveal enlarged lymph nodes and these can be visible on laparoscopy. McClure *et al* (1986) should be consulted for information on culturing *Yersinia.* Treatment with broad-spectrum antibiotics may help if the condition is recognised early enough. Lesions are usually found in the liver and spleen on *post-mortem* examination.

Viral diseases

Rabies

All primates imported into the UK are required to undergo six months quarantine.

Herpesvirus simiae (B virus) infection

This condition is primarily seen in macaques. The clinical signs are rarely serious in non-human primates and usually involve oral vesicles and ulcers. However, it is transmissible to humans (via bites, scratches and handling infected tissue) and is generally fatal. Prevention of transmission to humans requires avoidance of contact with monkeys or their tissues (Centers for Disease Control, 1987; Medical Research Council, 1985, 1989).

Herpesvirus tamarinus (platyrrhinae)

This disease exists subclinically in squirrel monkeys and some other New World monkeys but may be fatal in marmosets and owl monkeys. Therefore, these species should not be housed in the vicinity of each other.

Herpesvirus hominis or *simplex*

Oral lesions ('cold sores') can occur in man, the host species, but more serious disease can develop in owl monkeys, marmosets and apes including cutaneous ulcers, conjunctivitis and encephalitis (Martin *et al,* 1986).

Marburg disease

This is a febrile condition, only to date reported in animals from Africa, which can be fatal in both monkeys and humans (Martin *et al,* 1986).

Viral hepatitis

There are several forms of viral hepatitis; both hepatitis A and B viruses can be transmitted from humans to various species of primates (Martin *et al,* 1986). Hepatitis B can be transmitted via bites and contact with body fluids and excreta. Vaccination against hepatitis B is possible for humans at risk, eg. zoo keepers. Hepatitis A is probably spread by the faecal oral route and is usually asymptomatic in non-human primates.

Measles

Measles occurs commonly in most types of primates but it can be asymptomatic. Mortalities are more frequent in New World monkeys. Clinical signs can include nasal discharge, cough, pneumonia (secondary bacterial), rash, facial oedema and diarrhoea. Vaccination can be considered (Welshman,1989).

Myxovirus infections (Common cold)

This is usually self-limiting but secondary bacterial infection may develop, leading to severe respiratory signs. Therefore, prophylactic antibiotic therapy may be useful.

Retrovirus infections

These have been increasingly reported in non-human primates (Lowenstine and Lerche, 1988). There is no evidence that they are communicable to humans but precautions against infection should be taken and testing of pet and zoo animals should be considered.

Miscellaneous

Fractures

These may occur as a result of nutritional bone disease (see earlier), in which case correction of the diet is the first, and frequently the only, requirement. Internal fixation is preferable to external since primates will quickly remove the latter. Well aligned fractures often heal well and rapidly, even if no fixation is performed.

Dental conditions

Dental disease is common in primates and is probably exacerbated by the feeding of sugary foods. Canine tooth root abscesses produce facial swellings in marmosets and in these cases, the canine should be removed. Abnormal tooth root eruption and 'floating teeth' in the jaw are usually secondary to nutritional bone disease.

Extraction of canine teeth to prevent injury to the owner is a mutilation for which there is no justification, but it is frequently requested.

Soft tissue injuries

Suturing of wounds may be tempting but even deep gaping wounds are best cleaned and left to heal. Regular irrigation may be advisable. Monkeys quickly remove sutures, especially those on the limbs. Bandaging wounds or placing other sutures in more accessible parts of the body may help.

Wasting marmoset syndrome (WMS)

Marmosets may lose weight for many reasons, but there appears to be a syndrome characterised by loss of weight, weakness and lethargy in which animals are frequently anaemic, hypoalbuminaemic (Richter *et al,* 1984) and have a high incidence of Heinz bodies in their erythrocytes (Hawkey *et al,* 1982). Treatment with anabolic steroids, antibiotics, vitamins (particularly vitamin E) and iron, coupled with nursing and hand-feeding, may help but cases are often unrewarding.

Infant mortality

This is frequently attributable to maternal neglect and is common in marmosets, tamarins and apes (Graham and Bowen, 1985; Sainsbury, 1987). Captive marmosets and tamarins often produce triplets but usually only two are reared. Hand-rearing is possible in most primates and suitable regimes are available (Anderson, 1986; Kirkwood and Stathatos, in preparation) but it is labour-intensive and can lead to behavioural abnormalities.

Skin conditions

External parasites and mycotic infections are rare (Migaki, 1986; Toft, 1986).

Deceptive situations

1. Accumulations of food in the cheek pouches are normal in certain species, eg. macaques, but owners often suspect oral disease.

2. Oedematous swelling and bright colouration of the perineal region are normal signs of oestrus in some species.

3. Primates are able to disguise clinical signs of ill-health; if signs are evident, then the prognosis should generally be guarded.

4. Primates are potentially dangerous animals, even if apparently reliable with their owners; this cannot be over-emphasised. Most species are covered by the Dangerous Wild Animals Act 1976 (as amended by The Dangerous Wild Animals Act 1976 (Modification) Order 1984) (see 'Legislation').

ADMINISTRATION OF DRUGS

Drugs can often be given hidden in food or mixed with a flavoured drink. This technique may be successful initially but primates quickly learn to reject substances on the basis of taste, the time of administration or the person involved. If different vehicles are used, the time of administration varied and the vehicles given at other times, without the drug, oral dosing can be successful.

Injections can be given as follows:

a) Intramuscular using the arms or legs (gastrocnemius or quadriceps muscles).

b) Intravenous using the brachial (radial) vein near the elbow or the recurrent tarsal (saphenous) vein on the laterocaudal aspect of the leg. Intravenous injections are difficult in marmosets and tamarins but may be possible in the femoral vein.

BLOOD SAMPLING

Of the veins mentioned earlier, the femoral vein is the most satisfactory for taking blood. The animal should be laid on its back and the femoral pulse identified by palpation. The vein is caudal and deep to the artery. The formation of haematomas is a potential problem following femoral sampling and appropriate digital pressure should be applied after needle withdrawal.

Many laboratories will not accept primate material for examination because of health risks so clinical and pathological specimens should never be submitted without prior consultation.

ANAESTHESIA

Chemical restraint

Ketamine hydrochloride (Vetalar, Parke-Davis)

A dose of between 5 and 15mg/kg i/m will produce restraint sufficient for handling, clinical examination etc. The dose varies with the species and temperament of the animal but ketamine has a wide safety margin (Sedgwick, 1986). Onset of sedation takes 2—10 minutes and the duration is 10—15 minutes depending on the species and the size of the animal.

Alphaxalone/alphadolone (Saffan, Coopers Pitman-Moore)

The volume required limits intramuscular use in larger animals but Saffan is useful by this route in marmosets and squirrel monkeys; 8mg/kg i/m will give light sedation; 12—18mg/kg gives deep sedation to light surgical anaesthesia. The duration of sedation is greater than for ketamine. The intravenous route can be used (see later).

Surgical anaesthesisa

Inhalation agents

Endotracheal intubation should be used in preference to a mask but the anatomy of some species makes the procedure difficult (Brancker, 1985). Primates have a short neck and so care must be taken to ensure that the tube does not reach the tracheal bifurcation (Green, 1979). Primates should be sedated prior to the use of a mask to avoid unnecessary excitement.

Halothane is the most commonly used inhalation agent. **Isoflurane** (Forane, Abbott) has potential though expense may preclude its use.

Alphaxalone/alphadolone

This agent is best given intravenously (10—12mg/kg) with incremental doses as necessary, but a suitable vein may be difficult to find in small species such as marmosets where it can be given intramuscularly (18—25mg/kg). Alternatively, small doses of alphaxalone/alphadolone can be administered intravenously to deepen animals sedated with ketamine.

Ketamine

Ketamine (20—40mg/kg i/m) supplemented with midazolam (Hypnovel, Roche) (0.5mg/kg i/m) or xylazine (Rompun, Bayer) (0.5mg/kg i/m) will provide anaesthesia sufficient for minor surgery (Sainsbury *et al,* 1989). Atropine is a useful premedicant (0.01—0.05mg/kg i/m) to reduce salivation and the possibility of vomiting.

Propofol (Rapinovet, Coopers Pitman-Moore)

Propofol (5—10mg/kg) will provide short-term surgical anaesthesia (10—20 minutes) but must be given intravenously.

Recovery

Warmth is necessary, especially for small monkeys. If a heated pad is used it is important to keep it out of reach as the monkey wakes up. Climbing should be discouraged by placing the animal in a small cage until it has fully recovered. Large animals should be given a deep cushion of straw. Analgesia can be provided by buprenorphine (Temgesic, Reckitt and Colman) (0.01mg/kg i/m every 8—12 hours) or pethidine (2—4mg/kg i/m every 3 to 4 hours). Both buprenorphine and pethidine are covered by the Misuse of Drugs Regulations 1985 (see 'Legislation'). It is preferable to return social primates to their group as soon as possible.

Acknowledgements

I should like to thank Dr. J. K. Kirkwood for commenting on the manuscript, Miss S. Elmhurst for producing the figures and *The Veterinary Record,* Mr J.E.Cooper and Mr B.D.Eaton for permission to reproduce them.

REFERENCES

ANDERSON, J. H. (1986). Rearing and intensive care of neonatal and infant non-human primates. In: *Primates: The Road to Self-Sustaining Populations.* (Ed. K.Benirschke) Springer-Verlag, New York.

BEARDER, S. and PITTS, R. S. (1987). Prosimians and tree shrews. In: *The UFAW Handbook on the Care and Management of Laboratory Animals.* 6th Edn. (Ed. T. B. Poole) Longman, Harlow.

BRACK, M. (1987). *Agents Transmissible from Simians to Man.* Springer-Verlag, Berlin.

BRANCKER, W. M. (1985). Primates. In: *Manual of Exotic Pets.* Revised Edn. (Eds. J. E. Cooper, M. F. Hutchison, O. F. Jackson and R. J. Maurice) BSAVA, Cheltenham.

CALLE, P. P., THOEN, C. O. and ROSKOP, A. H. T. (1989). Tuberculin skin test responses, mycobacteriologic examinations of gastric lavage and serum enzyme-linked immunosorbent assays in orangutans (*Pongo pygmaeus*). *Journal of Zoo and Wildlife Medicine* **20** (3), 307.

CENTERS FOR DISEASE CONTROL (1987). Guidelines for prevention of *Herpesvirus simiae* (B virus) infection in monkey handlers. *Morbidity and Mortality Weekly Report* **36**, 680.

FOWLER, M. E. (1986). Metabolic bone disease. In: *Zoo and Wild Animal Medicine.* 2nd Edn. (Ed. M. E. Fowler) W. B. Saunders, Philadelphia.

FRENKEL, J. K. (1980). Protozoan diseases of zoo and captive mammals and birds. In: *The Comparative Pathology of Zoo Animals.* (Eds. R. J. Montali and G. Migaki) Smithsonian Institution Press, Washington DC.

GRAHAM, C. E. and BOWEN, J. A. (1985). Eds. *Clinical Management of Infant Great Apes.* Alan R. Liss Inc., New York.

GREEN, C. J. (1979). *Animal Anaesthesia.* Laboratory Animals, London.

HAWKEY, C. M., HART, M. G. and JONES, D. M. (1982). Clinical hematology of the common marmoset *(Callithrix jacchus).* *American Journal of Primatology* **3**, 179.

HEARN, J. P. (1987). Marmosets and tamarins. In: *The UFAW Handbook on the Care and Management of Laboratory Animals.* 6th Edn. (Ed. T. B. Poole) Longman, Harlow.

KIRKWOOD, J. K. and STATHATOS, K. (in preparation). *Biology and Rearing of Primates in Captivity.*

LAPIN, B. A., CHERKOVICH, G. M., KUKSOVA, M. I. and ANNENKOV, G. A. (1972). Biological normals. In: *Pathology of Simian Primates.* (Ed. R. N. T-W. Fiennes) Karger, Basel.

LOWENSTINE, L. J. and LERCHE, N. W. (1988). Retrovirus infections of non-human primates: a review. *Journal of Zoo Animal Medicine* **19**, (4), 168.

MARTIN, D. P., OTT-JOSLIN, J. E. and LOEB, W. (1986). Primates. In: *Zoo and Wild Animal Medicine.* 2nd Edn. (Ed. M. E. Fowler) W. B.Saunders, Philadelphia.

MARTIN, R. D. (1990). *Primate Origins and Evolution.* Chapman and Hall, London.

McCLURE, H. M., BRODIE, A. R., ANDERSON, D. C. and SWENSON, R. B. (1986). Bacterial infections of non-human primates. In: *Primates: The Road to Self-Sustaining Populations.* (Ed. K. Benirschke) Springer-Verlag, New York.

MEDICAL RESEARCH COUNCIL (1985). *The Management of Simians in Relation to Infectious Hazards to Staff.* Medical Research Council, London.

MEDICAL RESEARCH COUNCIL (1989). *Addendum to the MRC Statement on the Management of Simians.* Medical Research Council, London.

MIGAKI, G. (1986). Mycotic infections of non-human primates. In: *Primates: The Road to Self-Sustaining Populations.* (Ed. K.Benirschke) Springer-Verlag, New York.

NATIONAL RESEARCH COUNCIL (1978). *Nutrient Requirements of Domestic Animals: 14 Nutritional Requirements of Non-human Primates.* National Academy of Sciences, Washington DC.

POOLE, T. B. (1988). Behaviour, housing and welfare of non-human primates. In: *New Developments in the Biosciences: their Implications for Laboratory Animal Science.* (Eds. A.C.Beynon and H.A.Solleveld) Martinus Nijhoff Publishers, Dordrecht.

RENQUIST, D. M. (1987). Selected biohazards of naturally infected non-human primates. *Journal of Medical Primatology* **16,** 91.

RICHTER, C. B., LEHNER, N. D. M. and HENRICKSON, R. V. (1984). Primates. In: *Laboratory Animal Medicine.* (Eds. J. G. Fox, B. J. Cohen and F. M. Loew) Academic Press, New York.

SAINSBURY, A. W. (1987). Reducing infant mortality in marmosets. *Proceedings of a British Veterinary Zoological Society Meeting, 14th November 1987.* Winchester.

SAINSBURY, A. W., EATON, B. D. and COOPER, J. E. (1989). Restraint and anaesthesia of primates. *Veterinary Record* **125,** 640.

SEDGWICK, C. J. (1986) Scaling and anesthesia for primates. In: *Primates: The Road to Self-Sustaining Populations.* (Ed. K. Benirschke) Springer-Verlag, New York.

SEGAL, E. F.(1989). Ed. *Housing, Care and Psychological Wellbeing of Captive and Laboratory Primates.* Noyes Publications, New Jersey.

TOFT, J. D. (1986). The pathoparasitology of non-human primates: a review. In: *Primates: The Road to Self-Sustaining Populations.* (Ed. K. Benirschke) Springer-Verlag, New York.

ULLREY, D. E. (1986). Nutrition of primates in captivity. In: *Primates: The Road to Self-Sustaining Populations.* (Ed. K.Benirschke) Springer-Verlag, New York.

WELSHMAN, M. D. (1989). Measles in the cynomolgus monkey *(Macaca fascicularis). Veterinary Record* **124,** 184.

WHITNEY, R. A. and WICKINGS, E. J. (1987). Macaques and other Old World simians. In: *The UFAW Handbook on the Care and Management of Laboratory Animals.* 6th Edn. (Ed. T. B. Poole) Longman, Harlow.

FURTHER READING

DUKELOW, W. R. and ERWIN, J. (1986). Eds. *Reproduction and Development. Comparative Primate Biology Vol.3.* Alan R. Liss Inc., New York.

FIENNES, R. (1967). *Zoonoses of Primates.* Cornell University Press, Ithaca.

FIENNES, R. (1972). *Pathology of Simian Primates.* Karger, Basel.

GRAHAM, C. E. (1981). Ed. *Reproductive Biology of the Great Apes.* Academic Press, London.

HIME, J. M. and O'DONOGHUE, P. N. (1979). Eds. *Handbook of Diseases of Laboratory Animals.* Heinemann Veterinary Books, London.

KALTER, S. S. (1986). Overview of simian viruses and recognized virus diseases and laboratory support for the diagnosis of viral infections. In: *Primates: The Road to Self-Sustaining Populations.* (Ed. K. Benirschke) Springer-Verlag, New York.

PRIMATE SOCIETY OF GREAT BRITAIN (1987). *The Welfare of Pet Marmosets.* Universities Federation for Animal Welfare, Potters Bar.

RUCH, T. C. (1967). *Diseases of Laboratory Primates.* W. B. Saunders, Philadelphia.

WHITNEY, R. A. (1979). Primate medicine and husbandry. Symposium on non-domestic pet medicine. *Veterinary Clinics of North America* **9,** 429.

CHAPTER TWELVE

WILD MAMMALS

James K Kirkwood BVSc PhD MRCVS

Attitudes to wild animals have changed dramatically in recent years. There is widespread concern for the welfare and conservation of species that were once considered to be, at one end of the spectrum, best left to get on with it, and at the other, pests, competitors, or outright dangers to be eradicated whenever possible. Opinions still differ widely. For example, the treatment and rehabilitation of foxes are thought to be as irresponsible and reprehensible by some, as not to do so is by others.

This chapter concerns animals that are neither 'exotic' nor 'pets' and the author has stretched the definition of 'manual' too. It is usual in a manual to concentrate on the methods rather than the rationale for doing the task. However, since the methods of treatment and care of wild animals are the same in principle as those for domestic mammals and, in practice, the most difficult questions for a veterinary surgeon asked to treat a sick or injured wild animal concern the ethics and rationale for doing so, it seemed appropriate to begin the chapter with some notes about these issues.

There are about 90 species of wild mammal resident in the UK and the coastal waters. Knowledge of the diseases of these animals is patchy. Many parasites of wild mammals have been classified but their role as potential causes of disease have rarely been studied. Nevertheless, the literature on the diseases of British wild mammals is extensive and there is room in this manual for only a rather idiosyncratic selection of notes on the diseases, medicine and rehabilitation of the more common species. Also included are brief notes on some of the physiological and ecological characteristics.

Treatment and rehabilitation of wild animals — rationale, ethics and some general comments

With a few exceptions the treatment and rehabilitation of wild mammals in the UK is unlikely to have had a significant effect on population sizes and is unlikely to do so for the foreseeable future. There are possible exceptions (Yalden, 1986); for example, the otter population of parts of East Anglia has been reinforced by releases (Jefferies et al, 1986) and it has been estimated that, even before the morbillivirus outbreak in 1988, 20% of the common seals in the Wadden Sea had been released from Dutch rescue centres over the previous 15 years (Harwood and Reijnders, 1988). From a conservation standpoint, habitat protection is usually more relevant than rehabilitation. From the welfare point of view, however, it is argued that since many rescued wild animals have been injured as a result of human activities, eg. driving cars, we have a responsibility to intervene.

The ethical aspects of wild animal rehabilitation have been given some preliminary consideration by the British Wildlife Rehabilitation Council and their publication on this subject is reproduced in Appendix 1 (see also Cooper, 1989). The International Union for the Conservation of Nature (IUCN) guidelines concerning reintroductions and translocations are also relevant to aspects of rehabilitation (IUCN, 1989).

The treatment of sick and injured wild mammals rests on the same principles as the treatment of domestic ones, although special consideration may have to be given to restraint and husbandry. In many cases the difficulty of successful rehabilitation is the bottleneck in the process. There are few statistics on the survival of rehabilitated mammals and little published information on the techniques for mammals which occur in the UK (but see Harris, 1989; Walsh and Stebbings, 1989) or elsewhere (Ludwig, 1982; Evans and Evans, 1985; Haufler, 1985; Ludwig and Mikolajczak, 1985a,b; Odell, 1985).

There is a growing number of wild animal rescue and rehabilitation centres. Some of these operate with very little veterinary assistance. It is likely that the wild animal treatment and rehabilitation industry will grow and this offers the opportunity for contributions to knowledge of wild animal pathology, medicine and husbandry.

Legal aspects

Many wild species are protected by laws restricting their taking, killing or injuring. In addition to the Wildlife and Countryside Act 1981, which covers many species, there is legislation concerned with particular species, eg. the Badgers Act 1973 and the Deer Act 1963. It is permissible, however, to take sick or injured individuals of protected species for treatment as long as the intention is to return them to the wild when they are fit for release, or for humane destruction if they are beyond recovery (Cooper and Sinclair, 1989). Some legal aspects are briefly mentioned in the following sections, but Cooper (1987) provides a thorough account of the legislation (see also 'Legislation').

INSECTIVORES

There are seven species of the Order Insectivora resident in the UK. The greater and lesser white-toothed shrews *(Crocidura russula* and *Crocidura suaveolens)* are confined to the Channel Islands and the Scilly Isles respectively. Their biology is broadly similar to that of the other shrews and they will not be described here. The ranges of the mole, common shrew, pygmy shrew and water shrew cover most of England, Scotland and Wales, but of these only the pygmy shrew is found in Ireland. Brief notes on the biology of the other four species are provided in Table 1. The hedgehog *(Erinaceus europaeus)* is covered in another chapter (see 'Hedgehogs').

Table 1
Insectivores.

Common name	Mole	Common shrew	Pygmy shrew	Water shrew
Scientific name	*Talpa europaea*	*Sorex araneus*	*Sorex minutus*	*Neomys fodiens*
Food	Earthworms, insects, molluscs.	Earthworms, beetles, other invertebrates.	Small invertebrates.	
Male weight (g)	110	7—10	2.5—5	10—15
Female weight (g)	85	7—10	2.5—5	10—15
Gestation (days)	28	13—19	20	20
Birth season	May-Jun	Spring-summer	Apr-Aug	Apr-Sept
Litter size	3—4	5—7	4—7	3—8
Neonate weight (g)	3.5	0.5	0.25	0.6
Lactation (days)	28—35			22—37
Weaning (days)		22	22	Begins 24 days.
Development	Fur appears 14 days. Eyes open 22 days.		2.5g by 14 days.	Eyes open 22 days, leave nest 24 days.

Sources of data: Corbet and Southern (1977); Michalak (1987).

Parasites

Fleas, ticks and mites are common. A variety of internal parasites has been described, including *Hyogonimus* species of trematodes in the mole and the nematode *Porrocaecum talpae* which is commonly found coiled in the subcutaneous tissues of the common shrew (Corbet and Southern, 1977). The pathogenicity of these parasites is unknown.

Infectious diseases

Rankin and McDiarmid (1968) in a survey of 550 common shrews found a 1.4% prevalence of *Mycobacterium tuberculosis* var *muris.*

Anaesthesia

Because of the small size and therefore rapid rates of respiration and metabolism in these animals anaesthesia is likely to be induced very rapidly using inhalation agents and the concentration of these needs to be carefully controlled. At a given halothane concentration, induction (or overdose) will occur in about one tenth of the time for a 20kg dog. The problems of size-scaling for inhalation anaesthesia of small animals have been described by Sedgwick, (1986). The author is not aware of any literature on the use of injectable anaesthetic agents in these species.

Husbandry

Moles and shrews have been maintained successfully in captivity (Michalak, 1987; Dryden, 1975; Rudge, 1966). Shrews have been kept in open-topped plastic boxes covered with wire mesh, and with a substrate of sand, peat, and dry leaves. A diet of mixed beef offal (30%), fish (10%), rabbit or chicken (30%), egg (10%) and sprouted wheat grain (10%), supplemented with mealworms, was used successfully by Michalak (1987).

Neonatal care

Some data on the milk composition of the water shrew and the greater white-toothed shrew are listed in Appendix 2. It appears that the milk of these animals has a high dry matter content and is very rich in fat. Hand-rearing a shrew would present a considerable challenge. Esbilac (Pet-Ag Inc, Illinois) would perhaps be a suitable replacer (see Appendix 3).

Therapy

These small insectivores have very rapid metabolic rates and this must be taken into account in any therapy that requires repeated doses (Pokras *et al,* 1991). In drugs, the clearance of which is related to metabolic rate, for example oxytetracycline, penicillin, gentamicin and other antibiotics, plasma half-life tends to decrease with decreasing size (roughly in proportion to the 1/4 power of bodyweight) (Kirkwood, 1983; Kirkwood and Widdowson, 1990; Kirkwood and Merriam, 1990). It follows that, all else being equal, an adult pygmy shrew is likely to need dosing about 10 times more frequently per day than a 20kg dog. (Furthermore, it may be that a 12 hour course of antibiotics in a shrew is equivalent to a 5 day course in a 20kg dog.)

BATS

There are 15 species of bats (Order Chiroptera) resident in the south of England but only two or three species have ranges extending to the north of Scotland (pipistrelle, common long-eared bat and Daubenton's bat). Brief notes on the biology of five of the more common species are provided in Table 2. Further general information on bat biology is provided by Yalden and Morris (1975). All bats are protected under the Wildlife and Countryside Act, 1981 (see 'Legislation').

Parasites

External parasites are common (Corbet and Southern, 1977). Chlorinated hydrocarbons are very toxic to bats and Racey (1987) has suggested pyrethrum for external parasite treatment. Ivermectin (Ivomec, MSD) has been found to be safe in a very wide range of species of animals (at a dose rate of 200µg/kg) and it is quite likely to be safe in bats either orally or by subcutaneous injection.

Table 2
Bats.

Common name	Natterer's bat	Daubenton's bat	Noctule	Pipistrelle	Common long-eared
Scientific name	*Myotis nattereri*	*M. daubentonii*	*Nyctalus noctula*	*Pipistrellus pipistrellus*	*Plecotus auritus*
Roosts	Hollow trees, buildings, caves in winter.	(as for Natterer's)	Trees	Buildings, trees.	Buildings, trees.
Weight (g)	7—12	6—12	20—40	4.5—8	6—12
Gestation (days)	c50	c50	c70	c44	
Births	Jun-Jul		Jun-Jul	Jun-Aug	
Litter size	l		1—2	1 occ 2	1
Development	Blind at birth, flight 21 days, adult size 42 days.	As Natterer's.	As Natterer's	As Natterer's.	As Natterer's.

Sources of data: Corbet and Southern (1977); Walsh and Stebbings (1989).

Anaesthesia

Halothane and oxygen can be used for anaesthesia. Induction is rapid because of the high respiratory rate and the concentration of anaesthetic gas should be carefully controlled (see note about anaesthesia of insectivores).

Torpor can be induced by cooling but this may be stressful and may not affect sensitivity to pain. It is not recommended as a technique for restraint for surgical procedures.

Husbandry

A variety of species of insectivorous bats has been maintained successfully in captivity (Kleiman, 1969; Racey and Kleiman, 1970; Racey, 1970 and 1987; Walsh and Stebbings, 1989). Walsh and Stebbings (1989) recommended small wooden cages with a smaller dark roost. The internal walls should be lined with plastic mesh to provide grip and the floor can be lined with newspaper. The wood and plastic should be untreated and weathered.

Mealworms have been used as the main part of the diet and can be supplemented with insects. Walsh and Stebbings (1989) reported the addition of the mineral and vitamin supplement Vionate (Ciba-Geigy) at a rate of 1mg/g bodyweight daily.

Neonatal care

Data on the composition of the milk of insectivorous bats are scarce. The milks of the UK species are likely to be similar to those of the North American species that have been analysed (Huibregtse, 1966; Jenness and Sloan, 1975). These results indicate a wide variation between species (which may be an artifact), a dry matter content of 12—40%, and fat, protein and carbohydrate forming about 40%, 33% and 20% (8—45)% of the dry matter respectively. Cow's milk has been used to feed juveniles from two weeks of age but failed to support the growth of neonates (Constantine, 1986). A replacer containing a higher proportion of fat, eg. Esbilac (see Appendix 3), would probably be more suitable.

Therapy

The dramatic reduction in metabolic rate in torpor during the day is likely to reduce the clearance rate of drugs. It is probably wise to avoid those with known toxic side effects, eg. gentamicin, if possible.

Walsh and Stebbings (1989) considered that minor holes in the wing membranes and fractures of one phalanx do not warrant treatment and have often seen repaired fractures in wild bats. Tears involving the edge of the wing membrane are reported to be impossible to suture (Walsh and Stebbings, 1989).

Rehabilitation

Juveniles which are too young to fly should be placed as near to the roost as possible, where they may be picked up by their mothers (Walsh and Stebbings, 1989). Walsh and Stebbings (1989) considered that, if juveniles are not successfully returned to their mothers, they can never be returned to the wild because there is no way of providing the necessary training for finding and catching food and finding suitable roosts. In a study of many ringed bats Stebbings (cited in Walsh and Stebbings, 1989) reported that very few bats that had been in captivity for more than a few days were subsequently recovered in the wild. Walsh and Stebbings (1989) strongly argued that bats that have been in captivity for over 20 days should not be released and that it would be cruel to do so.

LAGOMORPHS

Three species of the Order Lagomorpha are resident in the UK: rabbit, brown hare and blue or mountain hare. The rabbit is found throughout the UK. The brown hare has a wide distribution in England, Wales and Lowland Scotland, and the blue hare occurs in Ireland and the Highlands of Scotland. Some notes on the biology of these species are provided in Table 3 and sources of further general information include Corbet and Southern (1977) and McBride (1988). All are herbivorous. The hares are surface-dwellers, the rabbit commonly uses burrows.

Table 3
Lagomorphs.

Common name	Rabbit	Brown hare	Blue hare
Scientific name	*Oryctolagus cuniculus*	*Lepus capensis*	*Lepus timidus*
Food	Herbage	Herbage	Herbage
Male (kg)	1.5	3.5	2.7
Female (kg)	1.5	3.7	2.9
Births	Jan-Aug with a minimum of 30 days between litters.	Jan-Aug with a minimum of 30 days between litters.	Jan-Aug with a minimum of 30 days between litters.
Gestation (days)	30	42	
Litter size	3—7	2—3	2—3
Neonate (g)	30	110	
Lactation (days)	24		
Weaning (days)	21—28		
Development	Eyes open 7 days. Leave nest 18 days.	Precocial. Eyes open at birth.	As brown hare.

Source of data: Corbet and Southern (1977).

Parasites

The sucking lice *Haemodipsus ventricosus* is found on rabbits and *Haemodipsus lyrocephalus* is found on hares. The flea *Spilopsyllus* is found on all three and is responsible for transmission of myxomatosis in rabbits. Internal parasites include *Graphidium stigosum* in the stomachs of all three species and the intestinal nematode *Trichostrongylus retortiformis* (Corbet and Southern, 1977). Parasite burdens increase during myxomatosis outbreaks (Boag, 1988). Neither body condition nor fecundity was found to be related to intensity of infection with *Trichostrongylus* in hares (Iason and Boag, 1988).

Infectious diseases

Coccidiosis due to *Eimeria stiedae* is a very common disease in young wild rabbits. Although the infection can cause considerable liver damage, mortality does not appear to be high (McDiarmid, 1962).

Infection with *Yersinia pseudotuberculosis* is common in hares (Mair, 1968). It can cause pyaemia with widespread necrotic foci and is a significant cause of mortality (McDiarmid, 1962).

In the three years after its introduction into the UK myxomatosis killed about 99% of rabbits, and this led to declines in the populations of stoats, buzzards and (indirectly) tawny owls (Ross, 1982). Since then, although the virus has become more virulent, the level of genetic resistance to the disease has increased and mortality during epizootics varies from 4—14% in spring and summer, but can be much higher in winter (Ross, 1982).

European brown hare syndrome is a recently discovered disease that has been observed in several European countries and was first reported in the UK in 1990 (Chasey and Duff, 1990). It mainly affects brown hares but blue hares are also susceptible. It causes acute and severe liver damage, nephrosis and neurological disturbances, and is thought to have a viral aetiology (Gavier and Morner, 1989).

Anaesthesia

(See 'Rabbits').

Husbandry

The husbandry of wild rabbits and hares, their handling, feeding and accommodation can be based on methods used for domestic rabbits (Vaughan, 1987).

Neonatal care

Information on the composition of the milks of British lagomorphs is given in Appendix 2. The milks have a high dry matter content (31—40%) and are rich in fat (46—49% of dry matter). Bogue (1979) suggested KMR (Pet-Ag Inc, Illinois) for feeding infant rabbits and Oftedal (1980) suggested Esbilac and noted that egg-yolk could be added to increase the protein and fat content. Esbilac with added Multi-Milk (Pet-Ag Inc, Illinois) may be a useful replacer (see Appendix 3). Rabbits are difficult to rear artificially. They are fed once daily by their mothers in a nursing period lasting just a few minutes. Hares are much more precocial at birth. The successful hand-rearing of a brown hare has been described by French (1989a).

Therapy

(See 'Rabbits').

SQUIRRELS

The grey squirrel became established in the UK after multiple introductions beginning in 1876 and its range now covers most of England and Wales and parts of Scotland. The red squirrel was formerly found throughout the UK but its range has contracted and only scattered populations remain in England and Wales. Brief notes on these species are given in Table 4: further information on the general biology can be obtained from Corbet and Southern (1977), Holm (1987) and Gurney (1987). The grey squirrel is considered by many to be a pest and it is illegal to import, release, or keep in captivity except under licence from the Ministry of Agriculture (see 'Legislation'). Red squirrels are protected under the Wildlife and Countryside Act, 1981, and it is illegal to disturb, capture, or harm them.

Parasites

McDiarmid (1962) considered that *Capillaria* infestations were the cause of many grey squirrel deaths. A variety of external parasites occur including the fleas *Monopsyllus sciurorum* (of red) and *Orchopeas howardi* (of grey), and sucking lice (Corbet and Southern, 1977). Reports of *Sarcoptes* may be erroneous (Keymer, 1983).

Infectious diseases

Coccidial infections are common. Red squirrels examined at the Zoological Society of London have frequently been found to be excreting coccidial oocysts (*Eimeria* spp.) whilst showing no signs of ill health, but the infection can cause disease (Keymer, 1983). A review of other infectious diseases is given by Keymer (1983). Nutritional bone disease has been recorded in a free-living red squirrel which frequently fed from a bird table (Keymer and Hime, 1977).

Table 4
Squirrels.

Common name	Red	Grey
Scientific name	*Sciurus vulgaris*	*Sciurus carolinensis*
Food	Seeds, especially cones and foliage.	Seeds and foliage.
Male (g)	280	515
Female (g)	280	515
Births	Breed mainly spring and summer.	
Gestation	c. 38 days	42—45 days
Litter size	3(1—6)	3(1—7)
Neonate (g)	10—15	13—17
Lactation	7—10 weeks	7—10 weeks
Weaning	8—10 weeks (160g)	8—10 weeks (210g)
Development	Hairs erupt 8 days, lower incisors erupt 20—25 days, eyes open 28—32 days (50g), upper incisors 37—41 days, begin solids 7 weeks.	Hairs erupt 10 days, lower incisors erupt 21 days, eyes open 28—35 days (90g), upper incisors 37—41 days, begin solids 7 weeks.

Source of data: Corbet and Southern (1977).

Parapoxvirus infection, a disease characterised by slight bilateral ocular discharge, nasal discharge, stomatitis, pneumonia, and patchy alopecia, has been observed in red squirrels (Vizoso, 1969; Keymer, 1983). A virus has been isolated from a lesion in an affected animal (Sands *et al*, 1984). The epidemiology of the disease is unknown but evidence that it occurred in some locations prior to invasion by grey squirrels counters the suggestion that grey squirrels may have introduced it (Keymer, 1983).

Anaesthesia

There are few specific data on anaesthesia of squirrels. Lumb and Jones (1984) state that ketamine (10—20mg/kg i/m) can be used for immobilisation and that halothane or methoxyflurane are suitable by inhalation.

Neonatal care

Some data on the composition of the milk of the grey squirrel are given in Appendix 2. The milk has a high dry matter and fat content. Although young squirrels have been reared, at least during the later stages, using human milk replacers, formulae containing a higher percentage of fat, such as Esbilac or Lamlac (Volac), may be preferable (Anon in Taylor and Bietz, 1985). Babies have been kept in cardboard boxes filled with a nest of hay and kept warm with a hot water bottle, and Holm (1987) has provided an account of the techniques.

Therapy

Drugs suitable for use in rats are likely to be safe for use at similar dose rates in squirrels. Adverse effects to antibiotics in squirrels have not been noted by the author, but this is a possibility that should be borne in mind (Clark and Olfert, 1986).

Rehabilitation

Ten adult red squirrels were released singly or in pairs from a cage in which they had spent the summer acclimatising to the environment of London Zoo. Food hoppers were provided in surrounding trees and the squirrels quickly found them. The animals were tracked using radiotelemetry. Although initial rehabilitation was quite successful the animals failed to establish and breed (Bertram and Moltu, 1986).

VOLES

The three species of voles for which brief data are provided in Table 5 are all widely distributed in England, Scotland and Wales. The fourth British vole, *Microtus arvalis,* occurs only on Guernsey and the Orkneys.

Table 5
Voles.

Common name	Bank vole	Field vole	Water vole
Scientific name	*Clethrionomys glareolus*	*Microtus agrestis*	*Arvicola terrestris*
Food	Varied, eg. leaves, fruits, seeds, fungi.	Leaves and stems of grasses.	Grasses and other plants.
Male (g)	20	37	150—300
Female (g)	15	30	150—300
Births	Multiple April to September	Multiple April to September	1—3 litters/year Spring and summer
Gestation (days)	17—22		20—22
Litter size	3—5	4—6	about 5
Neonate wt (g)	2	2	5
Lactation	18 days		
Weaning (days)	14—28 Eyes open 12 days.	18	14 Eyes open 8 days.

Sources of data: Corbet and Southern (1977); Baker and Clarke (1987).

Parasites

Voles are hosts to a wide range and often large numbers of ectoparasites, including fleas, lice, ticks and mites (Corbet and Southern, 1977; Blackmore and Owen, 1968; Healing and Nowell, 1985). There is also an extensive literature on internal parasites (see papers cited above) but the impact of these on the host's health and population dynamics has received little attention (Healing and Nowell, 1985).

Infectious diseases

Lesions caused by infection with *Mycobacterium tuberculosis* var *muris* were found in 20% of over 4,000 voles examined (Wells, 1937 cited by Rankin and McDiarmid, 1968). *Mycobacterium bovis* was not found in any of 875 individuals examined by the Ministry of Agriculture, Fisheries and Food (1987). Leptospirosis may be a common subclinical disease because serological evidence of infection is frequent and leptospires were cultured from the blood of 11 out of 51 bank voles and 5 out of 86 field voles (Twigg *et al,* 1968).

Anaesthesia

Baker and Clarke (1987) found alphaxalone/alphadolone (Saffan, Coopers Pitman-Moore) (0.1 ml/kg i/p) to be an excellent agent for bank and field voles. Because of the high respiratory and metabolic rates of these small rodents the concentration of inhalation agents should be controlled carefully.

Husbandry

Bank and field voles adapt well to captivity and have been maintained under laboratory conditions. They can be fed on whole oats, meadow hay, chopped carrots and a rodent pellet (Baker and Clarke, 1987).

Neonatal care

A meadow vole, *Microtus pennsylvanicus,* an American species closely related to the bank and field voles, was successfully reared using Esbilac (see Appendix 3) (Moore, 1985).

Therapy

In the absence of specific information, therapeutic regimes found to be safe and effective in the mouse may provide a starting point. Antibiotics should be used with caution as several have been found to cause fatal disturbances to gut flora in other small rodent herbivores (see 'Rats and Mice').

MICE AND RATS

There are four species of mouse and two species of rat that occur in the UK: wood mouse (*Apodemus sylvaticus*), yellow-necked mouse (*Apodemus flavicollis*), harvest mouse (*Micromys minutus*), house mouse (*Mus domesticus*), ship (black) rat (*Rattus rattus*) and common (brown) rat (*Rattus norvegicus*). The ship rat has become rare in the UK in recent years. Since these mammals are rarely presented for treatment and rehabilitation and in view of the fact that there is a chapter elsewhere in this manual on mice and rats, little more will be said here.

There is an extensive literature on the parasites and diseases of rats and mice and useful, brief reviews are provided in Corbet and Southern (1977). The management of wild rats and mice has been addressed by Redfern and Rowe (1987). These authors point out that these animals can carry serious zoonotic diseases, eg. leptospirosis, salmonellosis, lymphocytic choriomeningitis and cestode (*Hymenolepis nana*) infestations.

DORMICE

There are two species of dormice in the UK: the fat dormouse (*Glis glis*) and the common dormouse (*Muscardinus avellanarius*).

The fat dormouse was introduced in 1902 near Tring in Hertfordshire and it has barely extended its range from there. It weighs about 140g, is much larger than the common dormouse and has a bushy, squirrel-like tail. It is largely arboreal but often enters lofts to hibernate. One litter of about five young is born between June and August (Corbet and Southern, 1977).

The common dormouse has a patchy distribution in southern parts of England and Wales. It produces one or two litters of about four young each year after a 23 day gestation. The eyes open at 18 days and the young leave the nest (sited in a shrub or tree) at 30 days.

There appears to be very little information on diseases of dormice in the UK and still less on their medicine. Therapies established for laboratory mice are likely to be applicable.

The common dormouse is protected under the Wildlife and Countryside Act, 1981 (see 'Legislation'). Harris and Jefferies (1989) suggest that taking in young of this, and some other species, that are too underweight to survive the winter, for release after feeding them up or overwintering, may require a licence from the Nature Conservancy Council. The Nature Conservancy Council should be consulted in cases where the need for intervention is not clearcut. Licences can be issued at short notice.

A description of the successful hand-rearing of the common dormouse has been provided by French (1989b).

WHALES, DOLPHINS AND PORPOISES

More than 20 species of cetaceans have been recorded in strandings around the British coast and among those most frequently found are the common porpoise (*Phocaena phocaena*), the bottle-nosed dolphin (*Tursiops truncatus*), the pilot whale (*Globicephala melaena*) and the lesser rorqual (*Balaenoptera acutorostrata*) (Fraser, 1974; Martin *et al*, 1987). About 100 strandings are recorded each year.

The cause of strandings is often not clear, but can be due to illness. The following first aid procedures have been recommended for the care of stranded cetaceans: keep the animal wet, keep the blowhole clear, provide shade, position the animal on its belly if possible and do not drag it (Royal Society for the Prevention of Cruelty to Animals/Scottish Society for the Prevention of Cruelty to Animals, 1988).

Blood samples can be obtained from pectoral flippers, dorsal fin or tail flukes (the last of these can, however, be extremely dangerous). Geraci and Sweeney (1986) described how one or more major arteries surrounded by periarterial venous retia which run towards the tips of the flippers and flukes may be detected by slight surface depressions.

It has been recommended that if the deep rectal temperature is 42°C or more, the animal is in a terminal condition and should be destroyed. The most humane method of euthanasia is to administer Large Animal Immobilon (C-Vet) by intramuscular injection (or intrablubber in the absence of a long enough needle) at a dose rate of 0.5cc per 1.5m body length (RSPCA/SSPCA, 1988).

All cetaceans are protected under the Wildlife and Countryside Act, 1981 (see 'Legislation'). Whales and sturgeon are 'Royal Fish' and belong to the Crown under Statute Praerogativa Regis, 17 Edward II (AD 1324) (Cooper, 1987). Strandings should be reported to the Natural History Museum (Tel: 071-938 8861).

Relatively little is known about the diseases of free-living cetaceans. Dailey (1985) has recently reviewed the literature on diseases of wild and captive animals.

FOX

Foxes are widespread and common throughout the UK and may be presented for treatment and care as a result of disease, road accident trauma, or when found as orphans (or mistakenly assumed to be orphans). Some short notes on the biology of the fox are given in Table 7.

Diseases and medicine

Because of the close taxonomic relationship between fox and dog, a knowledge of canine medicine and pathology can be readily applied in the diagnosis and treatment of diseases of foxes. Some parasites have been listed by Corbet and Southern (1977). *Toxocara canis* infestation is common. Epizootics of *Sarcoptes scabiei* associated with high mortality have occurred and *Otodectes cynotis* can cause severe ear infestations (Harris, 1986). 11% of urban foxes examined by Harris (1986) were thought to have died from infectious disease. Foxes are reported to be susceptible to canine distemper and are likely to be susceptible to parvovirus infections (Jacobson *et al*, 1988). They are also susceptible to leptospirosis (Twigg *et al*, 1968).

Harris (1989) pointed out that fractures often heal without intervention in foxes. He found that, in London, 32% of those aged six months or over had one or more broken bones (Harris, 1978).

Anaesthesia

Foxes can be immobilised with ketamine (10mg/kg) combined with xylazine (2mg/kg) given intramuscularly. Kreager *et al* (1990) recommended 30mg/kg ketamine plus 5mg/kg promazine or 20mg/kg ketamine plus 1mg/kg xylazine, with 0.1mg/kg yohimbine 45—60 minutes after the last ketamine administration. Methods and techniques of canine anaesthesia will generally apply.

Neonatal care

The composition of fox milk is similar to that of the domestic cat (see Appendix 2) and good quality cat or dog milk replacer formulae are likely to be suitable. Techniques of rearing cubs have been described by Harris and Macdonald (1987) but these authors stress the difficulties of future management in captivity or subsequent rehabilitation of these animals.

Rehabilitation

Harris and Macdonald (1987) recommended that cubs mistakenly thought to be orphans should be returned, in the evening, to the exact place where they were found, because there is a good chance that they will find their own way back to their earth or be retrieved by the vixen.

Cubs that have been hand-reared can be rehabilitated, in a suitable area, by allowing them to come and go from their accommodation as they please from an early age (about six weeks). They gradually explore the area and learn to forage by night but return for food during the day. With time they return less regularly and from August may suddenly leave the area (Harris and Macdonald, 1987). There are particular difficulties in rehabilitating animals that have been in captivity for longer periods.

MUSTELINAE

There are five members of the Subfamily Mustelinae (Family Mustelidae) in the UK and brief notes on the biology of these species are given in Table 6. The pine marten used to be widespread in the UK but is now mainly confined to the Scottish Highlands and Ireland. The stoat and weasel are widespread throughout England, Scotland and Wales, but the weasel does not occur in Ireland. The polecat used to have a wider distribution but now occurs only in Wales. Mink began to spread from the South West of England after escaping from fur farms from 1929 and their distribution now covers much of the UK. The medicine and management of these animals can be based on practices recommended for the ferret (see 'Ferrets').

Table 6
Subfamily Mustelinae.

Common name	Pine marten	Stoat	Weasel	Polecat	Mink
Scientific name	*Mustela martes*	*M. erminea*	*M. nivalis*	*M.putorius*	*M. vison*
Male	1.0—1.4kg	320g	115g	990g	1.8kg
Female	1.0—1.4kg	210g	60g	620g	0.9kg
Births/Breeding	Litters in March/April.	Spring	April/May		
Gestation (days)		Delayed implantation then 21—28 days.	34—37	42	Delayed implantation 39—76 days.
Litter size	3	6—12	4—6	5—10	5—6
Neonate (g)	28		1.5	10	
Lactation	8—10 weeks	7—12 weeks	<12 weeks		
Weaning	6—7 weeks	5 weeks			
Development	Eyes open 32—38 days. Milk teeth 3—5 weeks (200g). Leave nest 8 weeks.	Eyes open 35—42 days. Milk teeth 3 weeks.	Eyes open 28 days. Milk teeth 2—3 weeks.	Eyes open 35 days.	

Source of data: Corbet and Southern (1977).

Parasites

The nematode *Skrjabingylus nasicola* has received considerable interest. The 13—25mm long adults lie in the nasal sinuses and can cause deformities and perforations of the skull. The infestation occurs in pine martens, stoats, weasels and polecats. Heavy infestations are thought to compromise the health of stoats and martens, but although a survey of weasel skulls showed the prevalence to be high (69—100%), King (1977) found no evidence of an effect on bodyweight or mortality in this species. Larvae travel from the nose to the gut and, after excretion, enter molluscs. When these are eaten by shrews, wood mice or bank voles the larvae encyst until they are, in turn, eaten by a member of the Mustelinae. Later larval stages leave the gut and approach the nasal sinuses via the spinal cord (King, 1989).

Infectious diseases

Canine distemper has been described in the ferret, the mink, and the weasel (Keymer and Epps, 1969). The other British species may well be susceptible but the incidence of the disease in wild populations of any of these species is unknown.

Mink are susceptible to feline panleucopoenia/mink virus enteritis (Bittle, 1970; Burger and Gorham, 1970). The significance of this disease in the wild is unknown.

Anaesthesia

These animals can be immobilised with ketamine (10mg/kg) combined with xylazine (2mg/kg) given intramuscularly (Wallach and Boever, 1983). Ketamine has also been used alone.

Husbandry

All these species have been maintained in captivity and their management presents no great problems (see, for example, Evans and Lockie, 1965).

Neonatal care

Data on the milk composition of the mink are given in Appendix 2. There are no data available for the other British species. Replacers designed for dogs and cats (see Appendix 3) are likely to be suitable.

Therapy

Live vaccines to canine distemper should be avoided unless their safety for the species is assured (see 'Ferrets'). Black-footed ferrets are among those animals that have died as a result of vaccine-induced disease (Carpenter *et al,* 1976).

BADGER

The badger is widespread throughout the UK. The Badgers Act 1973 provides special protection under which it is illegal to take, injure, or wilfully kill a badger. This was reinforced by the Wildlife and Countryside Act, 1981 (see 'Legislation'). Humane euthanasia of seriously ill or injured animals or their capture for treatment is permitted. Notes on the biology of the badger are given in Table 7 (see also Corbet and Southern, 1977; Clark, 1988; Harris *et al,* 1988).

Table 7
Fox, badger, otter and wild cat.

Common name	Red fox	Badger	Otter	Wild cat
Scientific name	*Vulpes vulpes*	*Meles meles* Subfamily Melinae	*Lutra lutra* Subfamily Lutrinae	*Felis silvestris*
Male (kg)	6.5	11.6	10.3	5
Female (kg)	5.5	10.1	7.4	4
Births/breeding	Cubs are born in late March.	Cubs born Jan-Mar.	All seasons.	Kittens born late spring and summer.
Food	Omnivorous	Omnivorous	Fish, crustaceans.	Lagomorphs, rodents, birds.
Gestation (days)	53	Delayed implantation.	62	63
Litter size	4—5	1—4	2—3 (up to 5)	4 (1—8)
Neonate (g)	100—130	100	c90	c100
Mating		Feb-May		
Implantation		December		
Lactation	About 6 weeks			
Weaning (days)		12—16 weeks	10 weeks	About 16 weeks.
Development	Eyes and ears open 14 days.	Leave nest 8 weeks.	Eyes open 31—34 days. Eat solids 49 days, enter water 72 days.	Leave nest 4—5 weeks.

Source of data: Corbet and Southern (1977).

Parasites

Common external parasites include the louse *Trichodectes melis,* the flea *Paracerus melis* and ticks *Ixodes hexagonus* and *I. canisuga.*

Infectious diseases

Canine distemper has been reported in a wide range of species in the Order Carnivora (Budd, 1970) and has been confirmed in the badger (Keymer and Epps, 1969). Harris et al (1988) considered that badgers are prone to parvovirus infection.

The epidemiology of bovine tuberculosis in badgers has been the subject of considerable study since badgers were identified as a source of infection in cattle (Cheeseman et al, 1985; Wilesmith et al, 1986). The incidence of the disease is quite high in the South West of England and approximately 10% of the carcases examined in some counties have been found to be positive (MAFF, 1987). Although the incidence may be highest in the South West, the infection has been diagnosed in carcases from other parts of the country. Research aimed at developing diagnostic tests and a vaccine are underway (MAFF, 1987).

Anaesthesia

Harris et al (1988) reported that ketamine (20mg/kg i/m) was suitable to anaesthetise badgers. The ketamine/xylazine mixture suggested for the fox and the Mustelinae is also likely to be suitable.

Neonatal care

Harris et al (1988) considered that invariably very young cubs found outside the sett during the day have been orphaned. The milk composition of the badger appears not to have been investigated. Harris et al (1988) recommended Complan (Crooke's Healthcare) as a milk replacer because hair loss has been observed in some badgers fed on some dog milk substitutes. One of the replacers with a higher fat composition, for example Esbilac, KMR, or Lamlac (Volac), may be suitable (see Appendix 3).

Rehabilitation

The following brief notes are largely based on the detailed advice given by Harris et al (1988) whose publication is essential reading for anyone contemplating badger rehabilitation. Orphaned badger cubs should be reared, with others if possible, in accommodation in a suitable area for release. Human contact should be minimised. From June, cubs should be taken for walks (they will follow) around the area, and they will learn to forage. Later in the summer they should be allowed to come and go as they please. Prior to this free-living, adult badgers present a particular threat and may kill cubs. Most cubs cease returning during winter or spring.

Rehabilitating badgers that have been maintained in captivity for long periods is very much more difficult. Harris et al (1988) recommended that these animals should first be acclimatised in a large semi-natural enclosure. A suitable disused sett should be selected for the release site and the release should be made in autumn. Criteria for choosing a suitable sett for a release have been listed and discussed by Harris et al (1988) and other aspects of rehabilitation have been discussed by Harris (1989).

Wild badgers brought into captivity for treatment should be returned at night to the exact place they were found as soon they are fit for release. The sooner they can be released the better.

OTTER

The otter was widely distributed in the UK but the population has declined, particularly in the Midlands and South-East England (Jefferies et al, 1986). Its decline is probably due to changes in river water quality. Some notes on its biology are given in Table 7.

Diseases

The otter may be susceptible to canine distemper and has been reported to be susceptible to feline panleucopoenia (Duplaix-Hall, 1972). Renal calculi are quite common in captive otters but also occur in wild individuals (Keymer et al, 1981; Calle,1988). Rübel et al (1987) reviewed some of the other diseases of captive otters and discussed their prevention.

Anaesthesia

At the Zoological Society of London otters have been immobilised with ketamine (10−20mg/kg) combined with diazepam (0.3−1.0mg/kg) given intramuscularly (Kuiken, 1988). Anaesthesia has been maintained with halothane.

Husbandry

Otters are relatively easy to maintain in captivity, providing suitable accommodation is available. Their amphibious habits should be taken into account (Duplaix-Hall, 1972). Otters have bred in captivity (Wayre, 1972; Vogt, 1987).

Neonatal care

The composition of otter milk does not appear to have been investigated. Esbilac has been successfully used to rear an Asian short-clawed otter (Thomas, 1985). The growth of four individuals has been described by Schmidt (1972).

Rehabilitation

The factors mentioned earlier regarding the rehabilitation of foxes and badgers are broadly relevant to the otter. There appears to be no literature specifically on rehabilitation of otters but an account has been published on the re-introduction of captive-bred otters to the wild (Jefferies *et al*, 1986). Eighteen-month old animals selected for release were placed in a release pen close to the bank on an island in a suitable river. They were kept there for 20 days prior to release and food was made available to them there until they stopped returning a week after release. The animals were monitored using radiotelemetry and were found to adapt well to the wild and, in due course, bred.

WILD CAT

Once wild cats occurred throughout the UK but their range is now limited to the Scottish Highlands. There has been extensive hybridisation with feral *Felis catus.* Brief notes about the wild cat are listed in Table 7. Further information is provided by Corbet and Southern (1977).

Little is known about the incidence of diseases in free-living wild cats but it is unlikely that their susceptibilities to infectious diseases differs significantly from those of the domestic cat. Medicine is as for the domestic cat.

No literature has been traced on the rehabilitation of wild cats but the release methods and subsequent sightings of some hand-reared bobcats in Nebraska have been described by Odell (1985). A technique similar to that described for the otter would be appropriate.

SEALS

There are two species of seals resident in UK waters; the common seal and the grey seal. The common seal occurs from south of the Wash on the east coast up to and round the coasts of Scotland and much of Ireland. It is irregular on the western and southern coasts of England. The grey seal has a wider distribution and occurs around much of the entire coast except for the south east (Hewer, 1974; Corbet and Southern, 1977). Brief notes on the biology of these seals are given in Table 8.

Parasites

The louse *Echinophthirius horridus* occurs on both species and the mite *Orthohalarachne halichoeri* is common in the nose of grey seals. The lungworms *Otostrongylus circumlitus* and *Parafilaroides gymnurus* are common, as are a variety of stomach and intestinal nematodes including *Contracaecum osculatum* and *Terranova decipiens* (Corbet and Southern, 1977; Lauckner, 1985).

Table 8
Seals.

Common name	Common seal	Grey seal
Scientific name	*Phoca vitulina*	*Halichoerus grypus*
Male (kg)	55—105	230
Female (kg)	45—88	155
Food	Mainly fish.	Mainly fish.
Births/Breeding	Pups born June/July.	Sept/Dec, also in spring in Pembroke and Cornwall.
Swimming	From birth.	
Gestation	Delayed implantation.	Delayed implantation.
Litter size	1	1
Neonate (kg)	9—11	14
Lactation	4—6 weeks	16—21 days (40—55kg)

Source of data: Corbet and Southern (1977).

Diseases

Starvation is the main cause of death in grey seal pups during their first month (Baker, 1984; Baker and Baker, 1988) and a common cause of death in common seal pups (Steiger *et al*, 1989). Pneumonia caused by bacteria or viruses is the most common cause of death in juvenile and adult grey seals (Baker, 1989).

The phocid distemper epizootic that occurred in 1988 caused heavy mortality among the common seals of the North Sea (Harwood and Reijnders, 1988) but only mild disease in grey seals. The disease was caused by a morbillivirus (Osterhaus *et al*, 1989). The clinical picture altered and percentage mortality decreased with increasing latitude. Purulent bronchopneumonia occurred in more chronic cases and *Bordetella bronchisepticum* and *Corynebacterium* spp. were commonly isolated. An epizootic with high mortality in the common seal population of Cape Cod, Massachusetts was caused by an influenza virus (Geraci *et al*, 1982).

For a comprehensive review of seal diseases the reader is referred to Lauckner (1985). Useful reviews of diagnostic techniques and medicine have been provided by Wallach and Boever (1983) and Geraci and Sweeney (1986).

Anaesthesia

Baker *et al* (1988) found that a mixture of ketamine (6mg/kg) and diazepam (0.3mg/kg) was a reliable and reasonably safe agent for immobilising grey seals. However a 1:1 mixture of tiletamine and zolazepam (Zoletil 100, Laboratoires Reading, France) given at a combined dose of 1mg/kg was considered to have advantages over all other agents used previously (Baker *et al*, 1990). Ketamine and diazepam mixtures have been used to immobilise common seals (Geraci and Sweeney, 1986).

Husbandry

Both species have been maintained successfully in captivity. In a census of captive marine mammals in North America, Cornell *et al* (1982) recorded 37 grey seals and 247 common seals in 1979.

At the Oban Sea Life Centre orphaned seal pups are kept dry for the first two weeks. During the next two weeks they are given the opportunity to swim for a short period each day in a small tank and then they are introduced to an outdoor pool with adequate haul-out areas prior to release (Larmour, 1989a).

Pups have to be force-fed with a stomach tube for the first three weeks but will then usually start to eat small pieces of fish (Gage, 1987; Larmour, 1989a). Sick or injured adults are also likely to need force-feeding. This can be done by sitting astride the animal's back, and prising its mouth open to insert food (Geraci and Sweeney, 1986; Larmour, 1989b). Leather gauntlets should be worn.

Zoonoses

Severe local infections can occur in seal handlers at the site of skin abrasions or bites. The condition is known as 'seal finger' (Beck and Smith, 1976) and is thought to be caused by *Erysipelothrix insidiosa* (the same lesion caught from cetaceans is called 'whale finger'). Sealpox occurs in both grey and common seals (but has not been confirmed in UK populations) and is caused by a poxvirus of the parapoxvirus group. The infection is transmissible to humans but the lesions are mild and transient (Hicks and Worthy, 1987).

Neonatal care

The feeding technique is mentioned earlier. Some data on the milk composition of the grey seal are given in Appendix 2. Formulae used to rear pups are based on ground fish, and recipes have been provided by Gage (1987) and Larmour (1989a,b).

Rehabilitation

At the Oban Sea Life Centre common seal pups are offered live fish from an early age and can usually chase and kill these by about 8 weeks of age. The pups are kept until they have reached a weight of 25kg at about 12 weeks of age. They are then tagged and released (Larmour, 1989a).

DEER

There are six species of deer living wild in the UK, and a number of others in captivity in zoos. There is also a semi-domesticated herd of reindeer in the Cairngorms. Brief notes on the six wild species are given in Table 9. There is an extensive literature about the general biology of deer, eg. Corbet and Southern (1977), Putnam (1988), and, compared with most other wild mammals, a great deal has been published on their husbandry, diseases and medicine, eg. Rudge (1984), Dansie (1985), Alexander (1986). For this reason comments here are confined to a few points relevant to the care of injured, orphaned or sick wild deer.

Table 9
Deer.

Common name	Red	Sika	Fallow	Roe	Reeve's muntjac	Chinese water
Scientific name	*Cervus elaphus*	*Cervus nippon*	*Dama dama*	*Capreolus capreolus*	*Muntiacus reevesi*	*Hydropotes inermis*
Male (kg)	100—200	65	70	25	14	12
Female (kg)	60—100	42	44	24	12	10
Births	May—Aug	May—Sept	June—Oct	Apr—July	No seasonal pattern.	May—June
Gestation (g)	230	230	229	Delayed implantation (294).		180—210
Litter size	1(occ.2)	1	1	1—3	1	1—4
Neonate (kg)	c6	3—7	c4.5	c2	c1	0.89
Weaning	6—12 months	6—10 months	7—8 months	2 months +	3 months	1—2 months
Lie up until*	7—10 days	21 days	14 days	About 14 days.	7—21 days	
At foot**	3—4 weeks			By 8 weeks.		Fawns do not follow dam.

Sources of data: Corbet and Southern (1977); Rudge (1984); Kirkwood *et al* (1987).

*Period for which fawns lie, hidden, before following their mothers.
**Period for which fawns follow their mothers.

Anaesthesia

Jones (1984) has provided an extensive review of capture techniques for deer and his suggested first choice of agents is listed below.

Chinese water deer	10—14kg	0.9—1.2mg etorphine 4—5mg xylazine
Reeve's muntjac	8—11kg	0.8—1.1mg etorphine 4—5mg xylazine
Roe deer	17—25kg	1.0—1.2mg etorphine 15—20mg xylazine
Fallow deer	35—70kg	1.2—2.0mg etorphine 35—79mg xylazine
Sika deer	45—85kg	2.0—3.5mg etorphine 9—15mg acepromazine
Red deer	105—180kg	2.0—4.5mg etorphine 9—20mg acepromazine

The respiratory depression caused by etorphine compromises its safety. At a dose of 1ml per animal it was found to be suitable for restraint of Sika deer by Kock et al (1987), but these authors indicated the need for intubation and intermittent positive pressure ventilation (IPPV) unless reversal of the etorphine narcotisation was prompt. Likewise, Pearce and Kock (1989) recommended IPPV and the administration of atropine intravenously following etorphine administration to fallow deer stressed during capture, unless reversal is prompt.

Ketamine/xylazine mixtures have also been found to be suitable for some species (Hastings et al, 1989) and these authors found that dose rates of about 7mg/kg each of ketamine and xylazine gave satisfactory results in most cases. The sedation was reversed by the experimental agent RX821002A (Reckitt and Colman), or yohimbine (Sigma Chemicals).

Medetomidine (Domitor, SmithKline Beecham)/ketamine mixtures have been used to immobilise a wide range of mammals including several species of deer (Roeken, 1987; Jalanka, 1989). Effective doses can be prepared in low volumes for darting and the sedation induced using this combination can be reversed with the alpha 2 adrenoceptor antagonist atipamezole (Antisedan, SmithKline Beecham).

Cooper et al (1986) found methohexitone sodium (Brietal, Elanco) to be a useful intravenous short-acting immobilising agent for use in Reeve's muntjac captured in nets.

Neonatal care

Some data on the milk composition of red, fallow, roe and reindeer are presented in Appendix 2. Lamlac (Volac), a sheep milk replacer, has been used to rear red deer (Allen, 1989) and Chinese water deer (Kirkwood et al, 1988). This substitute was well accepted and supported a good growth rate in the latter.

Rehabilitation

Rescued neonatal deer mistakenly thought to have been abandoned may be accepted by the mother if returned to the exact spot within 24 hours. Allen (1989) considered that hand-reared deer should not be released because their tame disposition puts them at risk (and hand-reared red stags can be dangerous).

Injured deer should be returned to the area where they were found as soon as possible after treatment. If they have been in captivity for a prolonged period there may be difficulties for them in reintegrating with a herd or, in the case of the roe deer, in re-establishing a territory (Harris, 1989).

Acknowledgement

I am most grateful to Miss Moya Foreman for her assistance in preparing this manuscript.

APPENDIX 1: BRITISH WILDLIFE REHABILITATION COUNCIL'S NOTES ON ETHICS AND LEGAL ASPECTS OF TREATMENT AND REHABILITATION OF WILD ANIMAL CASUALTIES (published 1989)

There is growing interest in the rescue, treatment and rehabilitation of wild animal casualties. No doubt man has always felt compassion for wounded or sick animals, but perhaps the reasons why rehabilitation has gained momentum recently are the general awareness of the present man-made threats to the environment and the development of veterinary medicine to the stage at which wild animal medicine can be effective.

Wild animals are as they are — anatomically, physiologically, immunologically and behaviourally — as a result of the continuing process of natural selection of those best-adapted to the environment and we should be wary of interfering with this process. However, many wild animal casualties are due to man's very recent (in evolutionary terms) changes to the environment and may be caused by, for example, road traffic accidents, oil-spillage at sea, collisions with high-tension wires and poisoning by environmental contaminants. In these cases the argument for rehabilitation is particularly strong.

Concern for animal welfare and species conservation underlie efforts to treat wild animals and restore them to the wild. Whilst, in some cases, the restoration of an animal to the wild may benefit both the individual and the species, there are circumstances when neither animal welfare nor conservation are served by attempts to rehabilitate. Careful thought needs to given to each case and the purpose of this document is to provide some guidelines about ethical and legal aspects of wild animal treatment and rehabilitation.

THE ETHICS OF WILD ANIMAL TREATMENT AND REHABILITATION

This is a very difficult subject and opinions differ widely about what is and is not a justifiable level of intervention in the fate of individuals and thus the population dynamics of their species.

A good first principle which also guides medical and veterinary practitioners, but which also applies here, is 'first, do no harm'.

There are several ways in which inappropriate rehabilitation attempts may also do harm; either to the individual involved, to others of its own species, to other species, or the environment. It is important that these possibilities, examples which are listed below, are considered:

1. If the animal is not fit when released, and suffers as a result.

2. If a fit animal is released into an inhospitable environment, eg. one in which food is scarce, or in which all territories are already occupied.

3. If a released animal carries an infectious disease, which could spread into the wild population of its own or other species.

4. If it is a genetically distinct strain from those in the area where it is released, in which case its offspring may be less adapted to the local environment.

5. If it is a non-indigenous species which may damage the ecosystem.

6. If it displaces a resident of the same species, to the latter's detriment.

The welfare issues (points 1 and 2) are the most immediate and, perhaps, the most easily judged and must be carefully considered in each case. The genetic arguments are probably of little relevance in most cases involving common species, because rehabilitated animals are unlikely to form more than a tiny proportion of the breeding population. The potential for introducing infectious disease into the wild population demands consideration because of the opportunities for cross-species disease spread in wild animal hospitals, and the effects of introducing disease into wild populations could be serious. Both genetic and disease hazards could be particularly relevant when rehabilitating an individual far from the site where it was captured.

Rehabilitation of wild animal casualties can for these reasons be harmful and these considerations must be seriously addressed. The law permits the taking of injured or sick wild animals for treatment, although in the case of birds, only if the intention is that they are released when cured (see note on legal aspects below).

The preceding paragraphs point out that treatment and rehabilitation of injured or sick wild animals is not, in all cases, the kindest or wisest course of action. Practical and economic contraints alone dictate that not all rescued individuals of all species can be treated and rehabilitated. Maintenance in captivity or euthanasia are humane alternatives. Some circumstances under which rescue, treatment and rehabilitation may benefit the individual and/or its own or other species, are listed below:

1. If the individual, having been restored to complete fitness, is successfully reintroduced into the habitat that can support it, without compromising the success of other wild individuals. That is if the wild population is smaller than that which the environment can sustain (as may occur after a 'die-off' due to bad weather, a disease epidemic, environmental contamination, or persecution), or:

2. If what is learned in the process of treatment and rehabilitation may subsequently be of value in the care of individuals of rare and endangered species in the future.

Three criteria should be addressed before embarking on treatment and rehabilitation, namely, whether or not the attempt will improve welfare, conservation or our knowledge. From the welfare viewpoint, it is not easy to judge whether treatment and rehabilitation is preferable to humane euthanasia. Even when successful, treatment is unlikely to be accomplished without any fear, pain or stress.

The welfare of the individual must be the prime consideration, but it is appropriate to consider also the conservation status of the species. With the exception of a few rare UK species, rescue and rehabilitation is unlikely to have direct beneficial or harmful effects on population dynamics. However, the rescue, treatment and rehabilitation of wild animals provides an excellent opportunity to learn about their diseases, management, medical care and husbandry which may contribute to conservation in the future. The time and level of organisation required to collect, analyse and publish results and thus capitalise on the work in this way, should not be underestimated.

Preventative wildlife medicine

It is perhaps a small step from treating the common causes of diseases and injury in casualty animals to considering how these ills might be prevented. If the cause is man-made, for example environmental pollution, then steps should be taken to correct the situation. It is probably not justifiable, on the other hand, to interfere with the epidemiology of 'natural' diseases' by, for example, vaccination or routine anthelmintic treatment of free-living animals, unless this forms part of a scheme to prevent disease in man or his domestic livestock, eg. vaccination of badgers against tuberculosis, or perhaps to intervene to protect an endangered population, eg. vaccination of Mountain gorillas against measles.

LEGAL ASPECTS

Taking or killing of wild animals

Under the Wildlife and Countryside Act 1981 (WCA), it is an offence to take or kill or have in one's possession, wild birds. There are exceptions to this which allow, for example, the shooting of wildfowl and gamebirds at some times of the year and control of some species which may damage crops, for example, crow, sparrow or pigeon. Only specified mammals, reptiles, amphibians, insects and other animals listed in Schedule 5 of the WCA (as amended) are given such broad protection.

It is permitted to kill any wild bird which is so badly disabled that there is no reasonable likelihood of its recovery, and it is permitted to take a sick or injured bird solely for the purpose of tending it and returning it to the wild when it has recovered. Broadly, the same principles apply to other protected wild animals.

Release of wild animals

The WCA also forbids the release of non-indigenous species, including those such as grey squirrel and Canada goose that are already well-established in the UK.

The Abandonment of Animals Act, 1969 provides that it is an offence to deliberately abandon an animal in circumstances likely to cause it unnecessary suffering. Thus, careful estimation of an animal's physical condition and the environment must be made before the release of a wild animal.

Welfare whilst in captivity

Section 8 of the WCA requires that bird-cages must be large enough to allow spreading the wings, unless the bird is undergoing examination or treatment by a veterinary surgeon.

Treatment by lay persons

The extent to which lay persons are permitted to treat animals is described in the Veterinary Surgeons Act 1966 (as amended). Any person may provide first aid measures in an emergency to save life or relieve pain and the owner of an animal may give minor medical treatment. As one in possession of a wild animal casualty is its temporary owner, he or she is therefore permitted to give minor medical care.

The Veterinary Surgeons Act 1966 (as amended) provides that only people registered with the Royal College of Veterinary Surgeons are permitted to:

(a)   make diagnosis of diseases in, and injuries to, animals;

(b)   give advice based upon such diagnosis, and

(c)   undertake the medical or surgical treatment of animals (see, however, the exceptions above).

The BWRC is keen that lay wild animal rehabilitators and veterinary surgeons should work closely in this field.

Sources of Information

The inclusion of books in this list does not imply their endorsement by the BWRC.

COOPER, J. E. and ELEY, J. T. (1979). *First Aid and Care of Wild Birds.* David and Charles, London.

COOPER, M. E. (1987). *An Introduction to Animal Law.* Academic Press, London.

ENGHOLM, E. (1970). *Company of Birds.* Nevill Spearman.

HARRIS, S., JEFFRIES, D. and CRESWELL, W. (1988). *Problems with Badgers?* Royal Society for the Prevention of Cruelty to Animals, Horsham.

HARRIS, S. and MACDONALD, D. (1987). *Orphan Foxes. Guidelines on the Rescue and Rehabilitation of Fox Cubs.* Royal Society for the Prevention of Cruelty to Animals, Horsham.

JORDAN, W. J. and HUGHES, J. (1982). *Care of the Wild; Family First Aid for Birds and Other Animals.* Macdonald, London.

MCKEEVER, K. (1979). *Care and Rehabilitation of Injured Owls.* W F Rannie, Lincoln, Ontario.

Proceedings of the National Wildlife Rehabilitator's Association. Volumes 1 – 8 (1982 – 1988). D Mackey, Florida.

Proceedings of the Inaugural Symposium of the British Wildlife Rehabilitation Council (1989). (Eds. S. Harris and T. Thomas) BWRC, London.

Proceedings of Hawk Trust Symposium on Raptor Rehabilitation (1989). The Hawk Trust, London.

ROYAL SOCIETY FOR THE PREVENTION OF CRUELTY TO ANIMALS/SCOTTISH SOCIETY FOR THE PREVENTION OF CRUELTY TO ANIMALS (1988). *First Aid for Stranded Cetaceans.* RSPCA, Horsham; SSPCA, Edinburgh.

SANDYS-WINSH, G. (1984). *Animal Law.* Shaw and Shaw, London.

STOCKER, L. (1986). *We Save Wildlife.* Whittet, London.

YGLESIAS, D. (1962). *The Cry of the Bird.* William Kimber.

APPENDIX 2

The concentration, energy density and percentage of fat, protein, carbohydrate and ash in the dry matter of milks of some species of mammals found in the UK (from Kirkwood, 1989).

Order and species	Solids %	Kcal/ml	fat	protein	Carbo-hydrate (as % of solids)	ash	source
Marsupialia:							
Red-necked wallaby	13.0	0.83	33	29	32	6	a
Insectivora:							
Hedgehog	20.6	1.42	47	33	9	10	c
Water shrew	35.0	2.42	63	31	3	2	a
Greater white-toothed shrew	51.2	3.50	62	19	—	5	d
Lagomorpha:							
Rabbit	31.2	2.06	49	32	6	6	d
Hare	32.2	2.01	46	31	5	—	d
Mountain hare	40.0	2.92	48	49	2	—	a
Rodentia:							
Grey squirrel	39.6	2.85	67	20	10	3	a
Common rat	21.0	1.53	46	37	12	6	b
House mouse	29.3	1.84	50	34	11	5	b
Cetacea:							
Blue whale	c57	4.58	76	19	2	—	c
Bottle-nosed dolphin	c43	3.48	78	16	3	—	c
Carnivora:							
Red fox	18.1	1.10	32	35	25	5	d
Polecat	23.5	1.23	43	32	20	4	b
Mink	21.7	1.17	33	26	21	4	d
Domestic cat	c27		28	40	27		f
Pinnipedia:							
Grey seal	67.7	5.66	79	17	4	1	b
Artiodactyla:							
Red deer	19.6	1.26	39	36	19	6	e
Fallow deer	19.6	1.30	43	35	17	5	e
Roe deer	24.0	1.56	50	29	15	6	e
Reindeer	26.3	1.68	41	34	13	5	d
Sheep	18.2	1.10	39	23	27	4	d

Sources: a, Ben Shaul (1962); b, Jenness and Sloan (1970); c, Widdowson (1981); d, Oftedal (1984); e, Sugar et al (1986); f, Monson (1987).

APPENDIX 3

Approximate concentration, energy density and percentages of fat, protein, carbohydrate and ash in the dry matter of some milk substitutes. The percentages of solids and the energy density of the whole milk depend upon the amount of water added to the powdered products during their reconstitution (from Kirkwood, 1989).

Product	Solids %	Kcal/ml	fat	protein	Carbo-hydrate (as % of solids)
Cow's milk	12.4	0.71	26	26	39
Channel Island cow's milk	13.7	0.76	35	26	34
Goat's milk	13.0	0.71	35	25	35
Skimmed milk	9.1	0.33	1	37	55
Lactol			27	24	33
Welpi			>18	>27	41
Denkapup			22	24	46
Esbilac	33.0	1.78	43	34	15
KMR			26	43	22
Cimicat			22	34	34
Litterlac			30	25	35
Volac Easy Mix			20	25	40
Lamlac	20.0	1.08	30	25	35
Horsepower	13.8	0.63	12	24	53
Faramate			14	22	56
Gold Cap SMA	12.5	0.65	28	12	56
Primilac		0.82	25	20	51
Multi-Milk			30	55	—

The names and addresses of the manufacturers of these products can be found in the 'Appendix — Useful Addresses'.

REFERENCES

ALEXANDER, T. L. (1986). Ed. *Management and Diseases of Deer — a Handbook for the Veterinary Surgeon.* The Veterinary Deer Society, c/o British Veterinary Association, London.

ALLEN, R. L. (1989). Care and hand-raising of young red deer. In: *Proceedings of the Inaugural Symposium of the British Wildlife Rehabilitation Council.* (Eds. S. Harris and T. Thomas) British Wildlife Rehabilitation Council. London.

BAKER, J. P. and CLARKE, J. R. (1987). Voles. In: *The UFAW Handbook on the Care and Management of Laboratory Animals.* 6th Edn. (Ed. T.B. Poole) Longman, Harlow.

BAKER, J. R. (1984). Mortality and morbidity in grey seal pups *(Halichoerus grypus).* Studies on its causes, effects of environment, the nature and sources of infectious agents and the immunological status of pups. *Journal of Zoology London* **203**, 23.

BAKER, J. R. (1989). Natural causes of death in non-suckling grey seals *(Halichoerus grypus). Veterinary Record* **125**, 500.

BAKER, J. R., ANDERSON, S. S. and FEDAK, M. A. (1988). The use of ketamine-diazepam mixture to immobilise wild grey seals *(Halichoerus grypus)* and southern elephant seals *(Mirounga leonina). Veterinary Record* **123** 287.

BAKER, J. R. and BAKER, R. (1988). Effects of environment on grey seal *(Halichoerus grypus)* pup mortality. Studies on the Isle of May. *Journal of Zoology London* **216**, 529.

BAKER, J. R., FEDAK, M. A., ANDERSON, S. S., AINBORN, T. and BAKER, R. (1990). Use of tiletamine-zolezepan mixture to immobilise wild grey seals and southern elephant seals. *Veterinary Record* **126**, 75.

BECK, B. and SMITH, T. G. (1976). 'Seal Finger' — an unsolved medical problem in Canada. *Fisheries and Marine Service Research and Development Technical Report. No. 625.*

BEN SHAUL, D. M. (1962). The composition of milk of wild animals. *International Zoo Yearbook* **4**, 333.

BERTRAM, B. C. R. and MOLTU, D. P. (1986). Reintroducing red squirrels into Regent's Park. *Mammal Review* **16**, 81.

BITTLE, J. L. (1970). Feline panleukopenia. In: *Infectious Diseases of Wild Mammals.* (Eds. J. W. Davis, L. H. Karstad and D. O. Trainer) Iowa University Press, Iowa.

BLACKMORE, D. K. and OWEN, D. G. (1968). Ectoparasites: their significance in British wild rodents. *Symposium of the Zoological Society of London* **24**, 197.

BOAG, B. (1988). Observations on the seasonal incidence of myxomatosis and its interactions with helminth parasites in the European rabbit *(Oryctolagus cuniculus). Journal of Wildlife Diseases* **24**, 450.

BOGUE, G. L. (1979). Caring for wild orphans. *Defenders Magazine* February 1979, 30.

BONNER, W. N. (1977). Seals. In: *Handbook of British Mammals.* (Eds. G.B. Corbet and H.N. Southern) Blackwell Scientific Publications, Oxford.

BUDD, J. (1970). Distemper. In: *Infectious Diseases of Wild Mammals.* (Eds. J.W. Davis, L.H. Karstad and D.O. Trainer) Iowa State University Press, Iowa.

BURGER, D. and GORHAM, J. R. (1970). Mink virus enteritis. In: *Infectious Diseases of Wild Mammals.* (Eds. J.W. Davis, L.H. Karstad and D.O. Trainer) Iowa State University Press, Iowa.

CALLE, P. (1988). Asian small-clawed otter *(Aonyx cinerea)* urolithiasis prevalence in North America. *Zoo Biology* **7**, 233.

CARPENTER, J. W., APPEL, M. J. G., ERICKSON, R. C. and OVILLA, M. N. (1976). Fatal vaccine-induced canine distemper virus infection in black-footed ferrets. *Journal of the American Veterinary Medical Association* **169**, 961.

CHASEY, D. and DUFF, P. (1990). European brown hare syndrome and associated virus particles in the UK. *Veterinary Record* **126**, 623.

CHEESEMAN, C. L., LITTLE, T. W. A., MALLINSON, P. J., REES, P. J. and WILESMITH, J. W. (1985). The progression of bovine tuberculosis infection in a population of *Meles meles* in South-West England. *Acta Zoologica Fennica* **173**, 197.

CLARK, J. D. and OLFERT, E. D. (1986). Rodents. In: *Zoo and Wild Animal Medicine.* (Ed. M.E. Fowler) W.B. Saunders, Philadelphia.

CLARK, M. (1988). *Badgers.* Whittet Books, London.

CONSTANTINE, D. G. (1986). Insectivorous bats. In: *Zoo and Wild Animal Medicine.* (Ed. M.E. Fowler) W.B. Saunders, Philadelphia.

COOPER, J. E. (1989). Care, cure or conservation: developments and dilemmas in wildlife rehabilitation. In: *Proceedings of the Inaugural Symposium of the British Wildlife Rehabilitation Council.* (Eds. S. Harris and T. Thomas) British Wildlife Rehabilitation Council, London.

COOPER, J. E., HARRIS, S., CHAPMAN, N. G. and CHAPMAN, D. I. (1986). A comparison of xylazine and methohexitone for the chemical immobilisation of Reeve's muntjac (*Muntiacus reevesi). British Veterinary Journal* **142,** 350.

COOPER, M. E. (1987). *An Introduction to Animal Law.* Academic Press, London.

COOPER, M. E. and SINCLAIR, D. A. (1989). Law relating to wildlife rehabilitation. Abstract from the *Second Symposium of the British Wildlife Rehabilitation Council, Stoneleigh, 1989.* British Wildlife Rehabilitation Council, London.

CORBET, G. B. and SOUTHERN, H. N. (1977). Eds. *Handbook of British Mammals.* Blackwell Scientific Publications, Oxford.

CORNELL, L. H., ASPER, E. D. and DUFFIELD, D. A. (1982). Census update: captive marine mammals in North America. *International Zoo Yearbook* **22,** 227.

DAILEY, M. D. (1985). Diseases of Mammalia: Cetacea. In: *Diseases of Marine Mammals* Volume IV, Part 2. (Ed. O. Kinne) Biologische Anstalt Helgoland, Hamburg.

DANSIE, O. (1985). Deer. In: *BSAVA Manual of Exotic Pets.* Revised edition (Eds. J.E. Cooper, M. F. Hutchison, O .F. Jackson and R. J. Maurice) BSAVA, Cheltenham.

DRYDEN, G. L. (1975). Establishment and maintenance of shrew colonies. *International Zoo Yearbook* **15,** 12.

DUPLAIX-HALL, N. (1972). Notes on maintaining river otters in captivity. *International Zoo Yearbook* **12,** 178.

EVANS, A. T. and EVANS, R. H. (1985). Raising racoons for release. *Wildlife Rehabilitation* **3,** 92.

EVANS, K. and LOCKIE, J. B. (1965). Further observations on weasels (*Mustela nivalis)* and stoats (*Mustela erminea)* born in captivity. *Journal of Zoology London* **147,** 234.

FRAZER, F. C. (1974). *Report on Cetacea stranded on the British coasts from 1948 to 1966.* British Museum (Natural History), London.

FRENCH, H. J. (1989a). Hand-rearing the brown hare *Lepus capensis. International Zoo Yearbook* **28,** 260.

FRENCH, H. J. (1989b). Hand-rearing the common or hazel dormouse *Muscardinus arellanarius. International Zoo Yearbook* **28,** 262.

GAGE, L. J. (1987). Hand-rearing pinniped pups. *Proceedings of the First International Conference on Zoological and Avian Medicine, Oahu, 1987.* American Association of Zoo Veterinarians.

GAVIER, D. and MORNER, T. (1989). The European brown hare syndrome in Sweden. *Erkrankungen der Zootiere* **31,** 261.

GERACI, J. R., ST AUBIN, D. J., BARKER, I. K., WEBSTER, R. G., HINSHAW, V. S., BEAN, W. J., RUHNKE, H. L., PRESCOTT, J. H., EARLY, G., BAKER, A. S., MADOFF, S. and SCHOOLEY, R. T. (1982). Mass mortality of harbor seals: pneumonia associated with influenza A virus. *Science* **215,** 1129.

GERACI, J. R. and SWEENEY, J. (1986). Clinical techniques in marine mammals. In: *Zoo and Wild Animal Medicine.* (Ed. M.E. Fowler) W.B. Saunders, Philadelphia.

GURNEY, J. (1987). *The Natural History of Squirrels.* Christopher Helm, London.

HARRIS, S. (1978). Injuries to foxes (*Vulpes vulpes)* living in suburban London. *Journal of Zoology London* **186,** 567.

HARRIS, S. (1986). *Urban Foxes.* Whittet Books, London.

HARRIS, S. (1989). The release of wild mammals after treatment: rationale, problems and techniques. *Proceedings of the Inaugural Symposium of the British Wildlife Rehabilitation Council.* (Eds. S. Harris and T. Thomas) British Wildlife Rehabilitation Council, London.

HARRIS, S. and JEFFERIES, D. J. (1989). Working within the law: practical aspects of wildlife rehabilitation. *Abstracts of the Second Symposium of the British Wildlife Rehabilitation Council, Stoneleigh, 1989.* British Wildlife Rehabilitation Council, London.

HARRIS, S., JEFFERIES, D. and CRESSWELL, W. (1988). *Problems with Badgers?* Royal Society for the Prevention of Cruelty to Animals, Horsham.

HARRIS, S. and MACDONALD, D. W. (1987). *Orphaned Foxes: Guidelines on the Rescue and Rehabilitation of Fox Cubs.* Royal Society for the Prevention of Cruelty to Animals, Horsham.

HARWOOD, J. and REIJNDERS, P. (1988). Seals, sense and sensibility. *New Scientist* **1634**, 28.

HASTINGS, B. E., STADLER, S. G. and KOCK, R. A. (1989). Reversible immobilisation of Chinese water deer (*Hydropotes inermis*) with ketamine and xylazine. *Journal of Zoo and Wildlife Medicine* **20**, 427.

HAUFLER, J.B. (1985). Habitat selection for release sites of rehabilitated or orphaned wildlife. *Wildlife Rehabilitation* **3**, 139.

HEALING, T. D. and NOWELL, F. (1985). Diseases and parasites of woodland rodent populations. *Symposium of the Zoological Society of London* **55**, 193.

HEWER, H.R. (1974). *British Seals.* William Collins and Sons, Glasgow.

HICKS, B. D. and WORTHY, G. A. J. (1987). Sealpox in captive grey seals (*Halichoerus grypus*) and their handlers. *Journal of Wildlife Diseases* **23**, 1.

HOLM, J. (1987). *Squirrels.* Whittet Books, London.

HUIBREGTSE, W. H. (1966). Some chemical and physical properties of bat milk. *Journal of Mammalogy* **47**, 551.

IASON, G. R. and BOAG, B. (1988). Do intestinal helminths affect condition and fecundity of adult mountain hares? *Journal of Wildlife Diseases* **24**, 599.

IUCN (1989). *Translocation of Living Organisms. IUCN Position Statement.* International Union for the Conservation of Nature, Gland, Switzerland.

JACOBSON, E. R., KOLLIAS, G. V. Jr. and HEARD, D. (1988). Viral diseases and vaccination considerations for non-domestic carnivores. In: *Exotic Animals.* (Eds. E. R. Jacobson and G. V. Kollias Jr.) Churchill Livingstone, New York.

JALANKA, H. H. (1989). Chemical restraint and reversal in captive markhors (*Capra falconeri megaceros*): a comparison of two methods. *Journal of Zoo and Wildlife Medicine* **20**, 413.

JEFFERIES, D. J., WAYRE, P., JESSOP, R. M. and MITCHELL-JONES, A. J. (1986). Reinforcing the native otter (*Lutra lutra*) population in East Anglia: an analysis of the behaviour and range development of the first release group. *Mammal Review* **16**, 65.

JENNESS, R. and SLOAN, R. E. (1975). The composition of milks of various species: a review. *Dairy Science Abstracts* **32**, 599.

JONES, D. M. (1984). The capture and handling of deer. In: *The Capture and Handling of Deer.* (Ed. A.J.B. Rudge) Nature Conservancy Council, Peterborough.

KEYMER, I. F. (1983). Diseases of squirrels in Britain. *Mammal Review* **13**, 155.

KEYMER, I. F. and EPPS, H. B. G. (1969). Canine distemper in the Family Mustelinae. *Veterinary Record* **84**, 204.

KEYMER, I. F. and HIME, J. M. (1977). Nutritional ostrodystrophy in a free-living red squirrel *Sciurus vulgaris. Veterinary Record* **100**, 31.

KEYMER, I. F., LEWIS, G. and DON, P. L. (1981). Urolithiasis in otters (Family Mustelidae, Subfamily Lutrinae) and other species. *Erkrankungen der Zootiere* **23**, 391.

KING, C. M. (1977a). The effects of the nematode parasite *Skrjabingylus nasicola* on British weasels. *Journal of Zoology London* **182**, 225.

KING, C. (1989). *The Natural History of Weasels and Stoats.* Christopher Helm, Bromley.

KIRKWOOD, J. K. (1983). The influence of size of animal in health and disease. *Veterinary Record* **113**, 287.

KIRKWOOD, J. K. (1989). Artificially rearing young wild animals: rationale and techniques. In: *Proceedings of the Inaugural Symposium of the British Wildlife Rehabilitation Council.* (Eds. S. Harris and T. Thomas) British Wildlife Rehabilitation Council, London.

KIRKWOOD, J. K., GASKIN, C. D. and MARKHAM, J. (1987). Perinatal mortality and birth season in captive wild ungulates. *Veterinary Record* **120**, 386.

KIRKWOOD, J. K. and MERRIAM, J. (1990). Variation in plasma half-life of gentamicin between species in relation to bodyweight and taxonomy. *Research in Veterinary Science* **49**, 160.

KIRKWOOD, J. K. and WIDDOWSON, M. A. (1990). Interspecies variation in the plasma half-life of oxytetracycline in relation to bodyweight. *Research in Veterinary Science* **48**, 180.

KIRKWOOD, J. K., WILLIAMS, P., MOXEY, T., WALLBANK, H., STADLER, J., HOWLETT, J., MARKHAM, J., DEAN, C. and EVA, J. K. (1988). Management and formula intake of young hand-reared Chinese water deer *Hydropotes inermis* and their growth compared with mother-reared fawns. *International Zoo Yearbook* **27**, 308.

KLEIMAN, D. G. (1969). Maternal care, growth rate and development in the noctule *(Nyctalus noctula),* pipistrelle *(Pipistrellus pipistrellus),* and serotine *(Eptesicus serotinus)* bats. *Journal of Zoology London* **157**, 187.

KOCK, R. A., HARWOOD, J. P. P., PEARCE, P. C. and CINDEREY, R. N. (1987). Chemical immobilisation of Formosan sika deer *(Cervus nippon):* a physiological study. *Journal of the Association of Veterinary Anaesthetists* **14**, 120.

KREAGER, J. J., SEAL, U. S., CALLAHAN, M. and BECKEL, M. (1990). Chemical immobilisation of red foxes *(Vulpes vulpes). Journal of Wildlife Diseases* **26**, 95.

KUIKEN, T. (1988). Anaesthesia in the European otter *Lutra lutra. Veterinary Record* **123**, 59.

LARMOUR, L. J. (1989a). Hand-rearing seal pups at the Oban Sea Life Centre. In: *Proceedings of the Inaugural Symposium of the British Wildlife Rehabilitation Council.* (Eds. S. Harris and T. Thomas) British Wildlife Rehabilitation Council, London.

LARMOUR, L. J. (1989b). Hand-rearing and rehabilitation of common seal pups *(Phoca vitulina)* at the Oban Sea Life Centre. *International Zoo Yearbook* **28**, 272.

LAUCKNER, G. (1985). Diseases of Mammalia: Pinnipedia. In: *Diseases of Marine Mammals.* Volume IV, Part 2. (Ed. O. Kinne) Biologische Anstalt Helgoland, Hamburg.

LUDWIG, D. R. (1982). Selection of release sites and post-release studies for rehabilitated wildlife. *Wildlife Rehabilitation* **1**, 25.

LUDWIG, D. R. and MIKOLAJCZAK, S. M. (1985a). Post-release behaviour of captive-reared racoons. *Wildlife Rehabilitation* **3**, 144.

LUDWIG, D. R. and MIKOLAJCZAK, S. M. (1985b). Post-release studies: a review of current information. *Wildlife Rehabilitation* **4**, 111.

LUMB, W. V. and JONES, E. W. (1984). *Veterinary Anesthesia.* 2nd Edn. Lea and Febiger, Philadelphia.

McBRIDE, A. (1988). *Rabbits and Hares.* Whittet Books, London.

McDIARMID, A. (1962). *Diseases of Free-Living Wild Animals.* Food and Agriculture Organization of the United Nations, Rome.

MAIR, N. S. (1968). Pseudotuberculosis in free-living wild animals. *Symposium of the Zoological Society of London* **24**, 107.

MARTIN, A. R., REYNOLDS, P. and RICHARDSON, M. G. (1987). Aspects of the biology of pilot whales *(Globicephala melaena)* in recent mass strandings on the British coast. *Journal of Zoology London* **211**, 11.

MICHALAK, I. (1987). Keeping and breeding the Eurasian water shrew *(Neomys fodiens)* under laboratory conditions. *International Zoo Yearbook* **26** 223.

MINISTRY OF AGRICULTURE, FISHERIES AND FOOD (1987). *Bovine tuberculosis in badgers.* 11th Report. Ministry of Agriculture, Fisheries and Food.

MONSON, W. J. (1987). The care and management of orphaned puppies and kittens. *Veterinary Technician* **8**, 430.

MOORE, D. (1985). Meadow vole. In: *Infant Diet/Care Notebook.* (Eds. S. Taylor and A. Bietz) American Association of Zoo Parks and Aquaria, Wheeling.

ODELL, C. H. (1985). Selection of release sites and post-release findings on five hand-reared bobcats. *Wildlife Rehabilitation* **3**, 155.

OFTEDAL, O. T. (1980). Milk composition and formula selection for hand-rearing young animals. In: *Scholl Nutrition Conference on the Nutrition of Captive Wild Animals.* (Eds. E. R. Maschgen, M. E. Allen and L. E. Fisher) Lincoln Park Zoological Gardens, Chicago.

OFTEDAL, O. T. (1984). Milk composition, milk yield and energy output at peak lactation: a comparative review. *Symposium of the Zoological Society of London* **51**, 33.

OSTERHAUS, A. D. M. E., BROEDERS, H. W. J., GROEN, J., UYTDEHAAG, F. G. C. M., VISSER, I. K. G., VAN DE BILT, M. W. G., ORVELL, C., KUMAREV, V.P. and ZORIN, V.L. (1989). Different morbilliviruses in European and Siberian seals. *Veterinary Record* **125**, 647.

PEARCE, P. C. and KOCK, R. A. (1989). Physiological effects of etorphine, acepromazine and xylazine on the black fallow deer *(Dama dama). Research in Veterinary Science* **46**, 380.

PLOWRIGHT, W. (1988). Viruses transmissible between wild and domestic animals. *Symposium of the Zoological Society of London* **60**, 175.

POKRAS, M. A., KARAS, A. M., KIRKWOOD, J. K. and SEDGWICK, C. J. (1991). An introduction to allometric scaling and its uses in raptor medicine. *Proceedings of the 2nd International Symposium on Raptor Diseases, Minnesota, 1988.*

PUTNAM, R. (1988). *The Natural History of Deer.* Christopher Helm, London.

RACEY, P. A. (1970). The breeding, care and management of vespertilionid bats in the laboratory. *Laboratory Animals* **4**, 171.

RACEY, P. A. (1987). Keeping, handling and releasing. In: *The Bat-workers Manual.* (Ed. A.J. Mitchell-Jones) Nature Conservancy Council, Peterborough.

RACEY, P. A. and KLEIMAN, D. G. (1970). Maintenance and breeding in captivity of some vespertilionid bats with special reference to the noctule *Nyctalus noctula. International Zoo Yearbook* **10**, 65.

RANKIN, J. D. and McDIARMID, A. (1968). Mycobacterial infections in free-living wild animals. *Symposium of the Zoological Society of London* **24**, 119.

REDFERN, R. and ROWE, F. P. (1987). Wild rats and mice. In: *The UFAW Handbook on the Care and Management of Laboratory Animals.* 6th Edn. (Ed. T. B. Poole) Longman, Harlow.

ROEKEN, B. O. (1987). Medetomidine in zoo animal anaesthesia. *Proceedings of the First International Conference on Zoological and Avian Medicine, Oahu, 1987.* The American Association of Zoo Veterinarians.

ROSS, J. (1982). Myxomatosis: the natural evolution of the disease. *Symposium of the Zoological Society of London* **50**, 77.

ROYAL SOCIETY FOR THE PREVENTION OF CRUELTY TO ANIMALS/SCOTTISH SOCIETY FOR THE PREVENTION OF CRUELTY TO ANIMALS (1988). *First Aid for Stranded Cetaceans.* Royal Society for the Prevention of Cruelty of Animals, Horsham.

RÜBEL, A., HAUSER, B., BAUMGARTNER, R. and ISENBUGEL, E. (1987). Veterinarmedizinische prophylaxe bei der haltung des Europaischen fischotters *(Lutra l. lutra). Erkrankungen der Zootiere* **29**, 285.

RUDGE, A. J. B. (1966). Catching and keeping live moles. *Journal of Zoology London* **149**, 42.

RUDGE, A. J. B. (1984). Ed. *The Capture and Handling of Deer.* Nature Conservancy Council, Peterborough.

SANDS, J. J., SCOTT, A. C. and HARKNESS, J. W. (1984). Isolation in cell culture of a pox virus from the red squirrel *(Sciurus vulgaris). Veterinary Record* **114**, 117.

SCHMIDT, C. R. (1972). New otter exhibit at Zurich Zoo. *International Zoo Yearbook* **12**, 83.

SEDGWICK, C. J. (1986). Scaling and anesthesia for primates. In: *Primates. The Road to Self-Sustaining Populations.* (Ed. K. Benirschke) Springer-Verlag, New York.

STEIGER, G. H., CALAMBOKIDIS, J, CUBBAGE, J. C., SKILLING, D. E., SMITH, A. W. and GRIBBLE, D. H. (1989). Mortality of harbor seal pups at different sites in the inland waters of Washington. *Journal of Wildlife Diseases* **25**, 319.

SUGAR, L., CZAPO, J., CZAPO, Z., HORN, A. and LEMLE, Z. (1986). Milk sampling and analysis of zoo-kept red, fallow and roe deer. *Erkrankungen der Zootiere* **28**, 213.

TAYLOR, S. and BIETZ, A. (1985). Eds. *Infant Diet/Care Notebook.* American Association of Zoological Parks and Aquariums, Wheeling.

THOMAS, J. A. (1985). Small-clawed otter. In: *Infant Diet/Care Notebook.* (Eds. S. Taylor and A. Bietz) American Association of Zoological Parks and Aquariums, Wheeling.

TWIGG, G. I., CUERDEN, C. M. and HUGHES, D. M. (1968). Leptospirosis in British wild mammals. *Symposium of the Zoological Society of London* **24**, 75.

VAUGHAN, J. A. (1987). The European wild rabbit. In: *The UFAW Handbook on the Care and Management of Laboratory Animals.* 6th Edn. (Ed. T. E. Poole) Longman, Harlow.

VIZOSO, A. D. (1969). A red squirrel disease. *Symposium of the Zoological Society of London* **24**, 29.

VOGT, P. (1987). Breeding European otters *(Lutra l. lutra)* in the new otter exhibit at Krefeld Zoo. *International Zoo Yearbook* **26**, 157.

WALLACH, J. D. and BOEVER, W. J. (1983). *Diseases of Exotic Animals.* W.B. Saunders, Philadelphia.

WALSH, S. T. and STEBBINGS, R. E. (1989). Care and rehabilitation of wild bats. In: *Proceedings of the Inaugural Symposium of the British Wildlife Rehabilitation Council, London.* (Eds. S. Harris and T. Thomas) British Wildlife Rehabilitation Council, London.

WAYRE, P. (1972). Breeding the Eurasian otter at the Norfolk Wildlife Park. *International Zoo Yearbook* **12**, 116.

WIDDOWSON, E.M. (1981). *Feeding the Newborn Mammal.* Carolina Biological Supply Company, Burlington, North Carolina.

WILESMITH, J. W., PRITCHARD, D. G., STUART, F. A., BREWER, J. I., BODE, R., HILLMAN, G. D. B. and SAYERS, P. E. (1986). Aspects of badger ecology and surveillance for tuberculosis in badger populations (1976—1984). *Journal of Hygiene, Cambridge* **97**, 11.

YALDEN, D. W. (1986). Opportunities for reintroducing British mammals. *Mammal Review* **16**, 53.

YALDEN, D. W. and MORRIS, P. A. (1975). *The Lives of Bats.* David and Charles, Newton Abbot.

CHAPTER THIRTEEN

CAGE AND AVIARY BIRDS

Brian H Coles BVSc MRCVS

SOME ASPECTS OF APPLIED CLINICAL ANATOMY

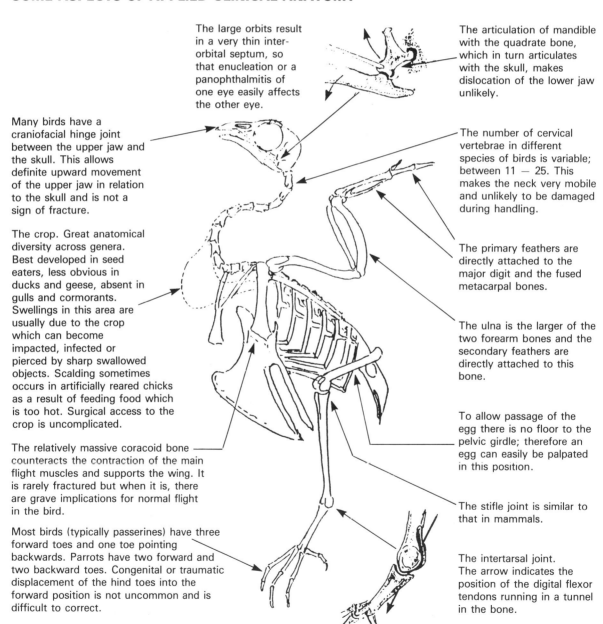

The large orbits result in a very thin inter-orbital septum, so that enucleation or a panophthalmitis of one eye easily affects the other eye.

The articulation of mandible with the quadrate bone, which in turn articulates with the skull, makes dislocation of the lower jaw unlikely.

Many birds have a craniofacial hinge joint between the upper jaw and the skull. This allows definite upward movement of the upper jaw in relation to the skull and is not a sign of fracture.

The number of cervical vertebrae in different species of birds is variable; between 11 — 25. This makes the neck very mobile and unlikely to be damaged during handling.

The crop. Great anatomical diversity across genera. Best developed in seed eaters, less obvious in ducks and geese, absent in gulls and cormorants. Swellings in this area are usually due to the crop which can become impacted, infected or pierced by sharp swallowed objects. Scalding sometimes occurs in artificially reared chicks as a result of feeding food which is too hot. Surgical access to the crop is uncomplicated.

The primary feathers are directly attached to the major digit and the fused metacarpal bones.

The ulna is the larger of the two forearm bones and the secondary feathers are directly attached to this bone.

The relatively massive coracoid bone counteracts the contraction of the main flight muscles and supports the wing. It is rarely fractured but when it is, there are grave implications for normal flight in the bird.

To allow passage of the egg there is no floor to the pelvic girdle; therefore an egg can easily be palpated in this position.

The stifle joint is similar to that in mammals.

Most birds (typically passerines) have three forward toes and one toe pointing backwards. Parrots have two forward and two backward toes. Congenital or traumatic displacement of the hind toes into the forward position is not uncommon and is difficult to correct.

The intertarsal joint. The arrow indicates the position of the digital flexor tendons running in a tunnel in the bone.

CLASSIFICATION OF COMMONLY KEPT CAGE BIRDS

Natural distribution	Genus	Common name	Particular characteristics
Class Aves **Order Psittaciformes** Contains 330 species with the commonest genera listed below.			
Family Psittacidae			
West and Equatorial Africa.	*Psittacus* (3 sub-species)	African grey parrot.	A medium-sized grey parrot with a short red tail.
Africa except the north.	*Poicephalus* (9 species)	Senegal and Meyer's parrot.	Small to medium sized parrots, usually with green bodies and grey or brown heads, napes and wings.
Africa except the north.	*Agapornis* (9 species)	Lovebird	Small parrots, slightly larger than budgerigars with a proportionately larger bill. So called because of mutual preening. Hybridise easily and many mutants produced in captivity.
Afro-Asia	*Psittacula* (15 species)	Ring necked parakeets.	Medium sized parrots with a long tail. Adult males have a black ring around the throat.
Australia	*Platycercus* (8 species)	Australian rosella parrots.	Medium sized parrots with long tails, variously coloured cheek patches and mottled plumage along the back.
Australia	*Neophema* (7 species)	Grass parakeet, Bourke's parrot, splendid parrot, turquoise parrot, elegant parrot.	The size and shape of budgerigars. Except for Bourke's parrot, predominantly green with blue, red and yellow colouring. Many mutants bred in captivity.
Australia	*Melopsittacus*	Budgerigar	Many different mutant varieties produced in captivity bearing little resemblance to the wild form.

Natural distribution	Genus	Common name	Particular characteristics
Spice Islands of South East Asia.	*Eclectus*	Eclectus parrot.	A rather large, medium sized bird with a short tail. Male is basically green colour whilst the female is basically red.
West Indies, Central and South America.	*Amazona* (22 species)	Amazon parrots.	Medium to large stocky birds with short tails. With few exceptions they are predominantly green with red, yellow or blue on the head, tail and wings of different species.
West Indies, Central and South America.	*Aratinga* (19 species) Other genera of conure occur.	Conures	Small to medium sized parrots with long tails. Often the periophthalmic skin is naked.
South America	*Cyanoliseus*	Patagonian conure.	A relatively large bird with a proportionately smaller bill than the other conures. Predominantly olive brown to green in colour. Mutants occur.
West Indies, Central and South America.	*Ara* There are other genera of macaw.	Macaws	Small to very large parrots with long tails and large beaks. The facial skin is usually naked.
Family Cacaduidae			
South East Asia and Australia.	*Cacatua* (11 species) 6 other species of cockatoo not in this genus.	Cockatoos	Medium sized to large birds with an erectile crest. Short broad tail and very strong bill. Plumage is predominantly white.

Natural distribution	Genus	Common name	Particular characteristics
Australia	*Nymphicus*	Cockatiel	A small sized bird with a body size a little larger than a budgerigar. Has a crest on the head. Many mutant strains produced. Sexually dimorphic; female has yellow cheeks and head.
Family Loriidae			
South East Asia, North, East and South Australia and Tasmania.	*Trichoglossus* 10 other genera of lory and lorikeet.	Rainbow lory	Small medium sized, brilliantly multi-coloured birds. Breast plumage barred. Feed mainly on pollen, nectar and fruit.

Order: Passeriformes
A large Order containing over half of all living species of birds; so called perching birds, the feet of which are specifically adapted for this purpose.

Natural distribution	Genus	Common name	Particular characteristics
Family Fringillidae			
Euro-Asia	*Serinus*	Finches, canary, European serin, African green finch.	All finches are small seed-eating song birds. They are sexually dimorphic. Aviculturists have produced many hybrids and there are over 40 varieties or breeds of canary.
Worldwide except Madagascar	*Carduelis*	Goldfinch, greenfinch, bullfinch, linnet.	
Family Estrildidae			
Tropics of Africa South East Asia.	*Estrilda*	Waxbills, zebra finch, munias (nuns).	Very small seed-eating birds which are usually highly sociable and kept in mixed groups. Many mutant plumage colours occur.

Natural distribution	Genus	Common name	Particular characteristics
Family Emberizidae			
North America, Euro-Asia and Africa.	*Emberiza, Pyrrhuloxia, Tangara.*	Buntings, cardinals, tanagers.	Small, stocky stout-billed mainly graniforous birds. The cardinals all have crests. Tanagers are often brightly coloured. Feed mainly on insects and fruits.
Family Sturnidae			
The Old World	*Lamprotornis, Gracula.*	Tropical starlings, eg. purple glossy starlings, mynahs.	All about the same size as the European starling. Territorial when breeding.
Order Clumbiformes			
Family Columbidae			
India and China.	*Streptopelia*	Barbary dove, red collared dove.	Size and form of a pigeon but rather smaller.
Family Phasianidae			
India and South East Asia	*Coturnix* Some taxonomists place this species in the genus *Excalfactoria.*	Painted quail, also known as: blue breasted, king button or blue quail.	Vary in size from 13—18cm in length; round-bodied birds with very short tails. Ground living.

Many other types of birds such as toucans (Ramphastidae), turacos (Musophigidae) and barbets (Capitonidae) are kept by specialist aviculturists.

References

Cameron and Harrison, 1978; Campbell, 1974; Forshaw and Cooper, 1978; Martin, 1980.

BIOLOGICAL DATA

Common name	Species	Number of eggs	Incubation in days	Fledging time in days	Age at maturity	Average weight in grammes	Weight range in grammes
Budgerigar	*Melopsittacus undulatus*	4—6	16—18	22—26	6 months	40	30—85
Lovebird	*Agapornis* sp.	4—6	18—21	40	6 months	45	42—48
African grey parrot	*Psittacus erithacus*	3—4	26—28	50—65	4—6 years	450	310—534
Orange winged Amazon parrot	*Amazona amazonica*	2—4	23—24	45—60	4—6 years	400	300—480
Lesser sulphur crested cockatoo	*Cacatua sulphurea*	2—4	23—25	46—60	5—6 years	250	228—315
Moluccan cockatoo	*Cacatua moluccensis*	2—4	24—26	66—80	5—6 years	700	658—1,000
Cockatiel	*Nyphicus hollandicus*	5	18	28—35	6 months	80	70—108
Blue and gold macaw	*Ara ararauna*	2—4	26—28	70—80	5—7 years	1,000	850—2,000
Diamond dove	*Geopelia cuneata*	2	13	11	5 months	40	35—45
Indian hill mynah	*Gracula religiosa*	3—4	14—16	15—25	1 year	200	180—260
Zebra finch	*Peophila guttata*	6	12	14—21	6 months	12	10—16
Canary	*Serinus canaria*	4	13—14	28	1 year	15	12—29

References

Coles, 1985; Harrison and Harrison, 1986.

HAEMATOLOGICAL DATA

There are considerable variations in the Class Aves and it is wise to consult standard texts, eg. Harrison and Harrison, 1986; Hawkey and Gulland, 1988.

The values below are only a very rough guide:

White cell count	$3-11 \times 10^9$/l
Red cell count	$2.5-4.5 \times 10^{12}$/l
Haemoglobin	11—19g/dl
Packed cell volume	0.4—0.55 l/l

Differential white cell count:—

Heterophils (equivalent to mammalian neutrophils)	30—75%
Lymphocytes	20—65%
Monocytes	0—5%
Basophils	0—5%
Eosinophils	0—4%

BIOCHEMICAL DATA

There are even greater interspecies variations for biochemical data and reference must be made to standard texts, eg. Harrison and Harrison, 1986; Hawkey and Gulland, 1988; Lumeij, 1989; Vanderheyden, 1989. The most comprehensive data are held on the 'Lynx' computer data base by Dr. Hawkey at the Zoological Society of London.

HOUSING

Cages

It is true to say that no cage is large enough and all birds are fitter if kept in aviaries. Exercising birds in a living room is hazardous and particular attention must be given to protecting windows. Hygiene is of paramount importance and all caging should be designed so that it can easily be cleaned. No cage should be so small that the bird cannot fully extend its wings (see 'Legislation') and the tail should be well clear of the floor when the bird is perched. Many parrot and cockatiel cages are very near this minimum. All birds feel more secure and less stressed if the cage has meshwork or bars on only one side — a situation partially simulated by having the cage in the corner of a room or partly covering it with a cloth. All cages should be well above ground level, preferably at human head height, with the exclusion of the ground living species, eg. quail. Most birds spend most of their time above human eye-level, either in flight or perching. There is little chance of human eye to bird eye contact and therefore less implied threat and thus less stress.

Perches

Perches need to be of varying diameter to exercise the feet. Uniform plastic and wooden dowels are easier to clean but not as good as natural branches, which can be replaced regularly. Slip-on sandpaper tubes for the perches and sand sheets do not help to keep nails in trim and predispose to foot excoriation and infection. Shelf liner or other plain paper or even newspaper is best used on the floor. Some birds will eat soiled particles of sand or sandpaper if they do not have access to grit or, possibly, if they have a dietary deficiency. If the sand is contaminated with faecal droppings, this behaviour could result in the bird's ingesting infectious agents. Coprophagia is not uncommon in budgerigars (personal observation; Baker, personal communication).

Food and water containers

Column water containers are preferable since they are less liable to be used by the bird for bathing; also they are easier for keeping a check on water consumption and less liable to contamination. Again, to reduce the risk of faecal contamination food containers should be above floor level and never under a perch. A container with a large surface area allows easier selection of food items.

Aviaries

Aviaries should have a double safety door and preferably an inside perching/sleeping area. Suitable plants in tubs or pots add interest and encourage insect life. However, care must be taken as to which plants are placed in an aviary since most birds are destructive to all plants and some of these may be toxic. For example, the following should not be used in aviaries: cherry (Prunus spp.), clematis (Clematis spp.), juniper (Juniper spp.), laurels (Lauracae), privet (Ligustrum vulgare), rhododendron (Rhododendron spp.), azalea (Rhododendron spp.), Virginia creeper (Parthenocissus quinquefolia) or yew (Taxus baccata).

Shallow (1cm) water bowls, for bathing, should be provided early in the day. Aviculturists sometimes fit timed sprinkler systems to their aviaries.

Lighting and heat

There is no complete substitute for unfiltered sunlight, but for birds kept indoors a broad-spectrum fluorescent tube or bulb (as used for indoor plant growth) provides a practical alternative. Healthy birds will withstand wide ranges of ambient temperature (from $1^\circ - 26^\circ C$) providing there are not rapid fluctuations. For most species a relative humidity of $40 - 50\%$ is the optimum.

Boredom

Caged birds are liable to boredom and 'toys' should be provided. Pieces of suspended chain, bells or keys (be wary that leg bands do not get caught in open links), blocks of hardwood, bark covered branches from native British hardwoods and fruit trees provide interest for parrots. Also, stainless steel mirrors, rawhide dog chews, cardboard boxes and egg boxes are useful. All rubber items are potentially dangerous. Singly kept budgerigars can become sexually bonded to a particular toy. The cage should not become cluttered and it is wise to change the items in rotation.

NUTRITION

It is important always to take into account the nutritional status of a sick bird.

Chronic malnutrition

A large number of caged birds endure chronic malnutrition, usually a deficiency of more than one nutrient and an imbalance of the main dietary constituents. This persistent low grade debility often becomes critical during times of increased nutritional demand such as moulting, reproduction, exposure to infectious disease, transport and quarantine and when a young bird is growing rapidly. A malnourished birds looks dilapidated. The sheen on the beak and plumage disappears and the plumage is often damaged and disarranged. The scales around the legs and skin around the eyes and cere look dry and flaky. The bird is dull and lacks the sparkle of a healthy creature.

Hardbills and softbills

For practical purposes aviculturists divide caged birds into two broad categories which to some extent overlap: hardbills and softbills.

Hardbills include most of the parrot-like birds and finches. They extract the kernel of seeds or nuts by cracking the hard outer husk using their specially adapted beaks.

Softbills include those birds feeding on fleshy fruits or invertebrates, or on a semi-liquid diet of pollen and nectar. However, many hardbills take some soft fruit and insects, particularly when breeding; some softbills take grain and nectar feeders take a few insects.

Dietary considerations

Although suitable diets for many species have been determined, the dietary requirements for many lesser known species have not been well documented. Space does not allow the inclusion of standard diets and reference must be made to other texts, eg. Petrak, 1982; Stoodley and Stoodley, 1983; Harrison and Harrison, 1986; Price, 1988; Stoodley et al, 1988.

Factors for the clinician to consider in relation to cage bird nutrition

1. Hardbills need seed appropriate to their size, ie. canary seed, rape seed and millet for budgerigars and most finches; sunflower, peanuts and pine nuts for the larger psittacines (but these also take the smaller sized seeds). Although a seed container may look full, a careless and unobservant owner may have left this receptacle filled with unsustaining seed husks from which the nutritive kernel has already been extracted by the bird.

2. Birds are basically conservative feeders, only eating those foods they recognise or on which they have become imprinted during development. An unfamiliar food or a different feeding dish may even frighten a bird. Abrupt changes in diet can result in starvation. New foods and routines should be gradually introduced over a period of weeks. Nevertheless, many birds are inquisitive and can be said to be opportunist omnivores, so that dietary changes are possible.

3. Variety in the diet. All birds need at least six different food items in their basic diet; one or two types of seed are not sufficient. Failure to ensure variety is a major cause of malnutrition, eg. millet sprays and compacted seed honey bells can easily become the main diet of many pet budgerigars on which they can survive but not thrive. Inexperienced owners are better advised to feed the balanced, packeted products of a reliable, commercial company. Complete pelleted parrot diets are now becoming available and are often sold as maintenance, growth and breeding diets. These products are advertised in the bird fancy press.

4. Supplementary feeding. Most species will be in better health if, in addition to their basic diet, they are given a supplementary ration which aims to provide a comprehensive range of vitamins and minerals together with, possibly as yet undocumented, nutritional factors. This extra ration should consist of green food (lettuce, watercress, chickweed, parsley, dandelion, etc.), sprouted seeds, vegetables (carrots, turnip, beetroot) and fruit (oranges, apples, plums, grapes, tomatoes, etc.). Some of these items can be pureed or made into a mash with a little added animal protein, eg. dried or cooked egg, chicken, hard cheese or milk. To this is added extra vitamins, particularly A, D_3 and B_{12}. Some of the above constituents form the basis of most 'condition', 'tonic', 'song' or 'moulting' foods. When introducing these supplementary items one should mix very small quantities in the normal ration and gradually increase the amount.

5. Insectivores usually need live food, eg. mealworms, crickets and fruit flies — easily attracted and cultured on over-ripe fruit. However, if these items are not available, commercial insectile preparations such as Mynah Bird Food and Sluis Universal (EW Coombs Limited, Finsbury Road, Strood, Kent) can be purchased.

6. Frugivores and nectar feeders, which include lories, lorikeets, toucans, hummingbirds and sunbirds, need either syrupy fluids, ie. subsitute nectar, or a variety of ripe fruit — as described under 4 above — and sometimes both. Formulae for artificial nectar should not include molasses, but be mainly based on Mellins Food (a maltose/dextrose mixture with added thiamine mononitrate ferric glycerol, phosphate and potassium bicarbonate), evaporated milk and honey with added vitamins, minerals and a little animal protein. Because this type of food is easily contaminated, nectar feeders are susceptible to bacterial and *Candida* infections. Good hygiene is paramount.

7. Obesity in cage birds. In psittacines, particularly budgerigars and cockatoos, obesity is common. It is not only caused by a badly balanced diet but also by a sedentary life-style. Aviary birds are more active and healthier. Free-living wild birds, particularly insectivores, have actively to search for food if they are to survive. They also feed mostly at first light and again in the late afternoon. Consequently, feeding caged birds *ad libitum* is not good practice and it is better to feed a ration at regular times (irregularity contributes to stress) when a new food is more readily acceptable. Nevertheless, small birds, particularly those smaller than budgerigars and those that have lost weight or are kept in a low ambient temperature, will die if they do not feed fairly frequently, ie. at least six times daily during the daylight hours. High energy foods, eg. hemp, rape and niger seeds, should be reduced in summer. Very small birds should have low level background lighting to enable them to feed at night during midwinter since over twelve hours of darkness is too long a period without food.

8. Grit. Most seed-eating birds require access to grit for proper functioning of the gizzard. Grit must be of an appropriate size, be changed regularly and consist of both soluble (oyster shell and egg shell) and insoluble (quartz, igneous stone) kinds. A few birds with a digestive malfunction will overeat grit leading to impaction of the gizzard and overspill into the proventriculus. These birds should only be given grit once a month or at longer intervals.

HANDLING

All birds are more easily caught in subdued light. If possible a torch with a red, or better a blue, filter should be used in a completely dark room. How well birds see in light at the blue end of the spectrum seems to vary with the species.

A fine catching net, padded around the rim, is a great asset for catching birds loose in the surgery. If the bird has to be caught in its cage all 'toys', perches and feeding dishes should be removed.

If a parrot is in a cage, the bottom of which can be removed, this should be done and the cage turned on its side. Both hands can then easily be used to catch the bird through the much larger opening of the base. A hand towel (best provided by each owner, to reduce the risk of cross infection) or a paper towel caught between the fingers, should be dropped over the hand to hide it, so that if the parrot bites it will bite the towel rather than the hand. The parrot should be pushed against the bars of the cage and grasped quickly around the neck so that the thumb and forefinger are against the mandible with the rest of the fingers forming a loose ring around the neck. The other hand can loosely wrap the towel around the bird to stop movement of the wings and legs. Parrots tend to grip part of the towel with their feet. The bird will remain quieter if held on its back. Parts of the bird can then be separately exposed for examination. For very large birds a heavy pair of welders' gloves give added safety but the hands are less mobile, the gloves easily become contaminated and the birds soon become wary. Suitable gloves are described in the Introduction. A large macaw can quite easily amputate a finger since it can exert a pressure of approximately 16kg/sq.cm.

A small finch or budgerigar can be caught without a towel and held in one hand with the neck placed between the index and middle fingers. The thumb and forefinger can then be used to hold a leg or a wing. Thin (surgical) gloves help reduce bites but reduce the handler's sensitivity. A very small bird, eg. a Gouldian or African green singing finch, can be gently held in the cup of the hand.

One should not squeeze any bird so that movement of both the abdomen and sternum is restricted or the bird may be asphyxiated. In all birds the neck is fairly mobile and, provided undue pressure is not placed on it, the bird's head can safely be restrained by holding the neck.

Toucans and hornbills may look fearsome. Although they do not usually bite, they may stab with their beaks, the edges of which can be quite sharp and serrated.

SEXING

Some species of caged birds are dimorphic, eg. the ring-necked parakeets (genus *Psittacula*), budgerigars, cockatiels, hummingbirds, sunbirds, tanagers and some species of finches. In all these groups the male is more colourful than the female. In the adult white and pink cockatoos, the iris of the female is reddish brown whilst that of the male is dark brown to black. However, in many species of cagebird and most of the parrots the sexes look alike.

Non-invasive methods of sexing

1.   Steroid assay. The ratio of oestrogen to testosterone present in either a faecal or plasma sample has been used (Bercovitz, 1981; Harrison and Harrison, 1986). This method has not proved to be 100% reliable across the species range and is not readily available in the UK.

2.   Examination of the chromosomes. Fresh growing cells are required and to obtain these a newly emerging feather is plucked. The cytologist looks for the XX and XY chromosomes. The method has to be carried out by a specialist laboratory and at present is relatively expensive. However, it is almost 100% accurate (Herzog *et al*, 1986).

Invasive methods of sexing

This comprises the direct visual examination of the gonads using a laparoscope. With an experienced operator the method is 100% accurate and can be used on birds down to the size of a lovebird. However, the capital outlay on good quality apparatus is expensive. For the occasional medium to large sized bird an auroscope with a long fine speculum and good light has been used. This technique is described in Cooper (1974), Coles (1985), Harrison and Harrison (1986) and Eaton (1988).

REPRODUCTION

This is a large and complex subject and reference should be made to standard texts (Low, 1980; Woolham, 1987).

The most important factors for the veterinary clinician to consider when consulted about a reproductive problem are:—

1.   The presence of disease. Failure to breed is more likely to be due to bad husbandry than to disease; the latter is more likely to affect other organ systems rather than primarily the reproductive system. The use of hormone therapy is therefore contra-indicated until the above factors have been ruled out.

2. Stress. This must be reduced to a minimum. Stress can be caused by anxious, inquisitive owners constantly peering into the nestbox and the appearance of predators such as cats, foxes, rats, stoats, weasels and raptors around the aviary. Breeding success is usually greater in captive-bred or domesticated birds than in recently wild caught specimens. Many species, e.g. cockatoos, are territorial and aggressive when breeding. Aviaries for the same or related species need to be well spaced or, at the very least, the birds should be screened from each other.

3. Stimulants to trigger breeding. In contrast to territory holding, certain species, eg. some finches, Bengalese, Gouldians, Java sparrows, some weavers and budgerigars, need the stimulus of other birds in a colony to start breeding. Nevertheless, an occasional rogue bird in a colony can cause havoc by attacking fledglings and eating eggs. Even if a pair of birds is known to be of opposite sex and tolerant of each other's company, they may not be psychologically compatible breeders. Birds really need to choose their own mates. Display by the male to the female such as mutual preening and the offer of food or nest material are signs of impending breeding.

4. Nestboxes. The presence of a nestbox in a suitable (from the bird's point of view) position often acts as a stimulus to breeding. Most cagebird species, except canaries and doves, require the right type of nestbox. All nestboxes need to give the bird a feeling of security and therefore those that are solid and may appear too small often work best. It is good practice to offer several boxes per pair of birds, positioned in different sites, and let the birds choose.

   Most parrots require woodshavings as nesting material. This should be placed in the nestbox at least ten days before the eggs are due to be laid so that the humidity of this substratum can stabilise. Breeders sometimes moisten nest materials but this is bad practice; the birds are best left to control the humidity in the nest themselves.

5. Physical fitness. Breeding birds are fitter if kept in large exercise aviaries and there is often an increase in the number of eggs produced (Baker, personal communication). Selection by breeders for show characteristics has sometimes resulted in mating difficulties in budgerigars (Baker, 1989), cockatiels and canaries.

6. Maturity. Some species, eg. some lorikeets, Amazons and African grey parrots, take three to four years to become adult. Macaws take longer and in the wild only 10% of the larger macaws breed annually and of the two chicks hatched often only one survives.

7. Nutrition. A high level of nutrition is of paramount importance (see Nutrition).

8. Climate and microclimate. Birds have become adapted to specific habitats, eg. the hyacinth macaw comes from a relatively arid area whilst most other large macaws come from tropical rainforest. The local climate of the breeder's premises may influence breeding success.

9. The influence of light. A gradual increase in the photoperiod is an important breeding stimulus for birds originating from temperate climates but not in tropical birds. The quality of light may be important, particularly for birds kept indoors. A 'Thorn True Lite' (Thorn EMI) or similar broad-spectrum lamp may be beneficial. For very small birds increased light periods (up to 12 hours), using a low level background illumination provided by a child's night light, give longer feeding times and maintain condition.

10. Artificial incubation and rearing. This requires good quality, specialised equipment and expertise by the operator. Strict hygiene and good control of temperature and humidity are of paramount importance (Baker, 1988).

11. Record keeping. The problems of many breeders would be immeasurably improved if they were to keep consistent and accurate records. These should include: —

    a) Any changes in husbandry such as alterations in feeding times or constituents of food.
    b) The alteration and siting of aviaries and nestboxes.
    c) The introduction of new birds.
    d) The sighting of predators, eg. sparrow-hawks, kestrels, cats, rats, etc.
    e) The weather conditions.
    f) The occurrence of any disease or deaths.

DISEASES/CLINICAL CONDITIONS

For specific diseases reference must be made to other texts, eg. Petrak (1982), Coles (1985), Harrison and Harrison (1986) and Price (1988).

Respiratory system

Many respiratory problems have an underlying viral and/or nutritional origin. Birds do not often develop a primary pneumonia but infection and partial obstruction of the respiratory pathways is very common.

Clinical signs	Species usually affected	Possible aetiology	Confirmation of diagnosis
Nasal exudate. Staining or matting of feathers around nares.	Parrots, budgerigars.	Upper respiratory infection. *E. coli, Haemophilus,* Staphylococci, Streptococci, *Mycoplasma* (Gerlach, 1986), *Chlamydia,* viral, hypovitaminosis A.	Bacteriological culture and sensitivity of swab from nares and particularly choanal aperture. Visual examination of the oropharynx.
Para-orbital swellings.	All species, particularly parrots.	Infection of the para-orbital and adjacent sinuses.	Cytology. For treatment, aspirate after lancing under anaesthestic.
Abnormal sounds. Clicking, gurgling, wheezing, loss of voice.	All species.	Upper respiratory infection, usually in the region of the syrinx.	1. Microbiological culture and antibiotic sensitivity of tracheal and syringeal swabs. 2. Endoscopy. Both procedures are safer if carried out under isoflurane anaesthesia.
A high pitched 'squeaky wheel' sound.	Budgerigars.	Thyroid dysplasia usually due to iodine deficiency.	Response to treatment with iodine orally and by injection (Blackmore, 1969; Coles 1985).
Coughing.	Parrots.	Mimicking owner.	
Dypsnoea. Particularly when stressed.	All species	a) Air sacculitis. b) Space-occupying abdominal lesions.	1. Radiography. 2. Endoscopy of the abdomen.
Tail bobbing.	Usually the smaller species.	a) Aspergillosis of the syrinx. b) Air sac mites.	Endoscopy of the trachea.
Mouth breathing, gaping and head shaking.	All species but particularly passerines.	a) *Syngamus trachea* b) Foreign body. c) Tracheitis — viral/bacteriological.	1. Endoscopy of the trachea. 2. Swabs for microbiology.
Peracute dypsnoea.	All species	Irritant fumes, poly-tetrafluoroethylene vapour (non-stick pans), ammonia.	

Alimentary system

Many diseases of the alimentary tract have an underlying nutritional origin leading to disturbance in the normal gut flora. *E. coli* may often be isolated but it is not always significant. A virus may sometimes be implicated.

Clinical signs	Species usually affected	Possible aetiology	Confirmation of diagnosis
Retching and actual vomiting.	All species, particularly budgerigars.	a) Tumours/infection/ ulceration of the crop, proventriculus, gizzard or intestine. b) Trichomoniasis/*Candida* of the upper alimentary tract. c) Foreign body in upper alimentary tract. d) Poisoning by lead, zinc aflatoxin or disinfectants.	1. Crop washing for cytology. 2. Microbiological swabs. 3. Endoscopy. Radiography, endoscopy. History.
	Budgerigars.	Normal courtship behaviour. Neurotic behaviour in single male budgerigars.	Observation. Cessation when mirrors and other 'toys' are removed from cage or if a different person attends the bird.
	Budgerigars.	Enlarged thyroid.	Response to iodine therapy.
Dysphagia.	Macaws.	Proventricular dilation. (Macaw wasting syndrome. Cause unknown, possibly viral).	Barium contrast radiography.
	Parrots.	*Chlamydia.*	Sometimes together with respiratory signs.
	Artifically reared neonates.	a) Impacted crop. b) Microbiological infection of the crop.	Palpation. Microbiological culture and microscopy of crop contents.
Changes of character of the droppings. Watery droppings.	All species. Parrots.	a) Dietary changes, eg. more fruit leads to more fluid droppings. b) Stress: reduction in gut transit time. c) Excessive use of unsuitable antibiotic therapy leading to over-growth of yeasts. d) Anorexia due to pansystemic disease. e) Parasites, coccidia, *Giardia.* f) Starvation. g) Psychogenic polydipsia.	1. Microbiological culture. 2. Cytology. 3. Gram stain for excess numbers of Gram-negative bacteria. Blood for biochemical and haematological profile. Mostly in breeding colonies. Psychological stress, eg. separation from owner or from parent birds.

Clinical signs	Species usually affected	Possible aetiology	Confirmation of diagnosis
Changes of character of the droppings (continued). Yellow urate fraction of the droppings, the darker (green or brown) faecal fraction appears normal.	All species.	a) Hepatopathy, causing biliverdin excretion via kidney. b) Overdosage with B vitamins.	Often in obese birds. Sometimes after the use of medroxy-progesterone (see later). Radiography of the liver. Blood biochemistry profile for evidence of hepatopathy.
Blood in droppings. This may be fresh, mixed with either the urates or the faecal fraction. It may be tarry and partially digested.	All species. Cockatoos.	a) Normal in some egg-laying females. b) Cloacal prolapse/self trauma. c) Ulceration of lower alimentary canal. d) Tuberculosis. e) Sharp foreign body. f) Toxins. g) Tapeworms.	If necessary, radiography. Visual examination. Biochemical and haematological profile. Microbiological culture and microscopy. Check for possiblity of toxins. Parasitology of faecal sample.
Passing whole seeds, grit or undigested food.	All species.	Disease of the gizzard. Increased gut mobility. (Stress).	Radiography.
Excess faecal matter sometimes in the shape of popcorn faeces.	Particularly small grass parakeets, but also other species.	Pancreatitis.	Check faecal content for excess starch and/or fat.
Constipation, ie. no faecal matter, only urates, in droppings.	All species. All psittacines, particularly cockatoos. Particularly parrots. All species.	a) Cloaca and surrounding feathers impacted with an aggregate of urates. b) Impaction of intestine with ascarid worms. With wood shavings in cockatoos. c) Impaction of gizzard with grit. d) Egg binding.	Visual inspection. Contrast radiography plus faecal examination. Radiography. Radiography.

Urogenital system

Clinical signs	Species usually affected	Possible aetiology	Confirmation of diagnosis
Dull, brooding on floor of cage, plus blood in droppings and tenesmus.	All species.	a) Egg laying. b) Egg impaction. c) Egg peritonitis. d) Cloacal prolapse which may subsequently include oviduct.	1. Palpation of abdomen. 2. Visual examination: part of egg may be seen through cloacal opening. 3. Radiography.
Chronic egg laying.	All, but particularly cockatiels.	Hormone malfunction.	In budgerigars and cockatiels medroxy-progesterone acetate injection has been used for treatment, but in cockatiels this is often not effective and hysterectomy has to be carried out.
Abnormal eggs. 1. Soft-shelled. 2. Rough-shelled. 3. Yolk-less.	All species.	Deficiences of Ca^{++}, trace elements, vitamins A and D. Disease of the oviduct. Take into account excessive use of tetracyclines which bind available calcium.	One or two abnormal eggs in a normal clutch is of no significance. 1. Clinical examination. 2. Comparison of radiographs for medullary bone pre- and post-egg laying. 3. Microbiological culture, swab taken from dilated oviduct immediately post egg laying.
Polydipsia.	All species, but particularly mynah birds.	a) Hepatopathy.	1. Colour of urates (see earlier). 2. Radiography. 3. Blood biochemistry.
	All species.	b) Visceral gout. c) Enteritis.	Thin, sick bird. Microbiological culture and microscopy of droppings.
	All species.	d) Kidney disease.	1. Paralysis or paresis of one or both legs. 2. Blood biochemistry. 3. Radiography. 4. 12 hour water deprivation test to check increase in specific gravity above 1.025.
	Particularly psittacines. Budgerigar and small grass parakeets.	e) Psychogenic. f) Diabetes mellitus (permanent). Diabetes mellitus (temporary).	All other tests negative (see under 'watery droppings'). Plasma biochemistry. Increased appetite. The pathophysiology of diabetes mellitus in granivorous birds is quite different from that in mammals (Harrison and Harrison, 1986).

Clinical signs	Species usually affected	Possible aetiology	Confirmation of diagnosis
Polydipsia (continued).	All species.	Dehydration due to water deprivation. 1. Bad husbandry and unobservant owner. 2. Injury may prevent bird reaching rood and water bowl.	

Central nervous system and the sense organs

All the following signs can be due to pansystemic disease.

Clinical signs	Species usually affected	Possible aetiology	Confirmation of diagnosis
Loss of grip, leading to falling off the perch.	All species.	a) Old bird. b) Fractures. c) Tight leg bands. d) Gout, arthritis. e) Tumours. f) Hypocalcaemia. g) Spinal injuries. h) Kidney lesions. i) Abdominal tumours.	Radiography together with observation and palpation. Often with 'fits'. Plasma biochemistry. Radiography.
Constant shifting of weight on perch.	All species.	Inflammation/ulceration of the feet. Arthritis/gout.	Radiography. Clinical examination
Convulsions. Opisthotonos rotation of the head. Incoordination.	All species.	Head trauma/ear infection, acute ischaemic infection. Hypoglycaemia, hypocalcaemia, epilepsy, (ascarid larval migration). Toxins: lead, zinc, aflatoxin, insecticides. Neoplasms.	1. Clinical examination. 2. Radiography. 3. Blood chemistry.
	Pigeons, doves, grass parakeets.	Paramyxovirus.	Serology or virus isolation. Sometimes have a yellow to white chalky stool due to associated pancreatitis.
Dropped wing.	All species.	Fractures, soft tissue injury, neoplasms, luxations. Shamming injury (plovers).	1. Careful palpation of the injured area and examination of relaxed tissues under general anaesthesia. 2. Radiography.
Blindness.	All species.	Cataract, keratitis. Traumatic infections (particularly *Chlamydia*). Corneal opacity, uveitis. Head trauma, foreign body/nematodes beneath nictitating membrane.	Ophthalmological examination. Microbiology. Instillation of fluorescein/rose bengal. Radiography, examination under anaesthesia.

THERAPEUTICS

Methods of administration of drugs

1. In drinking water: least reliable.

2. In food: the medication must mix effectively with the food.

3. Via the crop (using a gavage tube): a metal tube or custom-made gag is needed for psittacines. Stressful.

4. Parenterally:
   a) i/m, the most reliable. The posterior part of the pectoral muscles is used; the leg muscles can be used but not in small birds. It is necessary to consider if the species of bird **primarily** runs, walks or flies.
   b) s/c injection: poorly absorbed.
   c) i/v via the right jugular or brachial (basilic) veins.
   d) via the infra-orbital sinus.
   e) intratracheally via the oropharynx.

5. Topically:
   a) Creams and ointments are not usually suitable unless used very sparingly. They damage the plumage.
   b) Tinctures or drugs combined with dimethyl sulphoxide are more suitable.
   c) Eye drops are preferable to eye ointments but require frequent handling of the bird which increases stress.
   d) Antiparasitic dusting powders can be used.

Calculation of appropriate dosage

The dose of a drug depends on its pharmacokinetics, ie. absorption, metabolism and clearance by the body. One important factor influencing metabolism is the mathematical relationship between the surface area of a body and its volume. As the size of the endothermic vertebrate decreases the proportional surface area, and hence, the metabolic rate increases. In practical terms small-birds require comparatively higher doses of drugs at more frequent intervals than larger vertebrates. This is expressed in the formula:

$$E = \left(\frac{W}{1000}\right) 0.75 \times D$$

W = weight of bird in grammes

D = dose of drug for the larger vertebrate, eg. cat, given in mg/kg

E = dose of drug for the bird of a specific weight (W) given in mg

The allometric scaling of doses has been described in the Introduction to this manual.

Doses of the most useful and commonly available drugs

Very few of the drugs listed have been given a veterinary products licence for use in cage birds. Some of the products are only licensed for use in human patients. However, under the Medicines Act 1968 (which at present has not been superseded by European legislation) a veterinary surgeon is allowed to use what drugs he considers necessary for the well being of an animal under his direct care.

Drug	Route of administration	Dosage	Comments

Antibiotics

If practicable, a bacteriological sensitivity test should be done before using an antimicrobial drug.

Penicillins

Drug	Route of administration	Dosage	Comments
Ampicillin Soluble powder, 20g bottles.	In drinking water.	100mg/litre drinking water for a minimum of 5 days (Clark, 1986).	
Long-acting injection, 100mg/ml.	i/m injection.	0.5ml/kg daily for a minimum of 5 days (Ensley and Janssen, 1981).	
Amoxycillin Long-acting injection, 150mg/ml.	i/m injection.	250mg/kg or 1.7ml/kg for a minimum of 5 days.	For parrots (Lawrence, 1988).
Palatable drops, dispensed as powder; when reconsiituted, 50mg/ml.	Orally (by gavage). In drinking water. In soft food.	150mg/kg or 3ml/kg bid. 150mg/kg or 3ml/kg tid. 200 – 400mg/litre drinking water. 300 – 500mg/kg soft food	For pigeons. In birds For parrots. there is For canaries. intermittent absorption from the gastro-intestinal tract (Dorrestein *et al,* 1984).
Clavulanate-potentiated amoxycillin Injection Suspension, 35mg/ml clavulanic acid and 140mg/ml amoxycillin.	i/m injection.	87.5mg/kg or 2.5ml/kg.	Dose extrapolated from dogs and cats (by author).
Palatable drops, dispensed as powder; when reconstituted contains 50mg/ml.	Orally.	125mg/kg or 2.5ml/kg bid.	Canaries, pigeons. Only reliable for gut infections (Dorrestein *et al,* 1981, 1984; Cooper, 1985).

Tetracyclines

Drug	Route of administration	Dosage	Comments
Oxytetracycline Long-acting injection, (50mg/ml 5% w/v).	i/m injection.	58mg/kg or 0.3ml/kg once daily for 5 – 7 days. 100mg/kg or 0.5ml/kg daily.	In parrots (Lawrence, 1988). For birds below 400g bodyweight. Tissue reaction often seen after i/m injection.

All tetracyclines are poorly absorbed from the gastro-intestinal tract and rapidly lose potency in drinking water. Calcium and magnesium in bird grit may affect absorption. These doses are only effective for prophylaxis and need to be increased tenfold for therapy. The frequent habit of putting a pinch of 'the dreaded yellow powder' in drinking water does no good and may actually be harmful.

Drug	Route of administration	Dosage	Comments
Feed Supplement. Soluble Powder.	In food. In food. In drinking water.	500mg/kg of soft food. 500/kg of soft food. 250mg/litre drinking water.	(Black, 1977). (Yoshida *et al,* 1975). (Clark, 1986).

Drug	Route of administration	Dosage	Comments

Doxycycline

More readily absorbed from the gut and twice as active as other tetracyclines since its half-life period in many bird species is longer (Westerhof and Lumeij, 1989).

Drug	Route of administration	Dosage	Comments
Dispensable tablets.	In drinking water.	500mg/litre drinking water.	
Vibramycin syrup, 50mg/5ml.	Orally (by gavage).	10mg/kg or 1ml/kg daily.	For parrots (Lawrence, 1988).
		25mg/kg or 2.5ml/kg bid.	For other birds (Westerhof and Lumeij, 1989). May cause emesis if dose exceeded.

Chortetracyline

Very unpalatable in drinking water and food due to offensive taste. Palatability may be increased by adding fruit juice, citric acid or sugar.

Drug	Route of administration	Dosage	Comments
Soluble powder.	Orally.	190mg/kg bid.	For budgerigars and canaries (Westerhof and Lumeij, 1989).
	In food.	1000mg/kg soft food for 30 days.	For prophylaxis only (Westerhof and Lumeij, 1989).
		5000mg/kg soft food for 30 days.	For treatment.
	In drinking water.	1000mg/litre drinking water for 30 days.	For prophylaxis only (Westerhof and Lumeij, 1989).
		5000mg/litre drinking water for 30 days.	For treatment.

Macrolides

Tylosin

Drug	Route of administration	Dosage	Comments
Tylosin 50% tylosin dissolved in propylene glycol, 50mg/ml.	i/m injection.	60mg/kg or 1.2ml/kg tid.	Non toxic for birds. For parrots 50−250mg bodyweight (Lawrence, 1988).
		25mg/kg or 0.5ml/kg tid.	For parrots 250−1000 grammes bodyweight and for pigeons and quail (Westerhof and Lumeji, 1989).
		15mg/kg or 3.3ml/kg tid.	For parrots over 1000 grammes bodyweight.
Tylosin tartrate soluble powder.	In drinking water.	500mg/litre water.	All species of birds (Clubb, 1986).

Antibacterial and antiprotozoal drugs
Trimethoprin-sulphadiazine

Drug	Route of administration	Dosage	Comments
Oral suspension.	Orally.	10−50mg/kg or 0.12−0.63ml/kg bid.	Dose is based on the sulphadiazine fraction (Dorrestein et al, 1984).
Injection (trimethoprim-sulphadoxine).	i/m or s/c injection.	25mg/kg or 0.4ml/kg bid.	

Drug	Route of administration	Dosage	Comments
Sulphadimidine 33⅓% Solution.	In drinking water. Orally.	A 0.2% solution (ie. 6.7ml/litre) is used for 3 days, 2 days of rest are given, then the dose is repeated for 3 days. 50mg/kg or 0.15ml/kg.	
Metronidazole Solution, 5mg/ml. Tablets. 0.5% w/v solution.	i/m injection. Orally. In drinking water.	5mg/kg or 1ml/kg bid. 50mg/kg tablet. 20mg/kg or 4ml/kg of the solution given at 12 hourly intervals for up to 7 days. 20mg/litre of drinking water.	May be toxic for finches (Harrison and Harrison, 1986). Has been used in parrots at these dose rates (Woerpel and Rosskopf, 1981). May reduce water intake considerably.
Dimetridazole Emtryl soluble.	Orally. In drinking water.	50mg/kg by gavage, first dissolved in warm water, daily for 3 days. 100 – 250mg/litre drinking water.	Very toxic if overdosed for parrots (Lawrence, 1986). Do not exceed 100mg/litre when dosing finches (Dorrestein et al, 1987a).

Antimycotic drugs

To be effective most antifungal drugs need to be used over a prolonged period. Often these drugs are most effective if used in combination. However, amphotericin B, ketoconazole and miconazole are all potentially hepatotoxic if used for prolonged periods.

Drug	Route of administration	Dosage	Comments
Nystatin Oral suspension, 100,000 iu/ml (medical preparation).	Orally (by gavage). In food. In drinking water.	300,000 – 600,000iu/kg or 3 – 6ml/kg bid or tid for 7 – 14 days. 200,00iu/kg soft food for 3 – 6 weeks. 100,000iu/litre of drinking water for 3 – 6 weeks.	Dall et al (1964). Westerhof and Lumeij (1989). Most useful for finches and other small birds.
Amphotericin Medical preparations, 50mg vial. Amphotericin suspension, 100mg/ml.	i/v injection. Intratracheally. Topically in the mouth.	1.5mg/kg tid for 7 days. 1mg/kg in 2ml sterile water bid for 12 days then use on alternate days for 5 weeks. Once to three times daily for 7 – 14 days.	Dilute with sterile water before use (Westerhof and Lumeij, 1989; Redig, 1981.)

Drug	Route of administration	Dosage	Comments
Ketoconazole Tablets, 200mg. Suspension.	Orally by gavage. Orally by gavage. In drinking water.	25 – 30mg/kg tid for 2 weeks. 1.25 – 1.5ml/kg for 2 weeks. 200mg/10ml/litre drinking water for 7 – 14 days.	Oral absorption is good but there is a delay of 5 – 10 days before the drug is active in pigeons and psittacines (Moriello, 1986). Westerhof and Lumeij, (1989). (Clubb, 1986).
Miconazole Medical preparation, 10mg/ml.	i/m injection.	10mg/kg or 1ml/kg daily for 6 – 12 days. 20mg/kg or 2ml/kg daily for 8 – 10 days.	For raptors (Furley and Greenwood, 1982). For psittacines (Gylstroff and Grimm, 1987).

Anthelmintic drugs

Drug	Route of administration	Dosage	Comments
Fenbendazole	Orally by gavage. In drinking water.	10 – 50mg/kg or 0.4ml/kg once. Repeat after 10 days for nematodes. For microfilariae and trematodes, give daily for 3 days. For *Capillaria* give daily for 5 days. 50mg/litre or 2ml/litre of drinking water.	Tasteless, generally safe broad-spectrum anthelmintic. Effective against trematodes and microfilariae. All benzimidazole derivatives can cause feather abnormalities in some birds during the moult and may also have adverse effects if used during the breeding season. Other drugs in this group, such as thiabendazole and mebendazole, have a variable toxicity in different species and are not recommended (Lawrence, 1983 and 1988; Westerhof and Lumeij, 1989). Useful for finches.
Levamisole 7.5% (75mg/ml) solution.	Orally	10 – 20mg/kg or 0.13 – 0.26ml/kg. 20mg/kg or 0.26ml/kg. Administered once and repeated after 14 days.	For Australian parakeets (Dorrestein, 1987). For Galliformes, Columbiformes and psittacines (Shanthikumar, 1987). Only effective against nematodes. Occasionally causes emesis.

Drug	Route of administration	Dosage	Comments
Levamisole (continued)	In drinking water.	100 – 200mg (1.3 – 2.6ml) of 7.5% solution for 3 consecutive days.	Normal drinking water is withdrawn overnight. Then dose is put in ½ quantity of drinking water consumed in 6 – 8 hours. After this period remainder of water is given. It has a bitter taste so to increase palatability fruit juice or honey is added. For finches.
	s/c injection.	80mg (1ml)/litre of 7.5% solution. 4 – 8mg/kg or 0.06 – 0.12 ml/kg.	For Columbiformes and psittacines. Has been shown to be toxic if these doses are exceeded and in all cases when given parenterally in finches (Clubb, 1986).
As an immunostimulant.	s/c injection.	2mg/kg or 0.026ml/kg in 3 consecutive daily injections given at intervals of 4 days.	
Ivermectin 1% w/v solution.	Orally.	1ml of the solution is diluted in 4.5ml propylene glycol (if diluted with water precipitation occurs); of this diluted solution 0.1ml/kg is given.	Broad-spectrum, effective against external parasites (*Cnemidocoptes* and feather mites) and some internal parasites (nematodes, air sac mites, microfilariae). Drug effect is prolonged.
	i/m or s/c injection.	0.1ml/kg or 0.2mg/kg.	May be toxic in some small birds, eg. some finches and budgerigars when given by injection (Clubb, 1986; Dorrestein, 1987; Pierey, 1988).
	Percutaneously.	1ml of the 1% solution is diluted with 10ml propylene glycol. One drop (approx 0.01ml) of this diluted solution is placed on the bare skin at the back of the neck. Dose used once monthly.	Has been used in canaries and small finches by the author. A similar amount and technique using the cattle pour-on preparation has been used in budgerigars and cockatiels (Baker, personal communication). 1 – 2 drops of the undiluted 1% solution has not been found to be toxic in budgerigars, cockatiels and cardinals by the author (personal observation).
Prazinquantel 50mg tablet.	Orally.	5 – 10mg/kg as a single dose repeated after 2 – 4 weeks.	Effective for cestodes and trematodes. May be toxic in some finches at high dose rates (Clubb, 1986).
Injectable, 50.8mg/ml.	i/m or s/c injection.	7.5mg/kg or 0.13mg/kg as a single dose, repeated after 2 – 4 weeks.	(Harrison and Harrison, 1986).

Drug	Route of administration	Dosage	Comments
Niclosamide	Orally.	100mg/kg. 75mg/kg for 3 days.	Effective against cestodes in passerines. In pigeons (Pierey, 1988).

Ectoparasiticides

Drug	Route of administration	Dosage	Comments
Dichlorvos Impregnated strips.	Strip suspended in ambient atmosphere.	Minimum air space per strip – 30 cubic metres.	Can prove toxic if used in a confined air space for more than 3 days.
Bromocyclen 20g sachet for use as a bath.	External application.	0.2% suspension is used, ie. 20g sachet in 10 litres of water. This is painted on to affected areas for *Cnemidocoptes* once weekly.	The aerosol preparation can prove toxic if inhaled (Turner, 1985). Do not use any preparation on female breeding birds as the residue can be detected in eggs and may affect the developing chick (Lawrence, 1988).
Dusting powder.	External application.	Feathering is dusted every 7 – 10 days.	Dusting powder on the bird is not effective against red mite (Lawrence, 1988).
Pyrethrins Dusting powder (piperonyl butoxide 1.137% w/w and pyrethrins 0.113%).	Dusted on feathers.	Sufficient is applied to penetrate the feathering to the skin surface. One application is usually sufficient but this can be repeated in a week.	Safe to use on all species (personal observation).

Miscellaneous drugs

Drug	Route of administration	Dosage	Comments
Medroxy-progesterone acetate 5% suspension, ie. 50mg/ml.	i/m or s/c injection.	5 – 10mg/kg or 0.1 – 0.2ml/kg.	Used to suppress persistent ovulation and stop continuous egg laying. Can cause polyuria and lead to fatty liver (see earlier) (Coles, 1985; Clubb, 1986).
Oxytocin 10iu/ml.	i/m injection.	0.3 – 0.5ml/kg or 3 – 5 iu/kg given once.	Used for egg retention, combined with calcium borogluconate 10% solution, 1 – 5ml/kg administered subcutaneously (Rosskopf and Woerpel, 1982).
Dexamethasone 2mg/ml.	i/m or i/v injection.	0.3 – 3mg/kg or 0.15 – 1.5ml/kg bid.	Treatment for shock. Anti-inflammatory.

Drug	Route of administration	Dosage	Comments
Doxapram hydrochloride 20mg/ml injection. 20mg/ml drops.	i/m injection. Drops.	5 – 10mg/kg or 0.25 – 0.5ml/kg once. One 0.5mg drop on tongue or choanal aperture.	Respiratory stimulant when apnoea occurs during general anaesthesia. Also to speed recovery from ketamine-xylazine anaesthesia (Clubb, 1986).
Frusemide Injection 50mg/ml.	i/m or s/c injection.	0.15mg/kg or 0.003ml/kg bid.	Ascites, confirmed oedematous subcutaneous swellings. Care must be taken not to overdose (Clubb, 1986).
Mineral oil, liquid paraffin	Orally, per cloaca.	4ml/kg once.	Used as a laxative to relieve cloacal impaction. To lubricate gavage tubes.
Bromhexine Injection 3mg/ml. Powder 1%, ie. 10mg/g.	i/m injection. In drinking water.	3 – 6mg/kg or 1 – 2ml/kg. 6.5mg/2g powder/litre drinking water.	Mucolytic and may help antibiotics to penetrate the respiratory mucosa (Ahlers, 1970; Centrale Cooperative Production Animale, 1981).
Multivitamins	i/m injection. Orally. In drinking water. In food.	In preparations containing vitamin A the dose should not exceed 20,000iu, Vit A/kg. Overdose can produce skeletal abnormalities and damage to membranes.	Can be used in conditions of stress or together with antimicrobial drugs in the treatment of infectious disease, and in the treatment of multifactorial malnutrition (Dorrestein, 1988).
Vitamin A 500,000iu/ml.	i/m injection.	0.04ml. Maximum dose 20,000iu/kg.	Supplemental treatment for upper respiratory and ophthalmic infections.
Vitamin B complex plus vitamin C 35mg thiamine hydrochloride /ml.	i/m injection.	10 – 30mg/kg weekly based on dose of thiamine hydrochloride.	As an aid in muscular weakness. Appetite stimulant. As an aid in the treatment of neurological disease. Given together with long-term oral antibiotics (Clubb, 1986).
Calcium borogluconate 10% solution.	s/c or i/m injection.	1 – 5ml/kg.	For the treatment of egg retention when combined with oxytocin. For the treatment of hypocalcaemic tetany, particularly in African grey parrots (Harrison and Harrison, 1986).

Drug	Route of administration	Dosage	Comments
Diazepam or midazolam	i/m or i/v injection.	1 – 1.5mg/kg.	For the control of convulsions and muscle spasms. Must be given slowly i/v (check differential diagnosis, see convulsions, etc.)
		0.5mg/kg.	In conjunction with ketamine for anaesthesia (see later) (Redig and Duke, 1976).
Diazepam syrup, 2mg/5ml.	Orally in food or drinking water.	1ml/120ml drinking water.	Is useful in some cases of chronic feather picking. Diluted solution only stable for a maximum of 14 days.
Iodine Lugol's iodine.	Orally in drinking water.	A stock solution is prepared by adding 2ml of Lugols iodine to 28ml of water; of this diluted solution one drop is added to 100ml drinking water.	Used as an aid in the treatment of thyroid dysplasia (Blackmore, 1969).
Sodium iodide 20% sterile solution.	i/m injection.	0.3 – 1ml/kg.	If diagnosis of thyroid dysplasia is correct there is considerable improvement within 3 days of giving injection (Lafeber, 1965).
Pancreatin Powder or capsules.	Orally in soft food.	Contents of one capsule/kg bodyweight mixed in daily food intake for that particular patient.	Used as an aid in the treatment of pancreatic insufficiency or pancreatitis when there is an associated paramyxovirus infection. A soft food, eg. Mylupa Baby Food, is used as a carrier. Some seed is sprinkled on top to start bird eating.
Lactulose Syrup	Orally via gavage.	0.25ml/kg.	Appetite stimulant. Discourages the growth of ammonia and other enterotoxin-producing organisms. Can act as a laxative so if diarrhoea results its use is stopped (Harrison and Harrison, 1986).

CAGE BIRDS AND POSSIBLE POISONING BY HOUSE PLANTS

A large variety of tropical and other plants are now sold as house plants to which cagebirds may have access. The oral toxicity of many of these plants has not been recorded. Many plants have evolved a multiplicity of chemical defences against predatory herbivores and so, in general, most tropical house plants must be considered potentially toxic. Broadly, those plants that have long, leathery leaves and are deep in colour, eg. philodendrons and dieffenbachia, are usually the most poisonous. Flowers are not usually toxic. Plants or their seeds which are poisonous for one species of birds are not necessarily poisonous for another species.

As a guide the following house plants are either known to be poisonous or must be considered suspect. This list is not exclusive.

Amaryllis	Amarylidaceae
Avocado pear	*Persea gratissima, Persea americana:* all parts of the plant including the fleshy fruit and the leaves are toxic and cause death (Hargis, 1989).
Azalea	*Rhododendron* sp.
Bay tree	*Laurus nobilis*
Bird of paradise	*Poinciana gilliesii*
Boxwood	*Buxus sepervirens*
Caladium	*Caladium* sp.
Castor-oil plant	*Ricinus communii (Fatsia japonica)*
Crotons	*Croton* sp.
Crocus	Iridaceae
Crown of thorns	*Euphorbia millisplendens*
Dumb cane	*Diffenbachia* sp.
English ivy	*Hedera helix* (Many varieties: leaves are only slightly toxic. The berries are most poisonous but are eaten by some British species with impunity.)
House plant ferns	Those in the genus *Pteris,* a popular group of ferns, eg. *Pteris cretica* – crested ribbon fern, *Pteris umbrosa major* – ribbon fern, *Pteris tremona* – trembling fern.
Hyacinth	*Hyacinthus orientalis*
Hydrangea	*Hydrangea* sp.
Iris	*Iris reticulata*
Ivy tree	*Fatshedera* (hybrid of *Fatsia* and *Hedera*)
Lily-of-the-valley	*Convallaria majalis*
Lobelia	*Lobelia*
Morning glory	*Ipomoea*
Narcissus	*Narcissus* sp. (including daffodil)
Oleander	*Nerium oleander*
Oxalis	*Oxalis* sp.
(Lucky clover)	*Oxalis deppei* (varieties of wood sorrel)
Philodendron	*Philodendron* sp.
Poinsettia	*Euphorbia pulchenia*
Poison primrose	*Primula obconia*
Rhododendron	*Rhododendron* sp.
Rose, miniature	*Rosa chimensis*
Tobacco plant	*Nicotiana affinis*
Winter or Japanese cherry	*Solanum capsicastrum*

References

Clarke and Clarke, 1967; Hessayon, 1980; Coles, 1985; Harrison and Harrison, 1986; Snow and Snow, 1988.

ANAESTHESIA

The bird should be on a heated pad and the ambient temperature of the room should be high during anaesthesia and during recovery. The bird should not be wetted excessively during the pre-operative preparation.

To guard against inhalation of vomit, most cagebirds should be starved for a period of about three hours prior to induction of anaesthesia, except for the very small species (smaller than 50 grammes) and in the frugivorous birds where the rate of passage of food through the alimentary canal is very rapid and half an hour without food should be quite sufficient. Except in the case of very small birds, it is always wiser to use an endotracheal tube when giving any method of general anaesthesia. This protects the airway from inhalation of vomit and may be useful if apnoea occurs.

The bird should always be weighed accurately to compute the dose of a parenteral anaesthetic. One should never try to guess the bird's weight (see 'Introduction').

Inhalation anaesthesia can be induced using a mask and then maintained via an endotracheal tube. A semi-closed 'T' piece circuit is most suitable.

Suggested anaesthetic methods for birds, listed in the author's order of preference:

1. **Isoflurane** (Forane, Abbot)

   For economy, an accurately calibrated, custom-made Fortec (Cyprane) vaporiser should be used. Induction is with 5% at an oxygen flow of 1.0 − 1.5 litres per minute and maintenance on 2−3%. The addition of 50% N_2O in the gas flow mixture helps slightly to reduce the percentage of isoflurane required for maintenance.

2. **Ketamine** (Vetalar, Parke-Davis) **and diazepam** (Valium, Roche) **or midazolam** (Hypnovel, Roche) by intramuscular injection.

   15 − 40mg/kg ketamine + 1.5mg/kg diazepam. Gives approximately 20 − 30 minutes deep sedation or light anaesthesia, depending on the size of the bird.

3. **Ketamine and xylazine** (Rompun, Bayer)

   20mg/kg ketamine + 4mg/kg xylazine. Gives a longer period of anaesthesia than ketamine and diazepam or midazolam. 2 − 3 hours recovery depending on size of bird. Sometimes there is a degree of bradycardia and respiratory depression. Avoid using in pigeons.

4. **Halothane**

   It is best to use an accurately calibrated Fluotec (Cyprane) or similar vaporiser. Induction is at 1% gradually increasing to 3−4%, maintenance on 1.5−3%. Cardiac failure easily occurs during induction if the operator is too impatient.

Balanced anaesthesia

If method 2 or 3 is used for induction and an endotracheal tube is placed in position, using a flow of oxygen the plane of anaesthesia can be increased slightly if necessary by adding a low level of inhalation anaesthetic.

Apnoea

If apnoea occurs, one drop of doxapram (Dopram-V, Willows Francis) (drops or injectable solution) can be placed on the mucous membrane of the oropharynx. The air sacs should be gently and repeatedly inflated with oxygen and any residual anaesthetic should be flushed out.

Fluid therapy

In emergency cases which are shocked, traumatized or dehydrated, fluid replacement therapy can be life-saving. A bolus of lactated Ringer's solution given i/v via the right jugular, brachial, or, in pigeons, the medial metatarsal vein, is the most effective method. Subsequent injections can be given s/c in the inter-scapula area. Total 24 hour maintenance requirements given in multiple doses are 50ml/kg. Approximate maximum doses i/v are: budgerigar (weight: 40 grammes) 0.5ml; cockatiel (90 grammes) 2.0ml; Amazon parrot (350 grammes) 7.0ml; cockatoo (500 grammes) 10ml; and macaw (850 grammes) 12ml. For more information, see Harrison and Harrison (1986).

REFERENCES AND FURTHER READING

AHLERS, W. (1970). Report on the use of Bisolvon in small animal practice. *Kleintier-Praxis* **15**, 50.

ARNALL, L. and KEYMER, I. F. (1975). *Bird Diseases.* Baillière Tindall, London.

BAKER, J. R. (1988). Poor reproductive performance in exhibition budgerigars; a study of eggs which fail to hatch. *Journal of Small Animal Practice* **29**, 565.

BAKER, J. R. (1989). Do's and don'ts of the budgerigar breeding season. *Cage and Aviary Birds.* Prospect Magazines, Cheam.

BAKER, J. R. (1989). A new treatment for budgerigar parasites. *Cage and Aviary Birds.* Prospect Magazines, Cheam.

BAKER, J. R. (1991). Infertility in exhibition budgerigars. *Journal of Small Animal Practice* **1**, 6.

BLACK, W. D. (1977). A study of the pharmacodynamics of oxytetracycline in the chicken. *Poultry Science* **56**, 1430.

BLACKMORE, D. K. (1969). In: *Diseases of Cage and Aviary Birds.* (Ed. M.L. Petrak) Lea and Febiger, Philadelphia.

BERCOVITZ, A. B. (1981). Fecal steroid analysis; a non-invasive approach to bird sexing. *Proceedings of the American Federation of Aviculture, Veterinary Seminar.* San Diego, California.

BERCOVITZ, A. B. (1984). Endocrine fecology of immature birds. *Watchbird Magazine* **2 (2)**.

CAMERON, A. D. and HARRISON, C. J. O. (1978). *Bird Families of the World.* Peerage Books, London.

CAMPBELL, B. (1974). *Dictionary of Birds.* Peerage Books, London.

CENTRALE COOPERATIVE PRODUCTION ANIMALE (1981). Report of the effect of Quentan (bromhexine) in pullets. *CCPA Report.* Gennes-sur-Seine, L'Ille et Vilaine.

CLARK, C. H. (1986). The pharmacology of antibiotics. In: *Clinical Avian Medicine and Surgery.* (Eds. G. J. Harrison and L. R. Harrison) W. B. Saunders, Philadelphia.

CLARKE, E. C. G. and CLARKE, M. L. (1967). *Garner's Veterinary Toxicology.* Baillière Tindall and Cassell, London.

CLUBB, S. L. (1986). Therapeutics. In: *Clinical Avian Medicine and Surgery.* (Eds. G. J. Harrison and L. R. Harrison) W. B. Saunders, Philadelphia.

COLES, B. H. (1985). *Avian Medicine and Surgery.* Blackwell Scientific Publications, Oxford.

COLES, B. H. (1987). Some clinical experience with soft tissue surgery in birds. *Veterinary Record* **120**, 178.

COLES, B. H. (1988). Anaesthesia; radiographic examination; surgery; the musculo-skeleton system. In: *Manual of Parrots, Budgerigars and Other Psittacine Birds.* (Ed. C. J. Price) BSAVA, Cheltenham.

COLES, B. H. (1989). Diseases of budgerigars. In: *The Henston Veterinary Vade Mecum - Small Animals 1989-90.* (Ed. J. M. Evans) Siebert Publications, Guildford.

COOPER, J. E. (1974). Metomidate anaesthesia of some birds of prey for laparotomy and sexing. *Veterinary Record* **94**.

COOPER, J. E. (1985). Safety and efficiency of clavulanate-potentiated amoxycillin in pigeons *(Columba livia). Research in Veterinary Science* **39**, 87.

DALL, J. A., BRANCKER, W. M., GRAHAM-JONES, O., JOSHUA, J. O. and KEYMER, I. F. (1964). *Handbook on the Treatment of Exotic Pets. Part I: Cage Birds.* British Veterinary Association, London.

DORRESTEIN, G. M., BUITELAAR, M. N. and WIGGELINKHUIZEN, J. M. (1981). Pharmakokinetische aspeckton von antibiotika bei voliervogeln und tauben. *Proceedings 11d. Symposium on Krankheiten der Vogel.* Munchen.

DORRESTEIN, G. M., van GOGH, H. and RINZEMA, J. D. (1984). Pharmocokinetic aspects of penicillins, aminoglycosides and chloramphenicol in birds compared to mammals. A review. *The Veterinary Quarterly* **6**, 216.

DORRESTEIN, G. M, van der HAGE, M. H. and ZWART, P. (1987a). *Examination, Diagnosis and Therapy of Diseases of Aviary Birds.* Beerse, Belgium.

DORRESTEIN, G. M. and MIERT van ASJPAM (1987b). Pharmocotherapeutical aspects of medication of birds. *Proceedings European Symposium on Birds' Diseases.* Belgium.

DORRESTEIN, G. M. (1988). Update in avian chemotherapy. *Proceedings Annual General Meeting Association of Avian Veterinarians.* Houston, Texas.

EATON, T. M. (1988). Surgical sexing and diagnostic laparoscopy. In: *Manual of Parrots, Budgerigars and Other Psittacine Birds.* (Ed. C. J. Price) BSAVA, Cheltenham.

ENSLEY, P. K. and JANSSEN, P. L. (1981). A preliminary study comparing the pharmocokinetics of ampicillin given orally and intramuscularly to psittacines. *Journal of Zoo Animal Practice* **12,** 42.

FORSHAW, J. M. and COOPER, W. T. (1978). *Parrots of the World.* David and Charles, Newton Abbot.

FUDGE, A. M. (1988). Avian microbial therapy. *Proceedings Annual Meeting Association of Avian Veterinarians.* Houston, Texas.

FURLEY, C. W. and GREENWOOD, A. G. (1982) The treatment of aspergillosis in raptors with miconazole. *Veterinary Record* **111,** 584.

GERLACH, H. (1986). Mollicutes *(Mycoplasma, Acholeplasma, Ureaplasma).* In: *Clinical Avian Medicine and Surgery.* (Eds. G. J. Harrison and L. R. Harrison) W. B. Saunders, Philadelphia.

GREEN, C. J. (1979). *Animal Anaesthesia.* Laboratory Animals Limited, London.

GYLSTORFF, I. and GRIMM, F. (1987). *Vogelkrakheiten.* Ulmer, Stuttgart.

HARGIS, A. M. (1979). Avocado *(Persea americana)* intoxication in cage birds. *Journal of the American Veterinary Medical Association* **194 (1),** 64.

HARRISON, G. J. and HARRISON, L. R. (1986). *Clinical Avian Medicine and Surgery.* W. B. Saunders, Philadelphia.

HAWKEY, C. and GULLAND, F. (1988). Clinical haematology. In: *Manual of Parrots, Budgerigars and Other Psittacine Birds.* (Ed. C. J. Price) BSAVA, Cheltenham.

HERZOG, A. HOHN, H., KLOPPER, G., MATERN, B. (1986). Cytogenetic methods of sex determination. *Kleintier Praxis* **31 (1),** 31.

HESSAYON, D. G. (1980) *The Houseplant Expert.* pbi Publications, Hertfordshire.

LAFEBER, T. J. (1965). Thyroid dysplasia. *The Budgerigar Animal Hospital* **1,** 208.

LAWRENCE, K. (1983). Efficacy of fenbendazole against nematodes of captive birds. *Veterinary Record* **112,** 433.

LAWRENCE, K. (1988). Therapeutics. In: *Manual of Parrots, Budgerigars and Other Psittacine Birds.* (Ed. C. J. Price) BSAVA, Cheltenham.

LINT, K. C. and LINT, A. M. (1981). *Diets for Birds in Captivity.* Blandford Press, Dorset.

LOW. R, (1980). *Parrots, their Care and Breeding.* Blandford Press, Dorset.

LUMEIJ, J. T. (1989). Blood chemistry reference values in psittaciformes. *Proceedings of 2nd European Symposium on Avian Medicine and Surgery.* Utrecht.

MARTIN, R. M. (1980). *Cage and Aviary Birds.* Collins, London.

McDONALD, S. E. (1988). Practical avian therapeutics. *Proceedings Basic Avian Medicine Symposium of Avian Veterinarians Annual Conference.* Houston, Texas.

MORIELLO, K. A. (1986). Ketoconazole: clinical pharmacology and therapeutic recommendations. *Journal of the American Veterinary Medical Association* **188,** 303.

PETRAK, M. (1982). *Diseases of Cage and Aviary Birds.* 2nd Edn. Lea and Febiger, Philadelphia.

PIEREY, E. K. J. M. (1988). *Anthelmintica/Anti-ectoparasitica.* Wegwizer 1st Edn. Maarssen Brocacef BV.

PRICE, C. J. (1988). Ed. *The Manual of Parrots, Budgerigars and other Psittacine Birds.* BSAVA, Cheltenham.

REDIG, P. T. and DUKE, G. E. (1976). Intravenously administered ketamine and diazepam for anaesthesia of raptors. *Journal of the American Veterinary Medical Association* **169**, 886.

REDIG, P. T. (1981). Aspergillosis in raptors. In: *Recent Advances in the Study of Raptor Diseases.* (Eds. J. E. Cooper and A. G. Greenwood) Chiron Publications, Keighley.

ROSSKOPF, W. J. and WOERPEL, R. W. (1982). Abdominal surgery. Pet Birds. *Modern Veterinary Practice* **63**, 889.

SHANTHIKUMAR, S. R. (1987). Helminthology. In: *Companion Bird Medicine* (Ed. E. W. Burr) Iowa State University Press, Ames, Iowa.

SNOW, B. and SNOW, D. (1983). *Birds and Berries.* T. and A. D. Poyser, Waterhouses.

STOODLEY, J. and STOODLEY, P. (1983). *Parrot Production.* Bezels Publications, Portsmouth.

STOODLEY, J., HADGKISS, I. M. and RANCE, L. A. (1988). Feeding, housing and breeding. In: *Manual of Parrots, Budgerigars and Other Psittacine Birds.* (Ed. C. J. Price) BSAVA, Cheltenham.

TURNER, W. T. (1985). Cagebirds. In: *Manual of Exotic Pets.* Revised Edition. (Eds. J. E. Cooper, M. F. Hutchison, O. F. Jackson and R. J. Maurice) BSAVA, Cheltenham.

WESTERHOF, F. I. and LUMEIJ, J. T. (1989). An introduction to avian therapeutics. *Proceedings of 2nd European Symposium on Avian Medicine and Surgery.* Utrecht.

WOERPEL, R. W. and ROSSKOPF, W. J. (1981). Avian therapeutics. *Modern Veterinary Practice* **62**, 947.

WOOLHAM, F. (1987). *The Handbook of Aviculture.* Blandford Press, Dorset.

VANDERHEYDEN, N. (1989). Haematology and plasma chemistry values in selected diseases of Amazon parrots. *Proceedings of 2nd European Symposium on Avian Medicine and Surgery.* Utrecht.

YOSHIDA, M., HOSHII, H., YONEZAWA, S., NOGAWA, H., YOSHIMURA, H. and ITO, O. (1975). Residue and disappearance of dietary oxytetracycline in the blood, muscle, liver and bile of growing chicks. *Japanese Poultry Science* **12**, 181.

CHAPTER FOURTEEN

PIGEONS

Ian F Keymer PhD FRCVS FRCPath CBiol FIBiol

All varieties of domestic pigeon belong to the Order Columbiformes, Family Columbidae, and are believed to derive from *Columba livia,* the rock dove (Hawes, 1984), an inhabitant of remote rocky coastal areas of Scotland, Ireland and parts of Southern Europe. So-called 'feral pigeons', which especially favour built-up areas in Europe, are the progeny of lost racing pigeons. Other free-living species of Columbidae in Europe comprise the woodpigeon *(Columba palumbus),* stock dove *(C. oenas),* turtle dove *(Streptopelia turtur)* and the collared dove *(S. decaocto).*

Domestic pigeons are kept primarily for racing, although there are numerous fancy breeds used for exhibition. Exotic species are also kept by some aviculturists and in zoological collections. Free-flying doves are widely kept as 'pets' and intensive pigeon keeping for food production appears to be on the increase. If a racing pigeon is not 100% fit, the owner regards it as 'ill'! Sick birds are often culled and no veterinary attention is sought. Pigeon breeders often attempt treatment, frequently using outdated or unconventional methods, or using antibiotics obtained by devious means (Hunter, 1989). It is traditional to make the 'study' of disease part of the hobby. However, with the increasing value of individual birds, some pigeon breeders now seek professional advice, but often by then a number of treatments will have been carried out and carcases burned or buried. Indeed, it is unusual for pigeon breeders not to use vitamin and/or mineral supplements as a routine, especially before racing, when some administer vitamin B_{12} as a 'booster' or give low doses of antibiotics, coccidiostats, herbal teas and even warfarin 'to thin the blood'! In the opinion of Kiessling and Gerlach (1989) the use of sub-therapeutic doses of antibiotics by pigeon breeders may be the reason for the high incidence of L-forms of bacteria in pigeons. Bacterial L-forms will not grow on the media commonly used for bacteriological examinations and are therefore easily overlooked. Kiessling and Gerlach also pointed out that they can survive 'therapeutic and vaccinal measures'. It is therefore necessary to question the owner closely, as initially he is sometimes reluctant to reveal the complete history, especially if unsupervised antibiotic treatment has been given. In the last two decades the general health of racing pigeons appears to have declined, probably due to the practice of mixing birds from different sources in lorries used to transport them to release points for racing.

BIOLOGICAL DATA

Bodyweight	350—550g
Body temperature (cloacal)	40°—41°C
Resting respiratory rate	25—30 per minute
Clutch size	Two. First egg is laid in late afternoon. Second egg is laid about 40—44 hours later.
Incubation period	17—18 days; 'light' incubation starts after the first egg is laid. True incubation commences with laying of second egg. Incubation is by both sexes.

Young are fed within a few hours of hatching. Feathers first appear at about six to seven days of age. Nestling period is about twenty one days. Plumage is complete in about one month. Moulting of this juvenile plumage commences after about six weeks. Adults moult annually, mainly August—September.

Sexual maturity is reached at about five months, but birds are not normally used for breeding until they are between seven and eight months old. Pigeons are relatively long-lived birds. There are longevity records of fifteen years or more. Cocks tend to live longer than hens. Hens become increasingly unproductive after six years of age.

The eye is very large relative to the size of the head with only the cornea and iris visible. Experiments show that pigeons have good colour vision and can learn to categorise a complex array of figures and photographs. Unlike most birds, pigeons do not raise their heads when drinking, but suck up fluid in a similar way to a horse. A pigeon will drink 30—60ml of water per day depending on the environmental temperature and eat about one tenth of its bodyweight (Schrag et al, 1974).

Flying speed can reach over 104km/hour.

Flying heights have been recorded at 3,800—5,700 metres but usually birds fly much lower.

Homing distances: 500km is not unusual. A few birds can be raced over 1,000km.

TERMINOLOGY

Squab	a nestling up to about one month of age.
Squeaker	a young feathered bird from one to two months of age, so named because it makes a squeaking sound.
Wattles or operculum	soft fleshy structure overlying the nostrils.
Cere	featherless, fleshy area around the eyes.
Crop milk	a secretion of the crop produced by both parents by the fourteenth day of incubation. The secretion stops about ten to thirteen days after the young are hatched. Composition 75—77% water, 11—13% protein, 5—7% fat and 1.2—1.8% mineral matter. It contains no carbohydrate and is low in calcium, phosphorus and vitamins A and C.

ANATOMY

The feet and legs have small, smooth scales covered with a fine powdery deposit. The crop epithelium of breeding birds is hypertrophied for 'crop milk' production. The crop wall and adjacent cervical subcutaneous tissues normally show hyperaemia. The hardened koilin layer (once believed to be keratin; King and McLelland, 1984) of the gizzard is usually stained bright green. The gall-bladder is absent. The pancreas is normally well developed. The pericardial sac is attached to the inner ventral surface of the sternum. The spleen is elongated and sausage-shaped. There are two rudimentary caeca, 2—7mm in length, which mark the division between small and large intestines.

CLINICAL CHEMISTRY AND HAEMATOLOGY

Lack of space precludes dealing with blood chemistry values in any detail. However, Harrison and Harrison (1986) have tabulated enzyme blood plasma-serum data in iu/l for GOT, GPT, LDH, AP and SP, and Lumeij (1987a) has dealt with the subject in some depth. He has published a series of papers in book form, some of which are original, whilst others have been published previously. They include blood chemistry reference values, enzyme activities in tissues and clinical endocrinology. Lumeij (1987b) has pointed out that contrary to common belief, plasma urea, and to some extent plasma creatinine concentrations, are useful for detecting prerenal and renal failure in pigeons whilst plasma uric acid concentrations are not.

There appears to be very little published information on haematology in pigeons, although the chapter by Campbell and Dein (1984) in *The Veterinary Clinics of North America* is useful and Tangredi (1985) included a table of haematocrit and leucocyte values. Hawkey and Dennett (1989) have provided colour illustrations of blood cells.

HOUSING AND MANAGEMENT

Racing pigeons are kept in 'lofts' and doves in 'dove-cots'. These comprise a shelter with box-like compartments against the wall that serve as nesting sites and, in the case of lofts, an enclosed 'flight' or aviary. Pairs may be isolated in cages. Dry, well ventilated quarters are essential.

Equipment for lofts and dove-cots, such as nest pans or bowls, cages or coops, perches, food and water receptacles, is available commercially. Metal bath pans (preferably round for easy cleaning) are essential and should be about 12cm deep.

Although domestic pigeons will use nesting material such as straw, shavings and sticks, they will also utilise standard earthenware nest pans without such material. The latter are preferable for hygienic reasons but may cause 'pinwheel'. Some breeders line nest receptacles with fine builders' sand.

SEXING

The male squab has a wider space between the eyes than the female and its head is flatter. The head of the adult male is larger. The male struts around, coos and drags his tail. The hen is normally quiet and holds her body horizontally. Sexes are alike in plumage, ie. there is no sexual dimorphism.

REPRODUCTION

Birds should not be mated before seven to eight months of age.

Courtship display is quite elaborate and involves the cock feeding the hen, bowing, strutting and cooing. The hen stands still at first and later stands more erect; the neck swells perceptibly and pulsates slightly. The cock may open his beak and the hen places her beak in his. She accepts the cock's advances by crouching for copulation. Pigeons are monogamous and remain paired for life.

FEEDING

Although adult pigeons have the ability to live and maintain reasonable health on a very limited variety of food, it is important to remember that requirements for racing, and especially for growth and reproduction, are much higher. Grains commonly fed are kaffir, maple peas, hemp, maize, vetch, millet, wheat, oats and barley. Some greenfood is usually given. Pigeons need both soluble and insoluble grit. Salt is also important and is seldom eaten excessively, so that poisoning is not a problem. Clean drinking water should be provided daily in small receptacles positioned to minimise contamination by excreta.

HANDLING

When catching a pigeon it should be grasped from above with one or both hands around the body and closed wings. When held in the hand (see Figure 1), the pigeon's feet should be placed side by side between the first and second fingers of the right hand (for a right-handed person) and the thumb placed to cover the primary flight feathers so that the wings are kept folded in the natural closed position. The palm of the other hand can be used to give more support for the pigeon's breast. A bird should never be held solely by its legs or wings. Some authors (Cooper, 1984) advocate holding pigeons for examination by using one or both hands around the body and wrapping the bird in a light cloth which, if necessary, can also be used to cover the eyes.

DOSING

Oral administration is simple (Cooper, 1984). Tablets and capsules should be placed at the back of the tongue and pushed with the index finger. Liquids are best given by passing a tube (attached to a syringe) down the oesophagus. This should be sufficiently wide to avoid accidentally entering the trachea through the laryngeal opening.

As pigeons drink regularly, some drugs can be administered by dissolving them in the drinking water.

Anthelmintics, eg. fenbendazole, and other potentially toxic drugs, eg. dimetridazole (Harrison and Harrison, 1986), should not be administered to parent birds orally when they are producing crop milk and feeding squabs. It is also better not to treat moulting birds with anthelmintics if this can be avoided.

Figure 1
Correct way of holding a pigeon.
(By courtesy of R.A. Clarke and T.J.Roe)

DISEASES/CLINICAL CONDITONS

Parasitic diseases

Trichomoniasis

'Canker' ('wet' or 'dry'), sometimes also called 'diphtheria' by bird keepers. Caused by *Trichomonas gallinae*, a fragile flagellate. Lifecycle is direct. Young birds (especially squabs) are most susceptible, especially to the visceral form affecting the liver. A very common disease, often associated with other infections, overcrowding and poor hygiene.

Membranous and/or focal, caseous, yellowish lesions affect the oral mucosa, especially the pharynx, and can extend into the oesophagus and crop. Commissures of the beak may be affected and occasionally discrete areas of necrosis are visible in the liver. In advanced cases lesions extend to nasal sinuses and cause respiratory signs. Inappetence and diarrhoea are often present. Death may occur in seven to ten days. Older birds may be healthy carriers or succumb to more chronic infections. Infection is spread from parents to squabs during feeding and probably through contamination of drinking water when drinking, but not via the faeces.

Diagnosis is by microscopical examination of scrapings from lesions of live birds, or within a few hours of death, when it is necessary to mix necrotic material in slightly warmed water or saline to reactivate the flagellates.

Differential diagnosis: pox and vitamin A deficiency.

Treatment. Dimetridazole 40% w/w (Emtryl Soluble, RMB; Pharmsure Dimetridazole 40% Soluble, PH Pharmaceuticals) is effective when given in the drinking water at 500mg/litre for seven days as the sole source of water. If necessary three courses of flock treatment can be given with seven day intervals. However, dimetridazole can be toxic to breeding birds when they 'transport large quantities of water to incubating hens' (Harrison and Harrison, 1986). One teaspoonful per gallon of drinking water caused death, whereas the same dose to non-breeding birds had no adverse effect. Increased medicated water consumption in hot weather can also lead to toxicity (Carwardine, personal communication). For prevention of trichomoniasis, adult birds may be treated before mating and also before and after the racing season. Young birds may be routinely treated every four weeks, commencing when squabs are self-feeding at about two weeks of age. Panigrahy et al (1982) found dimetridazole to be effective when given by mouth at a dose of 50mg/kg bodyweight. Coles (1985) suggested metronidazole (Flagyl, May & Baker Pharmaceuticals) one-tenth part of a 200mg tablet daily for five days orally.

Coccidiosis

Coccidiosis is not frequently encountered, at least in veterinary practice. However, certain *Eimeria* spp., especially *E. labbeana* and *E. columbarum*, are pathogenic, particularly to pigeons between three and four months of age (Pellérdy, 1974). Affected birds have a greenish diarrhoea caused by catarrhal enteritis, become emaciated and stunted. There is inappetence and polydypsia. Some pigeons may die. Old birds can act as carriers.

Diagnosis is by finding large numbers of coccidial oocysts on microscopical examination of the faeces or from scrapings of the epithelial lining of the small intestine at necropsy.

Treatment. Good hygiene is essential for prevention. Sulphadimidine sodium (Sulphamezathine Solution 33⅓%, ICI) at half the dose recommended for poultry is likely to be effective, ie. 15ml of the solution in 4.5 litres of drinking water for five consecutive days. Panigrahy et al (1982) stated that 0.5% solution of sulphadimidine in the drinking water for four days is also effective. Alternatively, amprolium hydrochloride 3.4% w/v (Coxoid, Harkers) can be given in the drinking water at a rate of 28ml/4.5 litres for seven days. More recently in Holland, Vanparijs et al (1988) have found clazuril capsules (Appertex), a new anti-coccidial agent (a benzene-acetonitrile derivative), to be effective using a single dose of 2.5mg.

All these treatments should be given in place of the normal drinking water.

Ascaridiasis

Ascaridiasis is caused by the roundworm *Ascaridia columbae.* The worms average about 2—6cm in length and 1mm in thickness and mainly infest the duodenum and the upper part of the small intestine. When present in large numbers they can cause impaction and occasionally rupture the gut and produce peritonitis. The lifecycle is direct and long, taking nine weeks or more, depending upon the circumstances. Larvae penetrate the intestinal wall and cause enteritis. Warm, moist conditions favour transmission. Young birds are more susceptible than adults; they lose weight and may or may not develop diarrhoea.

Diagnosis is based on necropsy or microscopical examination of excreta. Thick-walled, oval ova are seen in the latter.

Treatment. Cambendazole (Ascapilla, Univet) has been specially formulated for treating ascarids and *Capillaria* spp. in pigeons. Birds up to 400g bodyweight should be given one capsule a day for two days. Heavier birds can be given two capsules. Fenbendazole 2.5% suspension (Panacur, Hoechst) at a dosage rate of 4ml/kg of feed (= 100 ppm) can be given for three days (Kirsch and Degenhardt, 1979), or a single dose at 7.5mg/kg bodyweight (Kirsch et al, 1978). Care must be taken not to overdose because, even at comparatively low concentrations, feather abnormalities may occur (Devriese, 1983) but these are reversible. However, Lawrence (1983) advised against using fenbendazole in pigeons. Levamisole hydrochloride (Spartakon, Harkers) dissolved in water, at a dosage rate of 10−20mg/kg bodyweight given as a single dose orally, appears to be effective (Steiner and Davis, 1981). Although Harkers have formulated Spartakon specially for pigeons, they have warned that 'vomiting commonly occurs in both adult and young racing pigeons 1—2 hours after treatment'. Clinical efficacy is not affected because levamisole is rapidly absorbed from the gastro-intestinal tract. Levamisole has a bitter taste and it may be necessary to withhold water for eight hours before dosing (Coles, 1985). If necessary both treatments can be repeated at fourteen day intervals until no more ova are found in the faeces. Coles (1987) recommended a solution of 1% w/v of ivermectin (Ivomec, MSD) 10mg/ml for use in birds. The drug is preferably given orally using a single dose of 200 μg/kg. It is occasionally toxic if given intra-muscularly (Coles, 1985). Administration of liquid paraffin after anthelmintic treatment will facilitate elimination of the worms (Wagenaar—Schaafsma, 1984).

Capillariasis

Capillariasis is caused by the threadworms *Capillaria columbae* and *C. longicollis.* These worms are very slender and reach up to about 2.5cm in length. They infest the small intestine and less frequently the crop and oesophagus. The direct lifecycle takes about four weeks to complete. Transmission is favoured by poor hygiene, overcrowding and warm moist conditions. The worms can cause severe illness with diarrhoea (sometimes blood tinged), vomiting and death within a few days in young birds, and loss of weight in adults.

Diagnosis. As for ascaridiasis. Ova have bipolar plugs.

Treatment. *Capillaria* spp. are usually more resistant to treatment than *Ascaridia.* However, cambendazole (Ascapilla, Univet) is now available in the UK and also ivermectin (see Ascaridiasis). Fenbendazole or levamisole can also be used as suggested for ascaridiasis, but according to Kirsch *et al* (1978) the single dosage for fenbendazole needs to be increased to 20mg/kg bodyweight. Doses of fenbendazole at this level, however, may be toxic (see Ascaridiasis).

Ornithostrongylosis

Ornithostrongylosis is caused by *Ornithostrongylus quadriradiatus* and has been recorded only once in the UK (Rose and Keymer, 1958) but may have been overlooked. It has been recorded in many parts of the world outside Europe. The worms appear red due to the presence of ingested blood. They are slender and usually measure about 10—20mm in length. The lifecycle is direct. Infested birds rapidly lose condition, become listless and show profuse greenish diarrhoea. Anaemia develops because the worms suck blood. They also cause a catarrhal or haemorrhagic enteritis.

Diagnosis. As for ascaridiasis. The ova are oval and thin-shelled.

Treatment. Hungerford (1969) recommended methyridine (not now available in the UK except in conjunction with piperazine citrate 15.86% w/v as Harkers Roundworm Treatment by subcutaneous injection at a dosage rate of 200mg/kg bodyweight, given on six successive days. Alternatively, ivermectin (see Ascaridiasis) could be tried.

Tapeworm infestation

Many species of cestodes have been recorded in the pigeon and belong mainly to the genera *Raillietina, Hymenolepis* and *Cotugnia.* All species require intermediate, invertebrate hosts such as molluscs, earthworms and a wide variety of arthropods. In heavy infestations birds may show loss of weight and listlessness. Light infestations are unlikely to cause any visible effect except, perhaps, when birds are stressed, for example, after racing. During life, infestations can easily be overlooked as the tapeworm proglottides are only expelled intermittently in the faeces. The segments liberate ova which then have to be ingested by a suitable invertebrate in order for the lifecycle to be continued. Similarly, invertebrates carrying the tapeworm cysts need to be eaten by a pigeon if further development is to occur and adult tapeworms produced in the intestinal tract.

Diagnosis is based on the presence of tapeworm proglottides or ova in the excreta. Occasionally, a tapeworm may be seen protruding from the cloaca. Only birds allowed free flight and therefore regular access to intermediate hosts are likely to become infested.

Treatment. It is unusual for more than a few birds in a flock to be infested and it is debatable if treatment is worthwhile, as infestations are usually secondary to some other factor. Axworthy (1972) stated that dichlorophen (Harkers Improved Tapeworm Capsules for Pigeons, Harkers) is usually effective. Each capsule contains 100mg of the active principle and should be given orally after a period of twelve hours without food. If necessary the treatment can be repeated after ten days. It is usually impracticable to attempt control of the intermediate hosts. Niclosamide (Yomesan, Bayer) can be used in birds orally by crop tube (Coles, 1985) at a single dose of 250μg/kg. The tablets are not soluble and need to be suspended in water. However, Harrison and Harrison (1986) regarded this anthelmintic as lethal to pigeons. Ivermectin is probably preferable (see Ascaridiasis).

Lice

Biting lice of various species, eg. *Columbicola columbae,* are common. Heavy infestations usually indicate that the bird is chronically sick and that the lice have multiplied due to lack of preening. The lice feed on skin debris, cause irritation and restlessness and may damage the feathers. The entire lifecycle occurs in the plumage and takes about three weeks.

Mites

The normally non-pathogenic, very small feather mites, eg. *Falculifer rostratis,* may cause irritation if present in large numbers but several other mite species may be involved (see Table 2). The depluming mite *(Cnemidocoptes laevis)* sometimes causes broken feathers at a point a little above the skin (Levi, 1974), and the feather quill mite (*Syringophilus columbae)* can be associated with feather loss. The blood-sucking red mite *(Dermanyssus gallinae)* and also occasionally *Ornithonyssus sylviarum* cause trouble in lofts. *D. gallinae* mites, however, unlike *O. sylviarum,* do not breed on the birds, but in cracks and crevices from which they emerge at night. *C. mutans,* the scaly leg mite, attacks the skin of the feet and legs (see Table 2).

Diagnosis. Microscopic examination is necessary to make precise identification, although most types can be recognised with the naked eye.

Treatment. Bromocyclen (Alugan, Hoechst) in the form of a spray or dusting powder can be used on the birds against most of these ectoparasites. Malathion (Duramitex, Harkers) solution should be used against red mites by treating nesting areas, interior surfaces and cracks and crevices in lofts. According to Coles (1985) 3% w/v coumaphos, 2% w/v propxur and 5% w/v sulphanilamide (Negasunt, Bayer) is active against all external parasites. It is available in the form of a dusting powder.

For more information on ectoparasites, Levi (1974) should be consulted.

Fungal diseases

These are relatively rare in racing pigeons but may be encountered in less hygienically housed doves and other pigeons.

Candidiasis

Candidiasis or moniliasis caused by *Candida (= Monilia) albicans* affects the upper alimentary tract and is called 'thrush' or 'sour crop' by breeders. Infected birds become unthrifty and may vomit or develop diarrhoea. The young are more susceptible than older birds, in which the infection tends to occur only when the pigeon is debilitated or for some other reason. Candidiasis is most prevalent in damp weather and under overcrowded conditions. Damp, mouldy food may be the source of the fungus. Predisposing causes include prolonged oral administration of antibiotics and vitamin deficiencies.

Diagnosis. The presence of greyish-white focal lesions loosely attached to the buccal cavity, especially the pharynx, is characteristic. At necropsy, similar lesions may be found affecting the oesophagus and/or crop. As the disease progresses the lesions coalesce. Organisms can be found in scrapings and grow readily on blood agar and special media for fungal isolation.

Differential diagnosis. Easily confused with trichomoniasis, vitamin A deficiency and pox, especially the first. In pox, skin lesions are usually also present.

Treatment. Levi (1974) reported success by the removal of lesions in the mouth with a blunt instrument and application of one part tincture of iodine to four parts of glycerine. For severe cases, however, and when the lower oesophagus and crop are affected, direct administration of nystatin (Nystan Oral Suspension, Princeton) orally is more likely to be effective (Arnall and Keymer, 1975). In psittacines, Heidenreich (1980) obtained good results using 0.2g/litre of nystatin in the drinking water for seven days. Coles (1985) stated that nystatin can be used orally using Nystan Oral Suspension containing 100,000 units in a 30ml dropper at dosage rates of 2—7ml/kg bid or tid for 7—14 days. Multivitamin therapy should also be given (see also 'Cage and Aviary Birds').

Aspergillosis

Aspergillosis, caused mainly by *Aspergillus fumigatus*, is common in many species of birds, especially waterfowl, but is seldom seen in racing pigeons. It is occasionally encountered in doves and pigeons which are not allowed free flight and kept in overcrowded, poorly ventilated, unhygienic surroundings. The infection is usually confined to the respiratory tract. It is only likely to affect individual birds and, if suspected, these should be culled. It can normally be prevented by good hygiene and ventilation.

Bacterial diseases

Salmonellosis

Salmonellosis, known as 'paratyphoid' by breeders, is usually caused by *S. typhimurium* and is the most common bacterial infection of pigeons. The organisms can be egg-transmitted and cause poor hatchability due to mortality of embryos. Squabs under two weeks of age are most susceptible, but all ages can become infected. Young birds show prostration, dyspnoea and polydypsia, and die within a few hours. Sometimes the brain is affected. Nervous signs, blindness and incoordination may occur. A greenish diarrhoea may also be present, caused by a haemorrhagic enteritis. Chronically affected birds lose weight and often develop suppurative arthritis of the joints, especially of the wings.

Diagnosis is by *post-mortem* and bacteriological examination. The organisms can often be isolated from excreta or from purulent exudate taken from incised or punctured joint swellings.

Differential diagnosis. Other bacterial septicaemias, especially staphylococcosis and pseudo-tuberculosis, although these diseases are relatively uncommon and less likely to affect more than one or two birds in a loft. When nervous signs and diarrhoea are present the disease may be confused with paramyxovirus (PMV-1) infection (see later).

Treatment is unlikely to be satisfactory. A proportion of birds in a loft are likely to remain carriers after treatment with the result that the disease may flare up again, especially when birds are stressed during periods of breeding or moulting. The use of an autogenous vaccine has given good results (Keymer and Clarke, unpublished), coupled initially with slaughter of sick birds. Vaccination has also been used experimentally in Germany (Bechir, 1979). Alternatively, chlortetracycline (Aureomycin Soluble Powder, Cyanamid) can be used in the drinking water, made up fresh each day, at 120mg or more/litre for five to seven days. However, working in Holland, Uyttebroek *et al* (1989) have experimented with the use of enrofloxacin (Baytril) in the drinking water for the treatment of *S. typhimurium* var *copenhagen*. A dose of 12mg/kg for ten days prevented the resumption of *Salmonella* excretion after cessation of treatment. Trimethoprim, chloramphenicol and furaltadone reduced excretion of the organisms to some extent, but spectinomycin and lincomycin were ineffective.

Mycoplasma infection

'Mycoplasmosis' or 'mycoplasmosis catarrh' is regarded as a clinical entity by most racing pigeon breeders and some veterinarians (Axworthy, 1972; Schrag et al, 1974), but others have shown that the pathogenic role of *Mycoplasma* spp. is uncertain (MacOwan et al, 1981; Keymer et al, 1984; Reece et al, 1986). Gerlach (1977) considered that 'the pathogenicity of all types of mycoplasmas was negligible'. *Mycoplasma columbinum* and *M. columborale* have been isolated from the upper respiratory tract of healthy pigeons in Japan (Shimizu et al, 1978) and from the respiratory tract and other sites of apparently healthy pigeons in the UK (Jordan et al, 1981; Keymer et al, 1984). Keymer et al (1984) also isolated *M. columbinasale* from a healthy pigeon. However, *Mycoplasma* spp. have also been isolated from pigeons showing respiratory disease, viz *M. columbinasale* (Sinclair, 1980), *M. columborale* (MacOwan et al, 1981), *M. columbinum, M. columborale, M. synoviae* and *M. gallinarum* (Reece et al, 1986). Macowan et al (1981) demonstrated the potential pathogenicity of *M. columborale* to pathogen-free chickens, and on histopathological examination described tracheal lesions which were later observed by Keymer et al (1984) in a pigeon showing evidence of upper respiratory disease, associated with a natural infection of *M. columborale*. Keymer et al (1984) carried out serological examinations of both healthy and clinically affected birds, but the results of the metabolism inhibition (MI) tests for *M. columborale* appeared to 'give no more than a preliminary indication that *M. columborale* antibodies exist in some groups of pigeons infected with this organism'. It was not clear if negative MI results reflected the insensitivity of the method or simply lack of pathogenicity of *M. columborale*. A further complication was that in four of the five lofts investigated by Keymer et al (1984), there was evidence of disease caused by a variety of other organisms. However, of twenty racing pigeons infected with *Mycoplasma* spp. and examined by Reece et al (1986), in seventeen there was no evidence of any other pathogen playing a role.

Although there is no clear evidence that *Mycoplasma* spp. are aetiologically involved in natural respiratory disease of pigeons when unassociated with other potential pathogens, they are included here as possible pathogens for the convenience of practitioners who will be confronted by owners presenting pigeons with 'mycoplasmosis'. The history in such cases includes poor performance in races with a proportion of birds failing to return to the loft, manifested by mild, mucoid catarrh involving the nares and nasal sinuses, 'coughing' and respiratory râles, especially when disturbed and, less typically, unilateral or bilateral, watery, ocular discharge. There may be loss of appetite and reluctance to fly. Both young and adults may be affected and sometimes loss of weight occurs.

Diagnosis is on the basis of clinical signs, history and isolation of *Mycoplasma* spp. from the respiratory tract and other organs, together with histological examination of the trachea.

Differential diagnosis. *Mycoplasma* infections can be associated with salmonellosis, 'one-eyed cold' syndrome, *Herpesvirus* and pox, as well as trichomoniasis and other parasitic infestations (Keymer et al, 1984). They may also be associated with staphylococcoi, streptococci and *Escherichia coli*. Reece et al (1986) also found the organisms associated with *Pasteurella multocida* and lymphosarcoma. Ornithosis and paramyxovirus infections should be excluded when pigeons show evidence of respiratory disease. The possibility of aspergillosis and vitamin A deficiency should also be considered, but these are unusual in racing pigeons.

Treatment. Reece et al (1986) claimed satisfactory response to treatment using tylosin (Tylan Soluble, Elanco) followed by chlortetracycline (Tricon Powder, Apex Lab Pty Ltd, NSW) or oxytetracycline. The recommended dose rates were 0.5g and 0.1 — 0.2g of active ingredient/litre respectively in the drinking water. Each medicament was given for five days and the treatment 'repeated at times of stress'.

A compound call Mycosan-T (Univet) consisting of a mixture of erythromycin, sodium arsanilate, various sulphates, methionine and vitamins etc., has been specially formulated 'for the treatment of mycoplasmosis in racing pigeons'. It is available in capsules or as a water soluble powder in sachets. The recommended dose of capsules is 1 — 2/bird/day orally for 5 days, followed by a single dose 7 days later. The powder is added to the drinking water (1 sachet to 1 — 2 litres). One litre is sufficient daily for twenty pigeons. The dose for young birds should be reduced by a third.

This type of respiratory disease in pigeons appears to be stress-related and especially following communal transportation of birds to release points for racing. Birds may become reinfected in this way even after courses of treatment.

Other bacterial diseases

Tuberculosis caused by *Mycobacterium avium* has been described in the Carneaux breed by Pond and Rush (1981), but like most of the following infections it is relatively rare in domestic pigeons.

Other bacterial diseases include those caused by *Yersinia pseudotuberculosis, Erysipelothrix rhusiopathiae, Pasteurella multocida, Listeria monocytogenes, Klebsiella pneumoniae, Haemophilus,* streptococci, *Escherichia coli* and staphylococci. The last two named are usually associated with bumblefoot and other joint lesions (see Table 2). For further information on all of these infections the reader should consult Arnall and Keymer (1975) and textbooks on poultry diseases.

Ornithosis (Chlamydiosis)

Ornithosis is caused by a rickettsia-like organism *(Chlamydia psittaci)* which was originally classified as a virus. The infection is an important zoonosis causing psittacosis in man and psittacine birds. In pigeons it can be associated with other diseases such as trichomoniasis, pox and *Herpesvirus* infections. The infection is widespread throughout the world, including the UK (Alexander *et al,* 1989). Young birds are more susceptible to infection than adults. Diarrhoea is a common sign, associated with weakness and loss of weight. Other clinical signs include clear, ocular discharge and conjunctivitis giving rise to the so-called 'one-eyed cold' syndrome (see later). High morbidity is more frequent than mortality.

Diagnosis. The disease should always be suspected if several birds in a loft show clinical signs as above and especially if human contacts have recently shown influenza-like symptoms indicative of possible psittacosis. Whole carcases should be submitted for laboratory examination but not without prior arrangement.

Differential diagnosis. Eye affections are non-specific and can also be associated with *Mycoplasma* and *Haemophilus* spp., as well as pox and *Herpesvirus* infections or even trichomoniasis.

Treatment. If the owner is unwilling to sacrifice all his pigeons and carry out thorough disinfection before restocking, then birds can be treated with chlortetracycline (Aureomycin Soluble Powder, Cyanamid). However, a proportion of birds may remain latent carriers and there is always the possibility that the infection will flare up later, especially when birds are stressed. Birds showing clinical signs should be given 100mg chlortetracycline intramuscularly for 5 days (Arnstein *et al*, 1964) and all birds medicated by incorporating chlortetracycline in the drinking water at a rate of 120mg/litre (fresh each day). Medicated water is given for at least three periods of five days, with three day intervals (Keymer, unpublished). Vitamin supplements should be provided in the three day intervals. Alternatively, chlortetracycline should be incorporated into the ration and fed for thirty consecutive days (Arnstein *et al*, 1964). Coles (1985), however, regarded doxcycline (Vibramycin, Pfizer) to be the drug of choice for treating ornithosis in birds. Unfortunately, the drug is only available as a syrup (50mg/ml) or in 100mg capsules. The oral dosage is 18-26mg/kg (Coles, 1985).

Viral diseases

A good review of virus-induced infections in pigeons is provided by Fritzche *et al* (1981).

Paramyxovirus type 1 (PMV-I and Newcastle disease)

Strains of PMV-I which cause clinical disease in the domestic fowl are called Newcastle disease viruses to differentiate them from what appears to be a mutant strain of PMV-I pathogenic primarily to pigeons. True Newcastle disease in pigeons is apparently rare in the UK and causes predominantly nervous signs (Stewart, 1971). Until 1983 the pigeon strain of PMV-I had not been recognised in this country, but is now widespread. According to Wallis (1983) the pigeon strain of PMV-I causes a green watery diarrhoea, clearly audible upper respiratory sounds and some sneezing. However, respiratory signs are not a common feature (Alexander, personal communication). These are all signs that have not been reported in pigeons infected with the true Newcastle disease strain of PMV-I. In pigeon PMV-I, the initial onset of profuse diarrhoea may be followed in 5—20% (Richter *et al,* 1983) of birds by nervous signs such as incoordination, twitching, tremors, torticollis, drooping wings or partial paralysis of the legs. Some pigeons may circle in flight or fly backwards. Affected birds become listless, have ruffled feathers, excessive thirst and show inappetence. Some birds may show unilateral palpebral oedema (Richter *et al,* 1983). Young birds are more susceptible than adults. Those showing nervous signs are likely to die, but a proportion of the others may recover over a week or so, although lose condition. Morbidity may reach 70% and mortality 40% (Vindevogel and Duchatel, 1986). According to Alexander *et al* (1984) the incubation period is usually seven to fourteen days, sometimes three to four weeks or as long as six weeks or more. The pigeon strain of PMV-I is spread via the faeces and also by nasal secretions (Vindevogel and Duchatel, 1986), unlike true Newcastle disease which is mainly aerosol spread by inhalation. Pearson *et al* (1987) in the USA showed that experimentally infected pigeons shed the virus for up to twenty days after infection. Recovered birds do not become asymptomatic carriers (Vindevogel and Duchatel, 1986). A good account of the disease written especially for pigeon keepers is given by Vindevogel and Duchatel (1985).

Diagnosis. PMV-1 and Newcastle disease are suspected on clinical signs and are both notifiable diseases, the Fowl Pest Order of 1956 (Animal Health Act, 1981) having been extended to include PMV-1 in pigeons (see 'Legislation'). The disease can be detected using the haemagglutination inhibition (HI) test on sera and confirmed by inoculation on to the allantoic sac of 9 — 11 day-old embryonated domestic fowl eggs, or by tissue culture techniques, using suspensions of lung, trachea, brain, spleen, liver, small intestine and/or bone marrow. The brain and excreta are favoured for virus isolation by Alexander (personal communication).

Differential diagnosis. The disease is most likely to be confused with salmonellosis. When only one or two birds in a loft show nervous signs, deficiency of vitamin B (especially thiamine) should be considered. Respiratory signs and conjunctivitis may occur in the early stages of the disease (see *Mycoplasma* infection — differential diagnosis).

Treatment. None. Cases confirmed by the Ministry of Agriculture, Fisheries and Food (MAFF) Animal Health Division are kept under movement restrictions until the disease has been deemed by a Veterinary Officer to have disappeared. There is no compulsory slaughter of infected birds or compulsory vaccination, except for imported pigeons. An inactivated, oil adjuvant vaccine (Paramyx-1, Harkers) is available in the UK and may be purchased from a veterinary surgeon or through a registered pharmacy. The dose is 0.5ml injected subcutaneously at the cauda aspect of the base of the neck. Only healthy pigeons should be vaccinated. The first dose is given at four weeks of age followed by a second between four and six weeks later. Thereafter annual vaccination, preferably after the moult, is recommended in order to maintain immunity. It is advisable when young birds have been vaccinated early in the summer to vaccinate them again when the older birds are done, rather than wait until their second winter. Very occasionally, pigeons may collapse and show an anaphylactic type of reaction, dying within a few hours of vaccination when oil-based inactivated vaccines, especially those containing aluminium hydroxide or carbomen PD as adjuvants, are used. The reaction appears to be more severe after the second vaccination. Wallis (1984) stated that intramuscular injection of 0.25ml betamethasone (Betsolan Injection, Coopers Pitman-Moore) may be effective in treatment. However, Kaleta *et al* (1989) and Keymer (unpublished) suspect this acute mortality to be caused by accidental injection of the plexus venosus intracutaneous collaris located on both sides of the upper part of the neck at the site of subcutaneous vaccination. Kaleta *et al* (1989) stated that less than 1% of pigeons died immediately or within one to two hours following subcutaneous injection in the neck.

Other vaccines are now available in the UK. Nobi-Vac Paramyxo Vaccine (Intervet) contains PMV serotype 1 (from pigeons) and is also an inactivated, oil adjuvant vaccine. The dosage is 0.25ml given subcutaneously at the back of the neck, and the vaccination schedule is similar to that described earlier (but consult Compendium of Data Sheets for Veterinary Products 1990-91). Colombovac PMV (Salsbury Laboratories) is a non-oil based, water-soluble, inactivated vaccine and it is claimed that, unlike oil based vaccines, it does not cause a local reaction at the injection site and has no negative influence on feather development. All pigeons in a loft should be given 0.2ml by subcutaneous injection at the back of the neck not less than 14 days before the beginning of the racing or exhibition season. Young birds may be vaccinated from three weeks of age. Immunity lasts one year, after which a single booster vaccination is required; for further details consult Compendium of Data Sheets for Veterinary Products 1990-91.

Many pigeon fanciers use the Hitchner B1 live vaccine in spite of the fact that it is only recommended for poultry. However, in pigeons it is less effective than the inactivated vaccine, providing an immunity for only a few weeks. Similarly, the La Sota live vaccine, the use of which is not permitted by MAFF in the UK, also gives a short period of immunity. Strict attention must be paid to hygiene, because the infection can be spread mechanically in transport vehicles, pigeon baskets and by utensils etc.

Pigeon pox

Pigeon pox, contagious epithelioma or so-called 'diphtheria', is enzootic in the UK and many other parts of the world. Good accounts of the infection are given by Schrag et al (1974) and Dodd (1974). It is common, especially in squabs and squeakers. The incubation period varies from four to fourteen days, but is usually one week. Squabs are infected by their parents which can act as healthy carriers. Mosquitoes and other blood-sucking parasites may also play a role in transmission. Swellings develop on unfeathered areas of the body, especially the cere, wattles, commissures of the mouth and mainly the keratinised areas of the buccal cavity (Illustrated by Keymer, 1977). In a few days the lesions enlarge and may coalesce. Affected birds lose weight and a few, especially youngsters, may die of the acute form of the disease. Morbidity is often more than 90%. Those which recover have a good resistance for a year or more. Lesions of the acute form of the disease usually regress after about three to four weeks. Sometimes (especially in wood pigeons, *Columba palumbus*) chronic, firm tumour-like and occasionally melanistic, pedunculated or sessile nodules form near the carpal joints and other parts of the wing. The feet can also become affected in a similar way.

Diagnosis is based on clinical signs and virus isolation by inoculation of tissue suspensions of lesions on to the allantoic membrane of 10 day-old embryonated domestic fowl eggs. Electron microscopic or histological examination of lesions can also be used (Cooper, 1984).

Differential diagnosis. When lesions are confined to the buccal cavity, pox can be confused with trichomoniasis, candidiasis and vitamin A deficiency. Mixed infections can occur. Chronic, nodular lesions of the skin can be confused with neoplasms.

Treatment is unsatisfactory. Physical removal of scabs or swellings is not recommended because it is likely to spread the infection by releasing virus particles. Some owners paint lesions with a weak solution of tincture of iodine and on occasions this seems to assist regression. An attenuated, live pigeon pox vaccine is no longer available in the UK due to lack of demand. Severely affected birds are best destroyed. Others usually respond to careful nursing. Occasionally, pox lesions may become secondarily infected by bacteria, when topical application of a suitable antibiotic may be desirable. In the absence of a pigeon pox vaccine it is probably better not to attempt to restrict the spread of infection in the loft, because this may prolong the outbreak. The sooner more birds are exposed to the disease the quicker they will become infected and either die or acquire immunity. After the outbreak is over, thorough cleansing and disinfection of the loft and utensils should be carried out.

Pigeon Herpesvirus infection (PHVI) or inclusion body disease

Al Sheikhly et al (1980) pointed out that several strains of *Herpesvirus* had been isolated from pigeons in different countries. All the strains produce mainly respiratory signs and a 'coryza-like disease'. Pigeon Herpes Encephalomyelitis Virus (PHEV) related to PHVI occurs in the Middle East (Tantawi et al, 1983) but appears to be absent from the UK. It causes contagious, fatal, nervous disease.

Herpesvirus infection was first reported in the UK by Cornwell *et al* (1967), but even now little is known about its incidence, although a few cases are confirmed each year (Gough *et al*, 1988; Alexander, personal communication). Clinical signs comprise conjunctivitis, rhinitis and general malaise. Some birds show dyspnoea. Small diphtheritic lesions may occur on the mucous membrane of the larynx, pharynx and oesophagus. Duration of infection in the individual bird varies from a few days to several weeks. It may be present in a flock for several months and mortality can reach 40–80% (Mohammed *et al*, 1978). Birds may become asymptomatic carriers. The virus is probably not egg-transmitted but passed from parents to offspring, mainly during the first days of life (Vindevogel and Pastoret, 1980).

Diagnosis. *Post-mortem* examination is essential. On histological examination acidophilic, intra-nuclear inclusions can be found in association with necrosis in the liver and, sometimes, other organs. Virus can be cultured in chick embryo fibroblast cell cultures or isolated by inoculation of tissue suspensions (washing of throat swabs, trachea, lungs, liver and/or spleen) on to the chorioallantoic membrane of 10 day-old embryonated, domestic fowl eggs. Virus particles can also be found using electron microscopy.

Differential diagnosis. Clinically, the infection cannot be distinguished from ornithosis, the mucous membrane form of pox, trichomoniasis or vitamin A deficiency. It can also be associated with *Mycoplasma* infection (Keymer *et al*, 1984).

Treatment. None. However, Vindevogel *et al* (1982) have experimented with the use of both live attenuated and inactivated vaccines, with promising results.

Adenovirus infection or inclusion body hepatitis (IBH)

This is a relatively recently recognised disease of pigeons. Axworthy (personal communication) stated that, in the UK, examination of 325 pigeon sera by Barling using the gel-diffusion test revealed that 4% were positive for adenovirus type 1 and 10% for type 8. The first report of the disease, however, was not until 1984 in Holland (Coussement *et al*, 1984), since when it has also been recorded in Japan by Goryo *et al* (1988). However, McFerran *et al* (1976) described two outbreaks of IBH, but as they isolated both a *Herpesvirus* (see PHV1) and two types of adenoviruses, it is not clear which viruses were responsible for the clinical signs and lesions which they described. Coussement *et al* (1984) described the clinical signs and *post-mortem* lesions in ten young pigeons with diarrhoea. The infection was acute and resulted in death. In the UK "recently weaned birds showed diarrhoea, vomiting and death in two days." Adults also succumbed (Report, 1985).

Diagnosis. Numerous Cowdrey type A intra-nuclear inclusions can be found in the hepatocytes on histological examination. Electron microscopic examination is necessary to confirm the presence of adenovirus.

Differential diagnosis. The infection has to be differentiated from PMV-1 and other causes of diarrhoea and from PHV1 which, on histopathological examination of the liver, also reveals the presence of intra-nuclear inclusions. The possibility of rotavirus infection has to be considered although nothing appears to be known of its pathogenicity in pigeons. This is because in Belgium Vindevogel *et al* (1981) have found serological evidence of its occurrence (10.7%) in 75 birds presented at an avian clinic, and two strains of rotavirus have been isolated from feral pigeon excreta in Japan by Minamoto *et al* (1988).

Infectious bronchitis (IB)

This coronavirus infection was considered to be specific for the domestic fowl until it was confirmed in a flock of racing pigeons in Australia in 1985 by Barr *et al* (1988). The infection, therefore, should always be considered in pigeons with respiratory disease kept in close association with chickens.

Other diseases

'Pinwheel': extension of 'knee' joint in squabs

Unilateral or bilateral extension of the femoro-tibiotarsal joint may develop in squabs between twelve to thirty days of age (Levi, 1974; Ward, 1983). The abnormality arises when squabs are hatched in a nest with a flat base and insufficient nesting material. Under these circumstances the rapidly growing squab is unable to keep its feet beneath its body. The legs gradually slide further out until one or both are extended at right angles. This results in inability to articulate the femoro-tibiotarsal joint. When the squab struggles to stand up, it rotates on the keel of the sternum, which eventually produces bruising and further traumatic lesions of the skin and subcutaneous tissues. It appears to be more common in single squab clutches because lack of support from its twin leaves more space in the nest.

Diagnosis is based on clinical signs, age of the squab and examination of the nest pan.

Differential diagnosis. Other forms of trauma and nutritional bone disease, such as rickets and perosis.

Prevention and treatment. The deformity can be prevented by using nest pans with a concave base and plenty of nest material. Alternatively, a special nest ring can be constructed using a partition, so that the nest is divided in half, thus giving support to the squab (Ward, 1983). The best time to divide the nest in this way would probably be when the squab is between seven to ten days old, although Ward (1983) said it 'was most easily accomplished as soon as it was seen that only a single squab would be hatched in that nest'. He presumably meant when only one egg was being incubated. The adult birds quickly adjust to the partitioned nest ring.

Treatment, except in the very early stages, is unlikely to be successful.

'One-eyed cold'

This is a common syndrome. It is a non-specific disease also known by pigeon keepers as 'eye-cold', 'ophthalmia' or 'big-eye'. The condition is usually confined to one eye. The causes appear to be multifactorial and non-specific. Vitamin A deficiency may possibly be involved in some cases. Swollen eyelids with conjunctivitis and watery ocular discharge can also occur in association with ornithosis, pox, *Mycoplasma* spp., *Haemophilus* and PHV1 infections, or even trichomoniasis and PMV-1 infection. Unlike all these infections, however, only the eyes are affected in typical 'one-eyed cold' and the lesions do not appear to spread. The cause of such uncomplicated 'eye-colds' is unknown, although many cases respond to local treatment with antibiotic eye ointments.

Vitamin A deficiency

This is most likely to occur in permanently housed doves and pigeons, especially youngsters kept on a restricted diet with little or no greenfood or yellow seeds, such as maize, that contain carotene, the precursor of vitamin A. In addition to 'rattling' respiratory sounds and bilateral, ocular, mucoid discharge, examination of the buccal cavity will reveal whitish, necrotic foci and diphtheritic areas on the buccal and pharyngeal mucosa. These lesions may partially occlude the internal nares and/or the glottis and lumen of the pharynx. In chronic cases the infra-orbital sinuses may be distended with caseous, necrotic material. Affected birds lose weight, have a dull plumage, poor appetite and may show an unsteady gait.

Diagnosis is based on the clinical signs and close investigation of the diet. The condition may or may not be associated with specific infections such as trichomoniasis, candidiasis, aspergillosis, the pharyngeal form of pox or *Herpesvirus* infection. It must be remembered that vitamin A deficiency may be a predisposing cause of these diseases, especially the fungal infections.

Treatment. Birds should be dosed orally with vitamin A preparation and provided with foods containing the vitamin or its precursors. Antibiotic therapy may be necessary in some cases where there is evidence of secondary bacterial infection of lesions. When young birds are affected and stunted, euthanasia may be advisable because they are unlikely to grow into normal, healthy adults.

Neoplasms

Neoplasia is uncommon in pigeons in spite of the fact that many birds reach old age in captivity. Lymphosarcoma and tumours of the ovary (adenocarcinoma) appear to be the most frequent. The following is a selection of other recorded neoplasms:- granulocytic leukaemia, malignant lymphoma, lipomata, embryonal nephromas, capillary haemangioendothelioma, basal cell carcinoma, fibrosarcoma, seminoma and post-inflammatory cystadenoma (Chalmers, 1986), myeloid leukosis, exocrine pancreatic adenocarcinoma, haemangioma, haemangiosarcoma and cholangiocellular carcinoma (Coletti et al, 1988).

Diagnosis. Histological examination of tumours.

Differential diagnosis. Skin tumours can be confused with chronic pox lesions, especially when melanistic, and possibly joint swellings caused by salmonellosis.

Poisoning

Sometimes free-flying pigeons gain access to grain dressed with agricultural pesticides. Pigeons are susceptible to poisoning by certain organophosphorus and chlorinated hydrocarbon compounds. They are especially susceptible to the toxic effects of chlorfenvinphos (Bunyan et al, 1971). Alphachloralose, which is often used under licence for baiting food to control feral pigeons, may also be consumed by pigeons allowed free flight. When pesticide poisoning is suspected it is necessary to submit carcases or the following tissues to a MAFF Veterinary Investigation Centre for chemical analyses:- brain, liver, kidneys, skeletal muscle, body fat, crop and gizzard contents.

Poisoning may also occur with certain drugs, especially if used incorrectly. For example, the anthelmintic mebendazole (Mebenvet, Janssen) which is used for gallinaceous birds and waterfowl, is toxic to pigeons (Coles, 1985). It also inadvisable to use thiabendazole (Thibenzole, MSD). Coles (1985) stated that furazolidone can be toxic if pigeons are overdosed, leading to neurological damage. However, this drug, in the form of Coryzium (Crown Chemicals), has now been withdrawn. Similarly, care is needed when using fenbendazole, which can cause feather abnormalities (Devriese, 1983) (see Ascaridiasis and Capillariasis). Levamisole may cause vomiting (see Ascaridiasis). Niclosamide is also stated to be toxic (see Tapeworm infestation). Although dimetridazole is widely used for the treatment of trichomoniasis, it can be toxic under certain circumstances, causing 'temporary ataxia' (McLoughlin, 1966) or incoordination and inability to fly or eat properly (Reece et al, 1985) (see also Trichomoniasis). Reece et al (1985) also reported the toxicity of the nitrofuran furaltadone (Formula 10, Central Chemical Distributors, New South Wales) to pigeons. Affected birds showed neurological signs and abandoned nests and young. The coccidiostat, dinitolmide (3,5,-dinitro-ortho-toluamide; generic chemical) can cause similar signs of toxicity (Reece and Hooper, 1984).

Miscellaneous

A number of systemic and nutritional disorders such as **egg peritonitis, impaction of the oviduct, rickets, osteomalacia, 'rubber beak' (secondary hyperparathyroidism), perosis, thyroid and vitamin B (especially thiamine) deficiencies** occur occasionally (see Table 2). For more information the reader should consult Arnall and Keymer (1975), British Veterinary Association (1964), Harrison and Harrison (1986), Hungerford (1969), Levi (1974) and Schrag et al (1974). Other useful references on pigeons are Abs (1983), Cooper, (1984), Macrae (1972), Naether (1970), Rutgers and Norris (1970), Vogel et al (1983) and Wagenaar-Schaafsma (1984).

ANAESTHESIA

There are relatively few indications for anaesthesia, especially in racing pigeons, unless a valuable bird has sustained an injury that can be surgically repaired and at least enable the individual to be used for breeding. In the case of fractures there is little likelihood of the bird being used for racing. Pet or fancy pigeons, especially exhibition specimens, are therefore more likely to be presented for reasons that necessitate anaesthesia.

Pigeons appear to have no idiosyncrasies related to anaesthesia. In avian anaesthesia there is a choice of parenteral and inhalation anaesthetics or a combination of both (see 'Introduction' and 'Cage and Aviary Birds'). When using a parenteral anaesthetic it is essential to weigh the bird beforehand, because dosage is dependent upon bodyweight. The intraperitoneal route should be avoided because of the risk of injecting fluid into the abdominal air sacs. Care is also needed with intramuscular injection into the pectoral muscles, in order to avoid the large venous plexus which lies deep in these muscles. When using this route it is advisable to withdraw the plunger of the syringe and check that blood cannot be drawn back before injecting the anaesthetic. In most cases it is preferable to give intramuscular injections into a leg (Cooper, 1984).

Parenteral anaesthesia

Amand (1980) listed seven substances suitable for general anaesthesia in birds. At the present time, **ketamine hydrochloride** (Vetalar, Parke-Davies) appears to be the most popular of these. Cooper (1984) recommended a dose of 25—50mg/kg bodyweight i/m for pigeons. The bird will remain sedated for about thirty to sixty minutes. Both Amand (1980) and Cooper (1984) also recommended **alphaxalone/alphadolone** (Saffan, Coopers Pitman-Moore) for short acting anaesthesia. Although this can be given intramuscularly, Cooper (1984) recommended the intravenous route. The dose is 5—7mg/kg bodyweight and the effect lasts only about three to five minutes. However, maintenance can be achieved by administering incremental doses via a 'butterfly' attachment into the brachial or tarsal vein (Cooper, 1984). In a recent paper, Fitzgerald and Cooper (1990) described the successful use of **propofol** (Rapinovet, Coopers Pitman-Moore) in pigeons by the intravenous route, but pointed out that the safety margin was low.

Inhalation anaesthesia

Volatile agents are now widely used to induce surgical anaesthesia either following parenteral injection of an anaesthetic such as ketamine or alphaxalone/alphadolone, or alone. Volatile anaesthetics have the advantage of allowing more precise control over the depth of anaesthesia. It is important to intubate the patient. Two popular anaesthetics are **halothane** and **methoxyflurane.** Cooper (1984) recommended 2—4% halothane in oxygen with the addition of nitrous oxide (50:50) because this enhances the analgesic effect and reduces the amount of halothane required. Methoxyflurane is particularly safe and especially suitable for poor risk patients, but at the usual dose of 4% in oxygen is not likely to attain anaesthesia sufficiently deep for surgery (Cooper, 1984).

As with all avian anaesthesia, care should be taken to ensure that the patient is kept warm, both during and after the procedure, and that its fluid balance is maintained. Further information on these aspects can be found in the chapter on Cage and Aviary Birds.

Acknowledgements

The author would like to thank Mr P C Carwardine, of RMB Animal Health, for help in compiling the section on drug toxicity and Dr D J Alexander, Central Veterinary Laboratory, Weybridge, Surrey, for kindly checking the section dealing with viral infections.

Table 1
Lay terms for various pigeon diseases.*

Term	Disease to suspect
Air puffs	Subcutaneous emphysema.
Big eye	See 'one-eyed cold'.
Bird fever	Salmonellosis
Blind staggers	Congenital nervous disorder or any infection affecting central nervous system, especially salmonellosis.
Blow out	Eversion of cloaca or oviduct.
Bumblefoot	Swelling of tarsometatarsus-phalangeal joint (see Table 2).
Canker. Variously called dry, wet, lip or throat canker.	Usually trichomoniasis, but also pox, candidiasis, PHVI or hypovitaminosis A.
Cholera	Pasteurellosis
Contagious epithelioma	Pox or trichomoniasis, but more likely the former.
Coryza	Sinusitis. See roup, 'nasal discharge' (see Table 2).
Diphtheria	Pox or trichomoniasis. Synonymous with 'contagious epithelioma'.
Dysentery	Diarrhoea, especially when blood-tinged, eg. capillariasis, ornithostrongylosis, salmonellosis.
Eye-cold	See 'one-eyed cold'.
Going light	Any chronic wasting disease (see Table 2).
Megrims	Salmonellosis, Newcastle disease, or any agent affecting the CNS.
Odium	Candidiasis
One-eyed cold	Any localised eye infection or pox. If bilateral, possibly hypovitaminosis A, ornithosis, PHVI, *Mycoplasma,* or *Haemophilus* infection.
Ophthalmia	Any inflammatory lesion involving the eye. See also 'big eye', 'one-eyed cold', 'sore-eye', 'eye-cold' and Table 2.
Paratyphoid	Salmonellosis
Pasting of the vent	Diarrhoea or excessive fluid urate excretion causing matting of feathers in region of cloaca (see Table 2).
Prolapse	Eversion of cloaca or oviduct.
Roup	Sinusitis. See 'coryza', 'nasal discharge' (see Table 2).
Scours	Diarrhoea of any type.
Sore-eye	Synonymous with 'big-eye', 'one-eyed cold', 'eye-cold' or 'ophthalmia'.
Sour-crop	Any crop infection especially candidiasis. Also trichomoniasis and capillariasis.
Thrush	Crop candidiasis (see also 'sour crop').
Vent gleet	Cloacitis of any cause.
Vertigo	Incoordination, especially caused by salmonellosis, PMV-1 and Newcastle disease.

*Modified and reprinted with permission from State Veterinary Journal (1984).

Table 2
A guide to clinical signs.*

Anatomical system and related clinical signs	Possible causes
Skin and appendages Loss of feathers and areas of alopecia.	Normal or 'heavy' moult; ectoparasitism, especially depluming mite *(Cnemidocoptes laevis),* quill mite *(Syringophilus columbae).* Cannibalism. Nutritional or thyroid deficiencies.
Broken feathers and holes in feather barbs and web.	Trauma. Ectoparasitism, especially lice, eg. *Columbicola columbae* and other spp., and feather mites *(Megninia, Falculifer rostratus* and other spp.) when in heavy infestations.
Stunted feather development with growing feathers still enclosed within feather sheath or quill stumps containing powdery material.	Ectoparasitism, especially quill mite *(Syringophilus columbae).* Possible nutritional deficiency in some cases.
Pruritus with or without self-plucking of feathers and often associated with restlessness and fluffing up of feathers.	Ectoparasitism, eg. depluming mite *(C. laevis),* heavy infestations with lice or red mites *(Dermanyssus gallinae* or *Ornithonyssus sylviarum).*
Ruffled feathers.	Any systemic disease. Ectoparasitism.
Puffy swellings of skin especially cervical region.	Subcutaneous emphysema, apparently due to rupture of air sac.
Vesicles and harder swellings, especially head region, wings and feet.	Pox.
Soft swellings of skin, especially with loss of overlying feathers.	Abscesses (relatively rare) or haematoma, especially if over keel of sternum.
Scaly proliferation of skin of legs and feet including plantar surfaces. Pitted appearance of skin with epidermal debris on surfaces.	*Cnemidocoptes mutans* infestation (scaly leg). Uncommon.
Swelling of 'ball' of foot, ie. tarsometatarsus-phalangeal joint.	'Bumble-foot' or pedal arthritis caused by staphylococcal or *Escherichia coli* infection.
Musculo-skeletal system Joint swellings of feet and legs leading to lameness and swollen wing joints.	Salmonellosis *(Salmonella typhimurium* infection). Localised staphylococcal and *E. coli* infections. Usually confined to feet and hocks. More rarely articular or periarticular gout.
Lameness or reluctance to stand.	Trauma, salmonellosis, tuberculosis, rickets, osteomalacia.
Bent legs.	Rickets, osteomalacia, 'pinwheel' or healed fractures.
Swollen hock (ie. tibiotarsus-tarsometatarsal joint) with or without slipped tendon (gastrocnemius).	Nutritional bone disease, eg. rickets or osteomalacia. Perosis associated with nutritional deficiencies, eg. manganese.
Wasting of pectoral muscles and general loss of weight.	Chronic malnutrition; chronic infections, eg. trichomoniasis, helminthiasis, tuberculosis, pseudotuberculosis, salmonellosis or aspergillosis. Chronic egg peritonitis and/or impaction of oviduct (individual hens only).
Extension of femoro-tibiotarsal ('knee') joint resulting in splaying of the legs ('pinwheel') in squabs.	Occurs when squab is hatched in a nest with a flat base and insufficient nesting material.

Table 2
A guide to clinical signs *(continued)*.*

Anatomical system and related clinical signs	Possible causes
Digestive system Liquid discharge from beak and/or regurgitation associated with general malaise.	Trichomoniasis; capillariasis, especially when vomiting occurs and birds die within a few days.
Caseous lesions at commissures of mouth and in buccal cavity.	Trichomoniasis. Also, but less common, pigeon pox, candidiasis, PHVI or hypovitaminosis A.
Swollen throat and firm lumps palpable in cervical region.	Chronic trichomoniasis, candidiasis and/or impaction of crop.
Diarrhoea (ie. genuine and not excessive urate excretion), often associated with so-called 'pasting of the vent'.	Trichomoniasis (not a consistent sign); coccidiosis (in pigeons 3–4 months old); ascaridiasis and capillariasis (not a consistent sign); salmonellosis; ornithosis; PMV-1; PHVI; adenovirus (IBH) infection; poisoning, eg. seed dressings. Ornithostrongylosis (very rare in the UK, but possibly overlooked).
Inappetence.	Most infectious diseases.
Polydypsia.	Coccidiosis, salmonellosis, PMV-1.
Respiratory system Nasal discharge.	Trichomoniasis (advanced stage affecting nasal sinuses); mycoplasmosis (see text); PHVI; ornithosis; *Haemophilus* infection (uncommon).
Dyspnoea.	Trichomoniasis (advanced stage affecting nasal sinuses); aspergillosis (uncommon); PHVI; ornithosis.
Audible respiratory sounds.	PMV-1; *Mycoplasma* infection (see text); hypovitaminosis A.
Urinary system Excessive fluid urate excretion often associated with so-called 'pasting of the vent'.	Sequel to nephrosis (non-specific) or secondary to an infectious and systemic disease.
Reproductive system Distension of abdomen in hens, especially if associated with periodic straining.	Egg peritonitis and/or impaction of oviduct. (Sometimes associated with environomental disturbances or salmonellosis).
Circulatory system Sudden death.	Internal haemorrhage as a result of trauma, eg. ruptured liver or heart muscle. Ruptured spleen is sometimes associated with ornithosis.
Nervous system Paralysis (partial or complete) of legs, feet and/or wings.	Trauma; PMV-1; typical Newcastle disease; salmonellosis; hypovitaminosis B complex, especially thiamine. Possible Marek's disease, but not confirmed in pigeons. Some types of poisoning (see Poisoning).
Tremors, shivering, twitching, inco-ordination, torticollis, convulsions (usually terminal).	Salmonellosis; tuberculosis; PMV-1; typical Newcastle disease; some types of poisoning (see Poisoning).
Sensory system Watery muco-purulent, ocular discharge with or without apparent conjunctivitis.	Irritants, eg. dust, ammonia from excessive excreta in environment; ornithosis; 'one-eyed cold' syndrome; PHVI; *Mycoplasma* infection; *Haemophilus* infection.
Swollen eyelids and blepharitis.	As above. Pox.
Keratitis.	Sequel to chronic ocular infections or trauma.
Swellings on eyelids.	Pox.
Blindness.	Salmonellosis.

Modified and reprinted with permission from State Veterinary Journal (1984).

REFERENCES

ABS, M. (1983). *Physiology and Behaviour of the Pigeon.* Academic Press, London.

AL SHEIKHLY, F., TANTAWI, H. H. and AL FALLUJI, M. M. (1980). Viral encephalomyelitis of pigeons. III. Growth of the virus in embryonated eggs. *Avian Disease* **24**, 112.

ALEXANDER, D. J., BEVAN, B. J., LISTER, S. A. and BRACEWELL, C. D. (1989). Chlamydia infections in racing pigeons in Great Britain: a retrospective serological survey. *Veterinary Record* **125**, 239.

ALEXANDER, D. J., WILSON, G. W. C., THAIN, J. A. and LISTER, S. A. (1984). Avian Paramyxovirus-1 infections of racing pigeons. III. Epizootiological considerations. *Veterinary Record* **115**, 213.

AMAND, W. B. (1980). Avian anaesthetic agents and techniques — a review. *American Association of Zoo Veterinarians Annual Proceedings.* Washington DC.

ARNALL, L. and KEYMER, I. F. (1975). *Bird Diseases.* Baillière Tindall, London.

ARNSTEIN, P., COHEN, D. H. and MEYER, K. F. (1964). Medication of pigeons with chlortetracycline in feed. *Journal of the American Veterinary Medical Association* **145**, 921.

AXWORTHY, R. H. (1972). *Pigeon Care and Protection.* Harkers Veterinary Remedies, Lamberhurst.

BARR, D .A., REECE, R. L., O'ROURKE, D., BUTTON, C. and FARAGHER, J. T. (1988). Isolation of infectious bronchitis virus from a flock of racing pigeons. *Australian Veterinary Journal* **65**, 228.

BECHIR, R. (1979). *Experimental Studies on Parenteral Immunization of Pigeons with a Salmonella Mineral Oil Vaccine.* Inaugural Dissertation. Tierärztliche Hochschule, Hannover. *Veterinary Bulletin* (1980) Abst. 534.

BRITISH VETERINARY ASSOCIATION (1964). *Handbook on the Treatment of Exotic Pets. Part I. Cage Birds.* British Veterinary Association, London.

BUNYAN, P. J., JENNINGS, D. M. and JONES, F. J. S. (1971). Organophosphorus poisoning: a comparative study of the toxicity of chlorfenvinphos (2-chloro-1-2, 4,-dichlorophenyl vinyl diethyl phosphate) to the pigeon, the pheasant and the Japanese quail. *Pesticide Science* **2**, 148.

CAMPBELL, T. W. and DEIN, F J. (1984). Avian hematology. The basics. In: *Symposium on Caged Bird Medicine. The Veterinary Clinics of North America.* (Ed. G. J. Harrison) W. B. Saunders Philadelphia.

CHALMERS, G. A. (1986). Neoplasms in two racing pigeons. *Avian Disease* **30**, 241.

COLES, B. H. (1985). *Avian Medicine and Surgery.* Blackwell Scientific Publications, Oxford.

COLES, B. H. (1987). Dosage of ivermectin for birds. *Veterinary Record* **120**, 604.

COLETTI, M., VITELLOZZI, G., FIORONI, A. and FRANCIOSINI, M. P. (1988). Spontaneous neoplasms of the domestic pigeon, *Columba livia. Obiettivi e Documenti Veterinaria* **9**, 57 (In Italian). *Veterianry Bulletin* (1988). Abst. 4234.

COOPER, J. E. (1984). A veterinary approach to pigeons. *Journal of Small Animal Practice* **25**, 505.

CORNWELL, H. J. C., WEIR, A. R. and FOLLETT, E. A. C. (1967). A herpesvirus infection of pigeons. *Veterinary Record* **81**, 267.

COUSSEMENT, W., DUCATELLE, R., LEMAHIEU, P., FROYMAN, R., DEVRIESE, L. and HOORENS, J. (1984). Pathology of denovirus nfection in pigeons. *Vlaams Diergeneeskundig Tijdschrift* **53**, 277.

DEVRIESE, L. A. (1983). Fenbendazole treatment of nematodes in birds. *Veterinary Record* **112**, 509.

DODD, K. (1974). Pox in racing pigeons. *Veterinary Record* **95**, 41.

FITZGERALD, G., and COOPER, J. E. (1990). Preliminary studies on the use of propofol in the domestic pigeon *(Columba livia). Research in Veterinary Science* **49**, 334.

FRITZSCHE, K., HEFFELS, V. and KALETA, E. F. (1981). Virus-induced infections in pigeons. A review. *Deutsche Tierärztliche Wochenschrift* **88**, 72. (In German).

GERLACH, H. (1977). Über das Vorkommen von Mykoplasmen bei Tauben. *Berliner und Münchener Tierärztliche Wochenschrift* **90**, 140. (In German)

GORYO, M., UEDA, Y., UMEMURA, T., HARUNA, A. and ITAKURA, C. (1988). Inclusion body hepatitis due to adenovirus in pigeons. *Avian Pathology* **17**, 391.

GOUGH, R. E., ALEXANDER, D. J., COLLINS, M. S., LISTER, S. A. and COX, W. J. (1988). Routine virus isolation or detection in the diagnosis of disease in birds. *Avian Pathology* **17**, 893.

HARRISON, G. J., and HARRISON, L. R. (1986). *Clinical Avian Medicine and Surgery.* W. B. Saunders Philadelphia.

HAWES, R. O. (1984). Pigeons. In: *Evolution of Domesticated Animals* (Ed. I. L. Mason) Longman, London.

HAWKEY, C. M. and DENNETT, T. B. (1989). *A Colour Atlas of Comparative Veterinary Haematology.* Wolfe Publishing, London.

HEIDENREICH, M. (1980). Diseases of parrots. In: *Handbook of Lovebirds.* (Ed. Horst Bielfeld) TFH Publications, New Jersey.

HUNGERFORD, T. G. (1969). *Diseases of Poultry Including Cage Birds and Pigeons.* 4th Edn. Angus and Robertson, Sydney. (Useful, in spite of being out of date in some respects.)

HUNTER, B. W. (1989). Drugs for pigeons. *Veterinary Record* **125**, 334, 465.

JORDAN, F. T. W., HOWSE, J. N., ADAMS, M. P. and FATUNMBI, O. O. (1981). The isolation of *Mycoplasma columbinum* and *M. columborale* from feral pigeons. *Veterinary Record* **109**, 450.

KALETA, E. F., BUCKNER, D. and GOLLER, H. (1989). Acute fatalities following subcutaneous injection of paramyxovirus type 1 vaccines in pigeons. *Avian Pathology* **18**, 203.

KEYMER, I. F. (1977). Diseases of Columbiformes. In: *Poultry Diseases.* (Ed. R. F. Gordon) Ballière Tindall, London. (Brief account).

KEYMER, I. F., LEACH, R. H., CLARKE, R. A., BARDSLEY, M. E. and McINTYRE, R. R. (1984). Isolation of *Mycoplasma* spp. from racing pigeons *(Columba livia). Avian Pathology* **13**, 65.

KIESSLING, D. and GERLACH, H. (1989). On the importance of bacterial L-forms in pigeons. In: *Proceedings 1989, Annual Conference Association of Avian Veterinarians, Seattle.*

KING, A. S. and McLELLAND, J. (1984). *Birds, their Structure and Function.* 2nd Edn. Ballière Tindall, London.

KIRSCH, R. and DEGENHARDT, H. (1979). Efficacy of fenbendazole against immature and mature stages of *Capillaria obsignata* and *Ascaridia columbae* in pigeons in a controlled test. *Tierärztliche Umschau* **34**, 767, 770. (In German.)

KIRSCH. R., PETRI, K. and DEGENHARDT, H. (1978). Treatment of *Capillaria* and *Ascaridia* infections in pigeons with fenbendazole. *Kleintierpraxis* **23**, 291. (In German).

LAWRENCE, K. (1983). Efficacy of fenbendazole against nematodes of captive birds. *Veterinary Record* **112**, 433.

LEVI, W. M. (1974). *The Pigeon.* 2nd Edn. with minor changes and additions. Sumpter, S. G. The Levi Publishing Co., Columbia. (The standard text on all aspects of pigeons).

LUMEIJ, J. T. (1987a). *A Contribution to Clinical Investigative Methods for Birds, with Special Reference to the Racing Pigeon (Columba livia domestica).* Utrecht.

LUMEIJ, J. T. (1987b). Plasma urea, creatinine and uric acid concentrations in response to dehydration in racing pigeons *(Columba livia domestica). Avian Pathology* **16**, 377.

MACOWAN, K. J., JONES, H. G. R., RANDALL, C. J. and JORDAN, F. T. W. (1981). *Mycoplasma columborale* in a respiratory condition of pigeons and experimental air sacculitis of chickens. *Veterinary Record* **109**, 562.

MACRAE, R. R. (1972). Management, feeding, breeding and training of racing pigeons. (Presented to BVZS 1969). In: *Proceedings BVZS 1961–1970.* (Eds I. F. Keymer, A. D. Irvin and J. E. Cooper) British Veterinary Association, London. (A useful article written by a veterinary surgeon who keeps pigeons).

McFERRAN, J. B., McCRACKEN, R. M., CONNOR, T. J. and EVANS, R. T. (1976). Isolation of viruses from clinical outbreaks of inclusion body hepatitis. Avian Pathology **5**, 315.

McLOUGHLIN, D. K. (1966). Observations on the treatment of *Trichomonas gallinae* in pigeons. *Avian Disease* **10**, 288.

MINAMOTO, N., OKI, K., TOMITA, M., KINJO, T. and SUZUKI, Y. (1988). Isolation and characterisation of rotavirus from feral pigeon in mammalian cell cultures. *Epidemiology Infection* **100**, 481.

MOHAMMED, M. A., SOKKAR, S. M. and TANTAWI, H. H. (1978). Contagious paralysis of pigeons. *Avian Pathology* **7**, 637.

NAETHER, C. (1970). Practical methods of maintaining native and foreign seed-eating doves and pigeons in captivity. In: *Encyclopaedia of Aviculture.* (Eds A. Rutgers and K. A. Norris) Blandford Press, London.

PANIGRAHY, B., GRIMES, J. E., GLASS, S. E., NAQI, S. A. and HALL, C. F. (1982). Diseases of pigeons and doves in Texas: Clinical findings and recommendations for control. *Journal of the American Veterinary Medical Association* **181**, 384.

PELLÉRDY, L. P. (1974). Pigeon coccidiosis. In: *Coccidia and Coccidiosis.* Verlag Paul Parey. Berlin.

POND, L. and RUSH, H. G. (1981). Infection of white carneaux pigeons *(Columba livia)* with *Mycobacterium avium. Laboratory Animal Science* **31**, 196.

REECE, R. L., BARR, D. A., FORSYTH, W. M. and SCOTT, P. C. (1985). Investigations of toxicity episodes involving chemotherapeutic agents in Victorian poultry and pigeons. *Avian Disease* **29**, 1239.

REECE, R. L. and HOOPER, P. T. (1984). Toxicity in utility pigeons caused by the coccidiostat dinitolmide. *Australian Veterinary Journal* **61**, 259.

REECE, R. L., IRELAND, L. and SCOTT, P. C. (1986). Mycoplasmosis in racing pigeons. *Australian Veterinary Journal* **63**, 166.

REPORT (1985). Ministry of Agriculture, Fisheries and Food, Animal Health. Report of the Chief Veterinary Officer. 115.

RICHTER, R., KÖSTERS, J. and KRÄMER, K. (1983). Paramyxovirus infection in pigeons. *Der Praktische Tierarzt* **64**, 915 (in German).

ROSE, J. H. and KEYMER. I. F. (1958). An outbreak of ornithostrongylosis in domestic pigeons. *Veterinary Record* **70**, 932.

RUTGERS, A. and NORRIS, K. A. (1970). Eds. *Encyclopaedia of Aviculture.* Blandford Press, London.

SCHRAG, L., ENZ, H. and KLETTE, H. (1974). *Healthy Pigeons. Recognition, Prevention and Treatment of the Major Pigeon Diseases.* Verlag L. Schober, Hengersberg. (English version of a German text).

SHIMIZU, T., ERNO, H. and NAGATOMO, H. (1978). Isolation and characterisation of *Mycoplasma columbinum* and *Mycoplasma columborale,* two new species from pigeons. *International Journal of Systematic Bacteriology* **28**, 538.

SINCLAIR, D. V. (1980). Respiratory disease in pigeons. *Veterinary Record* **106**, 466.

STEINER, C. V. and DAVIS, R. B. (1981). *Cage Bird Medicine: Selected Topics.* Iowa State University Press, Ames.

STEWART, G. H. (1971). Naturally occurring clinical Newcastle disease in the racing pigeon *(Columba livia). Veterinary Record* **89**, 225.

TANGREDI, B. P. (1985). Avian Paramyxovirus type 1. Infection in pigeons: clinical observations. *Avian Disease* **29**, 1252.

TANTAWI, H. H., YOUSSEF, Y. I., BASTAMI, M., AL-ABDULLA, J. M. and AMINA, N. (1983). Susceptibility of day-old chicks and ducklings, goslings and quails to pigeon herpes, encephalomyelitis and pigeon Herpesviruses. *Veterinary Research Communications* **6**, 145.

UYTTEBROEK, E., GEVAERT, D. and DEVRIESE, L. A. (1989). Effect of different chemotherapeutics on experimental salmonellosis in pigeons. *Vlaams Diergeneeskundig Tijdschrift* **58**, 51 (in Dutch). *Veterinary Bulletin* (1989) Abst. 5740.

VANPARIJS, O., HERMANS, L., FLAES, L. VanDer., VLAMINCK, K. and MARSBOOM, R. (1988). Clazuril: a new anticoccidial agent in the treatment of pigeons. *Tijdschrift voor Diergeneeskunde* **113**, 190 (in Dutch). *Veterinary Bulletin* (1988) Abst. 3496.

VINDEVOGEL, H., DAGENAIS, L., LANSIVAL, B. and PASTORET, P. P. (1981). Incidence of rotavirus, adenovirus and herpesvirus infection in pigeons. *Veterinary Record* **109**, 285.

VINDEVOGEL, H. and DUCHATEL, J. P. (1985). *Understanding Pigeon Paramyxovirus.* (Ed. Natural Granen N. V.) DS-Advertising O, Van Nooten, Schoten, Belgium.

VINDEVOGEL, H. and DUCHATEL, J. P. (1986). Paramyxovirus type I infection in pigeons. In: *Acute Virus Infections of Poultry.* (Eds. J. B. McFerran and M. S. McNulty) Martinus Nijhoff Publishers, Dordrecht.

VINDEVOGEL, H. and PASTORET, P. P., (1980). Pigeon herpes transmission: natural transmission of the disease. *Journal of Comparative Pathology* **90**, 409.

VINDEVOGEL, H., PASTORET, P. P. and LEROY, P. (1982). Vaccination trials against pigeon herpes virus infection (Pigeon Herpesvirus 1). *Journal of Comparative Pathology* **92**, 483.

VOGEL, K., LUTHGEN, W., MULLER, H., SCHRAG, L. and VOGEL, M. (1983). *Die Taube: Taubenkrankheiten.* VEB Deutscher Landwirtschaftsverlag, Berlin. (In German).

WAGENAAR-SCHAAFSMA, A. E. (1984). Ziertauben. In: *Krankheiten der Heimtiere.* (Eds. K. Gabrisch and P. Zwart). Schlütersche, Hannover. (In German).

WALLIS, A. (1983). Paramyxovirus infection. Virus Report. *The Racing Pigeon.* 22nd July, 1010.

WALLIS, A. S. (1984). Mortality associated with vaccination of pigeons against paramyxovirus type 1. *Veterinary Record* **114,** 51.

WARD. G. E. (1983). 'Pinwheel' in pigeon squabs; its appearance and prevention. *Animal Technology* **34,** 157.

CHAPTER FIFTEEN

WILD BIRDS

Francis T Scullion MVB PhD MRCVS

Recent growing public concern about the environment and its inhabitants has meant that the practising veterinary surgeon is being consulted about casualty wild birds more often. Under the Wildlife and Countryside Act 1981, the majority of British disabled wild birds can only be taken into captivity for attention to their ailments with eventual release as the objective (see 'Legislation'). Certain species of wild bird (Schedule 4 of the Act) must be registered with the Department of Environment if held in captivity. The unique value of veterinary expertise in relation to problems of wild bird casualties is recognised by the Department by the issue of a general licence permitting such birds to be kept in captivity under veterinary care for a period of up to six weeks before registration is required (see 'Legislation').

There is obviously a plethora of unfamiliar species that could be presented as patients. The ethical obligation of the veterinary surgeon towards unfamiliar species is outlined in the Royal College of Veterinary Surgeons' Guide to Professional Conduct (RCVS, 1990). At the very least, it is necessary to be prepared to provide proper emergency treatment. Although euthanasia is an appropriate option for some wild bird patients, advances in avian medicine and surgery are such that many birds can now be treated successfully. All veterinary surgeons should be aware of the possibilities that exist for wild bird patients and be capable of referring appropriate cases to colleagues with a special interest or expertise.

The overall objective in treating wild birds is to release a fit and healthy bird back into its own environment. Ideally this should be done as rapidly as possible. In many respects initial veterinary medical and surgical attention and nursing care are fairly straightforward and based upon basic principles (Cooper and Eley, 1979; Coles, 1985; Fowler, 1986; Harrison and Harrison, 1986; Hungerford, 1981; Petrak, 1982). In the majority of cases the prognosis for successful release is dependent on adequate rehabilitation procedures and release techniques. Rehabilitation is the restoration of injured birds to good health and activity and primarily involves the use of physiotherapy and various training procedures. Release is the act of returning a healthy active bird to the wild where, if the release is to be considered successful, the bird will survive and once again fend for itself in its natural habitat. There are many individuals and some charities that attempt with varying success to rehabilitate and release sick and injured wild birds. The interested veterinary surgeon can work in conjunction with such people to provide scientific advice and improve the welfare of the birds (Chaplin et al, 1988; Crawford, 1983; Derrickson and Carpenter, 1983; Harris and Thomas, 1989).

MANAGEMENT PROTOCOL FOR WILD BIRDS

It is imperative that any practice which decides to offer help to a wild bird casualty has a management protocol devised for the intake and throughput of such patients. The extent of involvement will vary for individual practices. A general programme is presented in Figure 1.

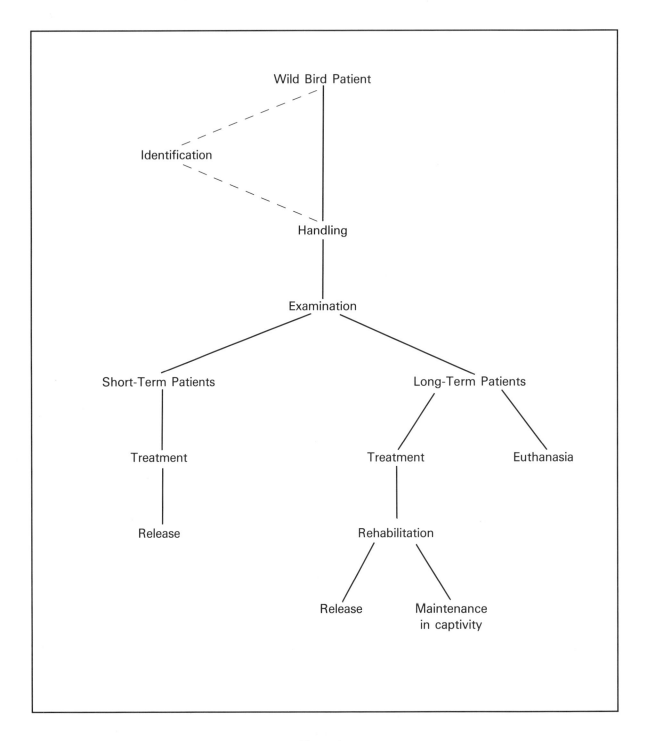

Figure 1.
Protocol for the management of wild bird patients.

IDENTIFICATION

The patient should be identified as far as possible. It is not necessary for every veterinary surgeon to be an ornithologist to identify wild birds. It is easy to find bird enthusiasts in local or national ornithological organisations who will delight in imparting their specialist knowledge (See 'Appendix — Useful Addresses'). The majority of the 200 species of wild birds that regularly frequent the UK belong to the Order Passeriformes but there are also 17 other Orders represented. Just over 50% of the species likely to be presented as patients are resident birds such as house sparrows *(Passer domesticus)*, carrion crows *(Corvus corone)* and barn owls *(Tyto alba)*; 30% are summer visitors such as terns *(Sterna* species), swifts *(Apus apus)*, swallows *(Hirundo rustica)*, sand martins *(Riparia riparia)* and house martins *(Delichon urbica)*; and the remainder (approximately 20%) are partial migrants of which a substantial part of the population winters outside the UK while the rest stay here throughout the year, and this group includes tits *(Parus* species), finches *(Fringilla* species) and some of the thrush family *(Turdus* species).

HANDLING

The safety of patient and handler is of fundamental importance. The majority of wild bird patients are presented in a subdued, weakened state which requires sensitive handling and restraint techniques in order to reduce stress-associated problems. Attempts to escape can exacerbate existing skeletal and soft tissue injuries and lead to traumatic feather damage. In the surgery, bird patients should initially be approached in conditions of dimmed lighting so as to avoid such problems. Windows should be draped to prevent accidental collisions in escape attempts and all possible exits must be closed. Some very nervous patients may need to be restrained in darkness with the aid of a torch light. Implements and perches should be removed from the holding cage without disturbing the occupant.

Although the use of thick leather gloves for handling birds that either peck or scratch is sometimes advocated, it can be argued that the loss of sensitivity and dexterity could result in injury to some birds.

The following procedures can be used for restraining most birds. A towel is held at two corners, allowed to drape down and slowly moved towards the bird keeping the hands out of sight. Sometimes a bird will attempt to move away from this perceived threat but the majority can be covered without much fuss. As a bird patient improves in health it becomes able to defend itself and it is useful to know which parts of the anatomy it uses in defence. Birds such as grey herons *(Ardea cinerea)* which use their beaks in defence will not do so when their heads are covered. They can safely be grasped through the towel at the base of the skull. Birds of prey strike with their talons and should be approached from above and behind. Their legs can be grasped through the towel as high up as possible to avoid pivotal struggling. The towel can be used to wrap the bird's wings and the bird can be picked up.

Once safely restrained the bird can be carefully extracted from the towel, always ensuring that the head, wings and feet are under control. The clinical examination can now be performed quickly under good illumination.

Birds which are being kept in large flights for rehabilitation purposes can be restrained using similar procedures, although it may first be necessary gradually to decrease the bird's available free space until it can be safely netted or persuaded to enter a small holding cage.

CLINICAL EXAMINATION

Clinical examination of wild birds follows basic principles and includes history taking, physical examination and special examination.

History

Reference books (see References and Further Reading) used for identification purposes will also provide information on the bird's natural history, its sex and age (if possible), the type of environment it usually inhabits, its normal behavioural patterns and its predominant dietary preferences.

Details should be taken about where, when and under what circumstances a bird was found. These, in combination with the supporting information acquired on identification of the bird, can lead to a presumptive diagnosis in many cases. For example, migratory birds found off their flight path, during inclement weather conditions at a time of year when they may just have finished a long flight, are likely to be suffering from exhaustion. The name and address of the finder of the bird should be noted so that he or she can be informed about the outcome of the case.

Physical examination

The physical examination is performed systematically as in other species (Cooper, 1983; Harrison and Harrison, 1986; Perry, 1981). It is important to determine whether life-threatening conditions are present and to assess the tolerance of the bird to the stress of handling and examination by observing its general attitude and respiratory rate. Diagnostic tests, initial therapies, weighing and other clinical measurements should be carried out in short periodic episodes in order to limit the duration of handling of the patient.

As a general rule, all wild birds are critically ill patients by the time they are capable of being found and caught by members of the public. In most cases they will be starved, in varying degrees of dehydration, suffering from hypothermia and often in a severe state of shock. The physical examination should help in assessing the severity of the presenting signs associated with the bird's critical condition. It should also be aimed at ascertaining the reasons why the bird became grounded and indicate the appropriate long-term therapeutic requirements.

It should be possible to classify casualties into two categories based on their anticipated recovery time, ie. long-term and short-term patients. Both groups will benefit from emergency therapy. Long-term patients will be suffering from conditions such as fractures, oil pollution, severe trauma or poisoning and will require a prolonged recovery period. Some of these patients may be so severely affected that their response to treatment could not be expected to lead to a full recovery, with the bird being destined to remain in captivity. An example is a compound wing fracture of long duration which requires amputation. It may be better to kill such birds unless there are ulterior reasons for keeping them, eg. rare species, possible use for breeding or educational display (Cooper, 1987; Evans, 1983).

Short-term patients suffering from conditions such as exhaustion, starvation or minor trauma could include fledglings which left the nest too early (many such youngsters are wrongly presented as being abandoned or orphaned), migratory birds after long flights and gulls or waterfowl entangled in fishing tackle. It would be inappropriate to kill birds in this category, since they should respond well to emergency therapy followed by basic nursing care. In the case of fledglings where no clinical conditions are obvious, it is best to replace the bird in the nest as soon as possible or, if the nest cannot be located, in a suitable sheltered spot near to where it was found initially, so that the parent birds will continue to care for it.

Special examination

Laboratory investigations can be of benefit in the complete assessment of any case (Woerpel and Rosskopf, 1984). It is possible to diagnose anaemia and monitor hydration status by collecting small blood samples into heparinised tubes for PCV and total solids estimation (Martin and Kollias, 1989). Radiographs will be necessary before treating fractures and are useful in diagnosing conditions such as air-sacculitis. Endoparasitic infections can be identified by performing simple procedures such as wet preparations or flotation techniques on faecal samples (Cooper, 1985).

EMERGENCY THERAPY

The bird should be put in a warm, dimly lit environment. Birds that are weak or perhaps suffering from anaemia or dyspnoea will benefit from oxygen therapy either in an incubator or a hospital cage converted to take a flow-through of oxygen, or, for very weak birds, via a face mask. Obvious bleeding must be dealt with immediately and haemostasis can be achieved by cauterisation, direct pressure or ligation of blood vessels.

Generally, critically ill birds will require and respond well to fluid therapy. Stable patients and small birds, in which it may be difficult to find veins, can benefit from oral fluids. Injectable fluids (normal saline 50ml/kg/day for maintenance) and corticosteroids (dexamethasone 0.1mg/kg) are useful for treating birds in shock. Intravenous catheters are not usually practicable in birds but it is possible to administer calculated doses of intravenous fluids as boluses over a period of 1−2 minutes. Critical patients may need multiple intravenous boluses. Fluid deficit can be calculated as a percentage of bodyweight. Maintenance requirements plus 50% of the fluid deficit are administered during the first 24 hours. The remaining deficit plus maintenance is given over the next 48 hours in multiple doses. Recently a technique involving the use of an intra-osseous ulnar catheter has been suggested as a means of supplying fluid requirements to critically ill birds over a long period (Quesenberry *et al*, 1989a; Ritchie *et al*, 1990).

Critically ill birds are usually anorexic and require nutritional support. Their immediate requirement is for energy and this can be conveniently supplied in the short-term by using conventional high energy diets such as Complan (Glaxo) or baby foods. Gavage feeding into the crop is a route commonly used in critical patients. Diets are made up following the instructions on the pack. The volume administered depends on the size of the bird but a useful rule is to give up to 2% bodyweight (Cooper, 1984). For convenience of calculation 1ml of liquid diet is taken to be equivalent to 1 gramme weight. Thus a bird weighing 200 grammes could receive up to 4ml of liquid diet.

ARRANGEMENTS FOR SHORT-TERM PATIENTS

Fully recovered short-term patients can usually be released successfully. If possible, these birds should be released near the area where they were found initially.

ARRANGEMENTS FOR LONG-TERM PATIENTS

For long-term patients it will be necessary to consider housing, therapy, nutrition, rehabilitation and release.

Housing

Although extremely weak birds can be kept in cages without perches, using towels or thick paper on the floor, more appropriate housing will be required as the bird recovers. While in confined conditions, the bird's tail feathers should be protected by sandwiching them between two pieces of X-ray film. The film can be suitably trimmed and fitted to the tail with tape, taking care to avoid blocking the vent. Staples can be carefully positioned to help hold the protective film over the feathers.

Most veterinary practices will not have appropriate facilities to accommodate birds for prolonged periods. Obviously different birds will have different housing requirements and it will be necessary to consider means for exercising recovering birds. A large flight cage is most useful as is a covered pond environment for waterfowl and coastal birds. It is at this stage that the benefits of collaboration with licensed rehabilitation keepers (see 'Legislation') is appreciated.

Diseases/clinical conditions and therapy

It would be impossible to describe every affliction of birds that requires prolonged care. However, the majority of patients will be suffering from conditions resulting from trauma, pollution or poisoning.

Trauma

Fractures of the bones of the wings and legs are common. Basic orthopaedic principles of reduction and immobilisation are applied by a variety of techniques. A simple external fixation procedure has proved invaluable for many cases and involves the use of sterile needles which are passed initially through rigid soft plastic, such as a suitably fashioned piece of syringe casing, and then through the bone on either side of the fracture site, whilst the limb is supported on a polystyrene block. The sharp ends of the needles and the plastic hubs can be removed and a protective light bandage applied over the whole apparatus. Bird fractures heal very quickly and it is usually possible to remove the external fixation in about three weeks.

Pollution

Oil pollution can have devastating effects on wild birds. Oiled birds should be wrapped in insulating material to prevent further loss of essential body heat. This will also stop the bird from preening and ingesting more oil. After initial emergency therapy the oil should be removed with a warm detergent solution following which the bird must be well rinsed and dried. Alcohol or ether can be used sparingly to shift persistent stains. Oral kaolin may be of benefit for birds that have ingested oil (Clark and Kennedy, 1971; Croxall, 1979; Dolensek and Bell, 1977; Harris, 1980; Tottenham, 1982).

Poisoning

Much depends on the toxic substance involved. In many cases it is difficult to pin-point a specific factor and heavy reliance is placed on symptomatic treatment. Lead poisoning is common in waterfowl: treatment of this involves up to three subcutaneous injections of a 25% solution of sodium calciumedetate (Sodium Calcium Edetate, Animalcare) daily at a dose of 0.25mg/kg (Anon., 1990). Radiology is useful for the diagnosis of lead poisoning. It may be necessary to remove ingested lead shot surgically.

Nutrition

Initially, it can be useful to talk to aviculturists and seek information about special food preferences of individual bird species, but if a bird is being kept for more than a week it will be necessary to consider the patient's actual needs and calculate the nutritional requirements for maintenance and growth, including healing. As the bird improves and is being rehabilitated the requirements for exercise will need to be considered. Daily energy needs should be calculated by allometric scaling based on body weight (Kirkwood, 1983; Quesenberry *et al*, 1989b; Sedgwick, 1988).

Rehabilitation

Patients that have been confined for a number of weeks while recovering from a serious injury or disease often lose physical fitness. Disuse atrophy can lead to stiff joints; fibrous scar tissue may limit the movement of limbs; circulatory efficiency may be decreased; muscles can be weakened and co-ordination and agility can be impaired.

It is necessary to begin a programme of physiotherapy as early in the healing process as possible (Horowitz *et al*, 1983). In the primary stages of physiotherapy, which will involve handling, the bird may need to be blindfolded using a hood or, if this is not possible, then the exercises should be performed under dimmed lighting. Initially, the bird's joints are moved through their normal range by manually extending and flexing the wings and legs. This is followed by using reflexes as a means of exercise. Reflex wing flapping can be accomplished by supporting the bird and holding its legs above the stifle joints. The bird is quickly lowered and it responds by extending both wings. This technique also provides an opportunity to assess the bird's ability to use its wings. Other methods devised to enforce gentle exercise and assist the training of birds include using perches that can be moved either in a swinging or see-saw motion, or using a pond for gentle self-regulated exercise of birds such as waterfowl.

As the bird gradually regains its normal range of movements it is important to begin endurance training. Essentially this means forcing the bird to fly in a flight cage from one perch to another in both horizontal and vertical directions. Exercise periods are increased in number and duration over a few weeks and birds should be evaluated regularly to assess their progress. A fit bird will have firm resilient muscles and be alert and eager to fly. Blood lactate levels may also be useful in assessing physical fitness (Chaplin *et al*, 1988).

Release

The factors which affect the success of a release can be divided into those relating to the bird and those relating to the environment.

Factors relating to the bird

Fitness. As previously mentioned, rehabilitation programmes should be designed to allow a bird to regain physical fitness. All birds should receive a final fitness evaluation and clinical examination shortly before release but there are few guidelines to assist the assessment of wild birds for fitness to survive

(Cooper *et al,* 1980). Coles (1985) outlined some of the features worthy of consideration in relation to skeletal, soft tissue, sensory organ and plumage damage relative to locomotion and flying ability. Patients should not be underestimated in their capacity for survival since there are a number of recorded cases of birds surviving with various defects including malaligned healed fractures (Hurrell, 1968) and loss of an eye (Ingram, 1983). More importantly, veterinary expertise is required to assess the risk of reintroduction of infectious diseases into the wild from recovered birds, or their succumbing to diseases in the area of release (Cooper, 1989). Familiarity with the bird's medical history through its sojourn in captivity will allow decisions on these problems to be based on informed opinion. Future improvement of this area of wild bird care relies heavily on better monitoring of birds in the wild. There are many organisations and people that monitor the movements of wild birds — for example by ringing them (see 'Appendix — Useful Addresses' — BTO). Collaboration between these organisations and people involved in bird rehabilitation and release should be encouraged.

Behaviour. The bird's natural behaviour will need to be considered since, for instance, it is pointless releasing a bird which should have migrated with the rest of its companions a month earlier. It is also necessary to consider the possibility that the bird has become imprinted on humans while in captivity. This is more likely to occur in fledglings which have been reared artificially. It is difficult for an imprinted bird to survive after release. In addition, a bird's ability to establish itself will depend on the social structure of its species. Gregarious birds such as rooks *(Corvus frugilegus)* and starlings *(Sturnus vulgaris)* will stand a better chance of survival if released near a flock of their own kind, although rehabilitated birds which have been away from their environment for a long time will have to find their own niche again. Release of such birds during periods when territorial conflicts are likely to occur, such as the breeding season, should be avoided (Coles, 1985).

Factors relating to the environment

Weather. Climatic changes must also be considered and birds should not be released if inclement weather conditions are expected in the near future. Barn owls *(Tyto alba)* and other nocturnal species should be released at dusk to allow maximum time for feeding and orientation. Conversely diurnal species should be released early in the day.

Food. Food supply is a key factor in population density. Territorial species have a smaller area to defend in times of abundance. Although it would seem prudent to time any release to coincide with a seasonal flush of the bird's natural diet, a method whereby the bird can be assisted by gradually weaning it off a captive diet, called hacking, has been successfully used in many raptor species (see 'Birds of Prey'). Indeed such slow-release techniques, if employed in non-raptorial species, would allow the bird to overcome many of the difficulties outlined above and are thus preferable.

CONCLUSION

Anxieties about the health of our environment have raised many questions in recent times. It is recognised that the health of the environment is reflected in the health of its inhabitants and in this respect the extent of public consternation has been shown by an increased interest in sick wildlife. It is incumbent upon the veterinary profession to recognise legitimate concerns of the public and respond accordingly. This chapter has concentrated primarily on the individual bird patient and suggested one role for the interested veterinary surgeon. However, the veterinary surgeon also has expertise in pathology, epidemiology and other fields and can call upon colleagues over areas requiring scientific input, such as the investigation of disease in flocks and the role of disease in threatened bird populations. The Further Reading list provides examples of useful literature which hopefully will act as a catalyst to encourage more veterinary surgeons to become interested in such environmentally-related topics.

Acknowledgement

Thanks are due to my wife Geraldine for comments on the manuscript.

REFERENCES AND FURTHER READING

ANON. (1990). Poison. *In Practice* **12 (2)**, 53.

ARNALL, L. and KEYMER, I. F. (1975). *Bird Diseases.* Ballière Tindall, London.

CHAPLIN, S. B., MUELLER, E. R., DEGERNES, L. A. and REDIG, P. T. (1988). Physiological assessment of rehabilitated raptors prior to release. *Proceedings of the American Association of Zoo Veterinarians and American Association of Wildlife Veterinarians.* Toronto, Ontario.

CLARK, R. B. and KENNEDY, E. J. (1971). *How Oiled Seabirds Are Cleaned.* University of Newcastle upon Tyne.

COLES, B. H. (1985). *Avian Medicine and Surgery.* Blackwell Scientific Publications, London.

COOPER, J. E. (1989). Ed. *Disease and Threatened Birds.* Technical Publication No. 10. International Council for Bird Preservation, Cambridge.

COOPER, J. E. and ELEY, J. T. (1979). Eds. *First Aid and Care of Wild Birds.* David and Charles, Newton Abbot.

COOPER, J. E., GIBSON, L. and JONES, C. G. (1980). The assessment of health in casualty birds of prey intended for release. *Veterinary Record* **10**, 340.

COOPER, J. E. (1983). A practical approach to cagebirds. *In Practice* **5 (1)**, 29.

COOPER, J. E. (1984). First aid for wild birds. *In Practice* **6 (6)**, 195.

COOPER, J. E. (1985). Diagnostic techniques in birds. *The Veterinary Annual* **25**, 236.

COOPER, J. E. (1987). Raptor care and rehabilitation: precedents, progress and potential. *Journal of Raptor Research* **21 (1)**, 21.

CRAWFORD, W. C. (1983). Reintroduction of rehabilitated raptors. *Annual Proceedings of the American Association of Zoo Veterinarians.* Tampa, Florida.

CROXALL, J. P. (1979). Birds and oil pollution. In: *First Aid and Care of Wild Birds.* (Eds. J.E. Cooper and J.T. Eley) David and Charles, Newton Abbot.

DAVIS, J. W., ANDERSON, R. C., KARSTAD, L. and TRAINER, D. O. (1971) *Infectious and Parasitic Diseases of Wild Birds.* Iowa State University Press, Ames, Iowa.

DEPARTMENT OF ENVIRONMENT (1989). Information sheets 1-6. *Registration of Birds.* DOE, Bristol.

DERRICKSON, S. R. and CARPENTER, J. W. (1983). Techniques for reintroducing cranes to the wild. *Annual Proceedings of the American Association of Zoo Veterinarians.* Tampa, Florida.

DOLENSEK, E. P. and BELL, J. (1977). *Help! A Step-by-Step Manual for the Care and Treatment of Oil-Damaged Birds.* New York Zoological Society, New York.

EVANS, R. H. (1983). Wildlife rehabilitation: purposes and benefits. *Annual Proceedings of the American Association of Zoo Veterinarians.* Tampa, Florida.

FOWLER, M. E. (1986). Ed. *Zoo and Wild Animal Medicine.* 2nd Edn. W.B. Saunders, Philadelphia.

GOODERS, J. (1988). *The Complete Birdwatcher's Guide.* Kingfisher Books, London.

HARRIS, J. M. (1980). Management of oil soaked birds. In: *Current Veterinary Therapy* VII (Ed. R. W. Kirk) W. B. Saunders, Philadelphia.

HARRIS, S. and THOMAS, T. (1989). Eds. *Proceedings of the Inaugural Symposium of the British Wildlife Rehabilitation Council.* BWRC, Horsham.

HARRISON, G. J. and HARRISON, L.R. (1986). *Clinical Avian Medicine and Surgery.* W.B. Saunders, Philadelphia.

HOROWITZ, N., SCHULTZ, T. and FOWLER, M. E. (1983). Physical therapy and exercise in raptor rehabilitation. *Annual Proceedings of the American Association of Zoo Veterinarians.* Tampa, Florida.

HUNGERFORD, T. G. (1981). Ed. *Aviary and Caged Birds.* Proceedings No. 55. The Post Graduate Committee in Veterinary Science, The University of Sydney.

HURRELL, L. H. (1968). Wild raptor casualties. *Journal of Devon Naturalists' Trust* **19**, 806.

INGRAM, K. A. (1983). Release and survival of a one-eyed golden eagle. *Annual Proceedings of the American Association of Zoo Veterinarians.* Tampa, Florida.

KIRKWOOD, J. K. (1983). Influence of body size in animals on health and disease. *Veterinary Record* **113**, 287.

MARTIN, H. D. and KOLLIAS, G. V. (1989). Evaluation of water deprivation and fluid therapy in pigeons. *Journal of Zoo and Wildlife Medicine* **20 (2)**, 173.

MARTIN, M. M. (1984). *First Aid and Care of Wildlife.* David and Charles, Newton Abbot.

PARSLOW, J. (1973) *Breeding Birds of Britain and Ireland.* T and A. D. Poyser, Berkhampstead.

PERRINS, C. (1974). *Birds.* William Collins, Glasgow.

PERRY, R. A. (1981). The examination of individual caged birds. In: *Aviary and Caged Birds.* Proceedings No. 55. (Ed. T. G. Hungerford) The Post Graduate Committee in Veterinary Science, The University of Sydney.

PETRAK, M. L. (1982). *Diseases of Cage and Aviary Birds*. 2nd Edn. Lea and Febiger, Philadelphia.

QUESENBERRY, K. E. and HILLYER, E. (1989a). Hospital management of the critical avian patient. *Annual Conference Proceedings of the Association of Avian Veterinarians.* Seattle, Washington.

QUESENBERRY, K. E., MAUDLIN, G. and HILLYER, E. (1989b). Nutritional support of the avian patient. *Annual Conference Proceedings of the Association of Avian Veterinarians* Seattle, Washington.

RITCHIE, B. W., LATIMER, K. S., OTTO, C. M. and CROWE, D. T. (1990). Intra-osseous cannulation of birds. *Compendium on Continuing Education for the Practising Veterinarian* **12**, 55.

ROYAL COLLEGE OF VETERINARY SURGEONS (1990). *Guide to Professional Conduct.* Royal College of Veterinary Surgeons, London.

SEDGWICK, C. J. (1988). Finding the dietetic needs of captive native wildlife and zoo animals by allometric scaling. *The Proceedings of the American Animal Hospital Association 55th Annual Meeting.* Washington DC.

TOTTENHAM, K. (1982). Oil pollution. In: *Diseases of Cage and Aviary Birds*. (Ed. M. L. Petrak) Lea and Febiger, Philadelphia.

WOERPEL, R. W. and ROSSKOPF, W. J. (1984). Clinical experience with avian laboratory diagnostics. *Veterinary Clinics of North America: Small Animal Practice* **14**, 249.

CHAPTER SIXTEEN

BIRDS OF PREY

Neil A Forbes BVetMed MRCVS

Falconry is one of the oldest and most historic of sports. It has a reputation of being the sport of nobility; however, this is now far from the truth. Many birds of prey are now legally bred in captivity in this country and are available for purchase on the open market at affordable prices. The popularity of the sport has waxed and waned over the centuries but it has probably never been as great as it is at present.

In January 1990 there were some 18,000 diurnal birds of prey legally held in captivity in this country. 'Raptor' is a collective term used to describe both diurnal birds, mainly of the Order Falconiformes, and those which are generally nocturnal, the Strigiformes (owls).

It is the keeping of 'diurnal' birds that is controlled by their inclusion under Schedule Four of the Wildlife and Countryside Act (see 'Legislation'). Any veterinary surgeon treating diurnal birds of prey should be fully aware of the legal situation, not from the point of view of catching out villains, but for the sake of informing members of the public who may be unwittingly breaking the law. It should be remembered that ignorance is no defence in law for either the member of the public or the veterinary surgeon. All falconiform birds in captivity are required to be registered and such birds will have a closed or cable tie ring stating their Department of the Environment (DOE) number. There are certain exceptions (see 'Legislation').

The Falconiformes are divided into Families that include vultures, the secretary bird and ospreys as well as the more commonly encountered falcons and hawks. It is useful for the clinician to be aware of the difference of life style between the latter two groups as on occasion this will help in making a decision as to the most prudent method of treatment.

The falcons include such birds as the peregrine (*Falco peregrinus*), saker (*Falco cherrug*), lanner (*Falco biarmicus*), merlin (*Falco columbarius*) and kestrel (*Falco tinnunculus*). These birds tend to fly high in the sky, sometimes hovering but always swooping on their prey from a great height. They seem to enjoy aeronautical acrobatics, often flying spectacularly apparently for sheer enjoyment. In such species precision flight is essential and any damaged wing must be repaired to near perfection if the bird is to fly effectively again. In contrast, the hawks have a much more purposeful flight. Such birds include the goshawk (*Accipiter gentilis*), commonly known in years gone by as the larder filler, sparrow-hawk (*Accipiter nisus*), common buzzard (*Buteo buteo*) and the now very popular and convenient falconer's bird, the Harris' hawk (*Parabuteo unicinctus*). While falcons fly high to see and then swoop down on the prey (quarry), hawks tend to sit unobtrusively in some tree waiting for the unfortunate prey to come within easy range; at this point they give chase. As may be appreciated, precision flight is not so important for this group of birds.

The Order Strigiformes is the group more commonly known as owls. These birds do not need to be registered with the DOE, although they are covered by other aspects of the Wildlife and Countryside Act (see 'Legislation').

When treating an injured wild bird it should always be borne in mind that it is not only an ethical but also a legal requirement that every effort is made to return that bird to the wild.

However, if it is apparent at any stage of the treatment and rehabilitation process that the bird will be unsuitable for release, then a careful evaluation must be made as to whether it is right to condemn that bird to a lifetime of captivity. In such instances it may well be correct and proper to destroy the bird humanely instead. Of the total number of birds kept in captivity (18,000), some 6,000 are kestrels, many of which are flight-impaired invalids. The captive kestrel population is rising at an alarming rate and it is difficult to find suitable keepers for captive-bred birds. In the case of wild bird casualties, however hard it may seem, it is only sensible to preserve the lives of those that can in future be released or are valuable in breeding projects.

The legal implications of keeping and treating birds of prey are considerable (see 'Legislation').

HOUSING WILD BIRD CASUALTIES

Most birds will arrive at the surgery in scruffy cardboard boxes or wire cages. On no account should any bird of prey be kept in a wire basket since these give rise to feather damage and do not allow seclusion. The choice of housing will to an extent depend on the injury or illness. Generally, for a wild bird the ideal container should be clean, dark, quiet and warm. A solid-sided cat carrying box is suitable for all species up to the size of a goshawk (1kg in weight). Warmth can be supplied by a heated pad under the box. Such containers should be discarded after use to minimise the risk of cross infection between patients (Cooper and Eley, 1979).

Once the bird has recovered from the initial injury, shock etc. it may be placed in more spacious accommodation. For a kestrel or sparrow-hawk the minimum size should be 1 metre cube. Each case should be considered individually. Whilst some individuals will appreciate more space, others will simply use it to throw themselves even harder against the sides of the container. Whenever possible birds should be kept separate from all other species and should not be able to see each other. Falconers' birds, if hospitalised, will tend to be better behaved. Their accommodation should be of sufficient size for them to stretch their wings fully. A number of different sized perches should be available, preferably covered with different surfaces, such as carpet or 'Astroturf' (Monsanto) (a commercially available plastic grass substitute).

As soon as a wild bird has recovered from its initial injury, it is wise to pass it on to a 'Licensed Rehabilitation Keeper'(LRK), someone who is licensed by the DOE (see 'Legislation') and who usually has specific expertise and facilities for the care and rehabilitation of raptors to the wild. The names and addresses of LRKs can be obtained by contacting:-

> Department of the Environment,
> Wildlife Division,
> Tollgate House, Houlton Street,
> Bristol BS2 9DJ.
>
> Tel. 0272 218811

FEEDING

The staple diet of the majority of captive raptors is likely to be day-old male chicks. Supplies of such chicks may be obtained from local hatcheries, falconers, bird keepers and some pet suppliers, or as advertised in magazines such as *Cage and Aviary Birds.* Chicks are stored frozen and thawed daily as required. Other feeds which are used are quail, young chicken or turkey poults or wild casualties from the highway. However, one should be wary of wild rabbits or birds that might contain lead shot, wild birds suffering from trichomoniasis or avian tuberculosis, or other meat that might not be healthy and wholesome. If one is only presented with an occasional bird of prey for treatment, the most accessible food will be shin of beef or similar. This diet will be deficient in calcium and roughage 'casting'. However, when a bird is weak and in poor condition, so long as it is adult, calcium can be excluded for a few days. Roughage such as dog or cat fur may be added. Whilst one is building up the bird's condition, it may be best if casting material is left out; the bird can then be fed several times a day as one does not have to wait for it to 'cast' before the next feed is given. It is, however, still very important not to give a raptor a further meal until the previous one has left the crop. This is easily verified by checking the crop (situated in front of the thoracic inlet but not present in owls), prior to feeding. If further food is forced down before the crop is empty, the meat may decompose, a condition called 'sour crop', which rapidly leads to toxaemia and death. By way of guidance a female goshawk would require 4—5 chicks per day whilst a kestrel only one. Fresh water should be available at all times, although healthy birds drink little.

HANDLING

It is the feet of raptors that represent the major danger to the handler and not the beak. If the bird arrives in a box, the top should be carefully opened and a towel simultaneously placed over the entrance. One should be aware of where the head is and then grasp the bird firmly across the shoulders, with thumbs pointing forwards. The use of subdued red or blue light will often facilitate easier handling. In red or blue light the handler can see well, whilst the bird sees little. The bird is lifted out of the box and placed on its side on a table. As soon as possible both feet should be restrained: this is done by placing a finger between the 'ankles' from above and holding them together. A towel may be laid gently over the head to prevent the bird from biting the handler.

If the bird is trained the process is similar, although easier. In this case the bird will be cast from the falconer's fist, or he may well prefer to do it himself from a table. The process is facilitated if the bird is hooded: it is then unaware of the approach. Likewise, if the bird is wearing 'jesses' (leather straps around the 'ankles') these can be used to restrain the feet. It is not necessary for the aspiring raptor veterinarian to be equipped with hoods as they all vary in size and, if the bird is trained in the use of a hood, the falconer will come ready prepared.

The gauntlet is the traditional glove of the falconer, worn in Europe on the left hand. The most suitable type for a practice is a pair of motor cycle gloves (see 'Introduction'). When a bird is carried a common mistake is to lower the wrist. This is disastrous as the bird then walks up the arm, which is not protected. The handler's wrist should always be higher than his elbow.

At all times great care should be taken to preserve the feathers. A bird with missing or damaged primary or tail feathers cannot be satisfactorily flown or released to the wild; any such damaged feathers will not be replaced until the next moult, which usually occurs in the autumn.

SEXING

In diurnal (falconiform) birds of prey the female is on average 30% heavier than the male. Hence by weight alone the sexes can usually be determined. Sometimes, as in the European kestrel (*Falco tinnunculus*), the plumage is different.

REPRODUCTION

This is a complex subject. Many species are now bred in captivity. Interest in this has increased as taking birds from the wild under licence is now rarely possible and importations are restricted. Consideration of the methods of captive breeding are beyond the limits of this chapter. For further information see Hill (1987) and Parry-Jones (1988).

DISEASES / CLINICAL CONDITIONS

General

Raptors are susceptible to many avian diseases, such as Newcastle disease, salmonellosis and avian tuberculosis. Birds will suffer from as many and as varied a range of diseases as cats and dogs. However, in this chapter only the most commonly occurring ailments will be considered.

As with all other species, a full history and examination of the bird in a relaxed state prior to handling are important.

Birds tend to have very little reserve once they are unwell. Thus, if a falconer arrives with a bird which has lost weight unexpectedly, is off colour or is vomiting its food back, the condition is indeed serious and the bird will require rapid treatment.

Respiratory disease

The dyspnoeic bird is always a challenge. If treatment is commenced without proper evaluation then a proper diagnosis and prognosis may not be possible. The veterinary surgeon should always take a faecal (mute) sample and check that the bird has not received anthelmintic treatment in the preceding few days. The gapeworm (Syngamus trachea) is often the commonest parasite although other species of worm are also occasionally found. Treatment with fenbendazole (Panacur, Hoechst) or ivermectin (Ivomec, MSD) will be effective (see Table 1). However, the killed worm is likely to remain in the trachea and may cause dyspnoea for a further 5—6 weeks. During this period bromohexine (Bisolvon, Boerhinger) and broad-spectrum antibiotics may be helpful (see Table 1). If the faecal sample is negative for parasites, the bird should be cast and examined. The buccal cavity should be examined for signs of localised infection, eg. trichomoniasis, capillariasis, candidiasis or abscess formation. The eyes and infra-orbital sinuses should be examined for signs of infection. The latter is manifested by lacrimation, nasal discharge or swellings around the orbit. Treatment is with tylosin (Tylan 50, Elanco), lincomycin (Lincocin Tablets, Upjohn) or spectinomycin (Spectam Injectable, Sanofi) (see Table 1 for dose rates and routes of administration). If there is no response samples should be taken for microbiology. In such non-responsive cases organisms such as Pseudomonas are likely to be discovered.

Other causes of respiratory disease are bacterial or fungal infections. If a bacterial infection is suspected, doxacycline (Vibramycin, Pfizer) or tobramycin (Nebcin, Eli Lilly) are the drugs of choice (see Table 1). However, in this situation it is prudent to take a swab from the proximal trachea for microbiology and sensitivity. The author would not, however, advise waiting for laboratory results before instigating therapy. The pathogenic bacteria most frequently recovered from the trachea are Pasteurella spp., Klebsiella pneumoniae and Streptococcus spp.

Radiology is of limited value as a diagnostic tool for respiratory disease. It is more practicable to use a process of elimination. If parasitic and bacterial infection can be ruled out almost invariably the cause of the condition will be Aspergillus fumigatus. This is the single commonest cause of death in raptors in the UK (Cooper, 1969; Keymer, 1972). Diagnosis of aspergillosis is frequently very difficult. Current serological methods available in this country are unreliable; only approximately 10— 20% of infected birds are positive on blood testing (Forbes, unpublished data). This is probably due to their poor immune response to this pathogen. An ELISA serological test for use in raptors is currently being tested in the USA (Redig, personal communication). This, hopefully, will be more accurate and, therefore, of great value. Currently, diagnosis is made by elimination of other pathogens as the cause and confirmation by tracheal swabs, tracheoscopy and endoscopy. Tracheoscopy can only be carried out in the anaesthetised bird. If the diameter of the tracheoscope in relation to that of the trachea is likely to cause a significant fall in tidal volume, then air sac cannulation will be required. A cannula of similar diameter to the trachea is used and may be inserted into either the abdominal air sacs (Harrison, 1986; Rosskopf, 1988) or the clavicular air sac (Rode et al, 1990). The clavicular air sac is the least impaired by other organs; it is easily found subcutaneously directly cranial to the apex of the sternum.

Aspergillosis may be present as a latent infection which is triggered off by stress — in a falconer's bird this might be as a result of reducing a bird's weight in preparation for training. Aspergillosis may be an insidious chronic wasting disease, with or without obvious respiratory signs, or a rapidly fatal disease with acute onset characterised by either dyspnoea or vomiting. It is clear that diagnosis of aspergillosis in time to prevent the demise of the bird is a great challenge. Change or loss of voice is an almost pathognomonic sign. If diagnosis is confirmed or highly likely following the tests outlined earlier, therapy should be instigated using itraconazole (Sporonox, Janssen) or miconazole (Daktarin, Janssen) (see Table 1). It appears that, as in the case of waterfowl, certain species of raptor are more susceptible to aspergillosis, notably the golden eagle (Aquila chrysaetos), black sparrow-hawk (Accipiter melanoleucus) and gyr falcon (Falco rusticolus).

Gastro-intestinal disease

'Flicking food' is a term widely used by many falconers. It describes well the behaviour of a bird with a buccal or oesophageal disease. An important differential diagnosis is trichomoniasis (commonly known as 'frounce'). This disease is usually contracted from pigeons. If pigeons are fed to birds of prey they should be examined prior to feeding and preferably should have been frozen first in order to destroy any *Trichomonas*. A diagnosis of trichomoniasis is made by preparing a suspension of the lesion in saline and examining it for flagellates under low power. Treatment is carried out with metronidazole (Flagyl, RMB) (see Table 1). Any buccal, oesophageal or crop disease may result in birds being inappetent. Such birds may require 'crop tube' feeding in order to maintain condition and to prevent dehydration. Candidiasis causes similar clinical signs, with caseous or necrotic material in the mouth or crop. Affected birds frequently vomit their food and are unwell. Diagnosis is confirmed by looking at methylene blue-stained, air-dried smears. Recommended treatment for this condition is itraconazole or ketoconazole (see Table 1).

Capillariasis may also cause regurgitation. Endoscopy of the oesophagus and crop reveals a grossly thickened oesophageal and crop lining. Diagnosis is confirmed by examination of direct smears when the characteristic bipolar eggs are easily identified. Treatment is with fenbendazole or ivermectin. Similar signs may also be seen in cases of inflammation of the crop due to bacterial infection. In this situation treatment is with a trimethoprim/sulphamethoxazole (Septrin Paediatric Suspension, Wellcome). Metoclopramide hydrochloride (Emequell, SmithKline Beecham) is a safe and efficacious anti-emetic for the treatment of vomiting raptors (Forbes, unpublished data).

Nervous disease

There are several commonly occurring causes of 'fits' and other nervous signs in raptors and it is essential that a full diagnosis is made in order to facilitate treatment.

Birds of prey are trained via their food, ie. a bird is encouraged to fly to the fist by first allowing it to become hungry, then tempting it with food. As a result, when a bird is being flown it will normally be light in weight. Most falconers weigh their birds daily and are generally able to tell the veterinary surgeon the weight of their bird. However, during the training process such birds may become too light; this is especially the case with smaller birds such as the male sparrow-hawk. Diagnosis of hypoglycaemia can easily be made by assessing the blood glucose level. If this is not practicable, because the bird is having fits or has collapsed and is in a light condition, glucose should be given (10% solution) intravenously or by crop tube.

Hypocalcaemic fits are seen in three different situations, the first of these being in juvenile birds on a calcium deficient diet. In these cases the long bones of the body are likely to be affected; hence radiographic evaluation of the bird may be prudent prior to extensive medical therapy. Secondly, hypocalcaemia occurs in egg-laying birds due to failure to mobilise calcium from the bones quickly enough. This usually results in eggbinding, lethargy and inappetence. The female is seen sitting around showing little sign of activity, initially on the nest ledge and then on the floor of the aviary. If untreated the condition deteriorates, causing tremors and finally coma. The third situation is where a bird is being severely stressed. This is particularly prevalent in goshawks which are being trained ('manned'). Diagnosis can be confirmed on blood test; in many cases circumstantial evidence alone will be adequate. Treatment is by slow intravenous 5–10% calcium borogluconate (3ml/kg 10%). This should be followed by dietary supplementation (Collo-Cal D, C-Vet).

Thiamine deficiency has been implicated in causing fits (Prescott Ward, 1971). Although the characteristic star-gazing or opisthotonos is not an uncommon presenting sign, few of these birds respond to thiamine supplementation alone. More recently a number of Harris' hawks suffered from repeated fits which could be prevented by supplementing their diet on a daily basis with high levels of thiamine (Forbes, 1987). All affected birds were thought to be related; no new cases are thought to have arisen since the 1987 breeding season, after which time the breeding pairs which produced these affected birds are believed to have been split up.

Lead poisoning is a common cause of fits in raptors. Any bird exhibiting nervous signs, whether fits or simple muscle weakness, should have a whole body radiograph taken to rule out or confirm the possibility of lead poisoning. Characteristically, the affected bird sits back on its hocks with its feet turned medially and clasping each other. Treatment is by giving sodium calciumedetate (Sodium Calcium Edetate, Animalcare) followed by surgical removal of the lead source.

Other causes of fitting which should be considered are Newcastle disease, traumatic injuries and bacterial or fungal meningitis (Cooper, 1978).

Bumblefoot

Bumblefoot is probably the most common reason for presentation of raptors to veterinarians. The condition is an inflammatory and, usually, infected reaction in the plantar aspect of the foot — for further classification refer to Cooper (1978). Much has been written about the treatment of bumblefoot. In the author's opinion the major prognostic feature is the identity of the pathogen. If the primary pathogen is a *Pseudomonas* sp., *Proteus* sp., *Candida* or *Aspergillus* then the prognosis is poor. In the case of other pathogens treatment should be successful. Infection occurs following pressure necrosis or penetration of the dermis, which permits pathogens to enter. In all cases reducing the bird to flying weight to reduce the pressure load, and preferably flying the bird to increase pedal blood supply, will help. Aviary birds suffer from bumblefoot less frequently as they generally have a choice of perches and are more active. The exception to this seems to be during the courtship period, although even this is almost always a recurrence of a previous problem. In the author's opinion microbiology is useful in order to give a more accurate prognosis as well as to allow correct antibiotic treatment. Prior to sensitivity results being available, a good first choice of drug is amoxycillin (Clamoxyl, SmithKline Beecham). If the lesion does not regress with antibiotic therapy, surgery is indicated. A full understanding of the anatomy of the foot is important (Riddle, 1981). All necrotic and infected debris must be removed prior to surgical closure. Where infection remains, it may be preferable to leave the wound open, allowing second degree healing and granulation from the base of the abscess. Particularly in the heavier species there is an advantage in preparing a foot cast so that there is no pressure on the healing or granulating wound. In the author's opinion the easiest method of accomplishing this is to manufacture a shoe. This is carried out with the patient anaesthetised. The foot (including each toe) is covered in padding, whilst a ball of cotton-wool is placed on the plantar aspect of the foot. The whole foot is then set in casting material (Delta Cast, Johnson and Johnson). Once it has set, an incision is made all the way around the cast in the horizontal plane, so that one is left with two equal portions. The ventral portion is a perfectly fitting shoe for that individual bird, in which the weight is borne by the toes and not the ball of the foot. The shoe may be reinforced with epoxy resin if necessary. The affected foot can then be easily redressed each day so that adequate medication can be applied.

THERAPEUTICS

Medication may be given by oral, parenteral or topical routes. The easiest route is orally. In the majority of cases birds will readily take drugs in tablet form hidden in a food item which they would normally swallow whole. In the case of an obstinate bird or one which is too weak to eat, a crop tube is invaluable. A crop tube is easily assembled out of a 5 or 10ml syringe with 10cm of plastic tubing attached (giving set tube is ideal) (see Figure 1).

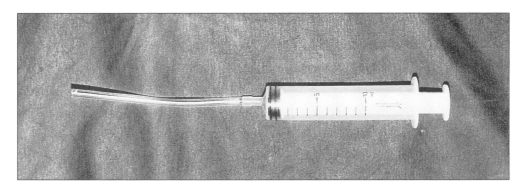

Figure 1
Crop tube made from 10ml syringe and 10cm of plastic tubing.

The bird is restrained and the tube passed down the oesophagus caudal to the tongue (see Figure 2). As the fluid is administered one should beware the level of fluid in the oesophagus rising over the opening to the trachea.

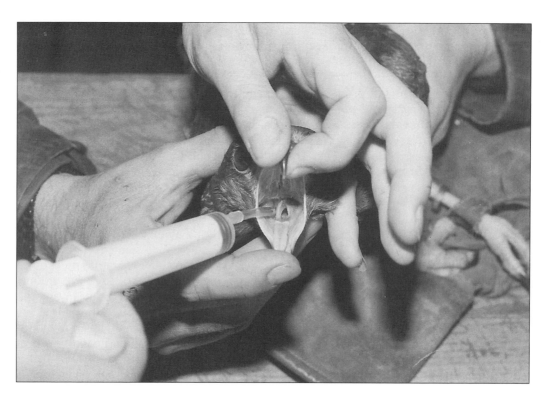

Figure 2
Crop tube being passed down the oesophagus.

TABLE 1
Recommended drug dosages.

Ampicillin	Soluble powder	100mg/kg po tid for 3-5 days
Ampicillin	Long acting injection	150mg/kg i/m sid for 3-5 days
Amoxycillin	Tablets	100mg/kg po tid for 3-5 days
Amoxycillin	Long acting injection	250mg/kg i/m sid for 3-5 days
Bromohexine	Powder	3mg/kg po bid for 3-5 days
Bromocyclen	Powder	Apply weekly for 3 weeks
Carbenicillin	Injection	100-200mg/kg i/m bid for 3-5 days
Calcium EDTA	Injection	35mg/kg i/m bid as required
Cephalexin	Tablets	50mg/kg po qid for 3-5 days
Chloramphenicol	Injection	30mg/kg i/m tid for 3-5 days
Ciprofloxin	Tablets	40mg/kg po bid for 5-7 days
Collo-Cal D	Liquid	0.5ml/kg po sid as required
Clavulanate-potentiated amoxycillin	Tablets	125mg/kg po bid for 3-5 days
Doxapram	Injection	10mg/kg i/v once
Doxycycline	Syrup	25mg/kg po bid for 3-5 days
Fenbendazole	Liquid	50mg/kg po once
Frusemide	Injection	15mg/kg i/m as required
Ivermectin	Injection	200ug/kg s/c once
Itraconazole	Syrup	10mg/kg po sid for 7-10 day
Ketoconazole	Syrup	5mg/kg po bid for 5 days
Lincomycin	Injection	20mg/kg i/m tid for 5 days
Lincomycin	Tablets	175mg/kg po bid for 5 days
Metoclopramide	Injection	2mg/kg i/m bid for 1-2 days
Metronidazole	Tablets	50mg/kg po bid for 5 days
Miconazole	Injection	10mg/kg i/m sid for 5-7 days
Oxytetracycline	Long acting injection	40mg/kg i/m sid for 3-5 days
Prednisolone	Injection	10-30mg/kg i/m or i/v as required
Spectinomycin	Injection	50mg/kg i/m bid for 3-5 days
Tobramycin	Injection	10mg/kg i/m bid for 5-7 days
Trimethoprim	Injection	50mg/kg i/m bid for 3 days
Trimethoprim/sulphamethoxazole	Syrup	80mg/kg po bid for 3 days
Tylosin	Injection	20mg/kg i/m bid for 3 days

Parenteral therapy may be administered by the intramuscular, intravenous or subcutaneous routes. Intramuscular injections are given into the pectoral or quadriceps muscles. If repeated injections are given the sites should be alternated to avoid muscle damage. Intravenous injections are given in the brachial (basilic) vein as it crosses the proximal ulna at the elbow joint, or in the right jugular vein. The subcutaneous route is used on occasions, particularly for fluid therapy. Any area of accessible skin can be used and a good site is the medial aspect of the thigh.

Topical treatment has few indications, the most significant being in the control of ectoparasites, for which bromocyclen (Alugan, Hoechst) is recommended.

ANAESTHESIA

Pre-operative evaluation of birds is important. The packed cell volume (PCV) is perhaps the most readily measured parameter. If the PCV is below 20% there is either severe anaemia or haemodilution present and surgery should be delayed if possible. If the PCV is greater than 55% then severe dehydration is present and rehydration should be carried out prior to surgery. Assessing the depth of avian anaesthesia can be difficult. Corneal, palpebral and pedal reflexes may be used but are not very consistent. Heart rate and respiratory rate are more useful indicators, although normal values vary greatly with the bird's bodyweight. The larger the bird and the deeper the anaesthetic, the slower the respiratory rate. The respiratory rate should not drop below half the normal resting rate (Coles, 1985). Hypothermia should be guarded against both during and after anaethesia (Cooper, 1978).

Parenteral anaesthetic agents

Birds should always be weighed prior to anaesthesia. Overdosage is a risk with parenteral agents; however, monitoring of gaseous anaesthesia is probably even more risky to the inexperienced. If the clinician falls into the latter category a minimum dose of a parenteral agent with the option of topping up with a volatile agent, is probably a good compromise.

Ketamine (Vetalar, Parke-Davies) is extremely useful but the dose should be computed carefully if prolonged recovery periods are to be avoided:—

Birds 100—150g bodyweight	30mg/kg
Birds 200—400g bodyweight	20mg/kg
Birds 750—1000g bodyweight	10mg/kg
Birds over 2kg bodyweight	5mg/kg

Ketamine is best given in combination with **diazepam** (Valium, Roche) (1.0—1.5 mg/kg) or **xylazine** (Rompun, Bayer) (0.25—0.5 mg/kg). Confusion often arises when variable dose rates are given; the general principle to follow is the smaller the bird the higher the metabolic rate and therefore the higher the dose of drug required. The above drugs may be given intramuscularly or intravenously. Surgical anaesthesia will last for approximately 15 minutes and may be prolonged by repeating the dose or topping up with a volatile agent.

Alphaxalone / alphadolone (Saffan, Coopers Pitman-Moore). This is a shorter acting agent which may also be given by the intramuscular (36mg/kg) or intravenous route (10mg/kg). Alphaxalone / alphadolone gives 10 minutes surgical anaesthesia. Recovery is rapid with no significant excitation. However, there are certain species, eg. red-tailed hawks (*Buteo jamaicensis*) (Cooper and Redig, 1975), as well as certain psittacines, eg. lories and lovebirds (Forbes, unpublished data), which react adversely to this drug. The author has used the drug safely in kestrels, merlins, Harris' hawks, peregrines, goshawks, sparrow-hawks, lanner and lugger falcons and buzzards: however, he would not advise its use in other more unusual species where insufficient anaesthesia has been carried out nor where adverse reactions have been recorded.

Volatile anaesthetic agents

Halothane has been widely used as both an induction and a maintenance agent. The principal difference between mammalian and avian volatile anaesthesia is due to the avian air sac system. This provides a greatly increased area for gaseous exchange. Also, the air sacs can act as a reservoir for volatile anaesthetic. Although the level of anaesthetic may be reduced when the desired effect is achieved, there is already a considerable volume of high concentration anaesthetic in the air sacs, able to cause further deepening. Induction and recovery are rapid (1—3 minutes) and in the hands of an experienced anaesthetist this is an extremely effective method of anaesthesia, particularly for quick procedures. Induction is carried out using a mask and 1—4% halothane. The lower the concentration the slower the induction and hence there is a potential risk of excitation and adrenaline induced cardiac arrhythmias. Anaesthesia is maintained using 0.5—2% halothane either by mask or, preferably, following intubation.

Isoflurane is the gaseous anaesthetic agent of choice for those contemplating anaesthetising large numbers of avian patients. Isoflurane is far less hepatotoxic than halothane and recovery is faster; the disadvantages are the very high cost together with the fact that one needs an additional vaporiser. It is probably less hazardous to the operator.

REFERENCES AND FURTHER READING

BREARLEY, M. J., COOPER, J. E. and SULLIVAN, M. (1991). *A Colour Atlas of Small Animal Endoscopy.* Wolfe, London.

COOPER, J. E. (1969). Some diseases of birds of prey. *Veterinary Record* **84**, 454.

COOPER, J. E. (1978). *Veterinary Aspects of Captive Birds of Prey.* The Standfast Press, Gloucester.

COOPER, J. E. and ELEY, J. T. (1979). Eds. *First Aid and Care of Wild Birds.* David and Charles, Newton Abbot.

COOPER, J. E. and REDIG, P. T. (1975). Unexpected reactions to the use of CT 1341 by red-tailed hawks. *Veterinary Record* **97**, 352.

COLES, B. H. (1985).*Avian Medicine and Surgery.* Blackwell Scientific Publications, Oxford.

FORBES, N. A. (1987). Fits in the Harris' hawk. *Veterinary Record* **120**, 264.

HARRISON, G. J. (1986). Selected surgical procedures. In: *Clinical Avian Medicine and Surgery*. (Eds. G. J. and L. R. Harrison) W.B. Saunders, Philadelphia.

HILL, D. J. (1987). Ed. *Breeding and Management of Birds of Prey.* Department of Extra Mural Studies, Bristol University.

KEYMER, I. F. (1972). Diseases of birds of prey. *Veterinary Record* **90**, 579.

PARRY-JONES, J. (1988). *Falconry Care, Captive Breeding and Conservation.* David and Charles, Newton Abbot.

PRESCOTT WARD, F. (1971). Thiamine deficiency in a peregrine falcon. *Journal of the American Veterinary Medical Association* **159**, 599.

RIDDLE, K. E. (1981). Surgical treatment of bumblefoot in raptors. In: *Recent Advances in the Study of Raptor Diseases.* (Eds. J. E. Cooper and A. G. Greenwood) Chiron Publications, Keighley.

RODE, J. A., BARTHOLOW, S. and LUDDERS, J. W. (1990). Ventilation through an air sac cannula. *Journal of the Association of Avian Veterinarians* **4**, 2.

ROSSKOPF, W. J. Jr. (1988). Surgery of the avian respiratory system. *Proceedings American College of Veterinary Surgeons 1988.*

REPTILES PART ONE CHELONIANS

Oliphant F Jackson PhD MRCVS

The shell is the hallmark of all chelonians; it provides protection for the chelonian but is a great hindrance to the veterinary surgeon who needs to know what goes on inside the 'bony box'. The possession of this bony box makes chelonians heavier and bulkier than other reptiles of comparable body length. They also have a greater capacity to store food and retain water than other reptiles of similar size. The capacious coelomic cavity is suitable for housing the bulky intestines necessary for the digestion of vegetable materials. The extended time that food and medicines take to pass through the gastro-intestinal tract has to be kept constantly in mind (Holt, 1981a).

ANATOMY

In most chelonians the bony plastron and carapace are covered by a superficial layer of keratin. This varies in thickness from about 5cm thick in the hawksbill marine turtle (*Eretmochelys*) to paper-thin in a Central American freshwater terrapin (*Dermatemys*). The nomenclature of the shields of the dorsal carapace, the ventral plastron and the lateral bridges that connect them is important when describing either a lesion or a site for surgery.

Identification of tortoises

Every tortoise has a unique pattern and colouration on the shields of the plastron and these are used as fingerprints for identification of individuals. The British Chelonian Group (see 'Appendix — Useful Addresses') has set up a tortoise registration scheme to assist owners. A close-up photograph of the clean plastron is sent to the Registration Officer (Dr R Lockhart, 9 Sutlej Road, Charlton, London, SE7 7DD) together with an application form. This is processed and put through a computer imaging system where it is recorded. Registration using such a dynamic computer system will act as a theft deterrent, as an aid to the recovery of lost tortoises, be useful to the Department of the Environment who issue licences for the sale of these endangered species (see 'Legislation') and be a valuable scientific tool for use by those undertaking breeding and research into Chelonia in the UK and overseas.

In the UK the term shields is used, while in America 'scutes' is preferred. On the carapace there are usually five unpaired central shields (called the vertebrals as they cover the ten vertebrae), flanked by paired rows of usually four pleurals (sometimes called costals). The small shields round the edges are known as marginals. In a few species there are also small, supra-marginal shields between the pleurals and the marginals. There is a single, often small, unpaired nuchal shield on the anterior edge and a large supra-caudal, which is sometimes divided, above the tail (see Figure 1). The shields of the plastron are arranged in six pairs known respectively as the gular, humeral, pectoral, abdominal, femoral and anal shields (see Figure 2), the names being derived from the parts of the body that they protect. The small shields on the bridges near the forelegs are the axillaries and the inguinals are in front of the thighs.

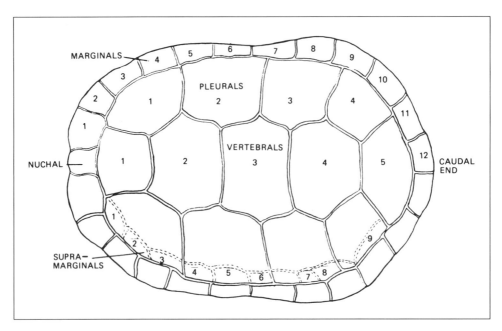

Figure 1   Carapace.

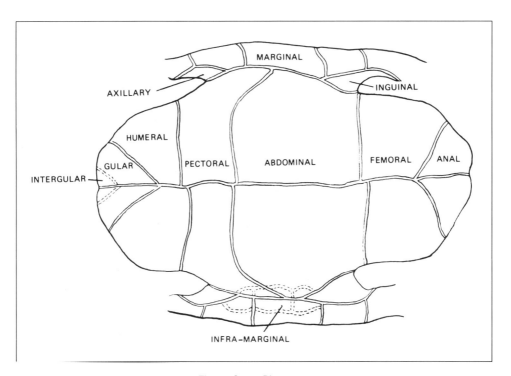

Figure 2   Plastron.

Inside the carapace the ten vertebrae and dorsal rib ends are substantial in many chelonians, the exception being the Mediterranean tortoises *(Testudo* spp.*)* where the vertebrae are of light construction and the rib ends are so thin that they virtually disappear.

The fact that both limb girdles are housed within the rib cage and the bony box is unique amongst vertebrates. The pectoral girdle, composed of scapula, acromion and coracoid (see Figure 3), provides a glenoid for the head of the humerus. In the forelimb, distal to the humerus, lies the radius and the ulna. The carpus lies at the cranial flexure of the limb and below this, pointing outwards and

222

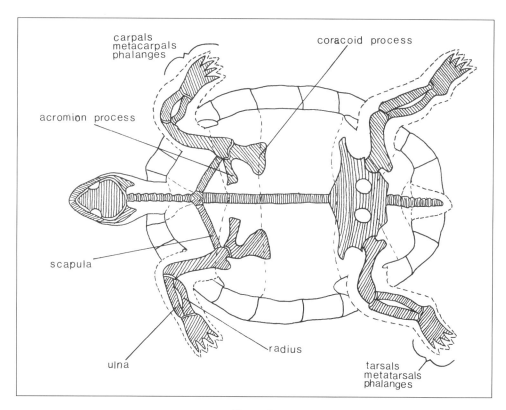

Figure 3a
Ventral view of skeleton superimposed on dorso ventral view of tortoise.

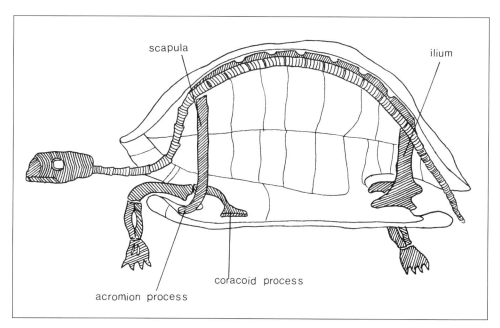

Figure 3b
Left side of skeleton and its relationship to the shell.

downwards, are the individual digits. The pelvic girdle has, as in mammals, a deep acetabulum into which fits the head of the femur. Distal to the femur are the tibia and fibula, the tarsal bones and the pes. Each toe has a single metarsal bone; the first and fifth toes have two phalanges while the others have three. In aquatic species the digits of both the manus and the pes are webbed.

223

A horizontal connective tissue sheet, with no muscle, forms the diaphragmatic membrane separating the lungs dorsally from the coelomic cavity lying ventral to it between the two girdles.

The trachea is short and divides behind the head into two bronchi that remain separate and run along either side of the neck until they reach the lungs. The lungs are sponge-like, occupying the dorsal half of the body cavity in the resting position but being reduced to one fifth when the head and all four legs are fully retracted. Each lung is divided into separate lobes by major vertical membranous plates, while an irregular meshwork of fibres between these plates divides the lung even further. The bronchi enter at about the middle of each lung and then branch into each lobe. Because the lungs are attached on all sides they do not collapse when punctured. Respiration takes place when the diaphragmatic membrane is pulled ventrally, which in turn pulls down the ventral surface of the lung. The expansion that occurs draws in air down the trachea and bronchi for inspiration (see Figure 4). Small volume expiration is achieved by rotating the forelimbs into the shell thus forcing the anterior part of the diaphragmatic membrane upwards.

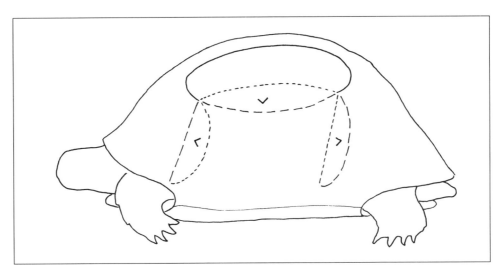

Figure 4   Movement during inspiration.

The alimentary system starts with a relatively immobile tongue behind the dorsum of which lies the longitudinal, slit-like glottis. The oesophagus follows the curvature of the cervical vertebrae which is why it is important to have the neck extended before passing an oesophageal or gastric tube. Within the body cavity the oesophagus merges on to the cardia of the stomach, which is situated in a depression in the ventral surface of the liver. The stomach is somewhat like a tobacco pipe; after a constriction it passes to the pylorus on the right side (see Figure 5). The duodenum is narrow. The small intestine is coiled and narrow before joining the large intestine, which consists of a thin-walled, bag-like caecum and a colon. The colon narrows to a rectum, which lies within the pelvic girdle and opens into the cloaca, which in turn opens at the vent on the underside of the tail.

The kidneys are large-lobed, reddish in colour and lie under the concavity of the carapace at the caudal end of the body cavity. A projected position for the kidneys is under the suture line that joins the 3rd and 4th pleural shields (see Figure 6). From each kidney a short ureter runs into the urogenital sinus. The paired testes are yellow, oval-shaped and closely attached to the cranial surfaces of the kidneys by peritoneum. The ducti deferentia run with the ureter to the urogenital sinus where they open very near to each other. The penis lies on the floor of the cloaca between the vent and the opening of the urinary bladder (see Figure 7). It rises like a mound but with the caudal end free. On the dorsal surface of this organ lies a shallow gutter, the seminal groove, which guides the semen into the female's cloaca at coitus.

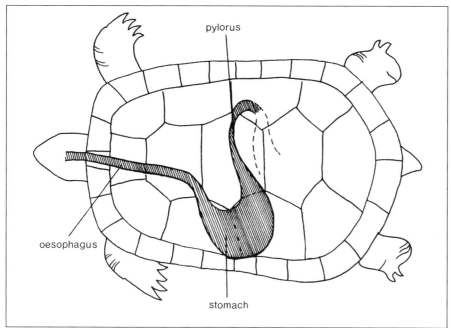

Figure 5
First part of
intestinal tract.

pylorus

oesophagus

stomach

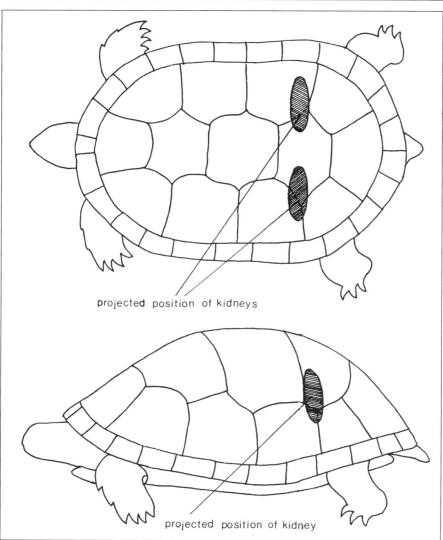

projected position of kidneys

projected position of kidney

Figure 6
Projected position
of kidneys.

225

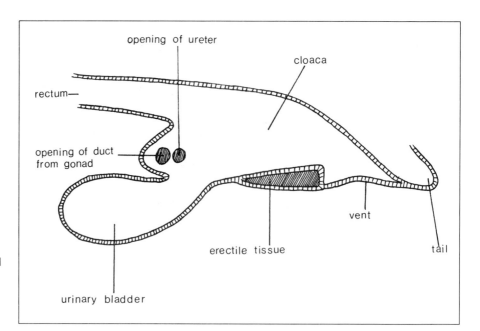

Figure 7
Median section of caudal
part of the gut and
urogenital sinus where
ureter and reproductive
duct open.

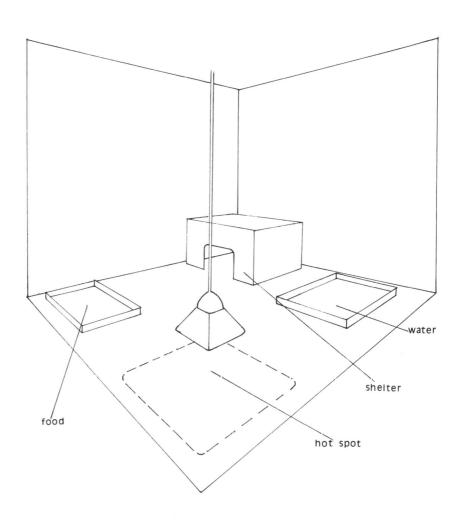

Figure 8
Indoor enclosure
for tortoises.

CLASSIFICATION

The Americans refer to all members of the Order Chelonia as turtles. In the majority of the world, land chelonians are called tortoises, freshwater chelonians are called terrapins and only the marine forms are known as turtles. There are about 4,000 different species but not all of them are kept as pets. Three types of Chelonia are likely to be kept in the UK; terrestrial tortoises, semi-aquatic box-tortoises and aquatic terrapins. There are many other different species from many regions of the world that have special requirements when kept in zoological environments, but these cannot be given full coverage in this manual. Some notes on their special care can be found in Pritchard (1979).

HOUSING AND ENVIRONMENTAL REQUIREMENTS

(a) **Mediterranean species *(Testudo* spp.)** If possible this species should have an escape-proof outdoor enclosure for the summer with a brick built shelter and a shallow water trough. Inside the enclosure there should be a grass bank mainly facing south. Where it is impossible to have an outdoor area then an indoor enclosure with infra-red and ultra-violet lighting in one area would be suitable. The minimum area should be 4 square metres per reptile. In this indoor area, in addition to the hot spot, there should be a solid shelter with a removable roof, a shallow sunken water area and a feeding area (see Figure 8). The hot spot and ultra-violet lights should be regulated by a time switch to allow for 14 hours on each day. If breeding is contemplated the time switch will have to be changed to simulate the varying seasons of the year. Underneath the infra-red lamp the ground temperature should be 30°C during the daytime and lower at night.

(b) **American box-tortoise *(Terrapene* spp.)** A very similar arrangement to that for *Testudo* spp. is required, but the water area must be larger as box-tortoises like to spend a considerable time each day partially immersed in water to a depth of approximately 5cm. They also like to bury themselves in leaf litter so a corner of the pen should have clean leaf litter available.

(c) **Terrapins of species such as the common red-eared terrapin *(Pseudemys scripta elegans),* the Eurpoean pond terrapin *(Emys orbicularis),* the mud 'turtle' *(Kinosternon),* the musk 'turtle' *(Sternotherus)* and the soft-shelled terrapin *(Trionyx).*** All these species, and many more, require a predominantly aquatic environment with a dry 'haul out' area which is under an infra-red lamp. To keep the water clean and free from serious bacterial contamination there should be a filtration system incorporated (see 'Ornamental Fish'). The water should have a thermostatically controlled water heater installed and be set at 20°–22°C. The water area may be a fibreglass pond or in a large, specially constructed tank. A suitable tank with a 'haul out' area is shown in Figure 9.

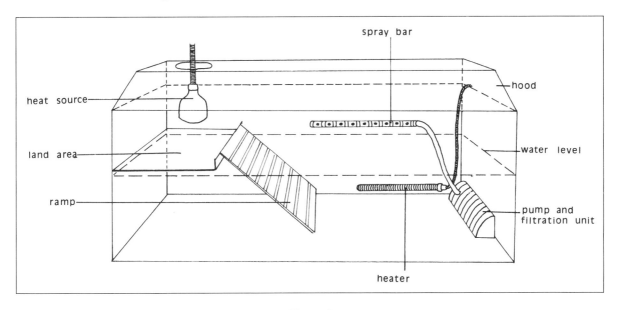

Figure 9
Suitable tank for terrapins.

FEEDING

It is important to recognise that a good and varied diet is essential to health. Not every food advocated in this list is freely available and some chelonians have seasonal food preferences.

Testudo spp. eat most of the following: cabbage, runner beans, French beans, cucumber, lettuce, peas, courgette, broccoli, clover, grass, dandelion, buttercup, hawkweed, chickweed, bindweed, sowthistle, cauliflower and other *Brassica* leaves, Brussel sprouts, cooked and raw parsnips, grated carrot and watercress (rich in vitamins and minerals). Bean sprouts are a useful source of food and vitamins in early spring and winter when fresh greens are scarce. Excesses of any one food should be avoided. For example, large amounts of *Brassica* plants, eg. cabbage or sprouts, may lead to goitre and an excess of buttercup flowers may be poisonous (Fenwick, 1989). Fruits such as apples, pears, melon, peaches, strawberries, raspberries, blackberries, plums, nectarines, tomatoes and small amounts of banana will also be eaten. Flowers such as rose petals, many succulent plants, eg. ice plant and sedums, are eaten with relish. Although primarily vegetarian, tortoises eat some meat in the wild, eg. dead birds, mice etc., so they should be given some animal protein, such as hard-boiled eggs or a spoonful of tinned cat or dog food, once a week. Vionate (Ciba Geigy) is an excellent vitamin and mineral supplement and is the one advocated by this author. There are others, eg. Nutrabal (VetArk), available which contain sufficient calcium but some products may not contain minerals and vitamins in the correct proportions for reptiles (Jackson, in press).

Terrapene spp. vary in the type of diet they eat depending on the age of the tortoise. Very young animals are almost entirely carnivorous, requiring meat or fish with lots of bone and calcium. As they become older they become more omnivorous eating insects, mealworms, crickets, slugs, snails, earthworms and woodlice. They enjoy raw mushrooms, watercress and blackberries as well as other fruits and vegetables. In captivity they will eat dog and cat food. All chelonians have a great requirement for minerals and vitamins in the diet, particularly when juvenile, and all food should be liberally sprinkled with Vionate or Nutrobal.

Terrapins are fish-eaters, eg. sprats, herring, mackerel, sardines, pilchards and whitebait, but they also enjoy prawns, shrimps and other creatures that they would find in their natural habitat. At other times of the year one should vary the diet by offering tadpoles, water beetles, insect larvae, water snails, earthworms and some water plants such as watercress. Trout pellets and the dried forms of cat food (soaked in water for 5 — 10 minutes) are accepted. For growing juveniles there should be a piece of cuttlefish in the tank. Terrapins like to take and eat their food in water but they should never be fed in their main tank as the fragments of uneaten food and the oils from the fish pollute the water. All terrapins should be fed in a separate feeding container. A hungry terrapin will eat sufficient food in about 20 minutes, after which it should be replaced in the main tank.

HANDLING

Handling and restraining tortoises of the *Testudo* spp. presents few problems. The occasional tortoise will be head-shy and keep its head withdrawn deeply within its shell. If imperative for examination the head can be withdrawn by applying sponge-holding forceps or small whelping forceps to the head over the cranium and under the mandible. The head should be withdrawn very slowly against the muscular pull of the retractor muscle. Once the head is sufficiently exposed the normal method of holding the head with finger and thumb behind the occipital condyles can be employed. The legs can usually be handled without difficulty provided one is patient and waits for a withdrawn leg to be extended. As the volume within the bony box is restricted it is possible to force the forelegs and the head out slightly by pressing both hind-legs deeply into the inguinal fossae; sometimes the opposite can be done by pressing both forelegs into the cranial opening when the hind-legs are forced slightly into the open.

Handling box-tortoises can be fraught with danger to the unwary. The closure of either hinge on a finger can be very painful. Speed is of the essence to catch at least one leg before the box-tortoise decides to withdraw it. Once a leg is held out it is impossible for the reptile to close the hinge at that end. If the box-tortoise has not closed the hinge fully then by closing, say, the back hinge between finger and thumb, the front hinge opens a fraction. A firm instrument, such as the heavy blade of a Mayo scissors, can be inserted into this split to act as a lever.

Handling terrapins at the back end is easy, but many terrapins bite hard with their beaks and some such as the snapping turtle *(Chelydra serpentina)* can inflict a severe bite and cause considerable damage. A useful safe hold is at the rear end of the carapace just cranial to the hind-leg (see Figure 10). Soft-shelled terrapins *(Trionyx)* also have a tendency to bite the hand that is holding them and with this species it is always advisable to wear leather gloves.

Figure 10
A safe hold for a belligerent terrapin.

SEXING

As with all reptiles, the males of each species have a longer tail than the females. Comparison is easy when both sexes are presented at the same time (see Figure 11) but, with practice, it is possible to identify the sex of certain common species when only one is presented. The males of some species of terrapin have longer claws than the females (see later).

REPRODUCTION

The males of the *Testudo* spp. dominate their females into both ovulating and submission by withdrawing their heads and crashing the front of their shells against the females' shell. The males also bite the legs and tails of the females. Male *Testudo* vocalise when mounting and copulating. The longer tail of the male is curved round under the female's tail and the penis, with its seminal groove, is introduced into the female's cloaca. There are many instances where the male does not succeed in intromission, which is why the fertility rate of eggs is sometimes poor (Jackson, personal observation).

Male red-eared terrapins *(Pseudemys)* have secondary characteristics - very long claws on the fore feet. With these they stroke the face of the female with a rapid fluttering motion with the palms facing outwards. The penis of *Pseudemys* is black and almost toadstool shaped (see Figure 12) and has a seminal groove which must be introduced into the female's cloaca for successful mating.

In both species the gonads are paired. In the female the ovary may contain several ova of different sizes from a few millimetres in diameter up to the size of the large yolk that almost fills the inside of the shell of the egg. The oviducts are divided into four main regions; infundibulum, magnum, uterus and vagina (see Figure 13). The infundibulum has a funnel-shaped end and a short tubular part, and is thin-walled with glandular and ciliated cells. The magnum is the albumen secreting region and accounts for two thirds of the total length of the oviduct. The uterus changes in shape from that of a

Figure 11
Ventral view of male terrapin.

Figure 12
Ventral view of male terrapin with penis extruded.

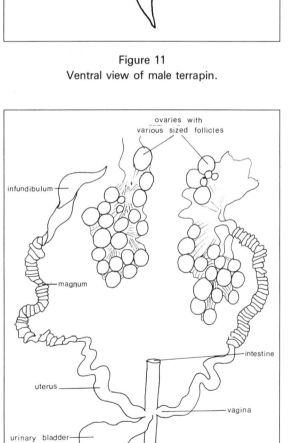

Figure 13
Ventral surface of genitalia from mature female.
On the left the infundibulum is shown separated
from the ovary. On the right it is adjacent.

'pleated ribbon' to a cylindrical cross section. The secretory cells provide the membranous and calcareous coverings of the egg. The completed eggs remain in the uterus until the stimuli are right for the entire clutch to be laid. In the UK climate single eggs are sometimes laid by females at unusual times of the year — for example by a female that has been right through hibernation with one or two eggs in her uterus. These females usually drop their eggs without nest building. Nest building (digging) is done in the summer. The females sense out suitable nest sites by testing for warmth and suitable soil. They may dig several test nests. When the nest is about 15cm deep the female urinates into the hole and lays eggs one at a time, carefully positioning each egg with a hind foot. Once the uterus is empty she carefully covers the eggs with the soil she has dug out so that the nest is hardly discernible to the naked eye. In the UK the temperature is too cold for eggs to incubate outdoors. The eggs have to be removed carefully and placed in vermiculate at 30°C (range 28°—32°) for about 60 days before they hatch out (Inskeep, 1983).

DISEASES/CLINICAL CONDITIONS

Clinical examination. This is not as difficult as it might appear. The eyes of the animal should be open and bright and the legs strong, well filled out and muscular. As in mammals, the degree of dehydration may be assessed by taking a pinch of skin. Both plastron and carapace should be a good shape for the species and firm and solid to the touch. There should be no obvious swellings anywhere — oedematous or fatty swellings in the clavicular or inguinal region must be considered abnormal. The mouth should be opened and the colour of the tongue examined. In certain species the relationship of bodyweight (g) to carapace length (mm) ('Jackson's ratio') is an important part of the clinical examination as it tells the clinician something of what is going on inside the bony box (see Figure 14).

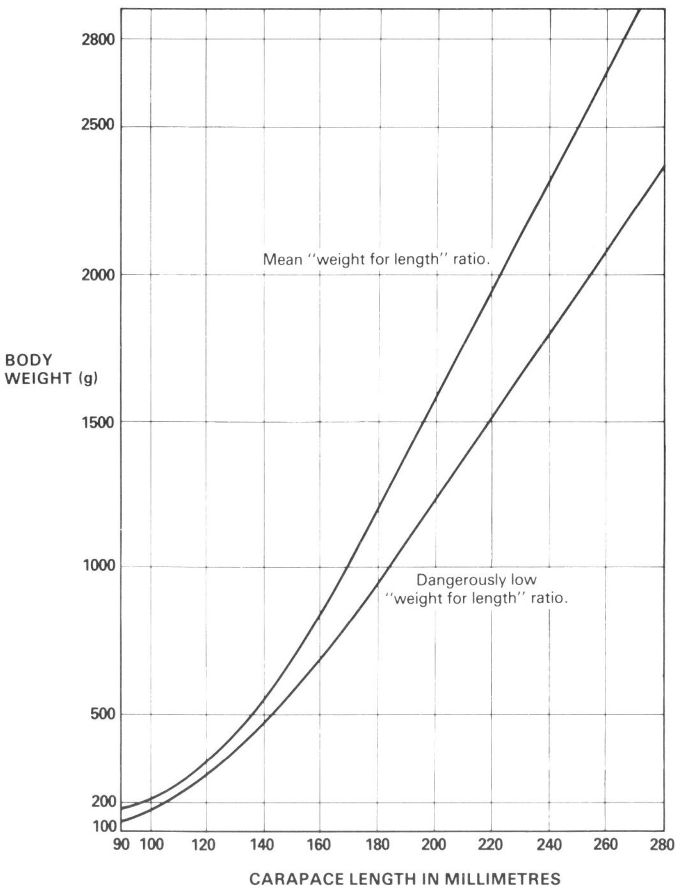

As adjuncts to the clinical examination, radiography and haematology are important in arriving at a diagnosis. Representative data for haematology and blood chemistry are listed in Table 1 for the red-eared terrapin (*Pseudemys scripta elegans*), the Mediterranean tortoises (*Testudo graeca* and *T.hermanni*) and the box-tortoise (*Terrapene carolina*).

The site of choice for blood sampling is the dorsal tail vein. This lies very superficial exactly in the mid-line. It is essential that the scales of the tail are scrubbed thoroughly, dried and a skin antiseptic applied prior to vene-puncture. It is best to have the bevel of the needle pointing upwards. It is not necessary to hold the tail; the tortoise should be turned so that the tail is pointing towards you. As an alternative, it is possible to obtain a few drops of blood by short clipping a nail of a hind limb. A third site is the venous plexus in the groin but as this is not always easy to find it is very much a last resort.

Figure 14

Growth of healthy *Testudo graeca* and *Testudo hermanni* in the UK, plotting mass against length.

Table 1
Haematology and blood biochemistry of chelonians.

Species	RBC count x 10⁶/mm³	PCV l/l	Haemoglobin g/dl	Blood glucose mmol/l	Blood urea mmol/l	Blood uric acid mmol/l
Red-eared terrapin *(Pseudemys scripta elegans)*	0.25—0.84	0.26	8.0	3.8	3.6	0.06
Mediterranean tortoise *(Testudo graeca; Testudo hermanni)* Spring Summer	0.82—0.96 0.67	0.34 0.28	10.1—11.3 9.1—9.5	11—12 1.4	100 0—3	Not available
Box-tortoise *(Terrapene carolina)*	0.27—0.45	0.28	5.9	1.9—2.4	5.0	0.12

Antimicrobials (see Table 2)

As the majority of bacteria affecting reptiles are Gram-negative, it is generally useless to use antibiotics such as penicillin. Care must also be taken when using tetracyclines as they can adversely affect the essential intestinal bacteria and also cause intestinal ulceration and fatal haemorrhage. Neuromuscular blockade can occur in reptiles that are treated with aminoglycoside antimicrobials. Affected animals show muscular weakness (Jackson and Cooper, 1981).

Reptiles must be maintained at a constant temperature during therapy. A fall of 6°C can double the half-life of the agent and may cause toxic blood levels.

Table 2
Antimicrobials agents.

Antibmicrobial	Dose	Maintenance temperature
Ampicillin (Penbritin, SmithKline Beecham)	4mg/kg i/m or s/c daily	26°C
Carbenicillin (Pyopen, SmithKline Beecham)	200-400mg/kg i/m daily	30°C
Ceftazide (Fortum, Glaxo)	20mg/kg i/m every 72 hours	30°C
Cefuroxine (Zinacef, Glaxo)	50mg/kg i/m every 72 hours	30°C
Cephalothin (Keflin, Lilly)	40mg/kg i/m every 48 hours	30°C
Framomycin 5% (C-Vet)	10mg/kg i/m every 48 hours	26°C
Framomycin Anti-Scour Paste (C-Vet)	100mg daily per os	26° C
Gentamicin (Nicholas)	2.5mg/kg s/c every 72 hours	24°C
Kanamycin (Kannasyn, Sterling Winthrop)	10mg/kg i/m or s/c every 72 hours	24°C
Streptomycin + dihydrostrep. (Dimycin, Coopers Pitman-Moore)	10mg/kg i/m or s/c every 48 hours	24°C
Tylosin (Tylan 50, Elanco)	25mg/kg i/m daily	30°C

NB. The aminoglycoside antibiotics, eg. gentamicin and kanamycin, may be MORE toxic in gravid females and the nephrotoxicity of gentamicin is enhanced at temperatures over 25°C.

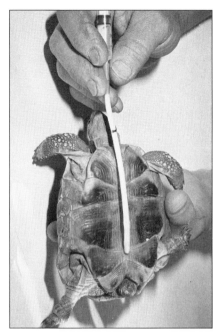

a) The length of tube from the caudal end of the abdominal shield to just beyond the gular notch is measured and this distance marked on the tube.

b) With the tortoise 'sitting' on its caudal shields the head and neck are extended to straighten the oesophagus.

c) After opening the mouth by depressing the mandible with the free hand it is possible to insert the tip of one's index finger into the commissure of the mouth to act as a gag.

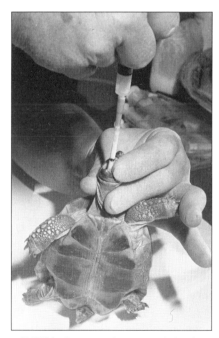

d) With the oesophagus straight the stomach tube slips down easily and one often feels the tip passing through the cardiac sphincter. The position of the mark on the stomach tube is additional reassurance.

Figure 15
Oral dosage of a tortoise by stomach tube.

Oral dosage of medicines. Measured medicinal doses can be administered to a tortoise by stomach tube. The tortoise is weighed and the required volume of liquid medicine for that weight is drawn up into the stomach tube and syringe leaving an air space in the syringe above the medicine equivalent to the dead space in the tube. The subsequent steps are illustrated in Figure 15.

Abscesses

These are extremely common, presenting as tympanitic abscesses, swellings on the limbs and swollen joints. With swollen joints and extremities it is essential to radiograph the lesion as there may be bone involvement. Certain bacteria cause osteolysis and the total destruction of bone is not uncommon, but not all abscesses involve bone and the course of treatment will therefore depend on the radiographic findings.

Tympanitic abscesses must be treated surgically under general anaesthesia as they involve the middle ear. In these cases it is usually possible to see a small bead of pus in the entrance to the Eustachian tube when the back of the mouth is examined. The external skin should be cleaned, an oculentum applied to the eye as a means of safeguarding the conjunctiva and the skin swabbed with a skin antiseptic solution. The swollen membrane should be incised and the pus, which is often inspissated, removed as a single mass if possible. The infection ascends the Eustachian tube and it is important that the core of pus that fills the Eustachian tube is removed at this stage.

After cleaning the cavity, it should be filled with an antibiotic cream such as Framomycin Anti-Scour Paste. The tympanic membrane must be sutured so that the wound does not become fly-blown.

Simple subcutaneous abscesses can be lanced under general anaesthesia. The majority of the abscesses are of inspissated pus, but on occasion smelly liquid pus produced by anaerobes is found. A similar regime of cleaning the inner cavity, closing up the dead space, suturing to ensure a waterproof seal and giving antibiotic cover is all that is required.

When bone is involved amputation is the only course of action. Limb stumps should not be saved as the wounds always break down and a second operation becomes necessary. A high amputation through the glenoid is relatively easy to perform; amputation through the acetabulum requires more surgical skill. A mass of muscle, detached from the bone with a periosteal elevator, should always be left to suture across the joint cavity. It has been the author's experience that some septic arthritis cases yield a sterile growth on culture; the reason is unclear!

Avitaminosis A

Most veterinary surgeons are familiar with this condition in juvenile terrapins but it seldom occurs by itself. Single injections of Vitamin A are of little value. The reptile should be dosed weekly for 4 consecutive weeks with an intramuscular injection of 1,000 - 5,000iu of vitamin A. The white, cellular debris should be removed from the conjunctival sacs and an oculentum applied. This condition also occurs in box-tortoises *(Terrapene* spp.*).* It is vital that the owner is instructed in the right diet for terrapins, which should include fresh whole fish, prawns, shrimps, tadpoles, cubes of cheese, hardboiled egg or trout pellets.

Bacterial septicaemia

This is seen in neglected cases, often *post mortem,* as petechiation and/or inflammation under the shields of the plastron. Sometimes, when the shield is pressed, fluid may be seen under the keratin. The keratin should be lifted and a swab taken for microbiology before cleaning the area and applying an antimicrobial agent. This is one of the few cases where it is necessary to start antimicrobial therapy before the culture and sensitivity results are available.

Balantidium coli

Balantidium coli is a large ciliated organism, rather like a *Paramecium,* easily seen under a microscope in a faecal smear. A heavy infestation will kill hatchling tortoises (Jackson, personal observation). Infestations have been found in adult tortoises, box-tortoises and terrapins. Treatment is with paromomycin (Humatin, Parke-Davis), 250mg daily for 4 days.

Beak deformities

There is a wide variety of deformities (Frye, 1981b) some of which can be corrected by trimming the beak with a nail forceps and filing down the excess that is protruding. Beaks are often badly deformed in cases of nutritional osteodystrophy.

Blindness

When tortoises are presented because they are anorexic or underweight for carapace length, it is wise to examine their eyes as part of the clinical examination. Blindness can be assessed by moving an object towards the head and observing if there is any flinch or head withdrawal reflex. The eyes should be examined with an ophthalmoscope looking at both the lens and the retina; +10 or +12 diopter lenses are required to see the back of the very small eye. It is the author's opinion that the eyes of tortoises can be damaged when the temperature drops too low in the hibernation box. Twenty blind tortoises were examined in the UK during the early summer of 1982 after the very cold winter. All chelonians must be able to smell and see their food before they will eat; blind tortoises must be hand-fed twice daily by their owners. Some tortoises improve and begin to feed on their own after a number of months of hand-feeding; it is possible that some peripheral vision returns.

Cataracts

Cataracts are sometimes seen when examining the eyes of a blind tortoise with an ophthalmoscope (see Blindness). When the lens is damaged and cataractous it is unlikely that vision will return and these animals have to be hand-fed on a regular basis. These tortoises can be taught to take food for themselves providing they learn to take exploratory bites at a pile of food placed in front of them.

Colic

The signs of colic are not impressive - an inappetent animal with a low weight for carapace length - but on radiography the gas-filled loops of intestine can be identified on both dorsoventral and lateral views. It is an impression that this condition occurs after owners have been feeding unsuitable foods by stomach tube. The careful use of carminative drugs such as metoclopramide (Emequell, SmithKline Beecham) (2—6mg) to promote gastric motility, or danthron (Dorbanex, Riker; Altan, RMB) (100mg of the suspension) to promote lower bowel motility, can be helpful.

Desquamated columnar epithelial cells

When these cells are seen in large numbers in fresh faecal smears, one must look carefully to find the cause of the intestinal irritation. Sometimes flagellates can be seen but on other occasions there is no obvious cause. In these cases a useful palliative treatment is kaolin suspension given by stomach tube.

Eggbinding/retention of eggs

When a female chelonian is unable to find a site for egglaying, a condition akin to uterine inertia occurs. It is not unusual to detect eggs on plain dorsoventral radiographs. One has to decide how long the eggs have been *in utero.* If the interior of the uterine horns is moist and receptive to the use of oxytocin, 1iu/kg can be injected intramuscularly. The concurrent injection of calcium borogluconate can assist by elevating the serum calcium level, but the author has found oxytocin by itself to be satisfactory. A repeat dose may have to be given 24 hours and again 48 hours later if some eggs remain. Massive doses (10iu/kg) must never be given as the uterine mucosa goes into spasm and the eggs are never passed. Examination of the cloaca by speculum, or even digital exploration, will occasionally be of assistance. Laparotomy as described by Frye (1981a), Holt (1979) and Jackson and Cooper (1981) involves creating a trap-door in the plastron followed by incision through the peritoneum to reach the viscera. The ventral veins are retracted as these form part of the hepatic portal system which traverses the visceral surface of the liver. After the eggs have been removed, the closure of the soft tissues is routine but the trap-door must be held in place by applying an epoxyresin (Technovit, Kurtzen) both to retain it in position and to ensure that the plastron remains completely waterproof. In terrapins, the use of metal sutures at the corners and then sealing the area over and around the resin with either silicone gel (as used on glass aquaria) or UHU All Purpose Adhesive (SmithKline Beecham) ensures a watertight covering.

Flagellate infections of the gastro-intestinal (GI) tract and bladder

This condition occurs in anorexic chelonians and is one of the reasons why it is essential to examine cloacal excretions whenever possible. Reptiles infected with flagellates usually drink a lot as the flagellate organisms live and multiply in a fluid medium. The bodyweight for carapace length may be within normal limits because the GI tract is distended with fluid. In fresh faecal material the flagellates will be seen moving across the field of view; sometimes desquamated, tall, columnar epithelial cells can also be seen. If the sample has been kept for several hours, many of the flagellates will be dead and unless one is acquainted with the microscopic picture it will be difficult to identify the mass of small, spherical, immobile organisms. *Hexamita* can be found in urine samples (see Nephritis). Metronidazole (Flagyl, RMB) (160mg/kg) or dimetridazole (Emtryl, RMB) are the drugs of choice and there are several preparations of the former available. Early treatment is effective, but in some cases, where much of the mucosa is damaged, the prognosis is grave. After treatment some chelonians are unable to digest food in the GI tract and measures must be taken to reinstate the normal intestinal flora by dosing with Vetrumex (Willows Francis), mixed with water, by stomach tube.

Foreign bodies

In the coelomic cavity. These are identified on radiographs. Air gun pellets and vesicular calculi from a ruptured bladder have been seen.

In the eye. Because chelonians use their front feet to tear apart food items, they also use this action to clear matter from their faces. They occasionally force foreign bodies behind the nictitating membrane. The irritation promotes more head rubbing, conjunctivitis, blepharospasm and swelling of the eyelids. The chelonian must be sedated (see Anaesthesia) before the eye can be examined, the foreign body removed and an oculentum applied. In chelonians the lower eyelid is the larger of the two and good access to the conjunctival sac can be achieved when this is depressed.

In the gastro-intestinal tract. These are identified on radiographs and are usually passed provided a small dose (5ml) of liquid paraffin is given daily by stomach tube. Follow-up radiographs are required to assess the passage of the foreign body down the tract.

Gross overweight/underweight for length

Gross overweight shows up when using the weight for carapace length curve (Jackson's ratio) (see Figure 14) even though the tortoise is presented as being anorexic. Often the huge pads of excess fat can be seen and palpated in the interclavicular fossa. The history may show that the tortoise has been in the family for many years and may have been fed on fattening foods such as custard, bread and butter, cake or cheese. The cause of the anorexia is not the palpable fat but the excessively fatty liver.

Treatment is prolonged, necessitating keeping the reptile metabolically active over winter and on medication. Initially methionine (250mg every 48 hours) for no more than 10 days will assist the hepatic cells. Thyroid tablets (Tertroxin, Coopers Pitman-Moore) (20mg every 48 hours) and anabolic steroid (Nandoral, Intervet) (0.5mg every 7 days) will help to increase metabolism. Many cases take up to 12 months to recover.

Underweight for length. Jackson (1980) reported on the relationship of bodyweight and length to the health status of long-term captive Mediterranean tortoises *(Testudo graeca and T. hermanni).* For each carapace length there is an optimum bodyweight (see Figure 14) but this must be assessed in conjunction with a clinical examination - for example, a tortoise that has not eaten all summer but has been seen to drink copiously will have a bodyweight in the mean range. This is due to excessive fluid retention; radiographically the coelomic cavity will be smaller than normal, there will be no fat reserves and the gastro-intestinal tract could well have a flagellate infestation. However, within limits 'Jackson's ratio' can be used to help assess the health status of these species of tortoise and can also be employed to predict whether or not an individual should be hibernated. It is also useful in monitoring the response to treatment. The relationship of weight to length has proved of little value to date in terrapins.

Helminthiasis

Nematode infestations in chelonians are common, and simple, wet smears of faecal material will demonstrate ascarid, trichostrongyle-like and oxyurid-like eggs. There appears to be no correlation between the number of eggs seen and the degree of infestation and all tortoises with a positive faecal egg count, especially hatchlings, should be treated. Oxfendazole (Systamex, Coopers Pitman-Moore; Synanthic, Syntex) is effective when given at the correct dosage and the author has not found viable eggs in faecal smears taken at monthly intervals from tortoises dosed with this drug. Albendazole (Valbazen, SmithKline Beecham) is slightly less effective. These drugs should be given as a 2.5% suspension at a dose rate of 60 — 66mg/kg. When dosing tortoises under 150g, the minimum dose is 1ml (22.6mg) and this can be given with safety. One must remember that the passage time for medicines and food in adult chelonians can be 28 days (Holt, 1981a). Despite the fact that fenbendazole (Panacur, Hoechst) has been used frequently, it is not totally effective in destroying all the nematodes; nor is mebendazole (Telmin, Janssen) as viable eggs can be found in faecal smears several weeks after treatment. Tortoises must not be dosed with ivermectin as they are very sensitive to this drug and a number of fatalities have been reported following its use (Teare and Bush, 1983).

Maggot infestation

During the summer months flies of the genus *Lucilia* will often lay eggs around the cloaca or in the pocket of skin at the base of the tail. The flies are attracted when this region is soiled by loose bowel motions. The maggots dislike hot, dry air and one method of removing them is by blowing hot air from a hair dryer into the region. It is essential that every single maggot is removed either by flushing or by removal using forceps. Where the maggots have eaten deeply into the tissues the operation to remove them should be done under general anaesthetic. Once the wound has been cleaned and disinfected with a povidone iodine solution, it should be packed with a broad-spectrum antibiotic powder and covered with a skin dressing. Unless the wound has completely healed and the tortoise's weight for length ratio is normal, it should not be hibernated as no healing takes place during hibernation.

Nephritis

Nephritis is usually discovered at *post-mortem* examination but can be diagnosed clinically if blood chemistry is performed. Nephritis has been associated with long-term hypovitaminosis A in terrapins; in the tortoise it is usually caused by the protozoon, *Hexamita.*

The signs of nephritis are obscure, with the tortoise failing to thrive during the summer, losing weight and, over a period of weeks or months, becoming apathetic with, occasionally, oedema of the limbs. The swollen kidneys are difficult to palpate. Nephritis can be diagnosed on radiographic features (Jackson and Fasal, 1981), microscopic examination of the urine and by changes in the blood chemistry.

If oedema of the legs is evident, radiological examination of the abdominal cavity will often show an accompanying anasarca. The presence of a vesicular urolith can also be identified radiographically. Microscopic examination of a fresh urine sample may reveal the flagellates, often *Hexamita,* swimming actively in all directions. As in other animals, the blood chemistry changes assist in confirming the diagnosis. Rosskopf and Howard (1983) demonstrated increases in SGOT and LDH levels in end-stage kidney disease in the Californian desert tortoise *(Gopherus agassizi)* as well as a rise in blood urea and uric acid.

		Normal	Nephritis
SGOT	(iu/l)	10 - 100	166 - 300
LDH	(iu/l)	25 - 250	800 upwards
Uric acid	(mmol/l)	0.13 - 0.52	1.8 - 2.7
Urea	(mmol/l)	0.35 - 10.0	18 - 20

Similar changes have been recorded in a small number of Mediterranean tortoises but with much higher blood urea levels, up to 200mmol/l. *Hexamita* nephritis can be prevented by attention to hygiene, removing faecal material as often as possible and ensuring that the reptiles are not kept in overcrowded conditions.

Treatment is not very successful, mainly due to the fact that the disease is well advanced by the time the patient is examined. Dimetridazole (Emtryl, RMB) can be used at a daily dose of 40mg/kg total bodyweight for 7 days. One must watch for any signs of CNS disturbance and stop the treatment immediately if signs are noticed. Several courses of treatment may be needed to eliminate *Hexamita*. Measures must be taken to reinstate the normal intestinal flora (see Flagellate infections).

In aquatic terrapins the water in a small tank may be medicated for 10 days - 15g dimetridazole in 10 litres of water. Nephritis can only be confirmed on histopathological examination of the kidneys, although the presence of enlarged, pale kidneys *post mortem* is suggestive of the condition.

Nutritional osteodystrophy

Many owners are hatching tortoise eggs and wanting to rear hatchlings. Young, rapidly growing hatchlings require a very high level of dietary minerals as well as adequate vitamins to ensure optimum mineralisation of the appendicular skeleton and the membranous bones of the shell. Unfortunately, many diets fed to young chelonians have a poor calcium/phosphorus ratio and some owners insist on feeding only soft, demineralised foods.

The signs of nutritional osteodystrophy differ between terrapins and tortoises. In the terrapin the most common feature is that of a soft shell which can be easily deformed by squeezing between finger and thumb. Advanced cases may also be associated with leg weakness and spontaneous fractures of the long bones. The owner usually admits that he/she has been feeding fish fillets or minced meat.

In tortoise hatchlings the condition is usually noticed as a progressive doming or pyramidal appearance to the shields of the carapace. There are other effects that become obvious and are worth pointing out to the owner. The beak is usually deformed so that the tortoise will have difficulty biting through food for the remainder of its life. The limb bones are bent so that the tortoise is unable to take the weight of the body on its legs. The hind legs are splayed out backwards and progress is by sliding the plastron along the ground. Often, as these osteodystrophic reptiles grow, the males develop penile phimosis.

Confirmation and an assessment of the degree of osteodystrophy can be made by taking radiographs (Jackson and Fasal, 1981); in some cases it will be very difficult to obtain good definition as the mineralisation of the bones is so poor.

Treatment depends on correction of the mineral and vitamin content of the diet. The diet of a growing chelonian should contain about 2% calcium (Kass *et al,* 1982) with a calcium/phosphorus ratio of 1.2:1 or even 1.5:1. There are now several good vitamin/mineral supplements. Table 3 gives the calcium contents in those that are suitable for reptiles. The Ca:P ratio in Nutrobal is due to the extremely low phosphorus content; this makes it useful for feeding to insects that are to be used as food for insectivorous reptiles.

Table 3

Name of product	Calcium content per 100g	Ca:P ratio
Vionate (Ciba-Geigy)	9.54g	1.49 : 1
Arkvit (Vetark)	1.8g	2 : 1
Nutrobal (Vetark)	20.8g	46 : 1

Terrapins should be fed a varied diet (see Feeding). Red meat and fish fillets must be avoided. Fresh fish is ideal because the skeleton, as well as the intestines and other nutritious organs such as the liver, are all of immense benefit to the terrapin. If meat is used to wean the terrapin off an addictive diet, vitamin/mineral supplements should be rubbed into deep cuts in the meat before feeding. Supplementation in this way can prove to be difficult as the mixture tends to be washed off in the water.

Tortoise owners should give every meal of mixed vegetables and fruits that they feed a liberal sprinkling with a vitamin/mineral supplement. In very severe cases it is useful to give Nutrobal as the additive but this has too much vitamin A and D for regular maintenance. Vionate has the correct balance for routine maintenance and growth. Arkvit is designed more as a supplement for fish than for reptiles. Although some tortoises will eat a small quantity of meat, they are, in the main, vegetarians and their intestine is not adapted to eating dog or cat foods except as an occasional small addition, no more than once per week.

There is one other essential for the prevention of doming of the shields in hatchling Mediterranean tortoises. Each winter they must have a short, controlled hibernation period to slow down the metabolism, as occurs in nature. Hatchlings under 150g bodyweight may lose 14% of their bodyweight during this hibernation. As they gain weight each year, they lose less each hibernation period; a hatchling weighing 200g (or over) usually loses only 6% of its weight.

Phimosis (Penile prolapse)

Phimosis is the inability of the male chelonian to retract its penis inside the cloaca. Whilst this is often associated with osteodystrophy (Jackson, 1980), bacterial, parasitic and fungal infections of the tissues as well as constipation, debility and trauma have also been implicated. If the prolapse is recent the cleaned, lubricated penis can be replaced and held *in situ* with a purse-string suture round the cloacal aperture. The suture should be left in for 5 or 6 days. If the penis has been extensively traumatised amputation may be required.

Amputation is a simple operation; under general anaesthesia 2 or 3 vertical mattress sutures are inserted cranial to the site of incision. Bleeding is minimal and little or no post-operative care is required. The operation does not affect the ability to urinate as there is no urethra in a chelonian, but it will be unable to copulate.

Post-hibernation anorexia (PHA)

During hibernation tortoises live on reserves of fat. An adult tortoise loses about 1% of its bodyweight every calendar month during hibernation as this fat is metabolised. If the body fat becomes depleted before the end of hibernation, the animal's own protein tissues start to be broken down to provide energy. With a total loss of body fat, all the fat-soluble vitamins will be lost leading to a deficiency. The level of liver glycogen will also be depleted. It is the store of liver glycogen that gives a healthy tortoise the energy to 'get up and go' on normal emergence.

These deficiencies are the cause of PHA, the tortoise being reluctant to eat anything, even after a drink. Many tortoise owners add a small amount of glucose to the first drink of water after emergence when as much as 70ml may be drunk.

The initial examination should include a close examination of the mouth, looking for any signs of stomatitis. The carapace length and bodyweight must be checked against the 'Jackson ratio' graph (see earlier) and blood samples may be taken to estimate PCV, blood urea and blood glucose. In cases of PHA the PCV is often as high as 0.5 - 0.6l/l (normal - 0.34), with blood urea levels of 100mmol/l (0.35 — 10) and blood glucose less than 1mmol/l (11 — 12). Treatment is aimed at maintaining the tortoise during the day at or near the preferred body temperature (25° — 30°C for Mediterranean tortoises; varies for other species), falling slightly at night. The essentials of treatment are threefold - rehydration, provision of an easily assimilated diet and replacement of the fat soluble vitamins. Fluids such as Hartmann's solution, lactated Ringer's solution or glucose rehydration products such as Lectade (SmithKline Beecham) are given at the rate of 4% bodyweight daily by stomach tube. Sterile fluids may be given by intracoelomic injection via the inguinal fossa, being careful not to damage the bladder or other viscera. The PCV and blood urea levels should be monitored to assess the effect of rehydration. An easily assimilated diet for these cases can be provided by using Complan (Farley Health Products), Build Up (Carnation Foods) or Protinaid (Veterinary Drug), giving 10ml by stomach tube every 48 hours.

Some multivitamin injections can be administered parenterally but the best method is to give them *per os* either as tablets, capsules or liquid added to oral medication. As always with tortoise medicine, recovery can be very slow and it is wise to inform the owner of this fact at the beginning of treatment.

Pneumonia

Chelonians have a simple respiratory system with no diaphragm. The lungs have large 'alveoli' and are attached to the inner surface of the carapace so there is no pleural space as in mammals. Ventral to the lung is a diaphragmatic membrane separating them from the coelomic cavity (see Anatomy). When there is a pneumonic lesion in the lung the denser, radio-opaque tissue shows up clearly on radiographs. It is useful to take dorsoventral, lateral and craniocaudal views so that the dimension, as well as the location of the lesion, can be identified (Jackson and Fasal, 1981).

Any bacteria involved must be identified. Nasopharyngeal swabs and those taken from the glottis are of little diagnostic value as the normal flora of the mouth will often mask the causal organism. The route of entry to the pneumonic lesion is via a wide hole (0.6cm) over the middle of the pneumonic area. This is drilled under aseptic surgical conditions through the carapace, using an orthopaedic drill. A nasopharyngeal swab can be introduced and pushed down into the centre of the lesion (the depth being measured accurately from the lateral radiograph) and submitted for culture and sensitivity. While awaiting the result the hole in the carapace can be blocked temporarily with sterile Blu-tack (Bostik) held in place with a strip of adhesive plaster. When the laboratory results are received the most appropriate antibiotic can be injected into the pneumonic lesion through the hole in the carapace (using aseptic technique) at regular intervals. Follow-up radiographs will demonstrate when the lesion is healed.

Antimicrobial therapy will depend on sensitivity testing. In serious cases treatment with a broad-spectrum bactericidal antibiotic should be initiated without delay. Ampicillin, carbenicillin or gentamicin have all proved successful (for dosage regimes see Table 2). No allowance is made for the weight of the shell; all recommended dose rates are based on the whole body weight (Lawrence, 1984). Diuretics have also been recommended in the treatment of respiratory disease in chelonians. Frye (1973) suggested frusemide (Lasix, Hoechst) at 5mg/kg by intramuscular or subcutaneous injection, whilst Jackson (quoted in Holt, 1981a) reported the use of bumetadine (Burinex, Leo) at a dose rate of 0.06mg/kg by intramuscular injection. Full supportive treatment including vitamins, fluid therapy (and in extreme cases the use of oxygen) and careful nursing will increase the success rate.

Tortoises affected with pneumonia should not be hibernated. To prevent hibernation the patient should be maintained at 25° — 30°C with a 14 hour day/10 hour night cycle.

Rhinitis

Runny nose syndrome (RNS) must not be considered a precursor of pneumonia. There are three main causes of rhinitis which can be distinguished by careful clinical examination.

1. **Rhinitis caused by sinusitis.** This is often unilateral, although bilateral cases do occur, and, as the condition may not be seen early, the secretion from the external nares may be fairly thick. By holding the head extended and opening the mouth, a finger can be placed on the hard palate and pressure applied to the internal nares, while an equal and opposite pressure is applied by the other hand to the nasal bones. This will cause the thick, mucoid secretion to be expressed from the external nares and this can be wiped away with cotton-wool. In long- standing cases secondary infection will have occurred and pus will be expressed. The associated eye may be closed with an ocular discharge as the infection may have ascended the nasolachrymal duct. The discharge must be expressed from the nares daily. In the surgery it is possible to block off the pharynx with a swab and reverse flush each nasal chamber with 1 — 2ml of water. The installation of suitable medication, such as antibiotic or antibiotic/anti-inflammatory drops, will usually clear the condition.

2. **Rhinitis caused by excess salivation in the mouth.** Because the posterior nares open freely above the tongue, excessive fluid in the mouth will flow from the nostrils. This is not a true rhinitis, although stagnant fluids that remain in the nasal passages may produce a sinusitis as mentioned in 1. The discharge from the nostrils tends to be intermittent in these cases. This condition can be assisted by subcutaneous injections of atropine sulphate (50mcg/kg daily).

3. **True rhinitis (RNS).** This condition appears to be highly infectious, spreading through whole collections of tortoises. The infectious nature of RNS is well recognised as those who take care of other people's tortoises over a holiday period have found to their cost.

True rhinitis is nearly always bilateral and appears as a continuous, thin, watery nasal discharge throughout the day and night. The mucous membranes of the nares, glottis, trachea and bronchi are difficult to examine but have been found to be inflamed. In serious cases there will be open-mouth breathing and, frequently, some degree of noise during respiration due to alterations in the architecture of the upper respiratory tract. The condition may be accompanied by a clear, ocular discharge due to excessive epiphora. Studies on cases of RNS in tortoises (Jackson and Needham, 1983) showed serum antibody titres to a Sendai-like virus. While the antibody titres remained low (below 1:32) the tortoise appeared to be unable to recover unaided.

Early cases must be isolated in an attempt to prevent the spread to other tortoises in the same ownership. Antibiotics appear to have no effect. What is required is a reduction of the inflammation of the mucous membranes. Currently there is no single treatment that produces a 100% cure. One very useful treatment producing resolution in 60% of RNS cases is filling each nasal chamber in turn with Framomycetin Anti-Scour Paste for about 10 days. The owner should be shown how to do this. If at the end of 10 days rhinitis persists, it is worth repeating the treatment for a further 10 days before abandoning this line of therapy. In long-standing cases vitamin A (10,000iu/kg i/m) helps the mucous membranes to heal.

Soft shell

All newly hatched chelonians have soft shells. Good calcification of the plastron and carapace during the early years depends on an adequate intake of calcium and a Ca:P ratio of 1.2:1. Soft shell in terrapins is very common because owners are inclined to feed meat or fish fillets. The normal diet of terrapins in the wild is whole fish fry, small crustaceans, eg. water shrimps, and snails. Treatment is based on firm advice over correct feeding regimes (see Feeding).

Steatitis

This condition occurs in terrapins which have been fed entirely on coldwater fish such as whitebait or herring. The terrapin metabolises the fat, laying it down in the fat stores as hard fat. These hard masses can be palpated in both the inguinal and clavicular fossae. Biopsy samples of this fat show it to contain necrotic islets which are characteristic of steatitis. Hepatic changes may also occur. Treatment is based on feeding fish which do not contain this polyunsaturated fat.

Stomatitis or 'mouth rot'

'Mouth rot' is a herpetologist's term. Stomatitis is a common condition of the tortoise occurring after emerging from hibernation. Workers in the UK (Cooper *et al*, 1988) and America (Jacobson *et al*, 1985) have detected virus in such cases and this may be the causal agent. By the time the veterinary surgeon sees these cases the dorsal surface of the tongue is covered with a white, diphtheritic membrane. The infection can spread rapidly to involve other tissues in the mouth, and secondary bacterial infections are known to extend down the trachea and oesophagus. The discomfort in the mouth prevents affected animals from eating, and examination of the oral cavity should be routine in all cases of post-hibernation anorexia. The initial treatment should be done under general anaesthesia and consist of debridement to expose the underlying ulcer. Cleaning with hydrogen peroxide followed by povidone-iodine solution is preferable to parenteral antibiotics. In severe cases the identification of bacteria (be they primary or secondary) by laboratory culture may be required. Daily cleaning of the lesion and supportive feeding by stomach tube are necessary, but great care must be taken when passing the stomach tube not to carry infection down the oesophagus. This means that the oral cavity must be filled with a suitable antibiotic cream, eg. Framomycetin Anti-Scour Paste, before a stomach tube is passed.

Trauma

Shells can be fractured or burned, while the limbs, as well as suffering fractures, can have scale damage to the skin. Cases of rodent damage can occur where rats or mice gnaw the limbs of the tortoise during hibernation when owners have not used vermin-proof hibernation boxes. Regular monthly inspection of tortoises over the winter period is of help in identifying such damage early when it can be more easily treated. Cuts across and into the carapace occur from the blades of hover mowers. Fractures to any part of the shell can occur accidentally when tortoises fall from balconies, are run over by motor vehicles or are damaged by falling rocks.

Burns on the carapace are seen when bonfires are lit without the owner realising that the tortoise has sought shelter under the pile of rubbish. These burns also occur in the wild from grass fires. After cleaning and debridement, shell defects can be repaired using an epoxyresin (Technovit, Kurtzer). After burns, the keratin shields lift off, exposing dead, grey bone. To prevent infection it is advisable to apply a thin layer of epoxyresin. The healing of shell lesions can take many years in the UK climate, especially if the animal is hibernated (Holt, 1981b; Jackson, 1978). During hibernation, when the metabolism slows, no healing occurs. Healing can be accelerated by keeping the tortoise awake, eating and metabolically active through the winter, when the shell lesion should resolve in 11 — 12 months. At the end of this period the dead bone will have separated; it can then be lifted off. Underneath there will be a layer of soft keratin over the new bone. There is no shield formation visible at this stage.

ANAESTHESIA

As a general rule chelonians should be maintained at 22°C during surgery and allowed to recover at 25°C, though there are variations in preferred body temperature. Should the body temperature fall the reptile's ability to detoxify the anaesthetic decreases rapidly and anaesthesia can become dangerous and very prolonged.

Injectable anaesthetics

Alphaxalone/alphadolone (Saffan, Coopers Pitman-Moore). This is the anaesthetic of choice for short procedures and as an induction agent prior to intubation for prolonged surgery. The intravenous route is preferred (9mg/kg) but if this fails intramuscular injection into the quadriceps muscle (15mg/kg) can be given.

Propofol (Rapinovet, Coopers Pitman-Moore) (1.0 - 1.4ml/kg i/v) has the advantages of a rapid onset and a fast recovery. As it is less viscous than Saffan it will pass easily through a 27G needle.

Ketamine (Vetalar, Parke-Davis). This must not be used in debilitated reptiles and those with any liver disease because ketamine reduces liver enzymes. It is not a true anaesthetic but a dissociative agent, and for this reason is not often used. Healthy tortoises show no effect at 50mg/kg bodyweight and require 100mg/kg. Once sedation has been achieved, intubation and a volatile anaesthetic must be given.

Volatile anaesthetics

Halothane (or isoflurane) is usually used as maintenance at 1½ — 2%, with oxygen, once the chelonian has been intubated. It has to be given by positive pressure technique using an Ayre's T-piece.

Methoxyflurane (Metofane, C-Vet) is also used as a maintenance anaesthetic with oxygen. Positive pressure using an Ayre's T-piece is required. Metofane must not be used in chelonians with liver disease or toxaemia. The depth of anaesthesia is best judged by the degree of muscle relaxation. Very little vapour is required to maintain anaesthesia.

REFERENCES

COOPER, J. E., GSCHMEISSNER, S. and BONE, R. D. (1988). Herpes-like virus particles in necrotic stomatitis of tortoises. *Veterinary Record* **123**, 554.

FENWICK, H. (1989). Feeding in captivity , with an appendix of plants poisonous to chelonia. *Testudo* **3 (1)**, 50.

FRYE, F. L. (1973). Miscellaneous drugs. In: *Husbandry, Medicine and Surgery in Captive Reptiles.* VM Publishing, Kansas.

FRYE, F. L. (1981a). Surgery. In: *Biomedical and Surgical Aspects of Captive Reptile Husbandry.* VM Publishing, Kansas.

FRYE, F. L. (1981b). Traumatic and physical diseases. In: *The Diseases of the Reptilia. Volume 2.* (Eds. J. E. Cooper and O. F. Jackson) Academic Press, London.

HOLT, P. E. (1979). Obstetrical problems in two tortoises. *Journal of Small Animal Practice* **102**, 353.

HOLT, P. E. (1981a). Drugs and dosages. In: *Diseases of the Reptilia. Volume 2.* (Eds. J.E.Cooper and O.F.Jackson) Academic Press, London.

HOLT, P. E. (1981b). Healing of a surgically induced shell wound in a tortoise. *Veterinary Record* **108**, 102.

INSKEEP, R. (1983). Incubation construction. *Testudo* **2 (2)**, 40.

JACKSON, O. F. (1978). Tortoise shell repair over two years. *Veterinary Record* **102**, 184.

JACKSON, O. F. (1980). Weight and measurement data on tortoises *(Testudo gracea and Testudo hermanni)* and their relationship to health. *Journal of Small Animal Practice* **21**, 409.

JACKSON, O. F. (in press). Diagnosis and treatment of diseases of captive chelonians. *Testudo.*

JACKSON, O. F. and COOPER, J. E. (1981). Anaesthesia and surgery. In: *Diseases of the Reptilia. Volume 2.* (Eds. J.E.Cooper and O. F.Jackson) Academic Press, London.

JACKSON, O. F. and FASAL, M. D. (1981). Radiology as a diagnostic aid in four chelonian conditions. *Journal of Small Animal Practice* **22**, 705.

JACKSON, O.F. and NEEDHAM, J. R. (1983). Respiratory virus antibodies in chelonians. *Journal of Small Animal Practice* **24**, 31.

JACOBSON, E. R., CLUBB, S., GASKIN, J. M. and GARDINER, C. (1985). Herpesvirus-like infection in Argentine tortoises. *Journal of the American Veterinary Medical Association* **187**, 1227.

KASS, R. E., ULLREY, D. E. and TRAPP, A. L. (1982). A study of calcium requirements of the red slider turtle *(Pseudemys scripta elegans). Journal of Zoo Animal Medicine* **13**, 62.

LAWRENCE, K. (1984). Drug dosages for chelonians. *Veterinary Record* **114**, 150.

PRITCHARD, P. C. H. (1979). *Encyclopedia of Turtles.* TFH Publications, New Jersey.

ROSSKOPF, W. J. and HOWARD, E. (1983). End stage kidney disease in a Californian desert tortoise. *Tortuga Gazette* **May 1983**, 5.

TEARE, J. A. and BUSH, M. (1983). Toxicology and efficacy of ivermectin in chelonians. *Journal of the Amercian Veterinary Medical Association* **183**, 1195.

CHAPTER SEVENTEEN

REPTILES PART TWO LIZARDS AND SNAKES

Martin P C Lawton BVetMed CertVOphthal FRCVS

There are approximately 6547 species of reptiles, of which 6280 are members of the Order Squamata (Hare and Woodward, 1989). The Order Squamata comprises four Sub Orders:- i) Sauria (lizards) - 3750 species, ii) Serpentes (snakes) - 2400 species, iii) Amphisbaenia (worm lizards) - 21 genera and 140 species, iv) Sphenodontia, the tuatara *(Sphenodon punctatus)* being the only species.

The Sauria (lizards) and Serpentes (snakes) will be covered in this chapter (see Tables 1 and 2).

Table 1
Families of lizards.

GEKKONIDAE	Geckos	85 genera	800 species
PYGOPODIDAE	Snake lizards		31 species
XANTUSIIDAE	Desert night lizards		16 species
DIBAMIDAE	Blind lizards		4 species
IGUANIDAE	Iguanas	55 genera	650 species
CHAMAELEONTIDAE	Chameleons	4 genera	85 species
AGAMIDAE	Agamas, flying dragons	53 genera	300 species
SCINCIDAE	Skinks	85 genera	1275 species
CORDYLIDAE	Girdle tailed lizards	10 genera	50 species
LACERTIDAE	Wall and sand lizards	25 genera	200 species
TEIIDAE	Whiptails	39 genera	227 species
ANGUIDAE	Anguids	8 genera	75 species
XENOSAURIDAE	Crocodile lizards		4 species
VARANIDAE	Monitor lizards		31 species
HELODERMATIDAE	Beaded lizard, gila monster		2 species

Table 2
Families of snakes.

LEPTOTYPHLOPIDAE	Thread snakes	2 genera	78 species
TYPHLOPIDAE	Blind snakes	3 genera	180 species
ANOMALEPIDAE	Dawn blind snakes	4 genera	20 species
CROCHROPIDAE	Pipesnakes, Asian wart snakes		2 species
ANILIIDAE	False coral snakes		9 species
UROPELTIDAE	Shield tail snakes	8 genera	44 species
XENOPELTIDA	Sunbeam snake		1 species
BOIDAE	Boas, pythons	27 genera	88 species
COLUBRIDAE	Colubrids, boomslang	292 genera	1562 species
ELAPIDAE	Cobras, mambas	61 genera	236 species
VIPERIDAE	Vipers	7 genera	187 species

ANATOMY

Skin

All reptiles have strong impermeable skin which prevents them from drying out on land. The epidermis is covered by tough keratin and in some species is thickened into a series of plates or scales which often overlap like roof tiles. In some species, such as geckos *(Gekko* spp.), there are fine bristles of modified scales clumped together on the toe pads; these give extra gripping power and enable them to climb up surfaces even as smooth as glass (Hare and Woodward, 1989).

A number of lizards, most noted being the chameleons, have clumps of pigmented cells (chromatophores) in the dermis. The pigment in these cells can be concentrated or dispersed by hormonal or nervous signals, enabling a change of colour. This is a means of camouflage that enables the reptile to blend into its surroundings. In many lizards this can also be taken as a sign of health or illness. Iguanas which are ill are more likely to be a dull grey or brownish colour.

Many lizards have glands on or near the hind limbs which produce scent; these 'femoral pores' are only present, or are more prominent, in males as opposed to females, and are a particular feature of the iguanas.

Skeleton

In snakes the limbs are greatly reduced, although there may be rudimentary pelvic and pectoral remnants - particularly in the boids (boas and pythons), where spurs are seen on either side of the cloaca. These spurs are usually present in both males and females and are of similar size; it is thought that they play a part in mating behaviour, where the male uses its spurs to stimulate the female (Obst *et al,* 1988).

Snakes have a greatly increased number of vertebrae and these may number over 400 in some species (Hare and Woodward, 1989). Each is attached to a pair of ribs that form a tubular cagework protecting the internal organs.

In snakes the two halves of both the upper and lower jaws, being only loosely attached, can stretch. This allows the snake to eat prey that is several times the size of the reptile's head.

Lizards have teeth which are generally peg-like structures; lost teeth are quickly replaced. Snakes' teeth are usually backward pointing and on the maxilla may consist of two rows. As in lizards, teeth are lost and replaced. In the Colubridae, Elapidae and Viperidae, teeth may be highly specialised and evolved into fangs for administration of poisons.

Special senses

A distinguishing feature between a snake and a lizard is that a snake has no external eardrum, since its earbones are attached to the jaw. Thus it is unlikely that snakes hear sounds in the usual way, but it is suspected that they detect vibrations from the ground via the jawbone.

Most boids are equipped with heat-sensitive pits, usually along the upper lip. These enable them to detect very small rises in the air temperature caused by the presence of warm-blooded prey. They are thought to be so sensitive that they can pick up changes of $0.001°C$ (Hare and Woodward, 1989). Partly for this reason some snakes are difficult to persuade to eat dead prey, especially if it is frozen and not thawed properly.

The basic sense of smell in reptiles is enhanced by the presence of Jacobson's organ, a region of chemically sensitive nerve endings in the roof of the mouth. In snakes and lizards the scent is carried to this organ by the long flexible tongue. As well as tasting the air, snakes and lizards use this organ to detect the presence of water.

Lizards have a number of bony plates within the eye (ossicles) that enable them to focus by distorting the shape of the eye, thus adjusting the distance between the lens and the retina. Snakes do not have these bones within the eye; they focus in much the same way as a mammal.

The shape of the pupil is usually a good guide to the lifestyle of the reptile. Round pupils are characteristic of activity during the day, whereas a vertical pupil is characteristic of a nocturnal species (Hare and Woodward, 1989). The eyelids of snakes are fused to form a transparent membrane, the spectacle, which covers the cornea. It is particularly important during ecdysis (shedding) that this spectacle is also shed, or ocular problems may develop (see later).

Respiration

In most legless lizards and snakes, the left lung tends to be reduced or even absent. This is an adaptation to their long slim shape. However, the right lung in these creatures is elongated and often there is an air sac that runs almost the entire length of the body cavity.

HOUSING

Lizards and snakes can loosely be divided into arboreal, terrestrial, burrowing, semi-aquatic and aquatic.

The housing requirements will depend on the individual needs of each species. The general rule is not to mix species which have different requirements or are from different parts of the world.

All reptiles are ectothermic (poikilothermic) and, therefore, rely on the external temperature, coupled with behavioural traits such as basking or burrowing, to influence their metabolism, reproduction and activity. The preferred body temperature (PBT) is the range of temperatures at which a reptile performs best. The PBT of a species is not a set temperature but a range, which can vary at different times of the year, or even at different times of the day. A comprehensive list of PBT ranges is provided by Jackson and Cooper (1981a). Therefore it is best to try and provide a temperature gradient in the vivarium. Generally a range is best provided by a heat source at one end of the vivarium; thus the reptile can select its own preferred temperature. It is also essential to have a thermostat or thermometer to monitor the temperatures.

Arboreal species, such as iguanas and pythons, require branches and a fairly high tank so that they can climb.

Substrate should be as simple as possible, so as to be easily cleaned. Peat, gravel or sand may look attractive in a vivarium but they hide urates and faeces which, if the temperature of the vivarium is high, encourage the growth of potentially pathogenic bacteria. Newspaper or kitchen towelling is recommended as substrate for the majority of species, although some, such as sandboas (Eryx spp.) which burrow, must be kept on sand.

Aquatic and semi-aquatic species should have a clean supply of water. Ideally, some sort of filtration mechanism should be utilised to prevent the water from becoming stagnant and a breeding ground for Pseudomonas and Aeromonas bacteria. Wherever possible a separate area for feeding should be provided, to keep the water clean. For fully aquatic species it is important that some sort of heating is provided for the water; thermostatic control is recommended.

All species of reptile require a ready source of water from which to drink. For most species this can be provided by using a simple bowl. For snakes the bowl should be large enough for the animal to bathe, as this is essential for normal ecdysis. Some species, such as chameleons, need to have their tanks sprayed daily as they will not drink from bowls of water, but only from droplets on the trees or plants.

FEEDING

Snakes are entirely carnivorous. Mammal-eating snakes seldom suffer nutritional deficiencies as the rodents provided in captivity are very similar to those that they would eat in the wild. However, the choice of rodent can be particularly important; for example the royal python (Python regius) is more likely to eat a gerbil, which is similar to the agouti coloured wild mouse, than an albino or fancy coloured mouse.

Some species of snakes are more difficult to feed in captivity - for example, Jackson's tree snake *(Thrasops jacksoni)* eats lizards. Careful thought should therefore be given to the suitability of keeping such a species.

Fish-eating snakes should be given a fish of a similar size to that which they would eat in the wild. If, for example, a garter *(Thamnophis* spp.) or dice snake *(Natrix* spp.) is fed pieces of a large fish such as cod, it is not receiving a natural and well balanced diet. Care must also be taken when feeding frozen fish, such as whitebait, because thiaminase activity can cause a deficiency (see Hypovitaminosis B_1).

Lizards can be insectivorous, carnivorous, omnivorous or herbivorous. The same species may change its eating habits during its life. For example, baby water dragons *(Physignathus* spp.) are almost entirely insectivorous but, as they grow, become first carnivorous and then omnivorous.

The diet for a captive lizard is unlikely to be the same as that which it would eat in the wild; thus nutritional problems are common. The choice of insects is particularly important as the average mealworm has a calcium:phosphorus ratio of 1:14 and the average locust a calcium:phosphorus ratio of 1:8 (Zwart, 1980). Thus, it is important to supplement insects on a diet high in calcium prior to feeding them to the lizard. A suitable supplement is Nutrobal (Vetark) which has a calcium:phosphorus ratio of 46:1 (see 'Reptiles Part One').

Pieces of meat should not be fed to lizards which are carnivorous or omnivorous as meat has a poor calcium:phosphorus ratio. 'Pinkies' (baby bald mice), 'furries' (young mice which have just grown a coat), adult mice, or cat or dog food are more suitable.

Herbivorous lizards can also present problems in that lettuce, cucumber and tomato have calcium:phosphorus ratios of less than 1:1 and therefore some sort of supplement is needed such as Vionate (Ciba-Geigy), Arkvit (Vetark) or Ace-High (Vetark).

HANDLING

A full description of handling techniques is given in Lawton (1991).

It is not unknown for poisonous snakes to be sold inadvertently by an importer or pet shop. Thus, if a species is not readily identifiable, it is best to assume that it may be poisonous and appropriate care should be taken. Most pet snakes are accustomed to being handled. One should not be unduly rough when handling a snake as this can result in bruising and autolysis of muscles which may even prove fatal (see Figure 1). Some species must be handled with care, as even though they are non-venomous they may be aggressive, eg. reticulated pythons *(Python reticulatus)* or anacondas *(Eunectes murinus)*. The large snakes such as Indian pythons *(Python molurus molurus)* and African rock pythons *(Python sebae)* should not be handled by one person alone; a second person should be available in case of an accident.

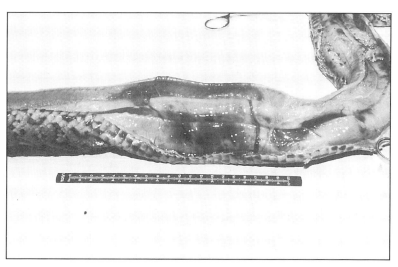

Figure 1
Bruising and autolysis of muscles
due to rough handling
(post-mortem specimen).

Care must be taken on handling lizards. One should not grasp them by their tail as some species practise 'autotomy', which is the spontaneous loss of the tail. This is due to an unossified fracture plane in the mid-region of the centrum of a caudal vertebrae (Davies, 1981). These lizards also have the ability for the tail to regrow, although not to its full former beauty. A lizard that has lost its tail should not have the stump sutured as this may interfere with the regrowth of the new tail. Application of an antiseptic such as povidone iodine solution is generally sufficient to prevent infection (see Figure 2).

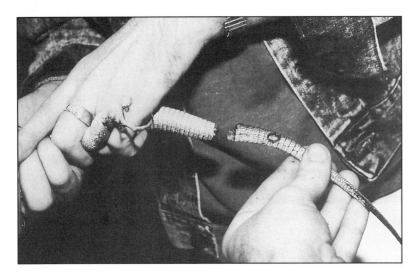

Figure 2
An iguana showing autotomy.

The majority of lizards, like cats, have five weapons; their teeth and four clawed limbs. Thus, when dealing with a species that is unused to handling, it may be necessary to wear gloves or to use a towel in order to protect oneself. The general rule for larger lizards is to support the animal with one hand around the pelvic girdle and limbs and one hand around the pectoral girdle and limbs.

As part of the clinical examination and at the time of handling, it is important to weigh both snakes and lizards for one's records. Although, at the moment, there is no equivalent of the 'Jackson's Ratio' (see 'Reptiles Part One') as there are for Chelonia, it is nevertheless important to know the weight of a patient to monitor its progress and it is essential prior to anaesthesia or chemotherapy.

SEXING

Sexual dimorphism is a feature of certain species such as Jackson's chameleon *(Chamaeleo jacksoni)*; the male has three horns on the front of its head (Frye, 1981, 1989). In some species of lizards, eg. the Iguanidae, it is possible to distinguish the male from the female by the presence and size of the 'femoral pores' on the inside of the thighs of the male lizards (Frye, 1989). Generally in lizards it is possible to see the bulges where the hemipenes are located at the base of the tail. By applying gentle pressure, distal to the cloaca, in a cranial direction it may be possible to evert the hemipenes and thus sex a male snake or lizard.

In snakes, males tend to have a longer tail than the female, so by comparing two or more individuals it may be possible to distinguish between a male and a female. There are also reference texts which state the number of paired sub-caudal scales (these lie between the cloaca and the tip of the tail) in males and females of different species. It is possible to count these sub-caudal scales in shed skins as well as on the live snake (see Figure 3).

The technique known as 'probing' requires a probe to be passed into the inverted hemipenes or paracloacal sacs (Marcus, 1981). It can be performed in snakes or lizards. In males, the probe generally travels more than eight sub-caudal scales, whereas in females it rarely goes beyond four.

For a more detailed description of sexing snakes, reference should be made to Coote (1985).

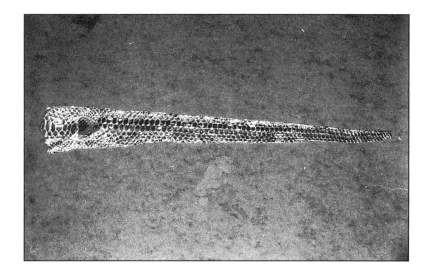

Figure 3
Paired subcaudal scale count
on fresh slough of a snake.

REPRODUCTION

In both lizards and snakes, the male possess paired hemipenes, although only one at a time is used during mating. Each hemipenis consists of a pouch that the male everts outwards through the cloaca during mating. The shape and appearance vary and often there are crests, nodules or spines; this is species-specific. The various protuberances help the organ grip the female's cloaca and stop it slipping out if the animals move.

Some reptiles retain sperm for a long time before fertilisation. Individuals of some species in captivity have laid fertilised eggs up to six years after their last contact with a male (Frye, 1981).

There are a number of species, such as the whiptail lizard *(Cnemidophorus* spp.) in the USA and the Caucasian rock lizard *(Lacerta saxicola)* in the USSR, which show parthenogenesis (Townsend and Cole, 1985). In these species the vast majority of the newly-born reptiles are female. Males are occasionally born but rarely survive. The major drawback with parthenogenesis is that there is no mixing of the genes; variation and evolution of the species are very slow and rely solely on mutation.

Most lizards are oviparous, laying eggs which have parchment-like shells and which are very much softer than those of tortoises or birds. A few, such as the European common lizard *(Lacerta vivipara)* produce live young.

Snakes may be oviparous, ovoviviparous or viviparous. Oviparous snakes produce eggs. Ovovivivparous snakes, such as boas *(Constrictor constrictor),* produce an egg which they retain within the oviduct until the young are ready to be born. The shell membranes of such eggs do not contain calcium salts, and they are reduced to varying degrees in different species (Davies, 1981). Viviparous snakes, such as garter snakes *(Thamnophis* spp), have gone one stage further where the eggshells have developed into a primitive placenta and there is exchange of materials including nutrients and excretory products across these membranes. Both ovoviviparous and viviparous snakes give birth to live young.

DISEASES/CLINICAL CONDITIONS

Marcus (1980) stated that poor husbandry, malnutrition and lack of sanitary and hygienic procedures are the major underlying causes of disease in captive reptiles. It is for this reason that, when dealing with a sick reptile, care must be taken to establish that the vivarium, temperature and other environmental factors are correct and are not predisposing factors in the reptile's illness.

For full description of diseases the reader should refer to the *Manual of Reptiles* (to be published in 1992) or *Diseases of the Reptilia* (Cooper and Jackson, 1981). Only the commonest problems are covered in this chapter.

Abscesses

These are very common in both snakes and lizards and must be considered in the differential diagnosis of any sub-dermal swelling. If the swelling is near a bone, especially in a lizard, it is wise to radiograph to make sure that it is not a pathological fracture.

Treatment of abscesses which are caseous in nature is surgical removal *in toto* and suturing of the wound afterwards.

Anorexia

Any reptiles presented with anorexia should be given a full clinical examination, as described by Jackson (1981), to rule out pathological causes such as bacterial or parasitic infection.

Careful consideration must be given to whether or not the reptile is being kept in the correct environment - for example, at the animal's PBT or with branches or water as required. One should then consider what type of food is being offered and whether or not it is the food that the species eats. It is pointless, for example, offering a baby corn snake *(Elaphe guttata)* an adult rat. Similarly, an adult water dragon *(Physignathus* sp.) will eat more insects and meat than vegetables, while an adult iguana *(Iguana iguana)* will eat more vegetables than meat.

Maladaptation syndrome is a recognised condition whereby the reptile does not adapt to captivity and therefore does not eat or thrive. If the animal is not force-fed and given supportive therapy, cachexia and starvation will result. The snake that suffers this most frequently is the royal python *(Python regius).*

When dealing with an anorexic royal python, one should not force-feed, as this may result in regurgitation or even death. First, one must rule out primary pathological factors. If there appear to be none, rehydration should be carried out as described under dehydration, culminating in building up the reptile with an amino-acid cocktail such as Duphalyte (Duphar). Once the animal is in a fit state, care must be taken to ensure that the environmental factors are correct and, most importantly, that the snake has a hide, as this is a shy species. Generally, it is those royal pythons that are handled as little as possible that feed best. Royal pythons will often take a gerbil in preference to white laboratory mice. If a royal python still fails to eat by itself, it may be necessary to stomach-tube it with a liquidised cat food mixture or force-feed it, sometimes for the rest of its life.

Bacterial infections

A full description of bacterial infections is given by Marcus (1980). Many of the pathogenic bacteria isolated from reptilian infections are Gram-negative organisms, which are often resistant to most antibiotics (Bush *et al,* 1980). For this reason any suspected bacterial infections should be cultured and sensitivity performed. The most important group of pathogens causing morbidity and mortality in reptiles are the Gram-negative bacilli, especially Pseudomonadaceae, of which *Pseudomonas* and *Aeromonas* spp. are the most important (Marcus, 1980; Cooper, 1985).

Conjunctivitis/sub-spectacular abscess

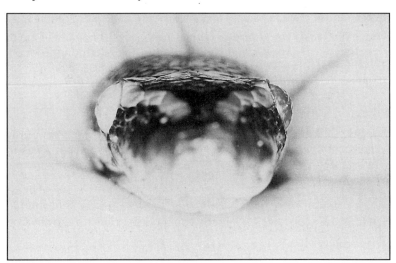

Figure 4
Royal python showing
sub-spectacular abscess
affecting right eye.

Conjunctivitis commonly occurs in lizards, but these animals do not usually produce a mucopurulent discharge; instead, a caseous plug forms which has to be removed from behind the third eyelid or flushed out of the eye. Treatment is with a suitable antibiotic ophthalmic solution such as gentamicin or tobramycin.

Sub-spectacular abscesses occur in snakes; this is where infection is below the spectacle (see Figure 4). The condition may occur due to ascending infection from previous necrotic stomatitis (Russo, 1987). Treatment is difficult; under anaesthetic the spectacle should be lanced at the lateral canthus (Millichamp, 1988) and all the infected material flushed out. Flushing is repeated daily and a suitable antibiotic preparation, based on culture and sensitivity, applied.

Dehydration

The main excretory product of reptiles is uric acid, which is highly insoluble, and even the slightest degree of dehydration can cause microcrystals to precipitate and form tophi, and cause visceral gout (Frye, 1984). Therefore, it is important that any dehydrated reptile is rehydrated as quickly as possible. Initially 3% of the bodyweight should be given by either intraperitoneal injection or stomach-tubing (Jarchow, 1988), using Hartmann's solution which helps to flush through the kidneys; after a few days Lectade (SmithKline Beecham) should be given. In very severely dehydrated cases, it is advisable to use allopurinol (20mg/kg) to prevent gout formation (Lawton, unpublished data).

Diarrhoea

Although this may be associated with liver dysfunction, it is more usually associated with parasitic problems such as flagellates, or, in the case of lizards, especially chameleons, coccidiosis (Marcus, 1981).

Ectoparasites

Virtually all imported reptiles have large ectoparasitic burdens (Jones and Llewellyn, 1989). Ticks are usually only found on imported species, whilst mites are commonly found on both snakes and lizards, captive-bred or caught. The problem is not so much an animal but an environmental problem. Thus, treating the animal may not get rid of the mite and treatment should routinely include the environment.

Ivermectin (Ivomec, MSD) (200μg/kg s/c) has proved extremely useful for the treatment of these external parasites (Matevsky and Mutafova, 1987) (see Table 3). It is recommended that the snake or lizard is placed in a hospital tank and its original environment made airtight — for example, by being covered and sealed with several dustbin bags and a Vapona strip (Dichlorvos, Shell) placed within this tank. The strip should be left for a minimum of 30 days (28 days being the minimum lifecycle, although it is influenced by the temperature). At the end of this time, the snake or lizard should be given another dose of ivermectin and returned to its old treated cage. The hospital tank must then be treated with Vapona as previously described.

Eggbinding

In lizards, eggbinding is often associated with calcium deficiency, renal disease or incorrect environment. Diagnosis is confirmed by gentle palpation of the abdomen. It is also possible to demonstrate the eggs radiographically or on ultrasound — although, being parchment-like and not having a hard shell, eggs are often difficult to see on radiographs, especially in an osteodystrophic lizard. The treatment consists of raising the ambient temperature to that of the PBT and providing an area suitable for laying of eggs, such as a seed tray filled with sand.

The majority of affected lizards are osteodystrophic so it is wise to give calcium (20%) by injection (1ml/kg) daily for five days before oxytocin (3 – 6iu i/m) is administered. It is the author's opinion that administering oxytocin and calcium at the same time is likely to result in the uterus clamping down around the egg, thus making a caesarian essential.

Should the eggs not be laid, a caesarian section is required. This is described more fully in the *Manual of Reptiles* (to be published 1992).

In snakes, eggbinding is most commonly associated with infection, abnormal eggs, eg. hyper-calcification, or uterine inertia.

As in lizards, calcium and oxytocin should always be used first; however, should this not work a caesarian section is required. It is often necessary to perform multiple incisions (Brown and Martin, 1990) as the uterus is usually not mobile enough to remove all the eggs through one incision.

Endoparasites

There are numerous endoparasites that can affect both snakes and lizards. Routine faecal examination of all reptiles is advised. A description of eggs and larvae that may be found in reptile faeces is given by Barnard (1986a,b).

Kalicephalus can be pathogenic in both lizards and snakes and is seen as either embryonated eggs or as free larva in the faeces (see figure 5).

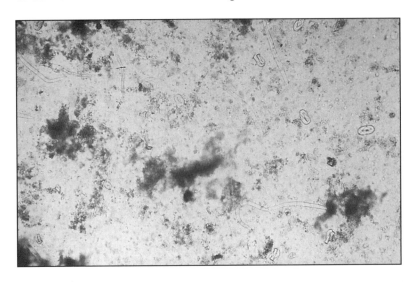

Figure 5
Microscopic view of faecal sample showing *Kalicephalus* spp. larvae and embryonated eggs.

Treatment of any endoparasites may be undertaken (see Table 3) using:-

(1) ivermectin (Ivomec, MSD) (200µg/kg s/c) which may be safe up to 400ug/kg (Matevsky and Mutafova, 1987);

(2) a suitable anthelmintic orally, such as oxfendazol (Bandit, Coopers Pitman-Moore) at a dose rate of 3ml/kg.

Table 3
Antiparasitic drugs.

Drug	Dose
Albendazole	50-75mg/kg orally
Bunamidine	150-300mg/kg orally
Fenbendazole	100mg/kg orally
Ivermectin	200mg/kg s/c (not Chelonia)*
Levamisole	200mg/kg orally
	50mg/kg s/c
Mebendazole	20-25mg/kg orally
Niclosamide	150-300mg/kg orally
Oxfendazole	3ml/kg orally
Praziquantel	3.5-7.5mg/kg s/c
Thiabendazole	50mg/kg orally

*Teare and Bush, 1983; Jacobson, 1988.

Infections with protozoa such as flagellates, ciliates or *Entamoeba invadens* occur in both snakes and lizards (Cowan, 1968). Treatment is by a single dose of metronidazole (Flagyl, RMB) (160mg/kg orally). It may be necessary to repeat this dose after two weeks. A single high dose is recommended as it is less likely to produce neurological signs than repeated smaller doses (Lawton, unpublished data).

Hypovitaminosis B$_1$ (Thiamine deficiency)

This is seen mainly in water snakes which are fed on frozen fish which have thiaminase activity. It can also occur in snakes fed on frozen chicks. The resultant lack of thiamine results in cerebrocortical necrosis (CCN) which causes blindness, postural defects and inability to strike at the prey (Lawton, 1989). In very severe cases it results in cardiac dysfunction and convulsions. Treatment in the early stages is dramatic. There is rapid response to thiamine supplementation at 25mg/kg orally. Long-term therapy consists of:

(1) changing the diet to foods with less thiaminase activity, ie. pinkies smeared with whitebait;

(2) denaturing the thiaminase by partially cooking the fish;

(3) supplementation with a vitamin supplement that contains thiamine.

Necrotic stomatitis

This is a problem in both snakes and lizards. Initially it is seen as petechiation of the membranes in the mouth, but this may lead to pus formation or, if not treated, osteolysis.

Ideally a swab for culture and sensitivity should be taken, but in the meantime the mouth should be cleaned with an antiseptic such as povidone-iodine or hydrogen peroxide and a topical antibiotic such as framycetin (Framomycin Anti-Scour Paste, C-Vet). There is unsubstantiated evidence to suggest that vitamin A and vitamin C improve mucous membrane repair (Wallach, 1979) and Hess and Rudy (1974) suggested that lack of vitamin C may pre-dispose towards ulcerative stomatitis. As well as treating the infection, supportive therapy (fluids) should be given and an increased temperature provided.

Neurological problems

For a full description the reader is referred to the chapter in the *Manual of Small Animal Neurology* (Lawton, 1989).

Nutritional osteodystrophy

This is the most common problem seen in lizards. A detailed description of the pathophysiology is given by Fowler (1986).

Any lizard that is presented with a swollen leg should be radiographed to make sure that this is not a secondary pathological fracture. Neurological signs due to hypocalcaemic tetany are often seen when blood calcium levels start dropping below normal (2.3mmol/l) (Lawton, unpublished data). Paralysis and paresis may also occur in osteodystrophy, in some cases due to secondary fractures of the spine, in others associated with the hypocalcaemic tetany.

Treatment is aimed at improving the diet together with calcium supplementation. Initially i/v calcium solution is advised. In severe cases, where the jaw is soft, force-feeding should be carried out with a baby food such as Milupa (Milupa) and calcium supplement (Nutrobal, Vetark; Vionate, Ciba-Geigy).

Obesity

This is a major disease problem of captive reptiles, especially snakes (Jones and Llewellyn, 1989). There is a tendency for an animal that is feeding well to be overfed (Frye, 1979); obesity can result in and cause debilitation. If lizards or snakes become obese there is a danger of liver damage due to fatty infiltration (Elkan, 1981). Obesity in reptiles may also predispose towards eggbinding.

Respiratory problems

These are common, especially in snakes. Respiratory disease may be associated with incorrect environmental conditions such as too low temperature or too high relative humidity. It also occurs due to bacterial, viral or parasitic infections.

A snake that is reported to be gasping or blowing bubbles must be given a thorough clinical examination to rule out respiratory signs associated with terminal septicaemia.

If there is excess accumulation of fluid in the mouth, originating from the glottis, a sample should be taken and examined under the microscope for presence of larvae, eggs or bacteria. This gives some indication of how the case should be treated.

Parasitic conditions, such as those due to *Rhabdias* spp. or pentastomes, as well as migrating larval stages of intestinal helminths, should be treated as described under endoparasites but may also warrant antibiotics.

The use of mucolytics, such as Bisolvon (Boehringer Ingelheim), helps to clear tenacious mucus. In very severe cases it may be necessary to give intratracheal installations of antibiotics.

Although viral respiratory problems are difficult to diagnose, they should be suspected, especially in cases that fail to respond to antibiotics. Paramyxovirus was first identified from an epizootic which swept through a snake farm in Switzerland (Clark *et al*, 1979), killing 128 of 431 Fer-de-lance snakes *(Bothrops atrox).* It has since been shown to effect other Viperidae in a zoological collection in the USA (Jacobson *et al*, 1981), and has recently been found to be a cause of death in a colony of Viperidae in this country (Cooper and Lawton, unpublished data). This should be borne in mind, as it appears that paramyxovirus is no longer restricted to Viperidae but can affect other families such as Colubridae and Boidae (Ahne *et al*, 1987).

In lizards, respiratory infections are often associated with cardiovascular complications or parasitic disease.

Skin diseases

Blister disease. This is seen as 'blisters' on the skin and occurs in lizards (especially water dragons) and most snakes. A sample of the fluid from the blister should be removed aseptically and examined under a microscope for larvae, as the nematode, *Kalicephalus,* can penetrate the skin and cause a vesicular reaction. Blister disease can also be associated with high relative humidity (Cooper, 1984) and secondary bacterial infection.

Treatment consists of eliminating parasites, if responsible, and cleaning the blister with an antiseptic such as povidone-iodine or (if necessary) antibiotics based on culture and sensitivity.

Ventral dermal necrosis ('Scale rot'). This is specifically seen in snakes and is associated with poor hygiene, leading to infection accumulating underneath the scales. Initially, this causes petechiation followed by echymosis of the ventral scales and eventually necrosis which may involve just a few scales or result in the total loss of skin down to the underlying muscles (see Figure 6).

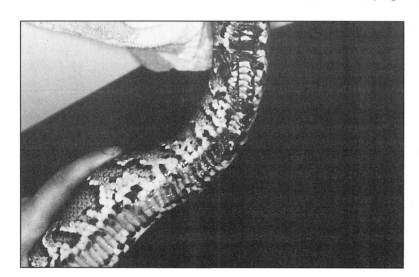

Figure 6
Reticulated python showing
severe ventral dermal necrosis.

Treatment consists of improving the environment, fluid therapy (there may be substantial fluid loss due to the damage of the skin) and treating the wounds with an antiseptic, such as povidone-iodine, and antibiotics. The latter can be given topically and, if necessary, systemically but use should be based on culture and sensitivity. As *Pseudomonas* and *Aeromonas* spp. are often involved, topical use of flamazine (Smith and Nephew) or Framomycin Anti-Scour Paste (C-Vet) may prove useful prior to sensitivity results.

Fungal infections of the skin may be primary or secondary (Jacobson, 1980) and should be considered in the differential diagnosis. Treatment of fungal infections is not easy.

Dysecdysis. This is the inability to slough (shed) the skin satisfactorily. Factors involved include low or high relative humidity and an unsuitable environment, such as the absence of an area in which to bathe or stones to rub against.

Old retained skin should be removed as quickly as possible, as it shrinks and may produce a tourniquet effect with necrosis of the tissues distal to the band of skin. This is particularly common in lizards where tips of tails and digits may be lost. In lizards, daily spraying is advised to prevent this. Skin is removed by gentle bathing with water; hypromellose (Isopto Plain, Alcan) softens the skin and aids its removal.

In snakes, failure to bathe or the absence of rocks to rub against are the commonest causes of dysecdysis. Occasionally, scarring or infection of the skin can also result in dysecdysis.

A snake with dysecdysis should be placed in a wet towel 'sandwich' in a box. The snake rubs against the wet towels, helping to remove the skin. If this does not work, one should rub the skin from nose to tail (the direction in which the snake would shed naturally), first with wet, then dry, pieces of cotton-wool.

Retained spectacles are a particular problem in snakes (see earlier). Care must be taken not to avulse the underlying spectacle as this will result in desiccation and loss of that eye. 'Sellotape' or forceps must **never** be used. A moistened cotton bud can be gently rubbed at the edges of the spectacle and should be sufficient to remove the retained spectacle. Alternatively, hypromellose can be used for several days to soften the spectacle. If the retained spectacle does not easily come away, it is best to leave it and deal with it after the next ecdysis.

Vomiting/Regurgitation

This is a particular problem in snakes. Causes include foreign bodies, parasites, dehydration, handling and environmental factors, especially incorrect temperature or inadequate water.

Long-term anorexic/cachectic species are likely to regurgitate if fed or force-fed, due to chronic changes of the gastro-intestinal tract which is no longer able to cope with solid food.

All snakes that regurgitate should be investigated. Dehydrated snakes should be treated for their dehydration and possible visceral gout (see earlier).

Endoscopy, rigid or flexible, is useful in the snake and is easily performed. The stomach and oesophagus should be examined for signs of abscesses, foreign bodies, blockages, parasites, ulceration or other problems. Enlargement of the stomach, due to hypertrophy, may require celiotomy and a sample taken for histopathology to rule out *Cryptosporidium* (Cooper and Lawton, unpublished data). Stomach washes and faecal examination should also be undertaken to rule out parasitic problems, eg. *Kalicephalus* or *Cryptosporidium.* If regurgitation and vomiting continue, a barium meal and radiography may also be helpful.

Blood samples for biochemistry may also prove useful. Table 4 lists the common sites for blood sampling Squamata; for further details see Esra *et al* (1975) and Samour *et al* (1984). Haematological and biochemistry normal values vary for each of the 6280 species of Squamata; there are also seasonal variations. Table 5 should therefore only be used as a basic guide to possible normal ranges for the Sub Orders of Sauria and Serpentes. Biochemistry normals for serpentes and sauria quoted in Table 6 should also only be used as a basic guide. The original authors (Dessauer, 1970; Frye, 1981; Lawrence, 1985; Frye, 1986; Jacobson, 1988) quoted the figures in gravimetric units which this author has converted to SI units and incorporated his own unpublished data on considered normal values.

Table 4
Sites for blood sampling.

Site	Technique	Comments
Sauria Ventral venous sinus.	This is located on the ventral mid-line aspect of the tail. Angle the needle at 45° cranially and advance to the midline aiming between the coccygeal vertebrae.	This is the vessel of choice.
Ventral vena cava.	Located in the midline of the abdominal wall.	This site is not advised as may result in large haematoma/ haemorrhage as complication.
Cardiac puncture.	May be approached from the ventral abdomen, angling needle cranially under the rib cage.	Potentially dangerous. Only advised in terminal or culled animals.
Serpentes Ventral venous sinus.	The needle is angled at 45° as described for Sauria, although it is initially placed between paired caudal scales.	Care must be taken in males not to damage the hemipenes.
Palatine veins and sub-lingual veins.	These vessels are readily seen when the mouth is open.	Sampling is easier if the reptile is sedated.
Cardiac puncture.	The heart may be palpated ventrally about 1/5 to 1/4 the distance between rostrum and cloaca.	Potentially dangerous. Only recommended in terminal or culled animals.
Jugular veins.	As per mammals.	Requires practice.

Table 5
Haematological data for Squamata.

Parameter	Units	Sauria	Serpentes
RBC	$10^6/mm^3$	0.4–2.1	0.4– 2.5
WBC	$10^3/mm^3$	12–22.5	6.7–81
Haemoglobin	g/dl	4.6–11.9	5.2–12
Haematocrit (PCV)	l/l	0.16–0.35	0.16–0.45

Table 6
Biochemical data for Squamata.

Test	Units	Sauria	Serpentes
Total protein	g/l	30—81	29—80
Uric acid	μmol/l	160—475	60—600
Urea	mmol/l	0.17—1.99	0.17—1.87
Creatinine	μmol/l	5—13	0—45
Glucose	mmol/l	3—11	0.5—6
Calcium	mmol/l	1.9—2.5	2.5—5.5
Phosphorus	mmol/l	0.6—1.66	0.9—1.85
Lactate dehydrogenase (LDH)	u/l	250—1000	30—600
Gamma glutamyltransferase (GGT)	u/l	0—10	0—15
Alkaline phosphatase (ALKP)	u/l	60—99	80—145
Aspartate aminotransferase (SGOT)	u/l	5—105	5—35
Alanine aminotransferase (ALT)	u/l	—	260
Triglycerides	μmol/l	0.6—1.2	0.6—2
Cholesterol	mmol/l	1.2—3.62	1.3—3.6

ANTIMICROBIAL AGENTS

It must be borne in mind that no antibiotics are licensed for use in reptiles in the UK, therefore particular care has to be taken when choosing an antimicrobial agent.

As reptiles are ectothermic, the temperature at which they are kept while being treated is important, as this affects the half-life of the antibiotic. Lawrence (1983) has stated that a 6°C fall in temperature can double the half-life of an antibiotic and may result in the accumulation of potentially toxic levels within the blood. It is for this reason that Table 7 lists the temperature at which the reptile should be maintained throughout the course of its antimicrobial treatment. If the reptile is kept at a temperature other than those stated, then the dose rate may be too high or even too low.

Table 7
Antimicrobial agents.

Drug	Dose	Temperature
Amikacin	2.5-5mg/kg i/m every 3rd day	25°C
Ampicillin	3-6mg/kg s/c i/m daily	26°C
Carbenicillin	200-400mg/kg i/m daily	30°C
Ceftazidime	20mg/kg i/m every 3rd day	30°C
Cefuroxime	100mg/kg i/m every 2nd day	30°C
Cephalothin	40-80mg/kg i/m every 2nd day	30°C
Cephaloridine	7mg/kg daily	24°C
Dimetridazole	40mg/kg orally every 5th day	PBT
Gentamicin	2.5mg/kg s/c every 3rd day	24°C
Kanamycin	10mg/kg i/m s/c daily	24°C
Metronidazole	100-275mg/kg orally once	PBT
Oxytetracycline	10mg/kg orally daily	26°C
Tobramycin	2mg/kg i/m daily	26°C
Trimethoprim/sulphadiazine	15mg/kg i/m daily	24°C
Tylosin	25mg/kg i/m daily	30°C

ANAESTHESIA

A full description is given by Cooper (1989) in the *Manual of Anaesthesia for Small Animal Practice.*

Sedation may be required to carry out a clinical examination, radiography or blood samples, while anaesthesia is generally required for more involved procedures and surgery (see Table 8).

It is always advisable to intubate reptiles by placing an endotracheal tube or catheter down the glottis. The latter is readily visible at the base of the tongue. It is difficult to monitor respiration and this, coupled with the fact that reptiles breathe sporadically under anaesthesia, makes it advisable to use intermittent positive pressure ventilation.

Table 8
Anaesthetic and sedative agents.

The following are recommended in Squamata.

Drug	Trade Name	Dosage	Site	Comments
Alphaxalone/ alphadolone	Saffan, Coopers Pitman-Moore.	6-9 mg/kg 9-15mg/kg	i/v i/m	Very good anaesthetic for reptiles when given i/v. I/m route less predictable.
Halothane	Halothane, RMB; Fluothane, Coopers Pitman-Moore.	1-4%	Inhalation	Induction slow, recovery slow. Contra-indicated with hepatic damage. Maintenance at 2%. Requires intermittent positive pressure ventilation.
Isoflurane	Forane, Abbots.	1-6%	Inhalation	Rapid onset, rapid recovery. Excellent muscle relaxation and good analgesia. Author's inhalation agent of choice.
Ketamine hydrochloride	Vetalar, Parke-Davis; Ketaset, Willows Francis.	20 – 100mg/kg	s/c i/m i/p	Start at lower dose rate and use incremental doses at 20-30 minute intervals until desired depth is obtained. Contra-indicated in debilitated or dehydrated reptiles.
Methoxyflurane	Metofane, C-Vet.	1-4%	Inhalation	Better analgesia than halothane, but 'hang-over' effect and prolonged recovery period. Requires positive pressure ventilation with oxygen prior to extubation.
Metomidate	Hypnodil, Janssen.	10mg/kg	i/m	Useful sedative for Serpentes. No analgesic property.
Propofol	Rapinovet, Coopers Pitman-Moore; Diprivan, ICI.	10mg/kg	i/v	Rapid onset, rapid recovery. Author's injectable agent of choice.

REFERENCES AND FURTHER READING

AHNE, W., NEUBERT, W. J., and THOMSEN, I. (1987). Reptilian viruses: isolation of myxovirus-like particles from the snake, *Elaphe oxycephala. Journal of Veterinary Medicine* **8 (34)**, 607.

BARNARD, S. M. (1986a). Color atlas of reptilian parasites Part I. Protozoans. *Compendium of Continuing Education* **8 (3)**, 145.

BARNARD, S. M. (1986b). Colour atlas of reptilian parasites Part II. Flatworms and roundworms. *Compendium of Continuing Education* **8 (4)**, 259.

BROWN, C. W. and MARTIN, R. A. (1990). Dystocia in snakes. *Compendium of Continuing Education* **12 (3)**, 361.

BUSH, M., CUSTER, R. S., SMELLER, J. M. and CHARACHE, P. (1980). Recommendations for antibiotic therapy in reptiles. The Society for the Study of Amphibians and Reptiles. In: *Contributions to Herpetology No.1. Reproductive Biology and Diseases of Captive Reptiles.* (Eds. J. B. Murphy and J. T. Collins) Cotswold Wildlife Park, Oxford.

CLARK, H. F., ANDERSEN, P. R. and LUNGER, P. D. (1979). Propagation and characterization of a C-type virus from a rhabdomyosarcoma of a corn snake. *Journal of General Virology* **43**, 673.

COOPER, J. E. (1974). Ketamine hydrochloride as an anaesthetic for East African reptiles. *Veterinary Record* **95**, 37.

COOPER, J. E. (1984). Physical influences. In: *Diseases of Amphibians and Reptiles.* (Eds. G. L. Hoff, F. L. Frye and E. R. Jacobson) Plenum Press, New York.

COOPER, J. E. (1985). The significance of bacterial isolates from reptiles. In: *Reptiles: Breeding, Behaviour and Veterinary Aspects.* (Eds. S. Townson and K. Lawrence) British Herpetological Society, London.

COOPER, J. E. (1989). Exotic animal anaesthesia. In: *Manual of Anaesthesia for Small Animal Practice.* 3rd Edn. (Ed. A. D. R. Hilbery) BSAVA, Cheltenham.

COOPER, J. E. and JACKSON, O. F. (1981). Eds. *Diseases of the Reptilia, Volumes 1 and 2.* Academic Press, London.

COOTE, J. (1985). Breeding colubrid snakes, mainly *Lampropeltis.* In: *Reptiles: Breeding, Behaviour and Veterinary Aspects.* (Eds. S. Townson and K. Lawrence) British Herpetological Society, London.

COWAN, D. F. (1968). Diseases of captive reptiles. *Journal of the American Veterinary Medical Association* **153 (7)**, 848.

DAVIES, P. M. C. (1981). Anatomy and physiology. In: *Diseases of the Reptilia Vol. 1.* (Eds. J. E. Cooper and O. F. Jackson) Academic Press, London.

DESSAUER, H. C. (1970). Blood chemistry of reptiles: physiological and evolutionary aspects. In: *Biology of the Reptilia Vol. 3.* (Eds. C. Gans and T. S. Parson) Academic Press, London.

ELKAN, E. (1981). Pathology and histopathological techniques. In: *Diseases of the Reptilia Vol. 1.* (Eds. J. E. Cooper and O. F. Jackson) Academic Press, London.

ESRA, G. N., BENIRSCHKE, K. and GRINER, L. A. (1985). Blood collecting techniques in lizards. *Journal of the American Veterinary Medical Association* **167**, 555.

FOWLER, M. E. (1986). Metabolic bone disease. In: *Zoo and Wild Animal Medicine.* 2nd Edn. (Ed. M. E. Fowler) W.B. Saunders, Philadelphia.

FRYE, F. L. (1979). Reptile medicine and husbandry. In: *Veterinary Clinics of North America, Small Animal Practice Symposium on Non-Domestic Pet Medicine.* (Ed. W. J. Boever) **9 (3)**, 415.

FRYE, F. L. (1981). Hematology. In: *Biomedical and Surgical Aspects of Captive Reptile Husbandry.* Krieger Publishing Co. Inc., Melbourne.

FRYE, F. L. (1984). Nutritional disorders in reptiles. In: *Disease of Amphibians and Reptiles.* (Eds. G. L. Hoff, F. L. Frye and E. R. Jacobson) Plenum Press, New York.

FRYE, F. L. (1986). Hematology of captive reptiles. In: *Zoo and Wild Animal Medicine.* 2nd Edn. (Ed. M. E. Fowler) W. B. Saunders, Philadelphia.

FRYE, F. L. (1989). Sexual dimorphism and identification in reptiles. In: *Current Veterinary Therapy X.* (Ed. R. W. Kirk) W. B. Saunders, Philadelphia.

HARE, T. and WOODWARD, J. (1989). *Illustrated Encyclopedia of Wildlife Vol. 26 - 28.* Orbis, London.

HESS, J. L. and RUDY, R. L. (1974). Ulcerative stomatitis in the python. *Veterinary Medicine - Small Animal Clinician* **69**, 1379.

JACKSON, O. F. (1981). Clinical aspects of diagnosis and treatment. In: *Diseases of the Reptilia Vol. 2.* (Eds. J. E. Cooper and O. F. Jackson) Academic Press, London.

JACKSON, O. F. and COOPER, J. E. (1981a). Nutritional diseases. In: *Diseases of the Reptilia Vol. 2.* (Eds. J. E. Cooper and O. F. Jackson) Academic Press, London.

JACKSON, O. F. and COOPER, J. E. (1981b). Anaesthesia and surgery. In: *Diseases of the Reptilia Vol. 2.* (Eds. J. E. Cooper and O. F. Jackson) Academic Press, London.

JACOBSON, E. R. (1980). Necrotizing mycotic dermatitis in snakes: clinical and pathological features. *Journal of the American Veterinary Medical Association* **177 (9)**, 838.

JACOBSON, E. R. (1988). Use of chemotherapeutics in reptile medicine. In: *Exotic Animals.* (Eds. E. R. Jacobson and G. V. Kollias) Churchill Livingstone, New York.

JACOBSON, E. R. (1988). Evaluation of the reptile patient. In: *Exotic Animals.* (Eds. E. R. Jacobson and G. V. Kollias) Churchill Livingstone, New York.

JACOBSON, E. R., GASKIN, J. M., PAGE, D., IVERSON, W. O. and JOHNSON, J. W. (1981). Illness associated with paramyxo-like virus infection in a zoological collection of snakes. *Journal of the American Veterinary Medical Association* **179 (11)**, 1227.

JARCHOW, J. L. (1988). Hospital care of the reptile patient. In: *Exotic Animals.* (Eds. E. R. Jacobson and G. V. Kollias) Churchill Livingstone, New York.

JONES, S. and LLEWELLYN, P. J. (1989). Precepts for the successful husbandry of lizards and snakes: how best to avoid disease. *The Veterinary Annual* **29**, 294.

LAWRENCE, K.(1983). The use of antibiotics in reptiles: a review. *Journal of Small Animal Practice* **24**, 741.

LAWRENCE, K. (1985). An introduction to haematology and the blood chemistry of the Reptilia. In: *Reptiles; Breeding, Behaviour and Veterinary Aspects.* (Eds. S. Townson and K. Lawrence) British Herpetological Society, London.

LAWRENCE, K. and JACKSON, O. F. (1983). Alphaxalone/alphadolone anaesthesia in reptiles. *Veterinary Record* **112**, 26.

LAWTON, M. P. C. (1989). Neurological problems of exotic species. In: *Manual of Small Animal Neurology.* (Ed. S. J. Wheeler) BSAVA, Cheltenham.

LAWTON, M. P. C. (1991). Reptiles. In: *Practical Animal Handling.* (Eds. R. Anderson and A. T. B. Edney) Pergamon, Oxford.

MARCUS, L. E. (1980). Bacterial infection in reptiles. Society for the Study of Amphibians and Reptiles. In: *Contributions to Herpetology No. 1. Reproductive Biology and Disease in Captive Reptiles.* (Eds. J. B. Murphy and J. T. Collins) Cotswold Wildlife Park, Oxford.

MARCUS, L. E. (1981). *Veterinary Biology and Medicine of Captive Amphibians and Reptiles.* Lea and Febiger, Philadelphia.

MATEVSKY, S. and MUTAFOVA, T. (1987). Effects of Ivomec on some helminths and ectoparasites of hedgehogs, snakes and tortoises. *Erkrankungen der Zootiere* **29**, 367.

MILLICHAMP, N. J. (1988). Surgical techniques in reptiles. In: *Exotic Animals.* (Eds. E. R. Jacobson and G. V. Kollias) Churchill Livingstone, New York.

OBST, F. J., RICHTER, K. and JACOB, U. (1988). *The Complete Illustrated Atlas of Reptiles and Amphibians for the Terrarium.* (Translated by U. E. Friese).(Ed. (English language edition) J. G. Walls) TFH Publications, Berkshire.

RUSSO, E. A. (1987). Diagnosis and treatment of lumps and bumps in snakes. *Compendium of Continuing Education* **9 (8)**, 795.

SAMOUR, H. J., RISLEY, D., MARCH, T., SAVAGE, B., NIEVA, O. and JONES, D. M. (1984). Blood sampling techniques in reptiles. *Veterinary Record* **114**, 472.

TEARE, J. A. and BUSH, M. (1983). Toxicity and efficacy of ivermectin in chelonians. *Journal of the American Veterinary Medical Association* **183**, 1195.

TOWNSEND, C. R. and COLE, C. J. (1985). Additional notes on requirements of captive whiptail lizards *(Cnemidophorus)* with emphasis on ultra-violet radiation. *Zoo Biology* **4**, 49.

WALLACH, J. D. (1979). The mechanics of nutrition for exotic pets. In: *Symposium on Non-Domestic Pet Medicine - Veterinary Clinics of North America, Small Animal Practice.* (Ed. W. J. Boever) **9 (3)**, 405.

ZWART, P. (1980). Nutrition and nutritional disturbances in reptiles. *Proceedings of the European Herpetological Symposium.* Cotswold Wildlife Park, Oxford.

CHAPTER EIGHTEEN

AMPHIBIANS

David L Williams MA VetMB MRCVS

Amphibians first evolved from primitive fishes around 350 million years ago. About 4,000 species exist today and these can be divided into three groups:

a.   Anura (tailless as adults, including frogs and toads)

b.   Caudata (adults with tails, including newts and salamanders)

c.   Apoda (tropical legless species)

These diverse animals have many features in common (Fraser, 1987), several of which are important to bear in mind when dealing with clinical cases. They are ectothermic (cold-blooded) and, as such, activity, food intake and drug metabolism change markedly with the ambient temperature — as is the case with other lower vertebrates and invertebrates. Perhaps the most important unusual feature is the amphibian skin. This is usually moist and water-permeable, often covered with a layer of mucus. Damage from handling without adequate lubrication can occur easily. Drugs and toxins can readily be absorbed by this route and thus the amphibian is even more sensitive to adverse environmental conditions than most other lower vertebrates.

HOUSING

Requirements for specific species will be covered below but several general points can be made concerning temperature and general accommodation. Apart from the completely aquatic species such as *Xenopus* (the clawed toad) and *Ambystoma mexicanum* (the axolotl) most amphibians require a vivarium with some land area and some shallow water. Adequate cover is essential to provide hiding places. Because little is known about the exact requirements of many of these animals, an environment with variations in microclimate — relative humidity, temperature and light intensity — should be designed so that the animal has the opportunity to regulate its own surroundings. These considerations go a long way to reducing the non-specific 'maladaptation syndrome' often seen in newly captive lower vertebrates (Cowan, 1968).

Some herpetologists prefer to design semi-natural habitats which are aesthetically pleasing but they are generally more difficult to clean than 'clinical' environments and provide more obstacles to rapid and efficient catching up of specimens. Most amphibians do well with a constant 12 hour light/12 hour dark photoperiodicity. Water quality is of prime importance and there are many similarities in this respect between amphibians and fish. This is especially true in the case of immature forms such as tadpoles.

FEEDING

There is a wide spectrum of size and behaviour in captive amphibians and this is reflected by differing feeding requirements. However, some general points can be made. Almost all adult amphibians are carnivorous and most should be fed earthworms and mealworms if aquatic, crickets, maggots or baby mice if terrestrial, or flies on the wing, from *Drosophila* to *Stomoxys* depending on size, if arboreal. Many can be trained to accept non-living food such as trout starter pellets (especially valuable in aquatic species) and raw meat or dog and cat food. Larval stages require vegetation in the water and later, when becoming carnivorous, small aquatic prey such as *Daphnia*.

BEHAVIOUR

While most amphibians are initially timid creatures many will become accustomed to captivity, to the presence of humans and to the feeding of dead food. Toads especially will become tame enough to accept food from the hand. The behavioural requirements for cover, water depth and climbing facilities (the latter especially in arboreal species) should be researched before the animal is brought into captivity.

BREEDING

Some amphibians are easy to sex because of sexual characteristics such as crest colouration in newts or forelimb gland swelling in toads but many of these features are only seen during the breeding season and a number of amphibians do not have externally identifiable male and female features.

Many of the temperate amphibians start breeding after a period of reduced temperature while tropical species will not breed unless the temperature is high enough. Seasonal breeding is the rule in most amphibians but in several species after a year or so in captivity this periodicity is lost. The vast majority of amphibians need to return to water to breed.

While some amphibians such as *Xenopus* have simple courtships, most terrestrial anurans have complicated mating behaviours with vocalisation, male competition and extensive physical contact (amplexus) followed by external fertilisation either with free sperm or a spermatophore picked up by the female. Hormonal induction of breeding can be performed with gonadotrophins as can artificial insemination in some species. A useful review of practical information on breeding in a number of species has been produced by the Institute of Animal Resources in America (ILAR, 1974). Nace (1977) should also be consulted.

COMMONLY KEPT AMPHIBIA

As amphibians may be found from the heat of tropical rainforests through to the Arctic Circle and from highly oxygenated streams to stagnant bogs, their environmental requirements in captivity will clearly be very varied and, as with any animal, attention to their natural habitat will allow the correct conditions to be set up. This is true whether in a vivarium in the home (Mattison, 1987) or a situation where animals are kept for experimental purposes (Nace, 1970). Some commonly kept amphibians are noted below, together with certain of our native species.

Xenopus laevis — African clawed toad. Commonly kept as a laboratory animal, care is very simple with an aquarium — 20cm warm water — and feeding twice a week. Tadpoles of *Xenopus* are unusual in that they feed on suspended food particles such as liquefied fish food.

Pipa pipa — Surinam toad. In the same family as *Xenopus*. An unusual but fascinating appearance with a triangular head and many small protuberances on the dorsal surfaces. Needs slightly acid water at around 26° –30°C, with ample plant material. Regularly eats live fish but also strips of meat if agitated to simulate live prey. Reproduction is unusual in that, after a complex courtship, eggs are deposited on the female's back and membranous cells, each with one egg, develop in the skin of the dorsum, through which the young toads emerge to 'hatch' after metamorphosis.

Bombina spp. — Fire-bellied toads. *B. orientalis* from South-east Asia is very colourful and requires a temperature of around 25°C with a 10° drop in winter and will readily breed. Others, such as *B. bombina* from Eastern Europe, are less colourful but will tolerate outside temperatures provided that a hibernation site is available.

Rana temporaria — European common frog. A less aquatic species, requiring damp vegetation and relatively low temperatures. Its North American cousin, the leopard frog *(R. pipiens),* needs slightly warmer conditions and is kept as a research animal, particularly to study Lucké virus-induced tumours.

Dendrobates spp. — Poison arrow frogs. Exceptionally colourful animals from Central and South America. They possess a highly toxic skin secretion which, although not dangerous unless ingested or injected, should dissuade one from handling the animals except with gloves. They require abundant tall vegetation, a high relative humidity and temperature around 30°C. *D. histrionicus* (a red and black species) is commonly available but does not do well in captivity, while *D. auratus* (the green poison arrow frog) is very easy to keep.

Bufo bufo — European common toad. Long-lived in captivity at temperatures not higher than 20°—23°C and is often only a semi-captive animal in a greenhouse or garden pond. Its North American counterpart, *B. americanus,* makes a good pet but is not often available, while *B. marinus,* the giant or 'cane' toad from Central America, is easily obtained but often dies after a period of maladaptation to captivity. Those which survive the first few months are very long-lived at medium temperatures and with good ventilation.

Hyla spp. — Tree frogs. A very large group of animals well worth the attention of the herpetologist. Most are arboreal and require good climbing vegetation and, while they do require reasonably warm environments, they are generally quite hardy. As with many other taxonomically related amphibians, these species range from tropical to temperate environments and temperature should be adjusted accordingly. The White's tree frog is the easiest species for the novice.

Ceratophrys spp. — Horned toads (see Figure 1). Together with the unrelated but visually similar *Pyxicephalus* species these toads have huge appetites and catholic tastes making them excellent captive animals. They are solitary and require leaf mould or sand into which to burrow and a temperature of around 25°—30°C.

Ambystoma mexicanum — Axolotl. This gilled amphibian is well known as the unmetamorphosed larva of the Mexican salamander, capable, in common with only a few other species, of reproduction in its larval state. It can easily be kept in an aquarium at anything between 10° — 25°C and will, with training, take dead food such as earthworms, meat or even cat food. Axolotls are large and clumsy and can be aggressive so overcrowding should be avoided.

Ambystoma tigrinum — Tiger salamander. A typical large salamander with colourful yellow bars or stripes. Excellent captives, living at between 15° — 20°C in damp moss or similar ground vegetation. These predominantly temperate conditions pertain to many of the salamanders although a few species, such as *Pleurodeles waltli*, do best in entirely aquatic displays.

Further information is available from several sources (Gibbs *et al*, 1966; Mattison, 1987; Smith, 1973; Verhoeff-de Fremery and Griffin, 1987; Verhoeff-de Fremery *et al*, 1987).

HANDLING

The mucus-covered skin of amphibians can make handling difficult for the operator and potentially hazardous for the animal. Hands should be wetted before attempting to catch the animal but not washed with soap or detergent. Often, plastic gloves are useful if the animal is to be apprehended directly and a palming technique should be used, either catching small frogs in the cup of the hand against the side of the cage or aquarium, or with larger species such as *Xenopus* catching the head between the first two fingers as it crosses the palm, followed by the thumb gently restraining the neck. In this way the forward straining movement of the escaping animal will only serve to push it further into the finger grip.

Other methods of restraint include capture in fine nylon nets but care must be exercised to avoid trauma. All amphibians can be transported in cooled, adequately ventilated waterproof containers with damp vegetation or sponge, apart from immature forms and the axolotl which, by virtue of its gill-mediated respiration, requires immersion in water.

APPROACH TO THE CLINICAL CASE

First the animal concerned should be identified. Several books can be invaluable in this regard, especially if the client is unsure as to the species or its requirements in captivity (Cochran, 1961; Mattison, 1987). History taking should concentrate on environmental conditions and any changes noted in general activity or feeding behaviour. Since environmental mismanagement is at the root of so many amphibian diseases, particular note should be made of temperature and temperature fluctuations, relative humidity, water quality and general cage hygiene. At this point, emphasis can be made on the importance of record keeping to facilitate observation, recording of the condition of the animal, its activity and feeding patterns and any untoward fluctuations in environmental conditions. If this can be encouraged in, for instance, the schoolboy bringing tadpoles in a jar, it will foster this good habit as the young herpetologist progresses to less familiar species.

As with any animal, full clinical examination should be performed on presentation. Examination of the animal in its environment before capture is mandatory. Many amphibians exhibit considerable changes in behaviour and physical characteristics, such as an increase in skin secretions, after a few minutes of attempted capture. Careful examination of the skin is important but a well ordered examination of orifices and sense organs will help ensure that no lesion is missed. Further techniques which may assist in diagnosis include bacteriological and mycological culture, faecal examination for parasites and skin scrapings or biopsies. Haematology may prove useful and some normal data are available (Fowler, 1986). *Post-mortem* examination is extremely useful in diagnosis and refuting or confirming clinical impressions in the living animal.

DISEASES

Useful general references are Anver and Pond (1984), Fowler (1986), Hoff *et al* (1984), Marcus (1981) and Reichenbach-Klinke and Elkan (1965).

Bacterial disease

Bacterial infections are very common in amphibians because of the intimate association with their aquatic environment and their thin and easily traumatised integument. Infections may be restricted to the skin, with ulcerative dermatitis, or may lead to a bacteraemia or septicaemia, especially in immunosuppressed animals (Glorioso *et al*, 1974b). Special considerations when diagnosing these infections include the use of low temperature incubation. Many of the organisms involved will grow well on blood agar, but only at $23^\circ - 25^\circ$C and not at temperatures used for mammalian pathogens. Also, many of these bacteria are either skin contaminants from the environment or normal commensals on the skin and only cause disease when other stressors, such as overcrowding, malnutrition or concomitant disease occur (Glorioso *et al*, 1974a). Poor tank hygiene will allow a build-up of these organisms and frequent water changes and cleaning away slime from the tank will lower the pathogen load. Steps should be taken to minimise trauma which can cause breaches in the integument through which bacteria can enter.

Aeromonas (Boyer *et al*, 1971; Hird *et al*, 1981; Hubbard, 1981; Shotts, 1984). The most common bacterial infection is that caused by *Aeromonas hydrophila.* This condition is often known as 'red leg' because of the intense hyperaemic and haemorrhagic focal lesions mainly on the hind limbs. In classical 'red leg' many animals may be found dead without having exhibited any clinical signs, while others may have terminal neurological signs such as incoordination, spasms or vomiting. In these cases *post-mortem* examination will often reveal hepatomegaly with a dark hepatic parenchyma and, sometimes, necrotic foci in other organs and musculature.

Isolation of *A. hydrophila* is not a sufficient criterion for a diagnosis, since the organism can be cultured from many healthy amphibians and may even be a commensal in the gut. Any skin lesion is thus likely to be colonised by these organisms whether or not they are the prime, or even contributary, cause of the lesion. Indeed, classical 'red leg' with death from septicaemia is uncommon compared with the prevalence of *A. hydrophila* isolation. Other bacteria, such as *Citrobacter, Proteus* and *Flavobacterium* spp., may be important in some outbreaks and such mixed isolates can prove difficult to interpret.

Figure 1
Ceratophrys horned frog.

Figure 2
Xenopus laevis with mycobacterial
infection giving ulcerated granulomatous
mass on hindlimb.
(Photograph courtesy of the Edward Elkan Collection.)

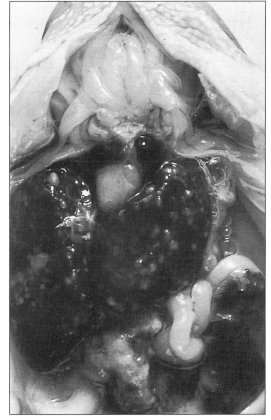

Figure 3
Hepatic phycomycosis in a Hyla frog.
Post-mortem specimen showing white fungal
masses in the liver parenchyma.
(Photograph courtesy of the Edward Elkan Collection.)

Amphibian **chlamydiosis,** caused by *Chlamydia psittaci,* is identical in clinical presentation to aeromoniasis with focal erythematous lesions and septicaemia. The similarity shows the importance of culture and biopsy or necropsy, since the histological features of chlamydiosis, while similar to those of aeromoniasis, include hepatic pyogranulomas with multiple intracytoplasmic inclusion bodies which are characteristic of the disease (Newcomer *et al*, 1982).

A certain degree of prophylaxis against bacterial skin lesions and septicaemia can be achieved by maintaining totally aquatic species in 0.4% sodium chloride solution; during epizootics this concentration may be raised to 4%. Other workers have suggested using 1:5,000 copper sulphate or 1:1,000 potassium permanganate, but these are empirical concentrations.

Treatment of affected animals and those in contact, can be attempted with tetracyclines, gentamicin or, possibly, chloramphenicol. Identification of the pathogen and antibiotic sensitivity of the isolate is mandatory, since many bacteria appear to be relatively resistant. Indiscriminate use of antibiotics in water is not to be recommended. Dose rates can be adhered to by gavage feeding by orogastric intubation and, if the animal is to be treated topically, it is preferable to place it in a small treatment tank for a predetermined length of time rather than applying drugs to the whole tank (Gibbs, 1963).

Salmonella. A number of different serotypes of *Salmonella* have been isolated from amphibians without clinical signs both in the wild, presumably from sewage contamination, and also from animals in aquaria (Scharma *et al*, 1974). Although these are probably of little significance to the animal, they should alert owners and veterinary surgeons to the zoonotic potential of organisms from these animals.

Diplobacterium ranarum is another bacterium thought to be merely a contaminant of many amphibian environments or a skin commensal in some individuals, only causing disease in stressed or injured animals, when septicaemia can supervene. Ulceration, enteritis and haemorrhagic exudates in the dorsal lymph sacs are common findings (Elkan, 1976).

Pseudomonas reptivora has been isolated from mud puppies *(Necturus maculosus)* with cutaneous hyperaemia and gill necrosis. Treatment with furantoin topically or chloramphenicol by stomach tube, has been successful (Marcus, 1981).

Mycobacterial disease. Tuberculosis, due to atypical mycobacteria, occurs in amphibians (Brownstein, 1984; Shiveley *et al*, 1981), either causing local skin lesions with entry of group IV mycobacteria through traumatic injuries, or resulting in internal tuberculous granulomas from ingested organisms. Skin lesions are often ulcerated masses which may invade muscles and surrounding tissue (see Figure 2). In general, it is considered that these lesions occur in immunocompromised amphibians and, as such, in-contact animals are not necessarily at risk. However, there is increasing medical interest in these atypical mycobacteria since they can cause lesions in humans, among which 'aquarist's nodules' are the most common, although primary pulmonary lesions have occurred. Affected animals should be culled on public health as well as animal welfare grounds.

Viruses

The Lucké tumour virus is an important cause of morbidity and mortality in captive and free-living leopard frogs *(Rana pipiens)* and has been the subject of much experimental investigation. Renal adenocarcinoma is always the cause of death in these cases but often no clinical signs are seen until late stage metastasis (McKinnel, 1984).

Other viruses of amphibians include the polyhedral cytoplasmic viruses, of little clinical importance apart from strains which are highly pathogenic to bullfrog tadpoles causing oedema and extensive internal necrosis.

Fungi

As with bacterial infections, the aquatic environment of amphibians is crucial in the pathogenesis of mycoses (Frank, 1976). Totally aquatic amphibians may, like fish, be affected with saprolegniasis and ichthyosporidiosis, while those which are predominantly terrestrial may be infected with the soil saprophytes causing chromomycosis and phycomycosis.

Saprolegnia causes grey-white mycelial mats on the skin starting at the head, with necrosis of underlying tissue. The condition should be treated with 1:15000 solution of malachite green for 15 seconds a day for 5 days or 1:2000 copper sulphate for 2 minutes a day for 5 days.

Ichthyosporidiosis is rarely seen in amphibians but, when it occurs, has the same appearance as in fish, with small granulomata in the skin and often throughout internal organs.

Chromomycosis is a chronic debilitating disease characterised clinically by weight loss and cutaneous ulcers with intense visceral granulomatosis as the main finding *post mortem.* The causative organisms are conidia-forming, brown, pigmented fungi. Grossly, the lesions are similar to those of mycobacteriosis but can easily be distinguished by detection of fungal hyphae rather than acid fast bacilli. Rapid diagnosis is by demonstration of pigmented fungal hyphae in a wet mount from a cutaneous ulcer (Rush *et al,* 1974; Schmidt, 1984).

Phycomycosis is caused by *Mucor*-like organisms and at *post-mortem* examination presents as white hepatic and splenic masses (see Figure 3). The organism in this instance is spherical and unpigmented. Treatment is not recommended for either of these soil-borne conditions. They are potential zoonoses and are not readily cured in affected animals. If treatment is attempted, drugs such as amphotericin B or nystatin might be useful.

Parasitic diseases (Kaplan, 1973).

Because so many parasites use the amphibian as a final or intermediate host in a complex lifecycle, there are considerable differences in parasite burden between captive-bred and wild caught animals. Clearly, captive-bred animals, such as those in laboratories, will only have parasites with direct life-cycles while those from the wild will have a much more varied parasitic fauna.

Protozoa.   Protozoan parasites appear to be less of a problem in amphibians than in reptiles, but amoeboid, ciliate or flagellate organisms may be found in the gastro-intestinal tract of normal and ill amphibians (Frank, 1984). Oral metronidazole (150mg/kg) repeated as necessary can be effective against such protozoal infections.

The dinoflagellate *Oodinium,* found on fish skin, has also been reported in aquatic amphibians and may cause mortality in captive newts. Haemosporidia may be identified in blood films. They do not cause clinical signs in the majority of cases although anaemia has been occasionally reported. Microsporidia such as *Plistophora* and *Glugea* have been reported as causing high mortality in captive wild caught common toads. Of the Haplosporidia, several cause skin nodules, including *Dermocystidium* in newts and *Dermosporidium* in tree frogs.

Nematodes.   Numerous helminth species are to be found in the intestinal tract of amphibians including several species of ascaridoid nematodes and *Capillaria* species (Kaplan, 1973). Often burdens are not sufficient to cause clinical signs but if weight loss is noted with high egg counts, levamisole (Nilverm, Coopers Pitman-Moore) (10mg/kg by injection) or oxfendazole (Systamex, Coopers Pitman-Moore) (5mg/kg) may be given. Rhabditid nematodes are extremely common in the lungs and rarely cause lesions except in very heavy infestations. Filarial nematodes are found in the cardiovascular system and can cause skin nodules, as can dermal capillariasis.

Trematodes. Of the monogenetic trematodes only some species associated with the urinary bladder are of importance as findings at *post-mortem* examination. Digenetic trematodes, often found in wild caught amphibians, include adults of species inhabiting intestine, oral cavity, urinary bladder and lungs. The larval metacercarial forms are of more clinical significance as they can invade organs such as the eyes, heart and pericardium and skin. Among the lesions caused are abnormal pigmentation, granulomas and vesicular skin disease in tadpoles.

Cestodes. Adult tapeworms can cause intestinal obstruction with either gradual weight loss or sudden foreign body obstruction and death. Bunamide at 50mg/kg or nicosamide at 160mg/kg have been used to treat cestode infestations (Brooks, 1984).

Other diseases (Cosgrove and Anderson, 1984; Cooper, 1984).

Management related changes. As has been emphasised earlier, many diseases in amphibians arise because of inappropriate environmental conditions. If problems are recurring it is always best to see the vivarium or aquarium in the home, rather than the animal presented in isolation in the surgery. Emphasis should be placed on providing a range of micro-environments with gradients of temperature and differences in vegetation so that the animal can find its own preferred microhabitat and move around as its environmental requirements change diurnally and through the year.

Diet-related disease. Metamorphosis failure is normal in the axolotl and in certain other species, but not in most amphibians. The diet may be deficient in iodine or goitrogens may be present precluding proper iodine metabolism.

Bone deformities are seen occasionally related to vitamin or mineral deficient diets but rarely is the deficiency well characterised. A varying diet, or one of fresh commercial trout starter pellets if taken, will prevent dietary deficiencies and if bone abnormalities occur calcium and vitamin D supplements should be given.

Poor skin sloughing may also be related to dietary deficiencies, as may claw abnormalities in species such as *Xenopus.*

Miscellaneous conditions

Rectal prolapse is not uncommon in amphibians and may be related to diet. Withdrawing food until the prolapse reduces itself is reported to be sufficient for resolution in about one week but the animal should be isolated in a tank where the prolapsed tissue cannot become traumatised. Replacement of the prolapse with a blunt probe and placement of a purse string suture may be necessary.

Tympany can occur in aquatic amphibians caused either by intragastric fermentation or simply by the animal swallowing air. While many of these cases recover spontaneously some may need removal of air with a stomach tube or transabdominal needle.

Anasarca or hydrops occurs sporadically in anurans. Lymph accumulates in the dorsal lymph sacs and sometimes in the coelom. The aetiology is unknown and fluid accumulates again after aspiration.

Apart from the renal adenocarcinoma of *Rana pipiens,* caused by the Lucké tumour herpes virus, **spontaneous tumours** in amphibians occur only rarely and most have been single case reports in the literature. The majority involve the integument but since so many other infectious and parasitic agents cause dermal nodules, biopsy is mandatory for a diagnosis (Balls and Clothier, 1974; Khudoley and Mizigirurev, 1980).

Trauma

The sensitive skin of amphibians is very prone to traumatic injury. Abrasions should be bathed in, or sprayed with, 2% sodium chloride solution and cleaned with 0.1% cetrimide or oxytetracycline solution. Lacerations may be sutured with 4/0—6/0 vicryl. Animals should be kept in a bath of normal saline until healing has occurred, as this will help prevent intercurrent infection.

DRUG ADMINISTRATION

The common practice of attempting drug therapy with dissolved agents in the water should be used much less frequently than it is, apart from topical administration of agents such as sodium chloride. In particular, dissolved oxytetracycline should be avoided since it can cause skin irritation.

Most agents can be given by the oral or intramuscular route. Doses are given below although many of these are empirical and reactions may vary between species and at different temperatures.

Drug	Dose	Route	Condition
Tetracycline HCl	150mg/kg for 5—7days	orally	bacterial diseases
Gentamicin	1.3mg/l water for 7days	bath bid	bacterial dermatoses
Metronidazole	150mg/kg repeated	orally	protozoan parasites
Levamisole	10mg/kg	i/m	helminthiasis
Oxfendazole	5mg/kg	orally	helminthiasis

ANAESTHESIA AND SURGERY (Kaplan, 1971)

Aquatic amphibia are best anaesthetised with either **tricaine methane sulphonate** (MS222, Sandoz) or **benzocaine** (Cooper, 1989). The latter is quite acceptable and very much less expensive. **Halothane** or other inhalation agents can be bubbled through the water and, with terrestrial amphibia, halothane or **methoxyflurane** vapour can be used as long as the animal does not come in contact with the liquid anaesthetic . **Ketamine** (Vetalar, Parke-Davis), (50mg/kg), can also be used by intramuscular injection into the hind limb, but MS222 or benzocaine are the more simple and more controllable alternatives.

MS222 is used at a dilution of 1:2500 in water and benzocaine at about the same concentration but dissolved first in a small amount of acetone which is then added to the large volume of water. The animal should be watched as it is induced in water up to its nostrils, which may take up to 30 minutes. After this the animal can be removed from the induction tank and laid on a damp cool towel. Depth of anaesthesia can be varied by syringing either oxygenated water or anaesthetic solution onto the animal. Axolotls or larval amphibians with gills should not be kept out of water for more than a few minutes.

The variety and complexity of surgical procedures attempted on amphibians are only limited by the surgeon's expertise and enterprise. Biopsies are simple and often diagnostically rewarding. Exploratory laparotomies are possible but one should take care not to perforate the large ventral vein in the midline. Amputations and excision of abscesses are likewise feasible but at all times the maintenance of a moist, cool, well anaesthetised patient should be a priority. Limb regeneration can occur in animals after traumatic or elective amputation.

EUTHANASIA

The preferred method of euthanasia for amphibia is by overdose of barbiturate by the intracardiac or intracoelomic route. A sharp blow to the head can be used, but decapitation, freezing or pithing with a needle inserted into the foramen magnum should not now be used (UFAW/WSPA, 1989).

REFERENCES

ANVER, M. R. and POND, C. L. (1984). Biology and diseases of amphibians. In: *Laboratory Animal Medicine.* (Eds. J. G. Fox, B. J. Cohen and F. M. Loew) Academic Press, New York.

BALLS, M. and CLOTHIER, R. H. (1974). Spontaneous tumours in amphibia. *Oncology* **29**, 501.

BOYER, C. I., BLACKLER, K. and DELANNEY, L. E. (1971). *Aeromonas hydrophila* infection in the Mexican axolotl, *Siredon mexicanum. Laboratory Animal Science* **21**, 372.

BROOKS, D. R. (1984). Platyhelminths. In: *Diseases of Amphibians and Reptiles.* (Eds. G. L. Hoff, F. L. Frye and E. R. Jacobson) Plenum Press, New York.

BROWNSTEIN, D. G. (1984). Mycobacteriosis. In: *Diseases of Amphibians and Reptiles.* (Eds. G. L. Hoff, F. L. Frye and E. R. Jacobson) Plenum Press, New York.

COCHRAN, D. M. (1961). *Living Amphibians of the World.* Doubleday Inc, New York.

COOPER, J. E. (1984). Physical influences. In: *Diseases of Amphibians and Reptiles.* (Eds. G. L. Hoff, F. L. Frye and E. R. Jacobson) Plenum Press, New York.

COOPER, J. E. (1989). Anaesthesia of exotic species. In: *Manual of Anaesthesia for Small Animal Practice.* (Ed. A. D. R. Hilbery) BSAVA, Cheltenham.

COSGROVE, G. E. and ANDERSON M. P. (1984). Aging and degenerative diseases. In: *Diseases of Amphibians and Reptiles.* (Eds. G. L. Hoff, F. L. Frye and E. R. Jacobson) Plenum Press, New York.

COWAN, D. F. (1968). Diseases of captive reptiles. *Journal of the American Veterinary Medical Association* **153**, 848.

ELKAN, E. (1976). Pathology of Amphibia. In: *Physiology of the Amphibia Vol 3.* (Ed. B. Lofts) Academic Press, New York.

FOWLER, M. E. (1986). Amphibians. In: *Zoo and Wild animal Medicine.* 2nd Edn. (Ed. M.E. Fowler) W. B. Saunders, Philadelphia.

FRANK, W. (1976). Mycotic infections in amphibians and reptiles. In: *Wildlife Diseases.* (Ed. L.A. Page) Plenum Press, New York.

FRANK, W. (1984). Non-hemoparasitic protozoans. In: *Diseases of Amphibians and Reptiles.* (Eds. G. L. Hoff, F. L. Frye and E. R. Jacobson) Plenum Press, New York.

FRAZER, J. F. D. (1987). Introduction to amphibians. In: *The UFAW Handbook on the Care and Management of Laboratory Animals.* 6th Edn. (Ed. T. Poole) Longman, Harlow.

GIBBS, E. L. (1963). An effective treatment for red-leg disease in *Rana pipiens. Laboratory Animal Care* **13**, 781.

GIBBS, E. L., GIBBS, T. J. and VAN DYCK, P. C. (1966). *Rana pipiens* in health and disease. *Laboratory Animal Care* **16**, 142.

GLORIOSO, J. C., AMBORSKI, R. L., LARKIN, J. M., AMBORSKI, G. F. and CULLEY, D. C. (1974a). Laboratory identification of bacterial pathogens of aquatic animals. *American Journal of Veterinary Research* **35**, 447

GLORIOSO, J. C., AMBORSKI, R. L., LARKIN, J. M., AMBORSKI, G. F. and CULLEY, D. C. (1974b). Microbiological studies on septicemic bullfrogs. *American Journal of Veterinary Research* **35**, 1241.

HIRD, D. W., DIESCH, S. L., MCKINNEL, R. G., GORHAM, E., MARTIN, F. B., KURTZ, S. W. and DUBROVOLNY, C. (1981). *Aeromonas hydrophila* in wild-caught frogs and tadpoles *(Rana pipiens)* in Minnesota. *Laboratory Animal Science* **31**, 166.

HOFF, G. L., FRYE, F. L. and JACOBSON, E. R. (1984). Eds. *Diseases of Amphibians and Reptiles.* Plenum Press, New York.

HUBBARD, G. B. (1981). *Aeromonas hydrophila* infection in *Xenopus laevis. Laboratory Animal Science* **31**, 297.

ILAR (Institute of Animal Resources) (1974). *Amphibians. Guidelines for the Breeding, Care, and Management of Laboratory Animals.* Report of the Subcommittee on Amphibian Standards, Committee on Standards. National Academy of Sciences, Washington DC.

KAPLAN, H.M. (1971). Anesthesia in amphibians and reptiles. *Federal Proceedings* **28**, 1541.

KAPLAN, H.M. (1973). Parasites of laboratory reptiles and amphibians. In: *Parasites of Laboratory Animals.* (Ed. R.J. Flynn) Iowa State Press, Ames.

KHUDOLEY, V. V. and MIZIGIRUREV, I. V. (1980). On spontaneous skin tumours in amphibia. *Neoplasma* **27**, 289.

MARCUS, L. C. (1981). *Veterinary Biology and Medicine of Captive Amphibians and Reptiles.* Lea and Febiger, Philadelphia.

MATTISON, C. (1987). *The Care of Reptiles and Amphibians in Captivity.* Revised 2nd Edn. Blandford Press, Poole.

MCKINNEL, R. G. (1984). Lucké tumour of frogs. In: *Diseases of Amphibians and Reptiles* (Eds. G. L. Hoff, F. L. Frye and E. R. Jacobson) Plenum Press, New York.

NACE, G. W. (1970). The use of amphibians in biomedical research. In: *Animal Models for Biomedical Research III.* National Academy Science, Washington DC.

NACE, G. W. (1977). Breeding amphibians in captivity. *International Zoo Yearbook* **17**, 44.

NEWCOMER, C. E., ANVER M. R., SIMMONS, J. L., WILCKE, B. W. Jr. and NACE, G. W. (1982). Spontaneous and experimental infections of *Xenopus laevis* with *Chlamydia psittaci. Laboratory Animal Science* **32**, 680.

REICHENBACH-KLINKE, H. and ELKAN, E. (1965). *The Principal Diseases of Lower Vertebrates. II: Diseases of Amphibians.* Academic Press, London.

RUSH, H. G., ANVER, M. R. and BENEKE, E. S. (1974). Systemic chromomycosis in *Rana pipiens. Laboratory Animal Science* **24**, 646.

SCHARMA, V. K., KAURA, T. K. and SINGH, I. P. (1974). Frogs as carriers of *Salmonella* and *Edwardsiella. Antonie van Leeuwenhoek* **40**, 171.

SCHMIDT, R. E. (1984). Amphibian chromomycosis. In: *Diseases of Amphibians and Reptiles.* (Eds. G. L. Hoff, F. L. Frye and E. R. Jacobson) Plenum Press, New York.

SHIVELEY, J. N., SONGER, J. G., PRCHAL, S., KEASEY, M. S. and THOEN, C. O. (1981). *Mycobacterium marinum* infection in Bufonidae. *Journal of Wildlife Diseases* **17**, 3.

SHOTTS, E. B. (1984). Aeromonas. In: *Diseases of Amphibians and Reptiles.* (Eds. G. L. Hoff, F. L. Frye and E. R. Jacobson) Plenum Press, New York.

SMITH, M. (1973). *The British Amphibians and Reptiles.* 5th Edn (revised by A. d'A. Bellairs and J. F. D. Frazer) Collins, London.

UFAW/WSPA (Universities Federation for Animal Welfare/ World Society for the Protection of Animals) (1989). *Euthanasia of Amphibians and Reptiles.* Report of a Joint UFAW/WSPA Working Party. Universities Federation for Animal Welfare, Potters Bar.

VERHOEFF-DE FREMERY, R. and GRIFFIN, J. (1987). Anurans (frogs and toads). In: *The UFAW Handbook on the Care and Management of Laboratory Animals.* (Ed. T. Poole) Longman, Harlow.

VERHOEFF-DE FREMERY, R., GRIFFIN, J. and MACGREGOR (1987). Urodeles (newts and salamanders). In: *The UFAW Handbook on the Care and Management of Laboratory Animals.* 6th Edn. (Ed. T. Poole) Longman, Harlow.

CHAPTER NINETEEN   # ORNAMENTAL FISH

Peter W Scott MSc BVSc MRCVS MIBiol

Fishkeeping has a long history which goes back to the Egyptians, who revered the mormyrids and kept tilapia for food, the T'ang Dynasty in China when goldfish began to be developed, and the UK around 1691 with the keeping of goldfish or paradise fish. Generally in fishkeeping the veterinary surgeon will be presented with teleosts, members of the Osteichthyes or bony fishes. There are over 20,000 species which in theory might be kept in home or public aquaria.

The vast majority of fish have a restricted distribution in the wild, possibly a whole continent down to a single water filled cave in Death Valley. Coldwater fish commonly encountered are members of the Family Cyprinidae and include goldfish (*Carassius auratus*), koi *(Cyprinus carpio),* orfe *(Idus idus)* etc. Cyprinids are also very commonly found in the aquarium and their body shape soon recognised. Scott (1991) gives a simplified guide to the Families which are too varied to be discussed here.

BASIC ANATOMY AND PHYSIOLOGY

Skin

Fish skin is comprised of living cells covered with a film of mucus (see Figure 1). When intact, the skin and mucus layer is a good waterproof coating, preventing the entry of water. It is very important to note that loss of scales is not just superficial; the scales are embedded and when lost a serious defect is often left. A large area of scale loss is analogous to a burn in mammals and results in loss of tissue fluids and entry of water.

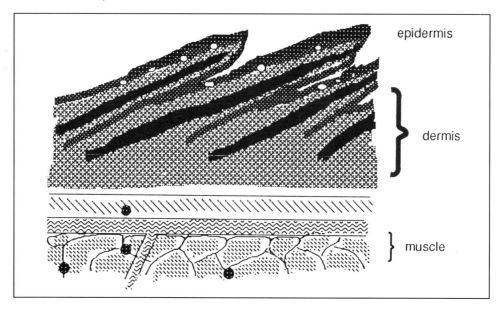

Figure 1
The skin.

Internal organs

The internal organs are essentially similar to those of any other animal (see Figure 2). The heart is single chambered with a phagocytic endothelium; this can cause problems if it picks up virulent bacteria which can produce a cardiomyopathy. The kidney lies dorsally along the spine and in some species sits like a saddle on the swim bladder; in addition to its excretory functions it is haemopoietic. The swim bladder helps fish maintain neutral buoyancy and thus save energy; in some species, eg. carp, it is bi-lobed and may be physostomatous, ie. with a duct connecting it to the gut, or physoclistous, closed and filled by gas secretion from the blood. The gastro-intestinal tract varies depending on the food of the species concerned.

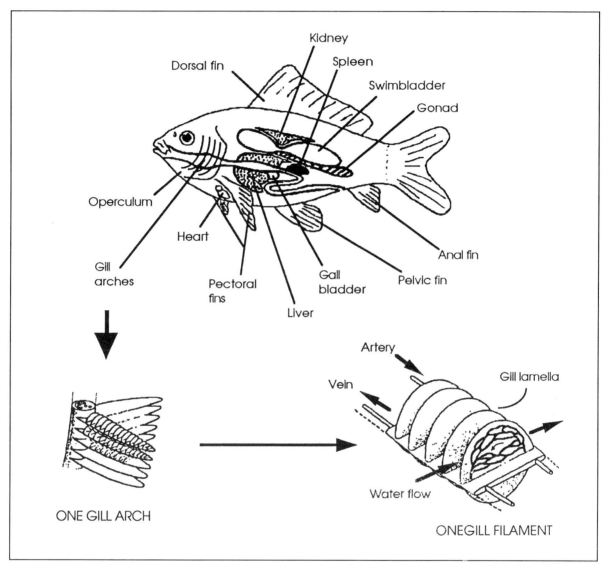

Figure 2
Basic anatomy, internal organs and gills.

The gills

When one thinks of fish, the first major anatomical feature considered as 'special' are the gills (see Figure 2). Although gills vary between species, the basic pattern is fairly consistent. The gills consist of a set of gill arches on each side from which project the finger-like filaments; these bear the lamellae which are the active areas of oxygen uptake. The lamellae have only a single layer separating blood from the water which flows over them. The blood flow through the lamellae is arranged as a countercurrent system and as a result water can have up to 80—90% of the available oxygen removed.

Principal excretory products of fish

The major nitrogenous excretory products of fish are ammonia (NH_3), carbon dioxide (CO_2) and undigested faecal solids which are high in phosphate (see Figure 3). These all have an effect on water quality (see later).

Ammonia is particularly toxic in its undissociated form and so in acidic water is less likely to be a problem. Most aquarium fish, however, are held in relatively hard, alkaline water where an accumulation of ammonia can cause problems. Low levels of ammonia cause gill hyperplasia and acute toxicity is caused by interference with oxygen transport mechanisms.

Fish are susceptible to ammonia in its unionised form which means that this is more of a problem in alkaline water. The nitrites produced by the nitrogen cycle are also highly toxic; fortunately, this is a short-lived stage before the final oxidation to nitrate. Only the final oxidative stage, nitrate, is safe. Nitrates are tolerated by most species but there is some evidence that marine fish and invertebrates are susceptible and elasmobranchs such as sharks and rays are certainly affected.

Levels of undissociated (unionised) ammonia-nitrogen above 0.02mg/litre are considered harmful to fish if exposure is prolonged. Such levels lead to chronic hyperplasia of the gills. Levels over 0.1—0.2mg/litre of nitrite-nitrogen retard growth of salmonids. Other species of fish may have different sensitivities.

Conversion factors

To convert	into	multiply by
$NH_3$3-N	NH_3	1.3
NO_2-N	NO_2	3.3
NO_3-N	NO_3	4.4

Dealing with ammonia

Biological activity is dependent on bacteria in the water or on a surface receiving sufficient oxygen via the water flow to thrive and use the ammonia as an energy source.

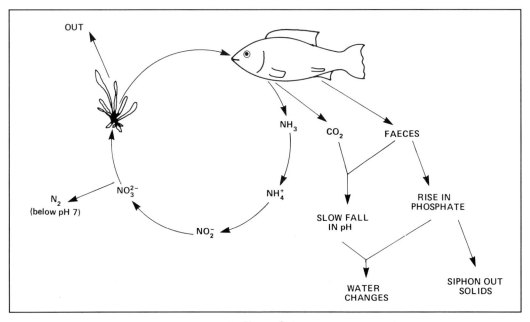

Figure 3
Waste products of fish and their fate.

274

The principal bacteria involved are *Nitrosomonas*, which oxidises ammonia to nitrite and *Nitrobacter* which oxidises nitrite to nitrate. These are both autotrophic organisms and so can use inorganic carbon from CO_2 as their source of carbon for growth.

$$NH_4^+ + OH^- + 1.5\ O_2 = H^+ + NO_2^- + 2\ H_2O$$

$$NO_2^- + 0.5\ O_2 = NO_3^-$$

Certain treatments may disturb the function of the bacterial filter system, eg. methylene blue, most antibacterials and antibiotics.

Time to establish a bacterial flora

A new tank takes time to establish its flora and hence to filter efficiently. It is for this reason that tanks should not be overstocked initially. The population of fish should be built up, starting with more hardy species. The term 'New Tank Syndrome' was given to the problems which occur through overloading a newly established filter, leading to ammonia and nitrite poisoning.

The bacterial population can be seeded using gravel from an established tank but generally three weeks are needed for a tropical tank to establish itself. A number of commercial products are available to seed tanks and so aid the start-up process. There is a timelag because *Nitrobacter* is actually inhibited by ammonia so the levels must fall before *Nitrobacter* can grow and convert the nitrite to nitrate. Fish are not the only source of ammonia in the tank; heterotrophic organisms will be breaking down organic waste such as faeces and excess food to release ammonia.

HUSBANDRY

Environmental conditions are paramount for fish keeping since in a closed system the fish are obliged to swim around in a relatively restricted body of water into which they must also excrete. In general, larger tanks are easier to establish and manage than small ones; popular sizes are 60 x 40 x 45cm and 90 x 40 x 45cm.

Basic environmental requirements for fish

Clean water— various methods of filtration are used, some highly sophisticated. The majority use some degree of bacterial action as the main filtration methods with enhancements, depending on the system.

Method of filtration	Type
Mechanical:	Box filters, power filters.
Biological:	Undergravel, power filters.
Ultra violet:	To kill algae or pathogens.
chemical:	Oozone, protein skimmers, activated carbon.

All of these types of filtration equipment are available, whether freshwater, tropical, marine or pondkeeping is being discussed. Water changes are also carried out to control the 'biological end products', normally ¼ — ⅓ every 2 weeks or $^1/_{10}$ per week. A very important point to remember is that these biological filters are alive and need a continual supply of oxygen, hence they cannot be turned off for more than a few minutes without requiring a major clean.

Undergravel filters should not have too many rocks etc. which will obstruct flow, nor should they be sloped too much since this creates zones which have more 'draw' and which block easily.

Temperature. This will depend on the type of fish being kept but broadly two distinctions are made; either 'coldwater fish' kept at ambient temperatures or 'tropical fish' kept in the region of 21°–29°C.

Light. Special fluorescent tubes are available which emit the particular spectral requirements for aquarium plants; these have been developed specially for the purpose. There are also mercury vapour and halogen lamps which are particularly used in deeper marine tanks where adequate light is essential to support the algae.

Stocking density is important; weight of fish per volume of water has a bearing on the rate of spoilage of the water. Normally, however, the suggested stocking levels for aquaria are given in terms of surface area, ie. allow 75cm² of water surface area for each 2.5cm of fish length (excluding the tail). This recommended level should only be exceeded by more experienced aquarists.

FEEDING

There are adequate proprietary foods on the market in the form of pellets, flakes and crumbs. Some fish, particularly marine species, find some form of fresh or even live food essential; deep-frozen gamma-irradiated food is available and is often acceptable. Many aquarists use live invertebrate foods at breeding time; these should preferably be of non-aquatic origin so as to avoid the introduction of disease. Small earthworms from the garden (not the ones from the compost heap which can be toxic) collected in an area well away from the use of weedkillers or fertilisers, are suitable as food.

Feeding should always be done carefully to ensure that all the fish receive some food yet none is left to pollute the tank. A maxim is FEED THE FISH NOT THE TANK. The amount consumed in two minutes twice daily is usually adequate as an initial guide until experience teaches differently. Fish fed to satiation can waste up to 30% of the ration, with food passing through the gut only partially digested.

Owners of large carnivorous fish should be cautioned against the use of fish from the aquarium shop as food for their pets. This is an ideal way of disease transmission, particularly of chronic diseases such as tuberculosis.

It is worth considering the fact that water-soluble vitamins leach out of pellets, particularly those which are not fat-coated. Chronic problems may occur and it is possible that in discus (*Symphysodon* spp.) and long-term captive marine fish, the skin ulcerations often seen may be in part due to a vitamin deficiency. Supplementation with fresh prawn supplies extra pigment which may be involved in survivability of eggs. Home-made diets can be made with prawn, tuna, beef, vegetables etc. and then set using gelatin. These can be medicated or have high potency vitamins which have minimal effect on taste, eg. ACE-High, Vetark, added as necessary. These can be frozen and scraped into the tank twice a week or put in small ice cube containers so that one can be put into the tank to thaw and be pecked at.

DISEASES/CLINICAL CONDITIONS

Most diseases affecting fish have a strong stress component. Avoiding or minimising stress is an integral part of recovery or prevention but it is still very important to be able to identify the pathogens present and treat them.

Whenever possible live fish should be examined. Dead fish are often unrewarding in terms of diagnosis; one should not freeze fish for subsequent *post-mortem* examination — in the vast majority of cases serious autolysis will occur during thawing and bacteriology will be of very limited value.

Routine

general backround	how long kept fish? tank size? how long established? history of any recent problems? any treatment carried out?
specific problem	odd behaviour? feeding? colour changes?
water quality	test for pH, NH_3, $NO_2{}^-$, hardness etc.

examination	fish are observed in water for obvious lesions, eg.
	    ulcers, fin erosion,
	    excess mucus,
	    exophthalmia,
	    ascites

General signs of ill health

The signs associated with most of the parasitic infections of the skin are similar. Fish are generally disturbed and often try to scratch on rocks and the gravel bottom (one should not mistake this for normal feeding behaviour as shown by some species). Their colours begin to look a little 'washed out' and dull because the parasites cause irritation and excessive production of mucus. The eyes are similarly affected and often appear slightly cloudy. If left untreated fins often begin to look raggy and frayed; eventually inflammation and ulcers may appear. Fish often die before this due to similar but unseen damage to their gills.

Bacterial diseases of the skin may appear as distinct white areas, sometimes with fine whitish filaments visible. In other fish there may simply be erosion of the skin showing as 'fin rot' or as ulcers. In fish that have become severely infected and the bacteria have caused septicaemia there may be skin wheals, ulcers, general petechial haemorrhages, bulging eyes or raised scales.

The signs of gill disease are not always immediately obvious. Fish become anorexic and tend to hang around the surface and the aeration stone or filter uplift where dissolved oxygen levels are highest. The gill covers (opercula) move more rapidly than normal and often the gills will be visible, and may be swollen and greyer than normal due to excess mucus.

Infectious diseases

Viruses

Spring viraemia of carp (SVC), caused by *Rhabdovirus carpio*

This disease has been found in the UK four times since 1977, associated with imported fish in recirculation systems. It affects cyprinids such as common or ornamental carp, goldfish, tench etc.

The disease manifests as a viraemia, with sick fish, dark and weak, hanging in the water. *Post mortem* general inflammation is seen together with petechial or ecchymotic haemorrhages on internal organs. Virology is the only reliable means of diagnosis as secondary infection with other, lesser, fish pathogens seems to be a prominent feature. The appearance of the disease is temperature-related, with the worst problems occurring at $13^\circ - 15^\circ$C; these decline around 20°C and disappear completely at 23°C. Infected fish will die or remain as carriers. Over 50% of fish could be expected to die in an outbreak over, perhaps, weeks.

Footdips and disinfection of nets etc. with iodophors, eg. Tamodine-E, Vetark; Wescodyne, Ciba-Geigy, are recommended for at-risk sites.

The disease is notifiable; even suspicion must be reported to MAFF by the owner (see 'Legislation'). Although, obviously, there are many diseases which may occur in the spring (or other times of the year) which can kill fish, these are often readily treatable, eg. bacterial septicaemias, costiasis, chilodonelliasis etc. Careful observation of fish and their maintenance in less stressful situations are critical factors in prevention of any disease.

Bacteria

Fish tuberculosis or mycobacteriosis is most commonly caused by *Mycobacterium marinum* or *Mycobacterium fortuitum*. The disease is spread by various methods; skin granulomas may release bacteria directly into the water, bacteria may be shed via the faeces from tuberculous granulomas in the liver or gut lining, or bacteria may be shed in the urine from the kidney. Another more direct route involves dead fish in the tank or pond being cannibalised. This is very common and usually the heavily infected abdominal organs are eaten first. Disease can also be spread by the aquarist who feeds live infected fish to his large specimen fish such as oscars (*Astronotus ocellatus*) or piranha (*Serrasalmus* spp.).

Fish tuberculosis is zoonotic and in man is often called 'aquarist's arm'; it is occasionally seen in people working in aquarium shops. The commonest sites of infection are the hands and arms due to minor scratches from the tank edges becoming infected. Because of the possibility of human infection, hygiene is very important when dealing with fish tanks. Hands and arms must be washed thoroughly after doing any tank servicing with particular attention to any cuts and scratches. Tank filters must not be washed out in the kitchen sink nor waste water poured down it. Simple, sensible hygienic practices should be more than enough to reduce greatly the already very low risk of infection.

Ulcer disease of goldfish is now accepted as being caused primarily by *Aeromonas salmonicida*, the same organism as that which causes furunculosis in rainbow trout and salmon. A carrier state exists in recovered fish which, when stressed, can release infectious organisms into the water. These can then attack healthy fish in the same body of water, particularly those under stress or with any skin damage, eg. caused by clumsy netting. The causal organism is shed from carriers at times of stress such as spawning, handling, high temperatures and sudden changes in environmental conditions. A wide range of other organisms may be associated with ulcers in goldfish and koi; *Aeromonas hydrophila* is a common isolate, as are *Flavobacterium* and *Pseudomonas* spp.

The misuse of antibiotics has encouraged resistant strains of many fish bacteria. Parenteral injections are of value in treating certain cases; short term (1-4 hour) baths are also used but are of uncertain merit in many cases. Various antimicrobial agents have been used including potentiated sulphonamides, neomycin, oxytetracycline (Microtet, Microbiologicals) and oxolinic acid (Microlinic, Microbiologicals; Aquinox, PH Pharmaceuticals), but efficacy will depend on resistance, the stage of the disease and the overall condition of the fish under treatment.

Care must be taken with nets to avoid transmitting disease between batches; netting a fish with an ulcer contaminates the net, and then, when used again, the net rubs the organisms into the skin of another fish. Disinfection of nets using benzalkonium chloride solution (Ark-Klens, Vetark; Marinol Blue, BK) is worthwhile since it is also a detergent and lifts mucus off which might protect bacteria from the effects of a disinfectant.

Treatment is aided by cleaning the ulcer using povidone-iodine (Tamodine, Vetark; Pevidine, C-Vet); then the fish is best held in a salt bath. The use of supplements high in vitamins A, C and E during the treatment period and prior to periods of prolonged fast (overwinter) is considered worthwhile, eg. ACE-High, Vetark or Aquace, PH Pharmaceuticals.

Parasites

Ectoparasites

Protozoa

Ichthyophthirius — 'Ich' or 'white spot', stress-related, responds well to many proprietary treatments (see later).

Trichodina etc. — range of pathogenicity, an aggressive parasite, reasonably responsive to treatment (see later).

Ichthyobodo (Costia) — under adverse conditions it rounds off, probably forming a cyst, reasonably responsive to treatment (see later).

Chilodonella — shown to produce resting cysts under adverse conditions. Increasingly resistant to treatment (see later).

Epistylis/Scyphidia/Glossatella — very much opportunistic invader of wounds etc. Indicative of water quality problems (see later).

Monogenea (one host flukes)

Gyrodactylids — primarily skin flukes, fish are seen 'flicking' as if scratching; the flukes are livebearing, often with several generations in one. Susceptible to trichlorphon or formalin.

Dactylogyrids — gill flukes are very common on imported coldwater fish. Approximately 10—12 days generation interval at optimal temperatures; produce 3—15 eggs per day. Fish develop a resistance to infection with larvae after an initial infection; they will still carry adults and transmit infection to other fish. Susceptible to trichlorphon; one should take care with formalin because of the potential for pre-existing damage to the gills being made worse.

Crustacea

Argulus — eggs laid during the summer hatch in 15—55 days and the larvae need to find a host within 24 hours. They grow and are sexually mature in 30—35 days. Susceptible to trichlorphon.

Lernaea (anchor worms) — male and female are parasitic as larvae and mate on the gill; the male then becomes free-living and the female moves on to the body and embeds her anchor, producing about 200 eggs in each clutch and several clutches per season. Susceptible to trichlorphon as larvae; adults need picking out and sites treating as ulcers.

Ergasilus — only the female is parasitic; she mates in the water and the male remains free swimming. The males do not live as long as the females which live on the gills, moving around and 'browsing'. Each female produces about 40 eggs per clutch and several clutches per season. They probably overwinter, the females producing a clutch in the spring prior to dying off and the cycle begins again.

Fungi

Saprolegnia — this is almost always a secondary problem; one should look for water quality problems, primary 'Ich', wounds etc.

Endoparasites

Nematodes, eg. *Camallanus*

Fish particularly commonly infected are the livebearers (especially *Poecilia* and *Xiphophorus* spp.), but all fish are susceptible. Signs are:- red 'paintbrush' out of the vent, anaemia, poor growth, emaciation, death. The worms have strong biting jaws with which they damage the mucosal lining of the small intestine where they live, causing bleeding. The worms are 8—10mm long and are red; their colour is due to feeding on blood. They are live-bearing, producing larval young. Transmitted by crustaceans such as *Cyclops, Asellus* etc. as intermediate hosts and possibly by cannibalism and direct pecking at the worms. The incubation period is about 9 weeks.

METHODS OF TREATMENT

Various methods are used, depending on circumstances. It is often best not to stress fish further and compound a problem by moving them to a treatment tank. Under circumstances where a treatment might be harmful to an established tank or involve risk to other fish or invertebrates, it may be considered essential to carry out treatment in a tank which might also be used for quarantine.

Short-term baths are a common method of treatment for fish. Formalin is normally used this way, the appropriate dose being mixed in a small watertight container. The affected fish are then transferred to this container for the required time, usually 5—60 minutes. Care must be taken with these treatments; the water needs to be aerated and to be the same temperature as the main tank. The procedure is quite stressful and fish with severely diseased gills may not tolerate it. It will be necessary to remove fish if they appear to show distress. Small tropical fish which are not feeding can be treated with certain antibiotics in this way although dosages are not worked out.

The hospital or quarantine tank

A tank for treating sick fish should have: —

> a suitable heater and thermostat for tropical species;
>
> simple mechanical filtration, a box filter or power filter;
>
> adequate aeration, since many treatments reduce the oxygen-carrying capacity of the water; filters should not contain activated carbon as this removes many treatments from solution;
>
> dim light — some treatments are neutralised by light and others sensitise the fish to light, causing skin diseases;
>
> plastic plants to give a sense of security; real plants may be killed by treatments;
>
> flowerpots for shelter;
>
> suitable water, as similar as possible to water from the tank where the fish live;
>
> marine fish hospital tanks should be at least half the size of the main tank, otherwise fish are stressed.

TREATMENT

Antimicrobial agents given via the water

N.B. These are generally not very useful and should not be used with bacterial filtration.

Oxytetracycline	13—120mg/litre (chelated by hard water)
Doxycycline and minocycline	2—3mg/litre
Chloramphenicol	20—50mg/litre
Potentiated sulphonamide	80mg trimethoprim and 400mg sulphadiazine/ml used at 1ml/100—120 litres
Nifurpirinol	0.1mg/litre
Metronidazole	7mg/litre (double for *Oodinium*)
Dimetridazole	5mg/litre (said to inhibit spawning)
Neomycin	50mg/kg (has been used in seawater)
Gentamicin	4—5mg/kg (has been used in seawater)
Kanamycin	50—100mg/litre

Care must be taken with soluble poultry formulas which may have very low concentrations of active drug and which may cause serious problems due to the carrier's changing pH, causing bacterial blooms or deoxygenation.

Antimicrobial agents via the food

Three antimicrobial agents are in relatively common usage in fish; these are oxytetracycline, oxolinic acid and potentiated sulphonamide. These can be incorporated into pelleted food or mixed into home-made food, such as 250g ox heart + 7g wheatgerm + 7g chopped spinach + vitamin mixture, which is used for many fish; this is then solidified with agar or gelatin. Similar home-made mixes can be made with prawns, or even simply flaked fish food mixed with the drug and then solidified.

Antimicrobial agents via the food	
Agent	**Dosage**
Oxytetracycline	7.5mg/g of food
Oxolinic acid	1mg/g of food
Potentiated sulphonamide	3mg/g of food
Doxycycline or minocycline	0.5mg/g of food

In the same way metronidazole is used in food at 1% for hexamitiasis in cichlids and gouramies.

Flaked food for tropicals and smaller coldwater fish is now available medicated with antibiotics, eg. Aquiflake with oxolinic acid and Tetraflake with oxytetracycline, PH Pharmaceuticals.

Benzalkonium chloride

Certain chain lengths of benzalkonium chloride (Ark-Klens, Vetark) are very useful for treating fish. They are powerful disinfectants with an additional detergent action and are particularly useful in treating external bacterial infections such as bacterial gill disease (BGD) where myxobacteria are multiplying within a film of mucus on the gills. The dual action is important since bacterial growth is inhibited and the mucus lifted off by the detergent effect. Other uses are as a net disinfectant where baths of other disinfectants might be dangerous, eg. shop premises.

For bath treatment in a static system 1ppm is used for 1 hour. In static ponds it will be necessary to use doses of less than 0.5ppm. The toxicity of benzalkonium chloride is increased in soft water so treatment levels should be at least halved. If in doubt it is wise to try lower doses first and increase as circumstances permit.

Chloramine T

The action of chloramine T (Chlorosal, Vetark) is based on a slow breakdown to hypochlorous acid releasing oxygen and chlorine. Because of this it should not be used at the same time as other chemicals such as formalin or benzalkonium chloride. It is very useful for external bacterial diseases and has the benefit of some effect against protozoal diseases. Doses can be repeated daily. One should not use high dose dip treatments.

Therapeutic dose		
pH	**Soft water**	**Hard water**
6.0	2.5	7.0
6.5	5.0	10.0
7.0	10.0	15.0
7.5	18.0	18.0
8.0	20.0	20.0

In general it is best always to err on the side of caution, starting with 2ppm and increasing carefully as necessary.

Copper sulphate

Stock — 400mg $CuSO_4.5H_2O$. in 1 litre — dose 1ml/litre

This gives a Cu concentration of 0.1ppm. The tank water should be tested with a good quality kit adding enough of the stock solution to bring the level to 0.2ppm. It is necessary to carry out daily tests and maintain the concentration at 0.1—0.2ppm for at least 10 days. One must be aware that this concentration of copper is toxic to invertebrates which are often kept in marine tanks.

Trichlorphon

Trichlorphon (Masoten, Bayer) breakdown depends on pH, taking up to 3 weeks in acid water.

pH	1/2 life at 20-23°C
7	21 days
9	1 day

Trichlorphon has been used widely as a fish ectoparasiticide in both fresh and salt water to kill a number of the larger parasites such as flukes, *Argulus* (fish lice) and *Lernaea* (anchor worms). Gill flukes need repeat treatments because they are egg layers. Claims of efficacy against protozoa are doubtful.

Trichlorphon is generally used at concentrations of: —

0.2 ppm active ingredient as a permanent treatment.

2—2.5% dip for cyprinids for up to 5—10 minutes but is not recommended; it is very dangerous and easy to overdose, and it is necessary to caution against this possibility.

Trichlorphon is an organophosphorus compound and potentially hazardous. It is particularly toxic to orfe, chubb and rudd in which neurological problems and death are seen. There are unconfirmed reports of problems in golden tench, although green tench have not shown problems. Characins in general are sensitive. Toxicity to other fish and higher animals is relatively low; its highest toxicity is to invertebrates and, in particular, Crustacea.

Formalin

Formalin is widely used for the treatment of ectoparasitic infections of fish, particularly the protozoa — *Costia, Trichodina* and *Chilodonella*. It is also effective against the monogenetic skin and gill flukes, eg. *Dactylogyrus* and *Gyrodactylus*. Formalin may be particularly needed for *Chilodonella* infections which are often resistant to many other treatments. Care is needed as it deoxygenates water and so is a major stressor; the 1 hour treatment should be avoided for use on fish with gill damage except with great caution.

Dose: — 1 ml of 40% formaldehyde in 4.55 litres for 1 hour — aerate
2 drops of 40% formaldehyde in 4.55 litres — permanent bath

Formalin can be used as a 200ppm dip; the dip must be aerated during use. It must be fresh; if any precipitate is present this must be filtered out prior to use.

Levamisole

Levamisole is used often in tropical fish infected with nematodes giving a single treatment directly into the tank at 10ppm.

Using 7.5% solution = 7500mg/100ml = 75mg/ml;   ie. dose at 1 ml/7.5 litres.

Leteux-meyer mixture

There are several variations on the basic combination of chemicals which aim to give a treatment dose of approximately 25ppm formalin and 0.05—0.1ppm of malachite green.

In static ornamental ponds a mixture of 3.3g of malachite green in 1 litre of formalin can be used at a dose of 1ml per 68 litres of pond water. If necessary it may be used at 3—4 day intervals, so long as dissolved oxygen levels remain above 5ppm and the temperature below 28°C.

There are several commercially available preparations based on this combination, usually at lower doses to be administered over a 5 day period.

Malachite green

This is used prophylactically and for treatment of fungal infections. Alone or mixed with formalin it has been used to treat protozoal infections (see Leteux-meyer mixture).

Dose: — 2 mg/litre for 30 minutes
0.1 mg/litre as a permanent bath

It is said to be important to use the zinc-free form; this is considered to be due more to the general purity than to the toxic effects of the zinc. It is toxic to several species of tetra so care needs to be taken not to use high levels. It may have a much wider range of efficacy than previously suspected since it has been found to be highly effective against a protozoan disease of the kidney in rainbow trout. The dose should be reduced to half if treating fish in soft water. Toxicity may be seen as respiratory distress; this is usually immediate and irreversible since malachite green is a respiratory poison.

Salt

Salt is used for the treatment of ectoparasitic infestations such as *Costia* and *Chilodonella*, particularly in fry, and is very important for reducing osmotic stress on individual fish especially koi *(Cyprinus carpio)* and goldfish *(Carassius auratus)*. In general, pure vacuum-dried (PVD) salt is preferred; table salt may be iodised and rock salt may have impurities. PVD salt is sold for cooking, dishwashers, water softeners etc.

Dose: — 3—5% for 2 minutes
1% for up to 1 hour
0.55% as a permanent bath until lesions heal; occasionally this concentration needs to be built up over 3 days if fish seem distressed by the treatment.

Methylene blue

This has been in use for many years as an antiprotozoal treatment. Methylene blue is extremely harmful to biological filter systems and for this reason should not be used in recirculation systems or aquaria with biological filters (most aquaria) without taking precautions for treatment off-circuit or stripping down and restablishing the filter.

Table 1
Common pathogens and suggested treatments.

WHITE SPOT — *Ichthyophthirius*	WQ, F and MG, ChT
'GREY SLIME DISEASES'	
Chilodonella	Formalin, F and MG
Cyclochaeta (Trichodina)	F and MG, ChT
Costia (Ichthyobodo)	F and MG, ChT
HOLE IN THE HEAD — *Hexamita*	metronidazole, dimetridazole
VELVET DISEASE — *Oodinium limneticum*	WQ, copper
CORAL FISH DISEASE — *Oodinium ocellatum*	WQ, copper
BACTERIAL INFECTIONS	
MOUTH FUNGUS — *Chondrococcus*	WQ, Ch T, BC, antibiotics
FINROT — eg. *Aeromonas* or *Pseudomonas* spp.	WQ, Ch T, BC, antibiotics
SEPTICAEMIA — eg. *Aeromonas* or *Pseudomonas* spp.	oral or parenteral antibiotics
TUBERCULOSIS — *Mycobacterium marinum*	doxycycline, minocycline, and
M. fortuitum	a very poor prognosis
FUNGUS — *Saprolegnia*	WQ, MG, topical povidone iodine
GILL FLUKES — *Dactylogyrus* spp.	trichlorphon, formalin
SKIN FLUKES — *Gyrodactylus* spp.	trichlorphon, formalin
ANCHOR WORM — *Lernaea*	trichlorphon, pick off adults
FISH LICE — *Argulus*	trichlorphon, salt baths
NEMATODES — *Camallanus*	levamisole

WQ = water quality; Ch T = chloramine T; BC = benzalkonium chloride;
F and MG = Formalin and malachite green mixture; MG = malachite green

ANAESTHESIA

Reasons for anaesthesia

Handling of fish, in or out of the water, is physically difficult and not without risk to the fish, and in some circumstances to the handler. Anaesthetics are useful in making any necessary handling procedures as "non-stressing" as possible.

There are a variety of reasons why anaesthesia may be required: —

handling broodstock for stripping, blood sampling, treatment etc;

vaccination by injection;

marking or tagging;

surgery/debridement, eg. removal of neoplasms;

long distance transportation;

handling of — valuable fish,
dangerous fish,
particularly large fish.

The needs of these various tasks are different so care must be taken with all applications. The transition between stages of anaesthesia can be very rapid so caution is needed.

Responses

The individual response of a fish to an anaesthetic and its transition between the various stages is dependent on a number of factors: — species; gill area to body weight ratio; size and weight; metabolic rate; lipid content; season, sex, maturity, diet; condition; disease.

Table 2
Stages of anaesthesia.

stage 1	light sedation	slight loss of reactivity
stage 2	deep sedation	total loss of reactivity except to strong pressure, equilibrium normal
stage 3	partial loss of equilibrium	erratic swimming, increased opercular rate
stage 4	total loss of equilibrium	reactivity only to deep pressure stimuli
stage 5	loss of reflex activity	total loss of reactivity, very shallow opercular movements
stage 6	medullary collapse	gasping followed by cessation of opercular movements

The transition between these stages is dependent on several factors, particularly dose used, species and activity. Stages 2/3 are often ideal for simple procedures; when the head and tail of the fish can be wrapped, struggling is minimised. The aim is generally to maintain the fish at a level of minimal activity which can be considered sedation rather than anaesthesia.

MS222 (tricaine methanesulphonate, Sandoz)

At present MS222 is the only anaesthetic licensed in the UK for fish; it also has the benefit of being water-soluble. Depth of anaesthesia needs to be watched carefully and the fish removed when the desired plane is reached. Its disadvantage is that it causes pH changes and may cause irritation. MS222 is fat-soluble so there may be some residual depression in large adult fish with well developed fat.

Normal dose: 1g/10 litres, ie. 100ppm

Benzocaine

Benzocaine is probably the cheapest of the available anaesthetics and it seems to work as well as MS222. Unfortunately, it is not very water-soluble. A stock solution can be made up in acetone or methanol (40g per litre). This can be kept for at least 3 months in a dark bottle (necessary to prevent the formation of toxic compounds).

		stock solution per 9 litres
gentle handling	25ppm	5.5ml
deeper surgical anaesthesia	50ppm	11ml

The figures above should be considered guidelines for providing a safe sedation in an acceptable period of a few minutes; experience will allow higher doses to be used for more rapid effect. When this is done, however, great care should be taken as fish can easily be overdosed and irreversible medullary collapse may occur. All anaesthetics carry a degree of risk and no warranty of safety should be implied from these guidelines; they are simply based on what has worked. The product is not licensed and the user carries the responsibility. Clients should be asked to sign an anaesthetic consent form (see 'Introduction').

There is considerable interspecies variation and one should always err on the side of caution. Relatively sedate species such as carp are slower to succumb than trout and can become very deeply anaesthetised without the operator's always appreciating it.

Resuscitation

Fish are normally placed into a container of the same water as they were kept in and moved gently to encourage a flow of water across the gills; a finger placed ventrally just behind the lower jaw will keep the mouth open. It is worthwhile when planning to anaesthetise a fish to have the client bring the fish in water in a container with a spare container with enough water in which to transport the fish home.

REFERENCES AND FURTHER READING

ANDREWS, C., EXELL, A. and CARRINGTON, N. (1988). *The Manual of Fish Health.* Salamander Books, London.

BREWSTER, B., CHAPLE, N., CUVELIER, J., DAVIES, M., EVANS, D., EVANS, G., PHIPPS, K. and SCOTT, P.W. (1989). *The Interpet Encyclopedia of Koi.* Salamander Books, London.

CARRINGTON, N. (1985). *A Fishkeeper's Guide to Maintaining a Healthy Aquarium.* Salamander Books, London.

GRATZEK, J. B. (1981). An overview of ornamental fish diseases and therapy. *Journal of Small Animal Practice* **22**, 345.

LAGLER, K. F., BARDACH, J. E. and MILLER, R. R. (1962). *Ichthylogy: The Study of Fishes.* J. Wiley and Sons, New York.

MILLS, D. (1987). *The Marine Aquarium.* Salamander Books, London.

POST, G. (1987). *Textbook of Fish Health.* TFH Publications, New York.

VAN RAMSHORST, J. D. (1978). *The Complete Aquarium Encyclopedia of Tropical Freshwater Fish.* Elsevier-Phaidon, Oxford.

SCOTT, P. W. (1985). Ornamental Fish. In: *Manual of Exotic Pets.* Revised Edn. (Eds. J. E. Cooper, M. F. Hutchison, O. F. Jackson and R. J. Maurice) BSAVA, Cheltenham.

SCOTT, P. W. (1991). *The Complete Aquarium.* Dorling Kindersley, London.

SPOTTE, S. (1979). *Seawater Aquariums: The Captive Environment.* Wiley Interscience, New York.

STERBA, G. (1978). *The Aquarist's Encyclopaedia.* Blandford Press, Poole.

VAN DUIJN, C. (1981). Tuberculosis in fishes. *Journal of Small Animal Practice* **22**, 391.

There are two major monthly magazines, *Aquarist and Pondkeeper* and *Practical Fishkeeping;* also the whole series of Interpet books is recommended for specific information. There are also many specialist societies and local aquarist clubs which can be rich sources of information.

CHAPTER TWENTY

INVERTEBRATES

John E Cooper BVSc CertLAS DTVM FRCVS MRCPath FIBiol

Many species of invertebrate are kept in captivity — as pets, for educational purposes, for display, for research and for food. In the past they have attracted little attention from veterinary surgeons but this situation is slowly changing as the profession becomes aware of the importance of such species and owners and breeders appreciate the potential value of advice on health and management (Collins, 1990; Cooper, 1980, 1986a; Frye, 1986, 1990).

The invertebrates comprise well over 90% of all living species. In the broadest sense they range from single-celled protozoa to complex and highly organised arthropods, molluscs and helminths. They are all ectothermic and thus unable to control their body temperature except by behavioural means. Some, such as the insects and crustaceans, have tough exoskeletons while others are composed solely of soft tissue. They vary greatly in their behaviour, nutrition and requirements.

Those invertebrates which are most likely to be presented for veterinary attention are as follows:

Arthropoda

Insects
Various species of butterfly and
   moth (Order Lepidoptera)
Stick insects (Order Phasmida)
Praying mantids (Order Mantoidea)
Cockroaches (Order Dictyoptera)
Grasshoppers, locusts and crickets
   (Order Orthoptera)

Arachnida
Many species of spider (Order Araneae)

Crustacea
Tree crabs *(Coenobita* spp.)
Crayfish (Family Astacidae)

Myriapoda
Many species of centipede and millipede

Annelids
Various species of worm

Coelenterata
Sea anemones and their allies

Mollusca
Various species of snail
(especially *Helix* and *Achatina* spp.)

The species listed are kept primarily for pets or for study. Other invertebrates — for example, the honeybee *(Apis mellifera)* — may be of agricultural or economic importance but are not discussed in this chapter. However, reference can usually be made to textbooks and papers which cover these species since these often provide data which appertain to other invertebrates (see, for example, Bailey, 1981; Provenzano, 1983; Singh and Moore, 1985). In this context veterinary surgeons may find it helpful to refer to MAFF publications which cover, *inter alia*, diseases of bees, eg. Anon, 1986.

Some of the species listed above, and others, are reared as food for captive mammals, birds and lower vertebrates. There is considerable interest in this subject and much work has been done on the culture and nutritive value of various species (Collins, 1990; Frye and Calvert, 1989; Martin *et al*, 1976; Webb and Webb, 1987).

In this chapter the word 'invertebrate' will be used mainly to describe the larger metazoan (mainly arthropod) species which are commonly kept as private pets or for study.

In the UK, certain invertebrates are covered by the Dangerous Wild Animals Act 1976 (see 'Legisation'). These comprise buthid scorpions and a number of species of spiders, including the black widow *(Latrodectus* spp.). Members of the public who keep such species require a licence from their local authority (Cooper, M. E., 1987).

Some invertebrates are poisonous, others bite and secrete irritant material and a few, such as certain spiders and lepidopterous larvae, can be the cause of urticarial skin reactions (Cooper, 1985). Pathogenic organisms may be harboured or transmitted by certain species (see later).

Notwithstanding these points, many invertebrates are innocuous and can serve as excellent pets, especially for young people and for those who, for a variety of reasons, cannot accommodate a more conventional mammal, bird or fish (Cooper, 1986a,b).

HOUSING

The type of housing required depends on the species. Thus, for example, a group of locusts will need a large heated tank or box while European pond snails are likely to thrive in a small jar containing water and weed. Some species require a 'natural' environment while others will do well — and generally remain healthier — in an artificial ('clinical') situation.

Whichever type of accommodation is used there are basic requirements:-

1. It should be sufficiently spacious to allow the animal to perform its normal range of activities.

2. It should provide the optimum environment, in terms of temperature, relative humidity and substrate, for the particular species. If this is not possible, or the requirements are not known, then a range of environments should be provided, with temperature gradients, so that the animal has some choice.

3. It should be easily cleaned and disinfected.

4. When heating is provided the source should be protected so that the inmates cannot burn themselves. Light and ultra-violet bulbs tend to attract certain species, eg. moths and flies, and may prove lethal.

Useful data on housing invertebrates are to be found in *The UFAW Handbook on the Care and Management of Laboratory Animals* (UFAW, 1976), in the publications by Crush (1982), Miller, (1975) and Murphy (1980) and in the recently published *Proceedings of a Conference on Management and Welfare of Invertebrates in Captivity* (Collins, 1990). The humane transportation of invertebrates is attracting increasing attention (see 'Legislation'). IATA (1990) should be consulted over size and design of containers.

FEEDING

Invertebrates vary greatly in their feeding habits. Some, such as spiders, are obligate carnivores and require living prey (Cooper *et al*, 1991) Others, such as stick insects, feed only on certain plants. A few — for example, cockroaches — will eat a variety of different foods of both plant and animal origin. Some herbivorous species are very selective, with (for example) larvae of certain moths and butterflies feeding on only one food plant. Others are more catholic in their tastes and will accept a variety. If there is doubt over the best food plant or prey species, a selection should be offered.

Some general rules for feeding invertebrates are as follows:-

1. Herbivorous species should always receive fresh food at regular intervals. Whenever possible, sprigs of foliage should be put in water so as to discourage wilting; however, the container must be plugged to prevent the animals from falling in and drowning. Old tough leaves and shoots should be avoided.

2. Live food must be used with care. In particular, it must not be so large as to prove unmanageable or so voracious as to pose a threat to the creature for which it is intended. Uneaten prey items should always be removed and not allowed to die in the cage. Live food should not be present when a spider or other animal is shedding its skin: it may be particularly vulnerable to attack at that stage.

3. All items of food, whether of plant or animal origin, should be of high quality. Herbicides and pesticides can present an important hazard to captive invertebrates. Live food which is unhealthy or kept under unhygienic conditions, may transmit disease. Whenever possible, prey items such as blowflies, crickets, locusts and mealworms should be purpose-bred.

4. If a species is catholic in its tastes a wide variety of foodstuffs should be offered. This will reduce the risk of nutritional diseases and will make feeding the animal easier if one item becomes unobtainable.

5. Molluscs should always receive a calcium supplement, such as limestone, powdered bonemeal or cuttlefish. Mineral additives may also prove beneficial for other species.

Figure 1
A tree crab (*Coenobita* sp.) is held in the hand by grasping the shell in which it has made its home. This presents no hazard to the handler but care must be taken not to drop the shell and damage the occupant.

HANDLING

Again, much depends on the species. Some, such as snails, millipedes and tree crabs (see Figure 1), can be grasped in the hand. Others, for example, large spiders and mantids, tolerate gentle handling but will bite if restrained. Certain species may require the use of nets, rubber gloves or padded forceps; examples are leeches, certain hairy caterpillars and scorpions respectively. Caution should always be exercised if there is any doubt as to the safety of handling — either to the animal or the handler. Under such circumstances the veterinary surgeon may find it useful to view the animal through a glass or plastic container (Cooper, 1987a) or to anaesthetise it lightly (see later). In most species hypothermia can be employed to facilitate handling — 30 minutes in a refrigerator (+4°C) is usually sufficient — but under no circumstances should this be used for surgical procedures.

SEXING AND REPRODUCTION

Some invertebrates show sexual dimorphism. For example, there is often a different wing colour or pattern in male and female butterflies; male moths tend to have feathery antennae and female grasshoppers have a distinct ovipositor. There are, however, no hard and fast rules and many species are difficult to sex on the basis of their external appearance.

Likewise, reproduction patterns vary greatly. Many invertebrates lay eggs but these may develop in a number of ways. In some species, eg. locusts and cockroaches, there is an incomplete metamorphosis, ie. the creature which emerges from the egg closely resembles the adult and merely grows bigger or changes slightly in appearance, while in others, eg. moths and beetles, there are distinct larval and pupal stages. Some species are hermaphrodites — for example, most molluscs — while in others — such as certain species of stick insect — parthenogenesis occurs and females will lay fertile eggs in the absence of the male.

Useful information on reproduction is to be found in many textbooks; a practical guide to breeding insects is by Stone and Midwinter (1975).

DISEASES/CLINICAL CONDITIONS

The 'higher' invertebrates are susceptible to a wide range of diseases, comparable in many ways to those seen in vertebrates (Cantwell, 1974; Cooper, 1986a; Sparks, 1972). Control of disease in captive invertebrates is based largely upon prevention and this in turn depends on (a) good management, and (b) hygiene.

Treatment of individual invertebrates is certainly possible but is generally restricted to the larger species (Cooper, 1980; 1987a,b). Wounds can be cleaned and escape of haemolymph stemmed. Minor surgery is feasible and may include the amputation of limbs or the debridement of wounds and infected orifices. Anaesthesia may be needed (see later).

Changes in management will often arrest mortality in captive invertebrates. For this reason, if a number of animals are affected the veterinary surgeon should suggest that some are separated and kept under different conditions pending proper diagnosis. Alternatively, altering the temperature, relative humidity or terrain may itself prove beneficial.

Hygienic precautions play an important part in disease control, especially amongst arthropods where many micro-organisms are recognised pathogens. In a few cases there may be a risk of zoonoses (see later). Regular cleaning of cages and the removal of sloughed skins and faeces will go a long way towards minimising the risk of an epizootic. Care must be taken over some species, however; giant land snails *(Achatina* spp.), for example, appear to prefer dirty conditions and will often thrive in the presence of decaying vegetation. Similarly, over-ripe fruit is a favoured food of Lepidoptera and is regularly provided in butterfly houses. One must, therefore, be selective when implementing hygienic measures.

Although many disinfectants can be used safely it is a wise precaution always to rinse thoroughly after their use. The author recommends cetrimide, hypochlorite or formalin for routine cleaning of cages.

Signs of ill health in invertebrates include anorexia, lethargy, change of colour, discharges and dysecdysis (difficulty in shedding the skin). Behavioural changes may also be seen; for example, mealworms *(Tenebrio molitor)* will assemble on the surface of their container if the carbon dioxide levels are high. However, some apparently aberrant behaviour may be perfectly normal; for example, spiders which are shedding their skins may lie on their backs and appear to be dead or dying. A full investigation must always be carried out and details taken of the history and method of management. The animal must be handled and examined (see Figure 2). Even small invertebrates can be examined using a hand lens. Clients who keep invertebrates should be encouraged to keep records and also to save shed skins, empty pupal cases etc. so that these can be examined for parasites or lesions.

Diagnostic samples can be taken from invertebrates. Swabs, for example, can be cultured or examined directly. In some cases it may be possible to take blood (haemolymph); a technique in lobsters *(Homarus* spp.) was described by Greenwood (1975).

Figure 2
A hissing cockroach
(Gromphadorina portentosa)
on the hand. In this position
the animal can be examined
for external lesions or
damaged limbs.

Post-mortem examination of invertebrates can prove useful. Even if the veterinary surgeon is not familiar with the normal anatomy of the species he/she should be able to detect gross lesions, to demonstrate the presence of parasites and to take samples for microbiology and histopathology.

Physical injuries

All invertebrates are susceptible to damage and this may occur if, for example, they are trodden upon or become trapped by the lid of the cage. Often no specific treatment is possible but in the case of arthropods the loss of haemolymph (blood) can sometimes be prevented if the wound in the exoskeleton is sealed with a small blob of glue, icing sugar or plasticine. Suturing can prove useful. Limbs which are lost will often regenerate and minor injuries will heal when the animal sloughs.

Alopecia is common in adult spiders, especially the large 'bird-eating' or 'tarantula' species; it is characterised by the loss of hairs (setae) from the dorsal surface of the abdomen. This can be pathological but often follows the shedding of setae as a defence mechanism; they can cause pruritus or an urticaria when they come into contact with the skin of a predator.

Infectious diseases

Insects appear to be particularly prone to outbreaks of disease due to bacteria, fungi or viruses (Rivers, 1976). The clinical signs vary considerably but larvae tend to become wet and 'liquefy' while adults show diarrhoea, regurgitation or discharges from the exoskeleton. Fungal infections may be apparent from the presence of mycelium on the skin.

Advice on the diagnosis of infectious disease may sometimes be obtained from those working in the field of insect pathology (Davidson, 1981; Poinar and Thomas, 1978; Weiser, 1977). Such persons are generally more concerned with the control of insect pests than with therapy but often they can provide information on such important matters as epizootiology and disinfection.

The isolation (quarantining) of incoming animals is important, especially if the client has large numbers of invertebrates at risk — on a commercial butterfly farm, for example. New arrivals should be isolated for at least two weeks; during this time they should be carefully examined and sick individuals investigated alive or *post mortem.* Incoming insect eggs can be disinfected (Cooper, 1980; Rivers, 1976).

Certain infections may be transmitted from invertebrates to humans. The most important are *Salmonella* spp. which may be harboured and excreted by cockroaches and other species. There has been concern that giant land snails *(Achatina* spp.) might harbour the zoonotic helminth *Angiostrongylus* but there is no evidence that animals bred in the UK are infected with this parasite (Cooper and Mews, 1987). Nevertheless, it is sensible to ensure that those coming into close contact with invertebrates of any species practise hygienic measures. This is particularly important when the invertebrates are kept in institutions such as schools or hospitals (Cooper, 1976; 1986b).

Parasites

Many parasites are associated with invertebrates and some may cause disease or death (Cooper, 1987; Rivers, 1976). The caterpillars of butterflies and moths and the eggs of mantids, in particular, are susceptible to attack by parasitic wasps and flies. The latter deposit eggs which subsequently hatch into voracious larvae; these eat the host alive. There is no known treatment but effective prevention can be achieved by erecting insect netting around cages.

Captive locusts and grasshoppers are subject to infestation by nematodes of the genus *Mermis.* Affected animals lose weight and die; at *post-mortem* examination they are found to have large numbers of worms in the body cavity. Again, there appears to be no treatment but since the parasite can be introduced on contaminated grass, careful selection of food (or even growing it specially) will help to prevent outbreaks.

Mites are found on many species of arthropod — for example, on millipedes and dung beetles — but they appear to be non-pathogenic and their removal is probably unnecessary.

Nutritional diseases

The most prevalent nutritional disorder of invertebrates is probably inanition. Captive specimens will often refuse to eat — and subsequently die of starvation — if the diet offered is unsuitable or if the temperature, relative humidity or environment is suboptimum. Many insects are voracious and regular feeders and will quickly succumb if insufficient food is provided.

While some invertebrates can survive long periods without drinking — for example, certain desert species — as a general rule water should always be provided. The method of presenting this is important; some species will drink from a bowl but for others it may be preferable to spray the cage as they drink only droplets on foliage. Terrestrial invertebrates readily drown if they fall into a water container.

Very few specific deficiency diseases are recognised in invertebrates. However, a definite syndrome occurs in molluscs which receive insufficient calcium in their diet; affected animals develop thin shells and may attempt to obtain the missing mineral by gnawing at the shells of their companions. The condition is easily remedied or prevented (see earlier — Feeding).

Miscellaneous conditions

A number of other problems can befall captive invertebrates and veterinary advice may be sought.

Chemicals.   Invertebrates are susceptible to insecticides and other agents. The clinical signs vary; often the animal is already dead but in some cases muscle spasms are seen and the victim may be incoordinated. There is no specific treatment; the invertebrate should be removed from the source of the chemical (or the agent blown or brushed off its body) and kept in a well ventilated cage. Aquatic species should be given fresh water.

Drowning. Terrestrial arthropods which fall into their water container will appear limp and dead. Some such individuals will recover if placed on blotting paper in a warm dry place.

Integumentary lesions. Lesions of the integument of arthropods are frequently due to, or associated with, dysecdysis. Small pieces of retained exoskeleton may be removed with a moistened paintbrush while larger portions can sometimes be clipped with scissors. Often the best solution to such problems is for the animal to undergo another full moult. This can be encouraged by generous feeding and by ensuring that the temperature and relative humidity are optimum. Shed skins should always be examined for evidence of damage or defects. Apparent deformities of the wings of newly emerged butterflies or moths and certain other insects are usually due to a failure of these to expand properly. This in turn may be attributable to a low relative humidity, or, in some cases, because no branch or similar perch has been provided on which the imago can rest following emergence from the pupa.

DRUGS

Relatively little is known about the safety or efficacy of chemotherapeutic agents in invertebrates although a certain amount of information is available on the use of antibiotics and other drugs in honey bees (Bailey, 1981). Sulphonamides have been used safely in grasshoppers (Henry, 1968) and Wallach (1972) recommended a number of agents for the treatment of colonies of mealworms *(Tenebrio molitor)*.

In the author's experience oxytetracycline and chlortetracycline solutions can be used safely either orally or topically in several species of insects and spiders. However, their efficacy is doubtful and as a general rule the isolation and/or culling of invertebrates is to be preferred to medication.

ANAESTHESIA

Anaesthesia may be needed to immobilise invertebrates or to permit the performance of procedures which are, it is assumed, liable to cause pain. In the past far too little attention has been paid to this subject but the author believes it important that veterinary surgeons are both acquainted with, and able to use, appropriate anaesthetic techniques. The higher invertebrates are not difficult to anaesthetise and most of the procedures recommended appear to be relatively safe. For a detailed account, reference should be made to Cooper (1989).

The following methods of anaesthesia are recommended:-

Terrestrial species

Inhalation anaesthesia using halothane (5–10%) or carbon dioxide (10–20%)

These agents are administered via a jar or anaesthetic chamber. Recovery may be prolonged (2–5 hours) but is usually uneventful.

Some insects tolerate these agents remarkably well. In a trial carried out by the author, American cockroaches *(Periplaneta americana)* were exposed to 100% carbon dioxide for two hours. Although recovery took several hours there were no fatalities. Cockroaches may be unusual in this respect but routine use of 20% carbon dioxide or 10% halothane has proved successful and safe in a number of other arthropods. If a procedure is likely to be painful there may be merit in using halothane in preference to carbon dioxide since the extent to which the latter induces analgesia is not known.

Aquatic species

Absorption anaesthesia using tricaine methanesulphonate (MS 222, Sandoz) or benzocaine

The former can be placed directly in the water but the latter must first be dissolved in acetone. 100mg of either agent is usually used per litre of water. When the animal is immobile it is removed and can be kept out of the water for up to 15 minutes. Recovery takes place on return to fresh water (Cooper, 1989).

Carbon dioxide

Another reliable and relatively inexpensive technique for aquatic species involves the use of carbon dioxide. Either the gas can be bubbled through the water or the latter can be diluted 50:50 with soda water. Again, some doubt exists as to the degree of analgesia produced by carbon dioxide but in practice the technique is tolerated well. The author has used it on many occasions to immobilise leeches *(Hirudo medicinalis)* for examination and swabbing (Cooper *et al*, 1986).

Recovery from all anaesthetics will be hastened if oxygen is administered. This can be pumped into the anaesthetic chamber or bubbled through the water.

REFERENCES AND FURTHER READING

ANON (1986). *Common Diseases of the Adult Honey Bee.* Ministry of Agriculture, Fisheries and Food, Alnwick, Northumberland.

BAILEY, L. (1981). *Honey Bee Pathology.* Academic Press, London.

CANTWELL, G.E. (1974). *Insect Diseases.* Marcel Dekker, New York.

COLLINS, N.M. (1990). Ed. *The Management and Welfare of Invertebrates in Captivity.* National Federation of Zoological Gardens, London.

COOPER, J.E. (1976). Pets in hospitals. *British Medical Journal* i, 698.

COOPER, J.E. (1980). Invertebrates and invertebrate disease; an introduction for the veterinary surgeon. *Journal of Small Animal Practice* 21, 495.

COOPER, J.E. (1985). Cats, dogs and caterpillars. *Veterinary Record* 117, 135.

COOPER, J.E. (1986a). Veterinary work with invertebrates: a new challenge for the profession. In: *Exotic Animals in the 80's.* (Eds. P.W. Scott and A.G. Greenwood) British Veterinary Zoological Society, London.

COOPER, J.E. (1986b). Animals in schools. *Journal of Small Animal Practice* 27, 839.

COOPER, J.E. (1987a). A veterinary approach to spiders. *Journal of Small Animal Practice* 28, 229.

COOPER, J.E. (1987b). Wirbellose (Invertebraten). In: *Krankheiten der Wiltiere.* (Eds. K. Gabrisch and P. Zwart) Schlütersche, Hannover.

COOPER, J.E. (1989). Anaesthesia of exotic species. In: *Manual of Anaesthesia for Small Animal Practice.* (Ed. A.D.R. Hilbery) BSAVA, Cheltenham.

COOPER, J.E., MAHAFFEY, P. and APPLEBEE, K. (1986). Anaesthesia of the medicinal leech *(Hirudo medicinalis).* *Veterinary Record* 118, 589.

COOPER, J.E. and MEWS, A.R. (1987). Health hazards from giant snails. *Veterinary Record* 120, 506.

COOPER, J.E., PEARCE-KELLY, P. and WILLIAMS, D.L. (1991). Eds. *Arachnida '87.* London.

COOPER, M.E. (1987). *An Introduction to Animal Law.* Academic Press, London.

CRUSH, M. (1982). *Handy Homes for Creepy Crawlies.* Granada, London.

DAVIDSON, E.W. (1981). Ed. *Pathogenesis of Invertebrate Microbial Diseases.* Allanheld and Osmun, Totowa, New Jersey.

FRYE, F.L. (1986). Care and feeding of invertebrates kept as pets or study animals. In: *Zoo and Wild Animal Medicine.* (Ed. M.E. Fowler) W.B. Saunders, Philadelphia.

FRYE, F.L. (1990). *Care and Feeding of Tarantulas and Some Invertebrates Kept as Pets, Study or Prey Animals.* Kreiger, Melbourne, Florida.

FRYE, F.L. and CALVERT, C. (1989). Preliminary information on the nutritional content of mulberry silk moth *(Bombyx mori)* larvae. *Journal of Zoo and Wildlife Medicine* 20, 73.

GREENWOOD, A.G. (1975). A simple technique for bleeding the lobster. *Veterinary Record* 97, 476.

HENRY, J.E. (1968). *Malameba locustae* and its antibiotic control in grasshopper cultures. *Journal of Invertebrate Pathology* 11, 224.

IATA (1990). *Live Animals Regulations.* International Air Transport Association, Montreal - Geneva.

MARTIN, R.D., RIVERS, J.P.W. and COWGILL, U.M. (1976). Culturing mealworms as food for animals in captivity. *International Zoo Yearbook* 16, 63.

MILLER, J. (1975). *How to Keep Unusual Pets.* Studio Vista, London.

MURPHY, F. (1980). *Keeping Spiders, Insects and Other Land Invertebrates in Captivity.* John Bartholomew and Son, Edinburgh.

POINAR, G.O. and THOMAS, G.M. (1978). *Diagnostic Manual for the Identification of Insect Pathogens.* Plenum Press, New York.

PROVENZANO, A.J. (1983). *The Biology of Crustacea. 6. Pathology.* Academic Press, New York.

RIVERS, C.F. (1976). Disease. In: *The Moths and Butterflies of Great Britain and Ireland. Vol. 1.* (Ed. J. Heath) Curwen Press, London.

SINGH, P. and MOORE, R.F. (1985). *Handbook of Insect Rearing.* Two volumes. Elsevier, Amsterdam.

SPARKS, A.K. (1972). *Invertebrate Pathology: Non-Communicable Diseases.* Academic Press, New York.

STONE, J.L.S. and MIDWINTER, H.J. (1975). *Butterfly Culture.* Blandford Press, Poole.

UFAW (1976). Ed. *The UFAW Handbook on the Care and Management of Laboratory Animals.* 5th Edn. Churchill Livingstone, Edinburgh.

WALLACH, J.D. (1972). The management and medical care of mealworms. *Journal of Zoo Animal Medicine* **3**, 29.

WEBB, A. and WEBB, F. (1987). *Breeding Live Food for Reptiles and Amphibians.* Fitzgerald Publishing, London.

WEISER, J. (1977). *An Atlas of Insect Diseases.* W. Junk, The Hague.

CHAPTER TWENTY ONE

LEGISLATION

Margaret E Cooper LLB FLS

The veterinary surgeon should be prepared to provide clients with basic information on the legal as well as medical aspects of pets which are presented at the surgery. It is not unknown for clients to consult a veterinarian about the prospective acquisition of an animal and legal requirements can be a significant factor, particularly in respect of exotic species.

The legislation most likely to be of use to veterinarians and their clients when dealing with exotic pets is outlined below and discussed briefly.

It should be borne in mind that legislation may be amended or repealed after the completion of this chapter (November 1990) and that Acts applying to England and Wales do not always extend to Scotland or Northern Ireland which may or may not have their own, comparable, legislation. The reader is also encouraged to keep up-to-date with developments in the law by reading the veterinary press and the Royal College of Veterinary Surgeons (RCVS) publication on legislation affecting the veterinary profession in the UK (RCVS, 1987). Many contemporary books on the care of pets in general or of specific species include a legal section - although the quality of the information provided is variable.

The legislation has been divided into sections for quick reference although the subject matter may overlap on occasion. The topics have been selected to indicate provisions that are particularly relevant to the species covered by this book or which are additional to legislation applicable to animals in general.

There are also other standard legal aspects of animal care or of veterinary practice, for example, relating to management, liability or safety, which apply no matter what kind of animal, exotic or domestic, is involved. For this basic information reference should be made to the books included in the General Reading list.

RESTRICTIONS ON KEEPING ANIMALS

A local government authority licence is required under the following legislation:

1. **Dangerous Wild Animals Act 1976 (as amended by The Dangerous Wild Animals Act 1976 (Modification) Order 1984)**

   The keeping at private premises of the exotic species listed in the 1984 Order must be licensed (British Veterinary Association, 1976; Cooper, 1978; Chapman 1989). This does not apply to zoos, petshops or circuses, or establishments designated under the Animals (Scientific Procedures) Act 1986.

   Most non-domesticated species which are likely to cause substantial harm are listed in the Order, including many larger species, all primates except marmosets, most venomous snakes, some particularly poisonous spiders and buthid scorpions. The only birds listed are the Rheidae (emu-like birds). The only UK species affected are the wild cat and the adder (viper).

   Basic standards of housing, safety and welfare are required. Insurance and an annual veterinary inspection are obligatory, and a fee is payable.

2.   Zoo Licensing Act 1981

This Act applies to all zoos and other collections of non-domesticated animals which are open (whether or not for a fee) to the public on more than seven days in any twelve-month period.

Zoos must be licensed and are subject to a major inspection by veterinarians, and others, every three years. There are lesser inspections in other years and fees are charged for licences and inspections (Cooper, 1983; Leeming, 1989).

Exemption from the Act, or more commonly, reduced inspection requirements, may be available for small collections and those with very few exotic species (Department of the Environment, 1988).

The Department of the Environment (DOE) has produced national standards for zoos and codes of practice are being developed to meet particular needs (National Federation of Zoological Gardens, 1990a; European Union of Aquarium Curators, in preparation). Zoo inspectors are provided with a report questionnaire. A supplement relating to invertebrates is now available (National Federation of Zoological Gardens, 1990b).

3.   Pet Animals Act 1951

A licence must be obtained to run a business (not solely the conventional high street petshop) of selling domestic and exotic vertebrate animals as pets or for ornamental purposes. Inspection may be by a veterinary surgeon or local authority official (British Veterinary Association, 1979).

4.   Performing Animals (Regulation) Act 1925
Performing Animals Rules 1925 and 1968

Although a licence as such is not required, the trainer of any vertebrate animal used in a performance or exhibit must be registered with the local authority where he or she resides and obtain a certificate of registration. Local authorities can inspect relevant premises.

There may be restrictions imposed upon the keeping of non-domesticated species at private or business premises. Clients should be advised to review their title deeds before they acquire a non-domesticated animal.

For more detailed information on this subject and the following topic of Welfare, see Porter (1987a) and Blackman *et al* (1989).

WELFARE

1.   Protection of Animals Acts 1911 - 88
Protection of Animals (Scotland) Acts 1912 - 88

It is an offence to treat any domestic or captive species of animal cruelly or to cause it any unnecessary suffering. This includes the failure to provide necessary food, water, care and veterinary attention (Todd, 1989).

Killing an animal is not an offence under these Acts provided that it is carried out humanely.

2.   Protection of Animals (Anaesthetics) Acts 1954 and 1964

Anaesthesia must be used in procedures which interfere with sensitive tissues or bones of an animal with the exception of minor procedures such as injections. Although these Acts expressly do not apply to birds, fish or reptiles, anaesthesia should be used to fulfil the general requirements of the main Protection of Animals Acts which require an operation to be carried out with due care and humanity and without unnecessary suffering.

3.   Abandonment of Animals Act 1960

Animals should not deliberately and without good cause be abandoned in circumstances likely to cause them unnecessary suffering. Although this Act is aimed primarily at pets, it should be borne in mind when assessing the suitability of wild creatures for release (see 'Introduction').

4. Wildlife and Countryside Act 1981

Section 8 of the Wildlife and Countryside Act provides that it is an offence to keep any bird in a cage which is not large enough to allow the bird to stretch its wings fully. A smaller cage is permitted only for poultry or for use while transporting or exhibiting a bird or while it is undergoing examination or treatment by a veterinary surgeon.

5. Animal Health Act 1981

Transit of Animals (General) Order 1973 (as amended)

Pet and exotic species, including invertebrates, must be transported with proper attention to their welfare. Appropriate containers and vehicles must be used and adequate food, water, ventilation and temperature must be provided. It is expected that from 1993 the Regulation (currently in preparation) on the transit of animals will supersede national transport laws in the European Community (EC).

Some public carriers such as British Rail have their own conditions for acceptance and transport; most airlines apply the International Air Transport Association (IATA)'s Live Animals Regulations (International Air Transport Association, annual). The Secretariat of the Convention on International Trade in Endangered Species of Wild Fauna and Flora (Washington Convention or CITES) (see Import and Export) has issued guidance for the transport by any means of endangered species (CITES, 1980). This primarily follows the IATA Regulations.

The Post Office forbids the transport by post of living animals apart from a few species of invertebrate, such as bees, although others, such as caterpillars, may be posted by prior arrangement with the Post Office. There are also special requirements for the mailing of animal pathogens (Post Office, annual).

WILDLIFE

Wildlife and Countryside Act 1981 (as amended by The Wildlife and Countryside Act 1981 (Variation of Schedules) Order 1988) (wild and game birds, listed wild creatures)

Deer Act 1963 and Deer (Scotland) Act 1959 and related legislation

Badgers Act 1973 (as amended)

Conservation of Seals Act 1970 (as amended)

Salmon and Freshwater Fisheries Act 1975

Game Acts (various) (rabbits, hares and game birds)

Destructive Imported Animals Act 1932 (mink, grey squirrel, etc).

While it is still popular to keep or help wild animals, there is now considerable legislation to protect wildlife.

The Wildlife and Countryside Act provides various degrees of protection for indigenous wild birds. There are close seasons for game birds, special penalties in respect of rare birds and the requirements of ringing and registration with the DOE in respect of diurnal birds of prey and other rare species (DOE, 1983 and various; Cooper and Cooper, 1983; Royal Society for the Protection of Birds, 1989 and undated).

Some mammals, reptiles, amphibians, insects and their habitats are also protected (Cooper and Cooper, 1987; DOE, 1988) and badgers are covered by a specific Act.

Schedules 1 to 6 of the Act list the various species according to the protection afforded to them (DOE, 1988).

The Act provides that it is an offence to take, injure or kill a protected species. It is also an offence to possess such animals unless it can be proved that the possession is legal. To do so, it is necessary to be able to show that the animal is captive-bred, or has been imported, sold or taken in accordance with the Act or under a licence. In this situation the burden of proof falls on the person alleging legal possession and it is therefore important to keep good records of any acquisition.

The sale of British wild birds and other protected species is controlled by either the CITES Regulation or the Act. The sale of many species is permitted under general or personal exemptions or licences. For the sale of other species, see Import and Export, Conservation controls.

It is, however, permissible to take from the wild a sick or injured protected creature in order to tend it until it is fit to be released. If it is injured or diseased beyond hope of recovery it may be killed. A humane method must be used (Protection of Animals Acts, see Welfare).

Diurnal birds of prey taken under this provision must be ringed and registered unless they are held under the six week exemption which has been issued by the DOE for veterinary surgeons and licensed rehabilitation keepers (LRKs).

Many activities which are *prima facie* prohibited, such as trapping, shooting or selling, can be authorised by licence from the appropriate authority if they are for purposes such as scientific studies, aviculture or crop protection. The provision permitting 'authorised persons' to kill or take wild birds listed in Schedule 2 Part II (for example, crows *(Corvus corone)* and rooks *(Corvus frugilegus)* may be amended to require such activities to be carried out under licence.

It is an offence deliberately to release a non-indigenous species into the wild unless, like the grey squirrel *(Sciurus carolinensis),* it is already established there and listed in the Act.

Animals such as game birds, deer, fish and seals which are hunted are protected by close seasons and certain methods of capture and killing are prohibited by various Acts.

Many other species are not protected by the Act; neither do the Protection of Animals Acts apply to free-living wildlife such as the hedgehog or fox. Under pest control provisions it is illegal to keep certain other species (particularly the grey squirrel) without a licence and occupiers of land can be required to destroy wildlife which are causing damage.

Deer are nowadays to be found wild, kept in parks and collections or farmed. All species are subject to the Deer Acts and, with the exception of marked, farmed deer, are protected during their respective close seasons. Deer are also protected at night, except in limited situations allowing for protection of property. Sick or injured deer may at any time be killed or taken for care.

A Nature Conservancy Council (NCC) licence is required if any drug-dart technique is to be used with deer in England or Wales to take or kill a deer; such licences are available only for scientific or translocation purposes.

Summaries of the law relating to deer are provided by Moss (1983) and Cooper (1984), while Porter (1982) and RCVS (1990) give guidance on the supply of drugs to dart-gun users.

IMPORT AND EXPORT

1.   **Health controls:**

     Animal Health Act 1981

     Importation of Animals Order 1977

     Rabies (Importation of Cats, Dogs and other Mammals) Order 1974 (amended 1977)

     Importation of Birds, Poultry and Hatching Eggs Order 1979

     Importation of Animal Pathogens Order 1980

     Importation of Animal Products and Poultry Products Order 1980

     Almost all imported animals (other than reptiles, amphibians and harmless invertebrates) and most animal derivatives and pathogens are subject to Ministry of Agriculture, Fisheries and Food[1] (MAFF) controls. These require that a licence to import, together with health certification, must be obtained prior to arrival and that some species are quarantined after landing in the UK.

[1] For England. The appropriate body for Scotland is the Department of Agriculture and Fisheries for Scotland and for Wales it is the Welsh Office, Agriculture Department.

Since the conditions of import vary from time to time and depend upon the disease situation in the country of origin, it is essential to obtain the current requirements from MAFF. There is little constraint on export but the country of destination will have its own import requirements, which can be obtained from MAFF or the relevant diplomatic mission. Both import and export arrangements are complicated and should commence well in advance of the actual journey, with enquiries in the first instance to MAFF.

2. **Conservation controls:**

    EC Regulation 3626/82 (as amended)

    The Endangered Species (Import and Export) Act 1976 (as amended by the Wildlife and Countryside Act 1981)) and (Modification) Orders 1977 and 1978

    Many exotic species are identified under CITES as threatened immediately or potentially with extinction and in need of protection from uncontrolled trade, and they are subject to import, export and sale controls, directly imposed by the EC CITES Regulation and managed by the DOE.

    The EC Regulation contains additional restrictions on the sale and display for any commercial purposes of endangered species, including birds of prey and Mediterranean tortoises. There are exemptions permitting the sale of ringed, captive-bred specimens of many species of bird of prey. In the case of Mediterranean tortoises, the exemptions authorise the sale of captive-bred specimens provided that, on the first occasion on which they are traded, they are sold to a dealer registered with the DOE. On any subsequent sale, proof of that first sale must be produced. Alternatively, an individual licence may be obtained. However, if clients are in any doubt about their position they should be referred to the DOE to ascertain their position before selling or putting such specimens on show.

    Species not subject to CITES controls may be regulated as to import, export or sale by the Endangered Species (Import and Export) Act 1976 as amended by the Wildlife and Countryside Act 1981.

    These and other provisions are described in notices issued by the DOE (1987) and are distinct from, and additional to, the MAFF documentation mentioned above. It is important to allow time to complete these formalities.

3. **Customs and Excise:**

    Animals imported into the UK will normally be subject to Customs Duty and Value Added Tax. Careful preparation for Customs clearance, particularly as to paperwork, should be made since delays can be harmful to the animals involved. Many frontier controls within the EC will be removed in 1993 although the UK rabies restrictions are expected to remain in force.

4. **Transport:**

    Due attention must be given to the welfare requirements (see Welfare) in respect of any movement of animals within UK jurisdiction. The CITES provisions require that animals subject to them must be packed and transported humanely.

MEDICAL

Veterinary Surgeons Act 1966

Medicines Act 1968

The Medicines (Veterinary Drugs) (Prescription Only) Order 1985

Misuse of Drugs Act 1971

The Misuse of Drugs Regulations 1985

General information on this subject can be obtained from Porter (1987b, 1989), Knifton and Edwards (1987) and the *Veterinary Record.* Points of particular relevance to those treating exotic pets are:

1. Veterinary Surgeons Act 1966

The Act restricts to veterinary surgeons and veterinary practitioners registered with the RCVS the right to practise in respect of mammals (including marine mammals), birds and reptiles; it is considered, however, that anyone may treat fish, amphibians and invertebrates, subject, of course, to the provisions of the Protection of Animals Acts (see Welfare).

The Act permits the owners of animals (and their employees and families) to give minor medical treatment and anyone may give first aid in an emergency (British Wildlife Rehabilitation Council, 1989; Cooper and Sinclair, 1989).

2. Medicines legislation

Procedures for complying with the medicines legislation such as prescribing, supplying and labelling Prescription Only Medicines (POMs) apply regardless of the species for which they are being prescribed.

Prescriptions for POMs issued by veterinarians must state that the drug is prescribed for animals under their care.

Some problems of interpretation occur in the application of the requirement that a veterinarian may only prescribe POMs for 'animals under his care' to exotic animal collections where there are large numbers or a rapid turnover. Guidance on the phrase appears in the RCVS Guide to Professional Conduct (RCVS, 1990), in Porter (1982) and British Veterinary Association (1990). This may be of help, but ultimately reference to the RCVS for guidance should be made.

LIABILITY FOR NON-DOMESTICATED ANIMALS

1. Animals Act 1971

Those who have in their possession (whether or not they are the owner) non-domesticated species which are likely to cause serious damage must take care to ensure that such creatures do not injure or damage other people or property. The law requires a stricter standard than that for domesticated species, imposing liability for any harm caused unless the person suffering it consented or contributed to it (North, 1972).

2. Negligence, nuisance and trespass

Liability can arise under these heads in respect of exotic, as with other, species.

3. Health and Safety at Work etc. Act 1974

A person who employs staff or has volunteers or students to work with non-domesticated species must provide additional safety procedures to take account of any special risks involved. This may include the provision of specialised guidance, training and working procedures and protective equipment. There is a specific code of practice for zoos (Health and Safety Commission, 1985).

DRUG-DART WEAPONS

Any weapon, such as a dart-gun, cross-bow or blowpipe which can be used to discharge tranquillising drugs must be authorised by the Home Office (Home Office, 1978). A Firearms Certificate issued by the police is also required. The use of a cross-bow (with or without drugs) for wild animals requires a Nature Conservancy Council licence.

CONCLUSION

The aim of this chapter has been to acquaint veterinarians with the law that is particularly relevant to exotic pets. It is hoped that it will enable them to expand their existing knowledge of the legislation applicable in general to veterinary practice, thereby adding another dimension to the service that they provide for their clients.

GENERAL READING

ACTS OF PARLIAMENT AND STATUTORY INSTRUMENTS. Available from Her Majesty's Stationery Office.

Halsbury's Laws of England. Butterworth, England.

Halsbury's Statutes of England. Butterworth, England.

Halsbury's Statutory Instruments. Butterworth, England.

BLACKMAN, D.E., HUMPHREYS, P. N. and TODD, P. (1989). *Animal Welfare and the Law.* Cambridge University Press, Cambridge.

COOPER, M.E. (1987). *An Introduction to Animal Law.* Academic Press, London.

CROFTS, W. (1984). *A Summary of the Statute Law Relating to Animal Welfare in England and Wales.* Universities Federation for Animal Welfare, Potters Bar.

PARKES, C. and THORNLEY, J. (1987). *Fair Game.* Pelham, London.

ROYAL COLLEGE OF VETERINARY SURGEONS (1987). *Legislation Affecting the Veterinary Profession in the United Kingdom.* 5th Edn (with annual supplements). RCVS, London.

ROYAL COLLEGE OF VETERINARY SURGEONS (1990). *Guide to Professional Conduct.* RCVS, London.

SANDYS-WINSCH, G. (1984). *Animal Law.* 2nd Edn. Shaw and Sons, London.

VETERINARY RECORD. Information and papers on legal subjects are published from time to time.

SPECIFIC REFERENCES

BRITISH VETERINARY ASSOCIATION (1976). *Dangerous Wild Animals Act 1976. Guide to Veterinary Surgeons concerned with Inspections under this Act.* BVA Publications, London.

BRITISH VETERINARY ASSOCIATION (1979). *Pet Animals Act 1951. A Guide for Local Authorities.* BVA Publications, London.

BRITISH VETERINARY ASSOCIATION (1990). Code of practice. Sale or supply of animal medicines by veterinary surgeons. *Veterinary Record* **127**, 236.

BRITISH WILDLIFE REHABILITATION COUNCIL (1989). *Ethics and Legal Aspects of Treatment and Rehabilitation of Wild Animal Casualties.* BWRC, London.

CHAPMAN, M.J. (1989). The Dangerous Wild Animals Act 1976. In: *Animal Welfare and the Law.* (Eds. D. E. Blackman, P. N. Humphreys and P. Todd) Cambridge University Press, Cambridge.

CONVENTION ON INTERNATIONAL TRADE IN ENDANGERED SPECIES OF WILD FAUNA AND FLORA (CITES) (1980). *Guidelines for Transport and Preparation for Shipment of Live Wild Animals and Plants.* International Union for Conservation of Nature, Gland, Switzerland.

CCOPER, J. E. and COOPER, M. E. (1983). A guide to the Wildlife and Countryside Act 1981 as it affects birds. *British Veterinary Zoological Association Newsletter* **15**, 7.

COOPER, M. E. (1978). The Dangerous Wild Animals Act 1976. *Veterinary Record* **102**, 457.

COOPER, M. E. (1983). The Zoo Licensing Act 1981. *Veterinary Record* **112**, 564.

COOPER, M. E. (1984). The law. In: *Guidelines for the Safe and Humane Handling of Live Deer in Great Britain.* (Ed. Deer Liaison Committee) Nature Conservancy Council, London.

COOPER, M. E. and COOPER, J. E. (1987). Wildlife and non-domesticated species. In: *Legislation Affecting the Veterinary Profession in the United Kingdom.* 5th Edn. (with annual supplements). Royal College of Veterinary Surgeons, London.

COOPER, M. E. and SINCLAIR, D. A. (1989). Law relating to wildlife rehabilitation. *Abstract from the Second Symposium of the British Wildlife Rehabilitation Council, Stoneleigh, 1989.* BWRC, London.

DEPARTMENT OF THE ENVIRONMENT (1983). *Wildlife and Countryside Act, Section 7. A Guide to the Registration of Species listed in Schedule 4 for Keepers and Owners.* Inspectorate of Rural Affairs, DOE, Bristol.

DEPARTMENT OF THE ENVIRONMENT (1987). *Controls on the Import and Export of Endangered and Vulnerable Species with Supplementary Notices 1-6.* Endangered Species Branch, DOE, Bristol.

DEPARTMENT OF THE ENVIRONMENT (1988). *Protecting Britain's Wildlife.* DOE, London; Welsh Office, Cardiff; Scottish Office, Edinburgh.

DEPARTMENT OF THE ENVIRONMENT (various). Information sheets and guidance notes on the implementation of the Wildlife and Countryside Act in respect of birds. DOE, Bristol.

HEALTH AND SAFETY COMMISSION (1985). *Zoos - Safety, Health and Welfare Standards for Employers and Persons at Work. Approved Code of Practice and Guidance Note.* Her Majesty's Stationery Office, London.

HOME OFFICE (1978). *The Use and Safe-keeping of Tranquillising Weapons.* Home Office, London; Scottish Home and Health Department, Edinburgh.

INTERNATIONAL AIR TRANSPORT ASSOCIATION (annual). *Live Animals Regulations.* IATA, Geneva.

KNIFTON, A. and EDWARDS, B. R. (1987). Controlled drugs and medicinal products. In: *Legislation Affecting the Veterinary Profession in the United Kingdom.* 5th Edn (with annual supplements). Royal College of Veterinary Surgeons, London.

LEEMING, D. B. (1989). Legislation relating to zoos. In: *Animal Welfare and the Law.* (Eds D. B. Blackman, P. N. Humphreys and P.Todd) Cambridge University Press, Cambridge.

MOSS, R. (1983). Legislation on the handling of deer. *Publication of the Veterinary Deer Society* **1** (4), 9.

NATIONAL FEDERATION OF ZOOLOGICAL GARDENS OF GREAT BRITAIN AND IRELAND (1990a). *Codes of Practice for the Care of Invertebrates in Captivity. IWG/2 Euthanasia of Invertebrates.* National Federation of Zoological Gardens of Great Britain and Ireland, London.

NATIONAL FEDERATION OF ZOOLOGICAL GARDENS OF GREAT BRITAIN AND IRELAND (1990b). *Codes of Practice for the Care of Invertebrates in Captivity. IWG/1 Notes for Inspectors.* National Federation of Zoological Gardens of Great Britain and Ireland. London.

NORTH, P. M. (1972). *The Modern Law of Animals.* Butterworth, London.

PORTER, A. R. W. (1982). Drugs for use in dart-guns. *Publication of the Veterinary Deer Society* **1**(2), 2.

PORTER, A. R. W. (1987a). Animal welfare. In: *Legislation Affecting the Veterinary Profession in the United Kingdom.* 5th Edn (with annual supplements). RCVS, London.

PORTER, A. R. W. (1987b). Practice of veterinary medicine and surgery. In: *Legislation Affecting the Veterinary Profession in the United Kingdom.* 5th Edn (with annual supplements). RCVS, London.

PORTER, A. R. W. (1989). The Veterinary Surgeons Act 1966. In: *Animal Welfare and the Law.* (Eds D. E. Blackman, P. N. Humphreys and P. Todd) Cambridge University Press, Cambridge.

POST OFFICE (annual). *Post Office Guide.* Post Office, London.

ROYAL COLLEGE OF VETERINARY SURGEONS (1987). *Legislation Affecting the Veterinary Profession in the United Kingdom.* 5th Edn (with annual supplements). RCVS, London.

ROYAL COLLEGE OF VETERINARY SURGEONS (1990). *Guide to Professional Conduct.* RCVS, London.

ROYAL SOCIETY FOR THE PROTECTION OF BIRDS (undated). *Information about Birds and the Law.* RSPB, Sandy, Bedfordshire.

ROYAL SOCIETY FOR THE PROTECTION OF BIRDS (1989). *Wild Birds and the Law.* RSPB, Sandy, Bedfordshire.

TODD, P. (1989). The Protection of Animals Acts 1911-1964. In: *Animal Welfare and the Law.* (Eds. D. E. Blackman, P. N. Humphreys and P. Todd) Cambridge University Press, Cambridge.

The following addresses may prove helpful to those who are dealing with exotic species. While every effort has been made to check that the list is correct at the date of publication, no responsibility can be accepted for mistakes or omissions. The inclusion of an organisation on the list should not necessarily be taken to imply recommendation or endorsement by the British Small Animal Veterinary Association or by the editors and authors of this manual.

SOCIETIES, CLUBS AND ORGANISATIONS

Amateur Entomologists' Society (AES)
22 Salisbury Road, Feltham, Middlesex TW13 5DP

Animal Welfare Foundation
British Veterinary Association, 7 Mansfield Street, London
W1M 0AT

Association of Avian Veterinarians
5770 Lake Worth Road, Lake Worth, Florida 33463-3299, USA

Association of British Wild Animal Keepers (ABWAK)
2A Northcote Road, Clifton, Bristol BS8 3HB

Association for the Study of Reptiles and Amphibians
(ASRA)
Cotswold Wildlife Park, Burford, Oxfordshire OX8 4JW

Avian Special Study Group
c/o BSAVA, Kingsley House, Shurdington, Cheltenham,
Glos GL51 5TQ

Avicultural Society (The) (Secretary)
c/o Windsor Forest Stud, Mill Ride, Ascot, Berkshire
SL5 8LT

Bat Conservation Trust
c/o Conservation Foundation, 1 Kensington Gore, London
SW7 2AR

Blue Cross
1 Hugh Street, Victoria, London SW1V 1QQ

British Bird Council
1577 Bristol Road South, Longbridge, Birmingham B45 9UA

British Chelonia Group (BCG)
PO Box 2163, London NW10 5HW

British Deer Society
Green Lane, Upton Nervet, Reading, Berkshire RG7 4HA

British Falconers' Club
Home Farm, Hints, Nr Tamworth, Staffordshire B78 3DW

British Herpetological Society (BHS)
c/o Zoological Society of London, Regent's Park, London
NW1 4RY

British Laboratory Animals Veterinary Association (BLAVA)
c/o 7 Mansfield Street, London W1M 0AT

British Marine Association
139 Bradford Avenue, Great Field Estate, North
Humberside HU9 4LZ

British Rabbit Council
Purefoy House, 7 Kirkgate, Newark, Nottinghamshire
NG24 1AD

British Small Animal Veterinary Association
Kingsley House, Shurdington, Cheltenham, Glos
GL51 5TQ

British Trust for Ornithology (BTO)
Beech Grove, Station Road, Tring, Hertfordshire
HP23 5NR

British Veterinary Association (BVA)
7 Mansfield Street, London W1M 0AT

British Veterinary Zoological Society (BVZS)
c/o 7 Mansfield Street, London W1M 0AT

British Waterfowl Association
New Gill, Bishopdale, Leyburn, North Yorkshire DL8 3TP

British Wildlife Rehabilitation Council
c/o RSPCA Headquarters, The Causeway, Horsham,
West Sussex RH12 1HG and 1 Pemberton Close,
Aylesbury, Buckinghamshire HP21 7NY

Budgerigar Society (The)
49-53 Hazelwood Road, Northampton NN1 1LG

Commercial Rabbit Association
Little On House, Little On, Stafford ST20 0AU

Fauna and Flora Preservation Society (The)
78-83 North Street, Brighton, East Sussex BN1 1ZA

Federation of British Aquarists' Society
46 Airthrie Road, Goodmayes, Ilford, Essex IG3 9QU

Game Conservancy (The)
Burgate Manor, Fordingbridge, Hampshire SP6 1ET

Hawk and Owl Trust (The)
c/o Zoological Society of London, Regent's Park, London
NW1 4RY

Institute of Biology
20 Queensberry Place, London SW7 2DZ

International Herpetological Society (IHS)
65 Broadstone Avenue, Walsall, West Midlands WS3 1JA

Mammal Conservation Trust (The)
c/o The Chapel, 2 Hobbs Hill, Welwyn, Hertfordshire
AL6 9DS

Mammal Society (The)
Burlington House, Piccadilly, London W1N 0LQ

National Bird of Prey Centre
Newent, Gloucestershire GL18 1JJ

National Cavy Club
21 Coleridge Close, Cefn Glas, Bridgend, Mid Glamorgan
CF31 4PB

National Council for Aviculture
87 Winn Road, Lee, London SE12 9EY

National Fancy Rat Society
19 Brown's Lane, Uckfield, East Sussex TN22 1RY

National Ferret Welfare Society
Meadow View, Pheasants Hill, Hambleden,
Henley on Thames, Oxon RG9 6SN

National Hamster Council
89 Forrest Road, Southport, Lancashire PR8 6HY

National Mongolian Gerbil Society
230 Crow Road, Broomhill, Glasgow G11 7LA

National Mouse Club
56 Claremont Grove, Shipley, Yorkshire

National Small Animals Society
2 Pound Green Cottage, Wokefield Green, Mortimer,
Berkshire RG7 3AT

National Young Fanciers' Society
53 Myrtle Avenue, Peterborough, Cambridgeshire

Parrot Society (The)
17 De Parys Avenue, Bedford, Bedfordshire

People's Dispensary for Sick Animals (PDSA)
Whitechapel Way, Priorslee, Telford, Shropshire TF2 9PQ

Pet Health Council (PHC)
4 Bedford Square, London WC1B 3RA

Primate Society of Great Britain
c/o Department of Social Studies, Oxford Polytechnic,
Oxford

Raptor Breeders Association
Orchard Cottage, Dexter Lane, Hurley, Warwickshire

Royal College of Veterinary Surgeons (RCVS)
32 Belgrave Square, London SW1X 8QP

Royal Entomological Society
41 Queen's Gate, London SW7 5HU

Royal Pigeon Racing Association
The Reddings, Near Cheltenham, Gloucestershire GL51 1HG

Royal Society for the Prevention of Cruelty to Animals
(RSPCA), The Causeway, Horsham, West Sussex
RH12 1HG

Royal Society for the Protection of Birds (RSPB)
The Lodge, Sandy, Bedfordshire SG12 2DL

Society for Companion Animal Studies (SCAS)
New Malden House, 1 Blagdon Road, New Malden,
Surrey KT3 4TB

Southern Gerbil Society
Common Side, Great Bookham, Surrey

South Western Herpetological Society (SWHS)
59 St Marychurch Road, Torquay, Devon TQ1 3HG

Ulster Society for the Prevention of Cruelty to Animals
Knockdeen, 11 Drumview Road, Lisburn, Co Antrim
BT27 6YF

Universities Federation for Animal Welfare (UFAW)
8 Hamilton Close, South Mimms, Hertfordshire EN6 3BD

Veterinary Deer Society
c/o Animal Diseases Research Association, Moredun
Institute, 408 Gilmerton Road, Edinburgh EH17 7HJ

Wildfowl and Wetlands Trust (The)
Slimbridge, Gloucestershire GL2 7BT

Wildlife Department
RSPCA Headquarters, The Causeway, Horsham, West
Sussex RH12 1HG

Wildlife Disease Association
PO Box 886, Ames, Iowa 50010, USA

Wildlife Hospitals Trust
1 Pemberton Close, Aylesbury, Buckinghamshire
HP21 7NY

World Association of Wildlife Veterinarians
(Chairman — Interim Executive Committee), Chartley
House, Studham, Dunstable, Bedfordshire LU6 2QB

World Pheasant Association
PO Box 5, Lower Basildon, Reading, Berkshire RG8 9PF

Worldwide Fund for Nature (WWF)
Panda House, 11-13 Ockford Road, Godalming, Surrey
GU7 1QY

World Society for the Protection of Animals (WSPA)
Park Place, 10 Lawn Lane, London SW8

Zoological Society of London
Regent's Park, London NW1 4RY

EQUIPMENT AND SERVICES

Arnolds Veterinary Products Limited
Cartmel Drive, Harlescott, Shrewsbury SY1 3TB
(veterinary equipment)

BCG Tortoise Registration
9 Sutlej Road, Charlton, London SE7 7DD

Bioserve Inc
PO Box 450, Frenchtown, New Jersey, USA
(for Primilac)

Biotech Consultants
Brook Street, Alva, Clackmannanshire, Scotland
FK12 5JJ
(cages)

Brindus Industrial Services Limited
Dartford Industrial Trading Estate, Dartford, Kent
(gloves)

British Denkavit
Patrick House, West Quay Road, Poole, Dorset BH15 1JF
(supplier of Denkapup)

British Trust for Ornithology
Beech Grove, Station Road, Tring, Hertfordshire
HP23 5NR
(spring balances)

Championship Foods Limited
Orwell, Royston, Hertfordshire SG8 5QX
(supplier of Horsepower)

Chas F Thackray Limited
PO Box 171, Park Street, Leeds, West Yorkshire
(endoscopes)

Databird Worldwide Scientific Limited
Queen Mary and Westfield College, Mile End Road,
London E14
(chromosomal sexing of birds)

Distinject
Peter Ott AGG, Postfach, CH-4007, Basel, Switzerland
(capture equipment)

John E Haith
Park Street, Cleethorpes, South Humberside DN35 7NF
(bird food manufacturers and suppliers)

Harlan Olac Limited
Shaw's Farm, Blackthorn, Bicester, Oxfordshire OX6 0TP
(specific bood test for Aleutian disease in ferrets)

International Market Supply
Dane Mill, Broadhurst Lane, Congleton, Cheshire CW12 1LA
(anaesthetic apparatus, heating pads and other equipment for
small mammal surgery; also bird crop tubes etc; animal
handling equipment)

King British Aquarium Supplies Limited
Hayfield Mills, Haycliffe Lane, Bradford, West Yorkshire
BD5 9ET
(fish food manufacturers)

MD Components
Hamelin House, 211-213 Hightown, Luton, Bedfordshire
LU2 0BZ
(animal capture and control equipment)

Medical Diagnostic Services Inc
PO Box 1441, Brandon, Florida 34299, USA
(diagnostic instruments including endoscopes)

Norfine Nets
15 The Drive, Fakenham, Norfolk NR21 8EE
(nets)

North Kent Plastics
1 Bilton Road, Erith, Kent DA8 2AN
(cages)

Olympus Optical Company Limited
KeyMed House, Stock Road, Southend on Sea, Essex
SS2 5QH
(endoscopes)

Peq-Ag Inc
30W432 Rt 20, Illinois 60120, USA
(supplier of Esbilac, KMR, Multi-milk)

Richard Wolf UK Limited
PO Box 47, Mitcham, Surrey CR4 4TT
(endoscopes)

Sherley's Division
Ciba-Geigy Animal Health,
Whittlesford, Cambridge CB2 4QT
(supplier of Lactol)

Special Diet Services
1 Stepfield, Witham, Essex CM8 3AB
(primate diets)

Telinject UK Ferrand Engineering Co Ltd
Riverside Works, Todmorden Road, Littleborough,
Lancashire OL15 9EG
(darting equipment)

Temple Cox Limited
Cray Avenue, Orpington, Kent BR5 3TT
(capture equipment including nets and pole syringes)

Tetra
Lambert House Court, Chestnut Avenue, Eastleigh,
Hampshire SO5 3ZQ
(fish food manufacturer)

Vetark Animal Health
PO Box 60, Winchester, Hampshire SO23 9XN
(specialist vitamin/mineral mixes and disinfectants)

Vetbed (Animal Care) Limited
Lotherton Way, Garforth, Leeds, West Yorkshire
LS25 2JY
(bedding material and supplier of Cimicat and Welpi)

Volac Limited
Orwell, Royston, Hertfordshire SG8 5QX
(supplier of Lamlac, Litterlac, Volac Easy Mix, Faramate)

Wyeth Nutrition
Wyeth Laboratories, Taplow, Maidenhead, Berkshire
SL6 0PW
(supplier of Gold Cap SMA)

JOURNALS AND MAGAZINES

Aquarist (The)
Buckley Press, The Butts, Half Acre, Brentford, Middlesex

Biologist (The)
c/o Institute of Biology, 20 Queensberry Place, London
SW7 2DZ

Bird World
PO Box 70, North Hollywood, California 91603, USA

British Journal of Herpetology
Available from British Herpetological Society

Cage and Aviary Birds
Surrey House, Throwley Way, Sutton, Surrey SM1 4QQ

Fur and Feather
Winkley Publishing, Preston, Lancashire

Journal of Avian Diseases
Available from Association of Avian Veterinarians

Journal of Wildlife Diseases
Available from Wildlife Disease Association

Journal of Zoo and Wild Animal Medicine
Available from Executive Director of American
Association of Zoo Veterinarians
34th Street and Girard Avenue, Philadelphia, Pennsylvania
19104, USA

Pet Product Marketing
EMAP Pursuit Limited, Bretton Court, Bretton,
Peterborough PE3 8DZ

Racing Pigeon Pictorial
19 Doughty Street, London WC1N 2PT

Small Exotic Animal Veterinary Journal
PO Box 70, Hollywood, California 91603, USA

Testudo (BCG Journal)
44 Ashdell Road, Alton, Hampshire GU43 2TA

Tropical Fish Hobbyist
PO Box 27, Neptune, New Jersey 07753, USA

INFORMATION AND ADVICE

Animals Information Bureau (Mr C Henwood)
179 Pavilion Road, Worthing, West Sussex BN14 7EP

Aquarian Advisory Service
P O Box 67, Elland, West Yorkshire HX5 0SJ

British Museum (Natural History)
Cromwell Road, London SW7 5BD
(identification of specimens including parasites)

Commonwealth Institute of Parasitology
395A Hatfield Road, St Albans, Hertfordshire, AL4 0XU
(identification of helminth parasites)

Focus Publications
PO Box 235, Harston, Cambridge CB2 5TL
(literature on exotic pets)

Institute of Terrestrial Ecology
Monks Wood Experimental Station, Abbots Ripton,
Huntingdon PE17 2LS
(examination of bird carcases for chemicals)

Liverpool Museum
William Brown Street, Liverpool 3
*(Dr Clem Fisher — contact regarding people willing to help
with nursing bats)*

Nature Conservancy
Attingham Park, Shrewsbury
*(Steve Woodfall — advice on what to do with unwanted
bat colonies)*

Nature Conservancy Council
Northminster House, Peterborough,
Cambridgeshire PE1 1UA

Pedigree Petfoods Education Centre
National Office, Waltham on the Wolds, Leicestershire
LE14 4RS
(general)

Weymouth Fisheries Laboratory
MAFF, The Lookout House, The Nothe, Weymouth,
Dorset DT4 8UB
(advice on fish diseases)

Zoological Society of London
Regent's Park, London NW1 4RY
(advice on care of exotic animals)

GOVERNMENT DEPARTMENTS

Agricultural Department (Welsh Office)
Crown Buildings, Cathays Park, Cardiff CF1 3NQ

Department of Agriculture and Fisheries for Scotland
(DAFS)
Pentland House, 47 Robb's Loan, Edinburgh EH14 1TW

Department of the Environment (DOE)
Tollgate House, Houlton Street, Bristol BS2 9DJ

Ministry of Agriculture Fisheries and Food (MAFF)
(Animal Exports and Imports)
Animal Health Division, Hook Rise South, Tolworth,
Surbiton, Surrey KT6 7NF
*(for Scotland see DAFS; for Wales see Agricultural
Department, Welsh Office)*

Pest Infestation Laboratory (MAFF)
Tangley Place, Worplesdon, Guildford, Surrey GU3 3LQ
*(for advice regarding pesticides used against wild birds
and mammals)*

APPENDIX TWO
Conversion Tables

Metric and Temperature Conversions

Length			**Volume**		
1 millimetre	=	0.03937 inch	1 litre	=	1.76 pints
1 centimetre	=	0.394 inch	4.546 litres	=	1 gallon
1 metre	=	1.094 yards			
Area			**Weight**		
1 square centimetre	=	0.155 square inch	1 gramme	=	0.03527 ounce
1 square metre	=	1.1960 square yards	1 kilogram	=	2.205 pounds

Temperature Comparisons

Centigrade	Fahrenheit	Centigrade	Fahrenheit
10	50	38.3	101
12.5	55	38.6	101.5
15.5	60	38.9	102
18.2	65	39.2	102.5
21	70	39.4	103
26.6	80	39.7	103.5
28	82	40	104
32.2	90	40.3	104.5
35	95	40.6	105
35.5	96	40.8	105.5
36.1	97	41.1	106
36.6	98	41.4	106.5
37.2	99	41.7	107
37.7	100	41.9	107.5
38	100.5	42.1	108